RESEARCH ADVANCES IN ALCOHOL AND DRUG PROBLEMS

Volume Two

ADVISORY PANEL

J. C. BALL

K. BRUUN

D. C. CAMERON

G. EDWARDS

L. E. HOLLISTER

O. IRGENS-JENSEN

J. H. JAFFE

K. F. KILLAM

C. M. LEEVY

J. MARDONES

W. H. McGLOTHLIN

H. McILWAIN

J. H. MENDELSON

W. D. M. PATON

H. POPPER

R. W. RUSSELL

J. R. SEELEY

M. H. SEEVERS

C. R. SCHUSTER

H. SOLMS

R. STRAUS

RESEARCH ADVANCES IN ALCOHOL AND DRUG PROBLEMS

Volume Two

Edited by

ROBERT J. GIBBINS

YEDY ISRAEL (*Executive Editor*)

HAROLD KALANT

ROBERT E. POPHAM

WOLFGANG SCHMIDT

REGINALD G. SMART

*Addiction Research Foundation
and University of Toronto, Toronto*

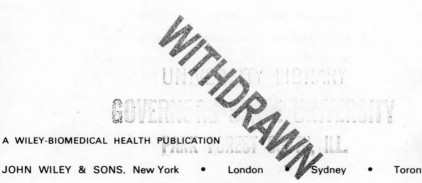

A WILEY-BIOMEDICAL HEALTH PUBLICATION

JOHN WILEY & SONS, New York • London • Sydney • Toronto

Library of Congress Catalog Card Number: 73-18088

ISBN 0-471-29738-0

Printed in the United States of America

10 9 8 7 6 5 4 3 2 1

CONTRIBUTORS

FREDERICK BAEKELAND, *Department of Psychiatry, State University of New York, Downstate Medical Center, Brooklyn, New York*

H. CAPPELL, *Addiction Research Foundation, Toronto, Ontario, Canada*

E. EIDELBERG, *Barrow Neurological Institute, St. Joseph's Hospital and Medical Center, Phoenix, Arizona*

G. GLOBETTI, *Department of Sociology, The University of Alabama, University, Alabama*

J. D. J. HARVARD, *British Medical Association, London, England*

D. B. HEATH, *Department of Anthropology, Brown University, Providence, Rhode Island*

B. KISSIN, *Division of Alcoholism and Drug Dependence, Department of Psychiatry, State University of New York, Downstate Medical Center, Brooklyn, New York*

H. H. LAU, *Informetrica, Ltd., Consultants in Economic Research, Ottawa, Ontario, Canada*

LAWRENCE LUNDWALL, *Department of Psychiatry, State University of New York, Downstate Medical Center, Brooklyn, New York*

PREFACE

During the last decade most parts of the world have experienced a growing interest in problems associated with the nonmedical use of drugs—specifically drug dependence. In part, this heightened awareness has corresponded to a real growth in the extent, diversity, and social impact of the use of drugs in many societies. Public concern, both reflected in and enhanced by the mass media of communication, has led to greater demands on experts of all types for information about the causes and consequences of drug use and about methods of coping with the perceived problems.

As a result, the amount of research and writing on the subject of drug problems has increased greatly. Thus as many clinical and scientific papers on the amphetamines have appeared since 1965 as were published from 1929 to 1965. This explosive growth of the scientific and clinical literature is not unique to the area of drug research. There is, however, an added difficulty—this field is an interdisciplinary one. It is almost a platitude to point out that the field of drug problems spans the entire range of investigation in social, behavioral, basic biological, and clinical disciplines. This means that the person who wishes to keep well informed about drug problems faces the difficulty of an expanding literature multiplied manyfold.

It is therefore impossible for one individual to keep up to date with all the relevant literature pertaining to the diverse aspects of the "drug problem." There is a particularly acute need in this field for critical reviews that assess the current developments, interpret them for the reader who is not expert in the particular area, and provide orientation in related areas of study. There are already a number of annual review publications, which have a well-established place in the continuing education of scientists. In general, however, they confine their attention to individual disciplines, such as biochemistry, physiology, psychology, medicine, and other traditionally defined fields of study. Many researchers and practicing professionals have felt a need for a single publication that would review the many aspects contributing to our understanding of drug use and drug problems. The present series, beginning with this volume, is intended to fill such a need.

Although one volume is to be published annually, the series is not intended to be an "annual review" in the usual sense. The aim is not to cover all the work reported during the preceding year in relation to a fixed selection of themes or disciplines. Rather, it is to present each year a number of critically evaluative papers dealing with selected topics in which enough recent progress has been made to warrant a review, or in which debate or confusion are such as to require an analysis and clarification of concepts. Consequently it is anticipated that a different selection of topics will be covered each year. Each paper will discuss the work appearing during a period of several years, the length of the period being determined by the relevance and amount of the material. The frequency with which any one topic is reexamined in later years will depend on the rate of progress of research on that topic.

Because of the multidisciplinary nature of problems of drug use and dependence, the papers published in each volume will be drawn from several disciplines or areas of research. It is even conceivable that an entire volume might be devoted to a particular problem, with individual reviews and papers examining various aspects of it. The desirability of such an approach will undoubtedly be easier to assess as the series evolves.

The composition of the editorial board and the international advisory board reflects these objectives of the series. The editors are members of the senior scientific staff of the Addiction Research Foundation of Ontario. Their own areas of special interest include the fields of biochemistry, pharmacology, anthropology, experimental and clinical psychology, sociology, and jurisprudence. The members of the international advisory panel are well known in this field. Their interests range over the relevant disciplines, and, they represent seven countries in Europe, North and South America, and Australia. On the basis of their knowledge of the relevant fields, and their reading of the literature in various languages, they propose to the editors each year a list of the subjects that are most appropriate for review, as well as the names of investigators in different parts of the world who might be best qualified to write the reviews. Obviously no publication can guarantee that it will fill the needs of all its readers with respect to sorting out fact from conjecture, the important from the trivial, or the permanent from the transitory. Nevertheless, we hope that this series will provide a lead in the desired direction and will stimulate the type of interdisciplinary inquiry that is widely advocated but seldom practiced. To this end the editorial board and the advisory panel will be happy to consider suggestions submitted by readers for reviews on subjects that they would like to see covered in future issues of the series.

The Editors

(Preface to volume 1)
July 1973
Toronto, Canada

CONTENTS

CHAPTER 4   ACUTE EFFECTS OF ETHANOL AND OPIATES ON THE NERVOUS SYSTEM   147

Eduardo Eidelberg

CHAPTER 7   METHODS FOR THE TREATMENT OF CHRONIC
ALCOHOLISM: A CRITICAL APPRAISAL   247

Frederick Baekeland, Lawrence Lundwall, and Benjamin Kissin

VOLUME ONE

Chapter One

A CRITICAL REVIEW OF ETHNOGRAPHIC STUDIES OF ALCOHOL USE

DWIGHT B. HEATH, *Brown University, Providence, Rhode Island*

1. INTRODUCTION

One of the peculiar features that distinguishes *Homo sapiens* from other animals is that species' early and persistent predilection for altering itself and the world about it. The accumulation of our efforts to reshape the world have begun, in recent years, to have a more visible and threatening impact. Our efforts to reshape our bodies have produced a remarkable range of deformations, redistributions, and other elaborations that are as attractive to one population as they are repugnant to another. Our efforts to reshape our consciousness have resulted similarly in a number of experiments, with varying effects and contradictory evaluations; this has been the case throughout human history, although the subject has received inordinate attention in recent years.

Among the best known and most widely used means of altering human consciousness is the ingestion of ethanol. For this readership, it would be extraneous to discuss the chemistry of alcohols; throughout this paper, I use the terms "alcohol," "alcoholic beverages," and "beverage alcohol" interchangeably, to refer to drinks in customary usage, with whatever distinguishable concentration of ethanol.

Early in the lifetime of most scientists living today, it would have been important to make a point that has become in recent years almost banal— among local groups of *Homo sapiens*, there is no universal use, meaning, or function for alcohol. In view of the fact that alcohols occur in nature throughout most of the inhabited areas of the world, and that their effects on the organism are strikingly similar in many respects, this would appear to be an especially fruitful topic for comparative research.

The intrinsic interest of the subject increases when we recognize that the use of alcoholic beverages is an ancient and widespread practice, and such beverages are almost universally subject to rules and regulations unlike those that relate to other drinks. Even where alcohol is not drunk, attitudes toward it are rarely neutral; among these societies that have historically known alcohol, abstinence is a highly emotional issue.

Although feeling runs high about alcohol almost everywhere, the quality of the feelings varies enormously, and the rules—both prescriptive and proscriptive—not only differ from one group to another, but are directly contradictory in many instances. For example, the Chamula of southern Mexico adhere strictly to the rule that individuals within a group drink only in sequence according to age, (375) whereas neighboring mestizos insist that everyone present drink simultaneously (225). The Zuni Indians of the southwestern United States generally do not drink, for fear of disturbing the harmonious relations each individual must sustain with the rest of the universe (143); the Apaches who live nearby strive to achieve a "high" state that they consider exhilarating; and the Navaho tribe includes a few teetotalers for whom use of the hallucinogen peyote is an integral part of religious worship, but more who actively seek alcoholic inebriation whenever they can (224, 272). In short, not only is alcohol a focus of considerable feeling, but it is also used and interpreted in a wide range of ways.

The rules and manner of use of many other substances also vary from one culture to another. One of the reasons that alcohol gained special attention among scientists was the belief that its effects on the human organism were fairly standard and that physiological processes could be analyzed to the point where quantitative datum points could be ascertained to serve as objective markers for particular kinds of reactions in individuals (9). Although this idea has not been sustained, it appears to have had considerable importance in shaping directions of research during the mid-twentieth century.

Despite abundant and detailed studies of physiological, nutritional, psychological, and sociological aspects of alcohol and alcohol use throughout much of Western history, there are still few unequivocal generalizations that can be made about the various meanings, uses, and effects of alcohol. Conflicting reports abound in the scientific literature concerning different effects and reactions to alcohol, on both the individual and social levels of observation and analysis.

These conflicting reports should be examined in the light of sociocultural factors relating to use, and also in terms of the possible means and extent to which these reactions may be conditioned. It is this concern with the range of variation in patterns of belief and behavior among human populations that I call an anthropological perspective.

My purpose in this chapter is to make the ethnographic literature as pertinent as possible to the readership of this volume, whose training and interests are exceptionally varied and interdisciplinary. In order to do this, I have attempted to organize my discussion in terms of categories that are prevalent in the literature on alcohol and other drugs, as described, analyzed, and interpreted by members of several disciplines. (A complementary survey of the same literature, organized in terms of categories that are more generally used by anthropologists, will soon be published elsewhere (179). Because my search of the literature was quite thorough, my intention is to focus on issues rather than to strive for exhaustiveness. Inevitably, I will have omitted reference to some work which other readers might have included, or given different attention to some sources that I do discuss. I feel confident, however, of not having overlooked any published research (except perhaps in eastern Asia) which would materially alter any of the generalizations that have emerged from this review. At the same time, I have systematically tried to communicate "an anthropological perspective" in a way that should reveal the diversity of strengths and weaknesses of works that treat alcohol in sociocultural context, as well as the past and potential contributions which I think such studies offer for an understanding of alcohol and human behavior.

2. AN ANTHROPOLOGICAL PERSPECTIVE

When I refer to "an anthropological perspective," I refer to a broad spectrum of methodological approaches and topical concerns that can be subsumed under the academic rubric "anthropology," as that term is generally used in the United States today. Among the "subdisciplines" represented are *cultural* (or *social*) *anthropology*, including ethnography (the detailed study of the way of life of nonliterate peoples); *ethnology* (the comparative study of such ways of life); *archaeology* (the study of ways of life that are remote in time, whether prehistoric or historic); and *physical anthropology* (the study of human biology, past and present). *Linguistics* and *folklore* are sometimes differentiated from cultural anthropology, and ethnology is sometimes called "comparative sociology," but it is important to recognize that, until a few years ago, most anthropologists prided themselves (whether justifiably or not) on having an unusually holistic perspective on the human animal.

Although the full implication of this becomes clear only in view of the review of the literature which follows, I must briefly characterize my understanding of anthropological approaches to alcohol as including studies of drinking beliefs and behavior (whether customary or pathological) in particular cultural contexts, and studies which have theoretical implications concerning cross-cultural similarities or differences with respect to such patterns of belief and behavior.

In my discussion of an anthropological perspective, I often use the words "culture," "cultural," and variants in ways that differ enough from the most common lay usage so that it seems appropriate to define my meaning. When an anthropologist refers to culture, he is not referring exclusively to classical expressions of the fine arts, or to an elite sphere of activity but, on the contrary, to the way of life of a people, including their simplest tools, their crudest forms of humor, their empirical attitudes, and all the rest of the patterns of belief and behavior that distinguish them as an identifiable group. For many years, anthropologists debated whether culture is a distinctive "superorganic" order of phenomenon, or a conceptual abstraction. Discussions about "cultural norms" encountered the necessity of distinguishing about norms *of* behavior ("the normal," in a descriptive sense of what most people say that they actually do), norms *for* behavior ("the normative," or "the ideal," in the regulatory sense of what most people should or should not do), or norms *from* behavior ("the real" or "the actual," in a statistical sense of what people are observed to do, as noted by a relatively objective reporter). There is still a great deal of discussion in some circles about whether culture has its locus in the minds of the participants, or only in the mind of the social scientist, or, as a few might suggest, "out there," as an objective reality.

For purposes of the present review, it seems enough to indicate that I have tried to deal with the entire range of literature that approaches drinking and drunkenness from *any* of those points of view. In my discussion of change, it will become clear that, despite charges to the contrary, anthropologists are competent to discuss social situations in other than static terms. In my discussion of ambivalence, it will become clear that the discrepancy between cultural ideals and the reality of workaday observation and experience is recognized by most of the people in the world. In my discussion of aspects of culture, it will become clear that the holistic ideal of research remains vital among anthropologists today.

One important factor that has shaped ethnographic studies of alcohol to date is their almost uniformly incidental or casual conception. Until the early 1970s, few anthropologists set out to study patterns of thought and action concerning alcohol. In virtually every instance cited here, descriptive and/or analytic studies of drinking by anthropologists have been felicitous by-products of field research that was undertaken with very different foci of concern.

In a sense, it is a striking endorsement of the traditionally esteemed holistic approach to ethnographic field work that such studies are often fairly comprehensive and sometimes even theoretically significant. In another sense, this could also be construed as a telling weakness of the ethnographic literature on alcohol; such individual studies cannot be replicated, and often do not even lend themselves to systematic comparison, since a wide range of variables is noted, and they are sometimes reported in strikingly different ways. Another obvious shortcoming of such studies, for certain purposes, is that the degree of integration between theory and data is often tenuous.

There are probably few who would seriously question the presumption that there is some intrinsic value in amassing more accurate information on drinking from as many different settings as possible. But the same could be said of studies concerning any other form of human behavior, and one is fully justified in asking what has been learned from what I have called "the anthropological perspective," and what special contributions it may make to our understanding of alcohol and alcoholism.

It is beyond the scope of this paper to provide a critical review of psychological approaches to drinking; our concerns are complementary, although our units of analysis are significantly different. Anthropologists are fully cognizant of the fact that the patterns we discuss both derive from and are expressed in the feelings of specific individuals. At the same time, we focus our attention on the fact that most individuals within a particular population share such feelings to a significant degree, even when they differ from—and often even contradict—the feelings shared by members of a neighboring population. We recognize the idiosyncratic physiology of each human being, and the fact that his or her life experiences are unique. At the same time, we consider it important to look closely at those ways in which members of a society share not only their experiences but also their expectations, shaped in large part by a worldview that is unlike that of other societies.

We recognize that the attitudes, sentiments, values, world views, emotions, needs, and other motivating factors do not exist "in culture," but in the individuals who express or manifest them in their actions. Our concern is with the striking degree to which the individual members of a society share similar motivations, and this is true whether we refer to the mode, a norm, or range of variation.

In a similar manner, although there is considerable overlap between the concerns and approaches of anthropologists and those of sociologists, there are also a few significant differences, at least in terms of emphasis. In general, sociologists have tended to study their own societies, or segments of them, whereas anthropologists have tended to focus on other societies, including those with institutions unlike the mainstream of Western culture, and especially nonliterate (or "primitive") societies throughout the world. Of course, exceptions can be identified on both sides of this disciplinary division of labor, but the predominant anthropological concern with describing and analyzing unfamiliar patterns of belief and behavior contrasts with the predominant sociological concern with quantifying or reinterpreting familiar patterns (370–373; 374).

The differences between anthropological and sociological approaches refer not only to subject matter but also to methods of investigation. Until the 1960s, ethnographers rarely paid much attention to representative or random sampling among the populations they studied, and their statements about patterned attitudes and actions were rarely phrased in quantitative terms; most sociological research contrasted in both respects.

For these reasons, I do not include in this chapter the many surveys of drinking that refer to the diverse populations within political entities (such as nations, states, provinces, and so forth) or to studies of such heterogeneous groupings in our society as "blue-collar workers," "collegians," "teen-agers," "women," and so forth. Similarly, only a small portion of the voluminous literature on "skid row" on "chronic drunkenness offenders" is included, specifically that which deals with the meanings as well as the forms of drinking in such a context. The sociological literature has been effectively reviewed elsewhere (e.g., 35, 135, 268, 293), so I will attempt to survey the specifically anthropological material, with particular emphasis on ethnographic data and their implications.

3. PREHISTORY AND HISTORY

We have already made the point that alcohol is the most widely used psychoactive substance among human populations today. It may also have been the earliest. Fermentation is a simple natural process that produces low concentrations of alcohol quickly in many fruit and vegetable juices or in gruels made of grain. Crude beer and wine may well have been invented (or discovered) independently at many times and places, so there is no firm evidence about man's earliest encounter with beverage alcohol, but drinking is undoubtedly an ancient pastime.

A variety of remains suggests that home brews may well be at least as old as agriculture throughout most of the world (excepting most of North America and Oceania); a symposium with the provocative (but misleading) title "Did Man Once Live by Beer Alone?" brings together pertinent data and theories summarized by outstanding archaeologists (60).

Because alcohol itself has been a part of culture for so long, and because it often produces noteworthy changes in behavior, it is no surprise that some of the earliest written documents refer to alcohol and its effects.

A few sources are useful for their attempt at providing virtually encylopedic coverage of the subject, although the quality of their historicity is grossly uneven; these include, among others, Cherrington (79), Crawley (95), Emerson (117), Gilder (146), McLeod (312), Morewood (340), Poznanski (376) and Redding (114), (384). With respect to ancient Egypt and the Near East, a variety of perspectives can be found in Crothers Drower 1966, (97), Gremek (160), Piga (360), Cornwall (94), Lutz (291), Modi (336), and others; biblical and ancient Jewish patterns are desribed and analyzed in Keller (231), Danielow (106), Fenasse (126), Goodenough (153), Jastrow (207), Raymond (382), and many other scholarly works. Drinking in ancient India is the subject of studies by Aalto (1), Bose (54), Mitra (334), Prakash (377), and Ravi (381); classical circum-Mediterranean antiquity is documented by Brown (62), Younger (483), Buckland (68), Rolleston (394), Hirvonen (188), Suolahti (431, 432), Jellinek (213), and McKinlay (300–310).

A variety of other emphases and perspectives on alcohol and culture have been offered by historians. A sampling of these illustrates the range of studies available: drinking in medieval England (395), alcohol and hashish in nineteenth-century England and France (148), drunkenness in puritan New England (269), chicha in South America (43), brandy in Canada (45), colonial Mexico (64), Indian-white relations in North America (205, 292, 311), pre-Columbian Mexico (34, 38, 73, 152, 322, 423), Pacific Island Missions (161), Scandinavia (206), seventeenth- and eighteenth-century Jesuit accounts of drinking among Indians of North America (105) and of South America (393, 398). Apart from regional studies, there are also a variety of richly detailed historical studies of specific aspects of alcohol: law (27), medical uses (62, 228, 476), alcoholism (187, 257, 328, 330), beer (190), folklore (396), symbolism (214, 238), wine (415), and so forth.

4. "ETHNIC GROUPS" IN WESTERN SOCIETIES

In many popular sources, the populations of whole nations often are characterized in terms of drinking patterns. It is true that most stereotypes have some basis in fact, but little of scientific value is to be gained from generalizations that give no indication of the range of variation around a mode, or even from studies that provide detailed data but no indication of how the sample relates to the population as a whole. This is not the place to do a worldwide itemization of the literature that deals with alcohol in reference to individual nations, whether in terms of "typical drinking patterns" or in terms of the epidemiology of alcoholism. Nevertheless, a few general statements about the strengths and weaknesses of this corpus of literature are in order.

Within the United States, there have been remarkably detailed studies of drinking in a few states, some selected populations, and even one representative of the population of the entire country (72). In most other countries, there are more fragmentary studies: in the Scandinavian nations, on young men; in France, for some provinces and for a sample of the national population (400); in Italy, again for a few regions, and for a sample of the national population who have close kinsmen in the United States (283, 216). A few richly detailed local studies are available for Austria, Greece (52), Spain, and Germany (412), but Portugal and Yugoslavia—similarly viticultural and oenophilic—have been virtually ignored in terms of alcohol studies. Historical data are often richer in description than contemporary reports.

Reference to ethnicity and to ethnic groups has had a variety of meanings in the social sciences during the past few decades. Following World War II, when social and physical anthropologists spearheaded a "scientific" attack on racism in the United States, there was a brief but vocal attempt to substitute the term "ethnic group" for the value-laden word "race," but it gained little support. Since the early 1960s, as cultural anthropologists have focused their attention increasingly on complex urban societies with diverse populations, and on the specific details of interpersonal relationships in peasant and primitive societies, the term "ethnic group" has come into increasing use to designate a subjective reference group within such situations where various kinds of groups have various kinds of importance; the differences often are those that used to be characterized as "subcultures," and the ways in which people define and maintain the boundaries between such groups are often more important and revealing than are the actual differences between them in terms of patterns of belief and behavior. It is striking that anthropologists who have written about alcohol rarely have referred to either of these usages of the term.

Nevertheless, there exists a large corpus of literature that deals with differences in drinking patterns among various "ethnic groups." Virtually all of this is written by sociologists, and the use of the terms has been remarkably consistent through time—ever though it has remained logically inconsistent as a classificatory system. The groups most often identified in such discussions are Jews, Irish, and ascetic Protestants—occasionally reference is also made to Chinese-Americans, Italians, Mormons, or others as "ethnic groups." It is clear that differentiation here is not on a uniform criterion, nor—since such data often are based on secondary sources—is self-identification pertinent.

However inconsistent the logic of such a classificatory scheme may be—combining broad religious affiliation (e.g., Jews) with paternal nationality (e.g., Irish), with narrowly sectarian religious affiliation (e.g., Mormon) it has been used frequently in alcohol studies. In fact, a number of articles that are couched in terms of such "ethnic groups" are probably thought to represent the perspectives of ethnography and cultural anthropology by those who are not familiar with those disciplines and the ways in which they differ from sociology.

Most studies are based on questionnaire surveys of local populations, and interpretations of variations in drinking patterns tend to emphasize either ideology or social structure. In the majority of such papers, the important point is made that the effects of alcohol—or the frequency of alcoholism—are not uniform among various "ethnic groups." It typically is noted that most Jews drink, but that few become drunk or alcoholic, whereas a high proportion of Irish males are public drunkards or even alcoholics, and ascetic Protestants rarely drink, but those who do so tend to become alcoholics at a rate even higher than the Irish. The ceremonial role of drinking for Jews is contrasted with the predominantly convivial role of drinking among Irishmen, and ambivalence or lack of guidelines "account for" the frequency of problems among those Protestants who transgress the rule of abstinence.

In summarily characterizing these articles, I do not mean to dismiss them as fruitless or misleading. On the contrary, they have served a crucial function in bringing the awareness of cultural differences to a readership who are largely unfamiliar with ethnographic data. Furthermore, occasional individual articles have gone far beyond the basic pattern, and a few have even made valuable contributions to the conceptualization of beliefs and behaviors concerning alcohol (e.g., 48). However, I presume that the readers of this volume will, in most instances, already be familiar with this widespread and recurrent genre, so that it would be redundant here to summarize the studies in detail. Excellent reviews of this literature already have been offered periodically, such as Riley and Marden (387), Lemert (262), Lucia (289), Reader (383), and Wechsler et al. (461).

Judaism has played a strange role in the history of alcohol studies; in contrast with other religions, there has been relatively little attention paid to systematic review of codified laws and interpretations, but drinking patterns of "the Jews," as a sociological category, have continued to receive more attention than those of any other population in the world. It is a widespread bit of folk wisdom that, although virtually all Jews drink, there are virtually no Jewish alcoholics. It is another commonplace that folk wisdom is often substantiated by systematic (i.e., "scientific") investigation, and this is one such instance. In a time when many people were looking to habituation, or simple exposure, to alcohol as a cause of alcoholism, this widespread case of customary drinking without accompanying drunkenness attracted curiosity that has not yet been fully satisfied.

Immanuel Kant addressed himself to the paradox as early as 1798, and suggested, in a way that earned him frequent attribution as "the father of sociology," that the almost universal and sustained prejudice that Jews confront around the world had forced them to be unusually circumspect in their behavior, so that they could not afford the risks of offending people that might occur if inebriation were permitted (223). In a sense, this might be considered a "cultural defense mechanism," and be casually dismissed by those who appropriately point out that "cultures don't act" and that Jews would be unlikely to articulate any such defense. One need not reify culture nor look to conscious planning on the part of individuals to accept that, in evolutionary terms, such defense would be eminently functional, regardless of whether it had been sought consciously.

Historical perspectives on Jewish drinking are offered by Jastrow (207) and Koplowitz (243), but the mystery of how and why Jews abandoned inebriety sometime between 500 and 300 B.C. remains (231). Bales (30) compared the high rate of alcoholism among Americans of Irish ancestry with the exceptionally low rate among Orthodox Jews, and "explained" the difference predominantly in terms of the different meanings of alcohol. For Jews, drinking was predominantly a familial act of sacramental and symbolic significance; for the Irish, it was predominantly a convivial activity among adult men. Synder elaborated and refined this view significantly (425), and also updated Kant's thesis by referring to the "ingroup-outgroup factor" (426).

Jewish and Irish populations were also compared by Glad (147); these and other groups were studied by Knupfer and Room (242), Skolnik (422), and Wechsler et al. (461). In only a few instances are the Jews specified as orthodox, and there is usually no reference to national or regional backgrounds. Studies of "the Irish" as an ethnic group are similarly inconsistent; most deal with samples drawn from the population of the United States, Canada, or Australia, and some use "at least two grandparents born in Ireland" as a criterion, whereas others seem content to identify "Irish" surnames. The other groups compared are even more vague; often "white Protestants," or "ascetic Protestants," but sometimes merely "urban ethnic groups" (defined in terms that sound like national citizenship but are "based on mother's birthplace").

Ascetic Protestantism is a relatively recent phenomenon, and one that was restricted to small portions of Euro-American civilization until recent years. Historians have documented some of the development of this diverse movement, and sociologists have often surveyed the behavior and attitudes of members of such sects. With respect to alcohol, the bulk of the literature is of three types: pleas for temperance written by ascetic Protestants; general histories of religio-political movements, in which temperance was one theme among many; or comparisons of patterns of attitudes (usually based on large-scale questionnaire surveys) of ascetic Protestants with those of members of other groups (notably Jews, Irish Catholics, and sometimes others). Few such studies deal with the kinds of data that are of interest to anthropologists.

However, the expansive missionary activities of such devoted people have contributed to our understanding of drinking behavior in a variety of cross-cultural contexts, sometimes in unexpected ways. The fact that Christian missionaries paid special attention to drinking and drunkenness means that their journals, letters, and other accounts of their travels provide a rich store of descriptive historical data that has not yet been analyzed systematically, except for a few limited regions (161, 465). An obvious concern of any investigator who might undertake such studies is the selectivity and value judgments of the observer-reporter, but this is a perennial problem in historical research and one which is not significantly limiting.

Another way in which ascetic Protestant missionary activity has played a role in anthropological studies of drinking among nonliterate peoples is in those instances where conversion to Christianity seems to provide an attractive alternative for some members of communities in which heavy drinking and frequent drunkenness are customary. It is not clear that any significant number of converts consciously select this as a means of escape, but it is apparent that that function is served, from an analytic point of view. A case study which focuses on this pattern is Kearney's account of the Zapotec Indians of Mexico (225); it also occurs among the Tzotzil (375), and others.

Another "ethnic group" who have received some attention are "the Chinese"; again, the groupings are highly equivocal. For example, Barnett's work on "Cantonese in New York City" (33) is often uncritically lumped with La Barre's (250) characterization of Chinese national patterns based on literary and documentary sources from throughout that enormous and diverse country. Wang (455), Chu (83), and Lee and Mizruchi (256) paid attention to other immigrant Chinese populations in the United States. Without reviewing each of the studies in detail, it is noteworthy that, in many respects, the Chinese pattern seems strikingly similar to that predominantly reported for the Jews. There may be a potentially important distinction between the groups with respect to the use of drugs other than alcohol; this suggestion, however, is based solely on my familiarity with other bodies of descriptive social science literature, since there is no mention of other drugs in the sources which focus on alcohol.

Attention to such "ethnic groups" is not restricted to the writings of the United States sociologists, however. Studies by a psychologist in Australia (404),and by a sociologist (397) and a psychiatrist (344) in Canada show the same classificatory irregularity, but are rather more rigorous in terms of their observation, reporting, and analysis than is the case in many of the previously mentioned works. Related studies include those of Gypsies in Sweden (436) and in Yugoslavia (448), or Erlich's (118) comparison of religious groups in Yugoslavia; many of the Amerindian and Eskimo groups in the United States and Canada have become acculturated to the point where they might fruitfully be considered "'ethnic groups' in Western societies," but, in keeping with popular usage, I will discuss them as "nonliterate societies" (see Section 6).

5. NON-WESTERN LITERATE SOCIETIES

Many of the shortcomings already noted concerning studies of alcohol and culture in various "ethnic groups" in Western societies are even more characteristic of studies of non-Western societies, both literate and nonliterate. For historical and ethnographic purposes, there is some logic for treating literate societies (which are usually also urban, with complex social stratification and division of labor, and other features of "civilization") as distinct from nonliterate societies (which are usually smaller, with more homogeneous experience and social organization, characterized as "folk" or "primitive").

In the section on prehistory and history (Section 3) I have already listed a number of studies that deal with ancient civilizations of India, Persia, Mesopotamia, and other areas. During the last few millenia, some strikingly different patterns also have emerged, some of which have been described in terms of major religious groups, others in terms of castes, and still others in terms of national populations. In short, the problem of lack of comparability among "ethnic groups" is just as acute in non-Western societies as it is in Western ones; fortunately, the "ethnicity" terminology is rarely used.

The so-called "Great Religions" are sometimes thought, by Western readers, to comprise significant unitary sociocultural entities, as if adherents to Islam, Hinduism, or Buddhism somehow shared a common pattern of belief and behavior that they know better than to expect among Jews or Christians. In reality, of course, sectarian differences are at least as many and as behaviorally significant in each of those systems.

To be specific, the prohibition on alcoholic beverages that is commonly supposed to characterize the entire Islamic world is not ancient nor, for that matter, is it uniformly respected among contemporary Muslims (113, 251, 401). Drinking by Muslims is often observed and remarked upon (78, 378), and occasional studies of hospitalized alcoholic Muslims (379) indicate that drinking poses problems for some individuals, but the only systematic description that has come to my attention is of an emigrant enclave in South Africa (352).

Hinduism, like Islam, is far more diverse than most Westerners realize and it includes groups who esteem particular kinds of drunkenness as valuable forms of religious experience, at the same time that others abhor any use of alcohol. The romantic and simplistic view that some outsiders hold concerning the ascetic spiritualism of many East Indian religions obviously does not include awareness of the fact that some of those groups for whom alcohol is an abomination use other drugs as means of achieving similar sensations. An informative and sympathetic study by Carstairs (76) compares the use of *daru* (liquor distilled from *Bassia latifundia*) by the warrior Rajputs within one Indian community and that of *bhang* (tea of *Cannabis indica*) by the higher caste Brahmins in the same community. Chopra et al. (82) offer other comparative studies in modern India, and a relatively rich literature traces the changing historical and religious meanings and uses of alcohol in Indian history (334, 377, 381). Although Gandhi's (141) attempt at nationwide prohibition was short-lived, some messianic groups have foresworn alcohol, in one instance a caste who had specialized in the production of palm wine (380). A peculiar "addiction" to sweets reported by Vatuk and Vatuk (449) is noteworthy as a uniquely Indian form of intoxication. Pertold (359) describes a tribal variant on Hinduism, in which orgiastic drunkenness is important, and, by contrast, Patnaik (354) traces the case study of a man who was expelled from his caste because his son drank wine.

As is the case with respect to the other religions already discussed, Buddhism is also diverse and complex, but a few general points deserve mention even in this brief summary of the relations of religion and alcohol. The sects represented in the Himalayas are not at all ascetic, and homebrew is a staple beverage throughout that area (see, e.g., 154, 362). Descriptions and interpretations of Chinese drinking patterns include La Barre (249), Larni (252), and Moore (339); Chinese in Hong Kong were studied by Singer (421). Japanese studies have focused largely on folklore and change (17, 477–480). In other portions of Buddhist Asia, data are sparse.

With respect to those countries that were under colonial domination until this century, we often find far more descriptive material regarding relatively small and isolated tribal populations than we do regarding the literate elites, many of whom are not only urbane but also strikingly cosmopolitan. Only in recent years has limited research been undertaken with respect to these latter important populations.

6. NONLITERATE SOCIETIES

One valuable way of gaining perspective on the diverse uses, meanings, and effects of alcohol, and on the degree to which these can be conditioned, is to compare data from the largest possible sample of societies. In a sense, each of the many cultures shared by local populations in human history represents a unique "experiment" in terms of man's experience. Because they are scattered through both time and space, studying them does not lend itself to the precise control of variables that is a hallmark of the experimental method in some of the physical sciences. Nevertheless, I would argue that systematic and controlled comparison, focusing on specific and limited variables of ecology, social organization, ethics, or other subjects of concern, does allow us to approximate—insofar as any feasible approach in the social sciences—experimentation.

In a paper expressly written to complement this one, I have provided a detailed review of the ethnographic literature on alcohol (179); that article is virtually comprehensive in terms of areal coverage, and includes an historical review of such studies as well as a discussion of the ways in which alcohol studies have shed light on the wide variety of topics that interest anthropologists in general. Anyone who is interested in learning about the immense range of beliefs and behaviors that have grown up around alcohol throughout the world will find that paper a helpful guide to the vast, diverse, and scattered literature on the subject; other useful introductions include Washburne (458) and Popham and Yawney (374). However, most readers of this volume presumably would profit more from a selective sampling that reveals not only quaint and curious customs but also some cases where the normal patterns of a population are so unusual as to bring into question widely held ideas about reactions to alcohol, the etiology of alcoholism, or other theoretically significant aspects of alcohol studies.

One of the most dramatic cases in this respect is the one that I know best: the Camba of eastern Bolivia (175). Virtually all the Camba drink to the point of passing out, at least twice a month. The beverage they drink is stronger in alcoholic concentration than that customarily drunk by any other population. Nevertheless, there is no one among them who suffers any economic, social, or psychological problems in relation to alcohol, nor are there fights, insults, or other aggressive acts in connection with drinking. In contrast with the Jews, the Cambas esteem drunkenness and actively pursue it; nevertheless there is no alcoholism in any of the widely used senses of the term. Neither is there *alcoolisation* of the sort that Ledermann (255) identified with the widespread French pattern of alcohol-induced illness among individuals who never were inebriated. Among significant features of the Camba situation are the secular rituals which are the only context in which drinking takes place, and the apparent importance of the drinking group as a primary reference group in a society that is otherwise extremely loosely structured, even to the point of being atomistic.

Another classic study set in Latin America deals with very different but equally unusual forms of drinking which are integrally related to other aspects of local culture: Bunzel's (69) paper on Chamula, Mexico, and Chichicastenango, Guatemala, is not only a pioneering contribution to the ethnography of alcohol but is also one of the earliest systematic attempts at controlled comparison, dealing with the interrelation of child rearing and other psychological indices with other aspects of culture.

In an unusually wide-ranging comparative article, Mandelbaum (317) tentatively drew attention to "culture areas in drinking patterns," citing some marked uniformities throughout sub-Saharan Africa, and also in Latin America. It should be mentioned that these similarities with respect to the role of alcohol are embedded in strikingly different cultural contexts, in terms of dress, economic activities, house style and residence pattern, and other aspects of the way of life of the various peoples. Geographical distributional studies are available for each of these areas (168, 414), and the abundant ethnographic descriptions do show striking similarities at a broad level of generality, even though specific local patterns are distinguishable.

Kaffir beer (or "Bantu beer") is a relatively mild home-brew of fermented maize and/or millet, esteemed as a food, a medium of exchange, a sacred liquid, and an integral part of any significant social interaction; the same is true of palm wine in areas where it dominates. In a few societies, however, the latter is also distilled to yield illicit gin, an economically important product for trade, with none of the ideological connotations of the popular beverage (e.g., 258, 353). Beer drinking is an integral part of virtually any social interchange among men in most African tribal societies; beer also is offered to gods and spirits, as a pledge of agreement between parties following adjudication, as a token of appreciation to those who have taken turns working one's land in the system of reciprocal labor exchange, and as a medium of interaction in many other contexts. In all such drinking, aggressive behavior is extremely rare and promptly squelched; pathological addiction does not occur, and the abstainer would be a social misfit. Among the many societies where such a pattern occurs are, as illustrative examples, the Tiriki (402), Kofyar (346), Kaguru (42), Ibibio (209) Henga

(159), and most of the Bantu-speaking peoples (4, 71, 182, 202, 333, 402, 416).

Features of the Latin-American pattern are not only widespread; they appear in some areas to have been remarkably consistent through time, and they characterize both Indian and mestizo components of plural societies. A basic style involves frequent drinking bouts in which men drink to the point of stupefaction; the beverage has no special religious connotation; although drinking in a group is a social imperative, solitary drinking is unthinkable; and so forth. The broad distribution of this style is characterized in Cooper (93) and Cutler and Cardenas (100); a few of the detailed local studies where it is exemplified refer to Peru (e.g., 150, 318, 420), Mexico (296, 297, 331, 469), Chile (284–286, 329), Ecuador (324, 326), Colombia (386), and Guatemala (385).

Oceania is one of the few areas of the world where one man has repeatedly studied drinking patterns among various peoples. Although Edwin Lemert's (264, 267) primary professional identification is as a sociologist, his many studies, are sound ethnography and provide rich data not only in terms of contemporary modal patterns but also in terms of local, historical, and class differences, and in terms of the diverse meanings of alcohol.

Much of the ethnographic literature on African alcoholic beverages is descriptive of technology, terminology, and patterns of social exchange, whereas there is little information on the ways people drink or the meanings that are attached to the act. Nevertheless, a few studies provide unusual insights. For example, Hellmann's (182) account of illicit beer gardens is one of the earliest analyses of ethnic groups and their boundaries among the tribally diverse migrant populations in African cities, and Seekirchner's distributional study (414) is virtually continental in scope. Nutritional analyses of home-brew were undertaken earlier here than in most other areas (e.g., 327, 367), and an imaginative epidemiological research project tested the association between local beverages and differential incidence of esophageal cancer (88, 89).

In view of the predominance of North Americans among the world's anthropologists, it is no surprise that Indians of that continent have been more studied than native peoples elsewhere. Again, I refrain from citing the vast number of general ethnographic monographs that include some reference to alcohol—often fairly detailed, but always embedded in a context of abundant cultural data on other subjects. If we pay attention only to those studies that are primarily concerned with alcohol, it is striking that a wide range of peoples has been studied, and a wide range of approaches has been used. The following list is intended merely to be illustrative of the rich variety of the available literature on North American Indian drinking, and is by no means comprehensive. The question of whether distilling had been known in pre-Columbian times was examined by Bourke (56, 57), Bruman (65), and by Driver (112); LaBarre (249) offered a survey of native beers. The excellent record kept by Jesuit missionaries provides a rich source for characterizing the rapid spread during the seventeenth century of drinking among various tribes in the Northeast, and the history of drinking on the Northwest Coast has been summarized by Howay (199). The changing uses of and reactions to alcohol among the Iroquois have been mentioned already (103–105, 227); the role of alcohol figures predominantly in the history of trade and diplomacy between various Indian and white populations (205, 311). A psychiatric approach to Mohave culture makes much of drinking and drunkenness (109); an early study of change in drinking patterns focuses on the Navaho (176); ethnic group differences in drinking and drunkenness within the same community are described and analyzed (194).

There is no reason why our frame of reference here should not include other "native peoples" of North America. In this connection, a few of the more influential studies include Berreman's refinement of the concept of "reference group," which grew out of his analysis of Aleut drinking (46); a series of articles on the Eskimos offer many insights into the ways in which people learn to drink (195); and the linkage of urbanization and anomie is often cited in recent welfare-oriented studies (see Section 9).

The major part of North America was, unlike most areas of the world, devoid of alcoholic beverages before Europeans introduced them. Among the earliest and most widely used items of trade and diplomacy, however, were gin, rum, and other aquae vitae, and the appetite of American Indians for them seemed to be insatiable. Even so, the popular image of "the drunken Indian," with supposedly little tolerance for alcohol, reacting violently against friend and foe alike after having a little "firewater," has had a curiously uneven history.

The Iroquois of upstate New York and southeastern Canada offer an illuminating case history. During the first decades of contact, they did indeed welcome distilled liquors, but they did not use them in drunken and disorderly revels. On the contrary, drunkenness became an aid in the vision quest, which was an integral part of the native religion. Thus not only was drinking a religious act, but often a group of Iroquois men would pool their resources so that one of their number could participate in that important religious experience, while the rest of them soberly watched. Only in the early eighteenth century did the Iroquois in effect "learn" brawling and aggression as drunken behavior, presumably following the model of white trappers and traders. By 1800, drinking and drunkenness had become commonplace and often problematic, until Handsome Lake—himself a reformed alcoholic—proclaimed abstinence as an article of faith in his popular messianic religion. The striking sequence of changing uses and attitudes toward alcohol on the part of the Iroquois is summarized and well documented in Dailey (103–105) and MacAndrew and Edgerton (292).

A number of other cases could be cited around the world to illustrate that nonliterate societies undergo drastic change just as do larger and more complex societies. Another point that such a comparison would underscore is similarly a truism to the anthropologist but perhaps a surprise to others: drinking not only serves different purposes in different cultures, but those purposes, as well as the associated patterns of belief and behavior, may change drastically through time.

Most anthropological studies of alcohol are descriptive, and some of those are also analytic; but few address themselves to social policy, and even fewer have been concerned with therapy for "problem drinkers" or "alcoholics." Among these few, most are in North America, especially in Canada and the United States. One of the most methodologically rigorous and theoretically sophisticated studies of drinking as a form of deviant behavior is the long-term multidisciplinary cross-cultural study by Jessor and his colleagues (215), in which Ute, Mexican-American, and Anglo-American populations in the state of Colorado are compared. A special symposium was devoted to "American Indian Drinking: Pathology or Perspective?" at the 1973 meeting of the Society for Applied Anthropology; those and some related papers are forthcoming in Everett and Waddell (121). As described in Section 10, a variety of new approaches, often developed by Indians themselves, are being used in both prevention and therapy during the early 1970s.

If one wishes to look at alcohol in a non-Western society from a wide range of perspectives, the Navaho probably offer the most salient case. The largest Indian tribe in the United States, they retain their own language, dress, religion, and other aspects of culture to a greater degree than most American Indians. The Navaho way of life probably has been studied more broadly and analyzed in greater depth by scientists representing a wide range of academic disciplines over the years than has any other outside of the literate Western or Eastern traditions. The same is true with respect to alcohol, a topic which is rarely covered in any detail in the worldwide ethnographic literature. An early paper described beliefs and practices associated with drinking in one community (174); another did the same after legal prohibition had been repealed (176); the same community's attitudes toward alcoholism were scrutinized closely and compared with attitudes toward other threatening events (143). Kaplan (224) interpreted Navaho heavy drinking as expressing a sort of counter-cultural inversion of dominant values. A series of papers deals with the relationship between alcoholism, homicide, and suicide (272, 271); another welfare-oriented focus that has received attention is the relationship between migration to cities and drinking problems (156, 157). A variety of approaches to treatment have been tried among Navaho alcoholics (e.g., 184, 407, 460), and Ferguson (128) has consistently sharpened our understanding of alcoholism by "working backward," comparing elements in the lives of recovered alcoholics rather than attempting to identify the etiological factors among practicing alcoholics. Henderson (183) pointed out the advantages and problems of cross-cultural and multidisciplinary research on the basis of his work among Navaho and Zuni alcoholics. Novel research methods are being applied in the hope of isolating the "cognitive maps" (or "folk models"), the views that the people themselves hold [which are often far removed not only from scientific views but also from the widespread views that are popular among other populations (438)].

In short, the literature on Navaho drinking represents a sort of microcosm of the approaches and concerns that characterize the ethnology of alcohol.

7. CROSS-CULTURAL STUDIES

Even if anthropologists restricted their efforts to making intensive studies of populations that would otherwise be ignored, their contribution to the understanding of behavior would nevertheless be valuable, in the sense of portraying the rich diversity of human experience. But another fundamental part of the anthropological perspective is that of comparison among diverse sociocultural systems.

Cross-cultural studies take a variety of forms, in keeping with the idea that individual ethnographic case studies lend themselves to various kinds of comparative analysis, using "mankind" as our population and "the world" as our laboratory. By introducing comparative studies in the broadest possible terms, I do not mean to imply that such efforts are directed only at the elaboration of pan-human scientific laws of behavior, or at the constriction of a universal theory to account for all forms of drinking. To be sure, that kind of generalization is the aim of a few cross-cultural efforts, using large-scale statistical correlation of variables, but a number of more limited comparisons have shed light on people and alcohol in different ways that are instructive from a variety of points of view.

Specific ethnographic details are not only distinctive of separate tribes but sometimes seem almost "illogical" or "unnatural" to those who do not bother to understand the internal logic of an alien cultural system or to recognize the natural variation among human societies. To such observers, paying meticulous attention to the drinking patterns of primitive peoples may appear to be a pointless academic exercise. Such observers might also question the relevance of comparisons between patterns found in relatively small and isolated societies and our own. Although it may at first sound paradoxical, it is especially this readership to whom cross-cultural studies may be most important.

In one sense, it is obvious that a cross-cultural perspective is valuable in providing a critical test for conceptions of reality—many of the customary ways of thinking and acting that people learn in the course of socialization and enculturation are erroneously thought of as universal, or part of "human nature." It is a truism that this simplistic view must be qualified in the face of the variety of "human natures" that appear in various cultures around the world.

Another value of cross-cultural studies is in terms of the "natural laboratory" approach to various cultures, outlined above. Throughout much of the twentieth century, some social scientists have been characterizing one of their major aims as the elucidation of "laws," or at least, general theories, of human behavior. A major portion of the "sociology" and "anthropology" (often called "social philosophy") written before World War II did, indeed, comprise just such general statements, but they were usually based on evidence concerning only a few societies, or were phrased in such general terms as to be almost allegorical in scope. Freud's tentative ventures into cross-cultural analysis (such as *Totem and Taboo*) and James Frazer's work on mythology and religion (notably, in *The Golden Bough*) exemplify the best of such work; much of the rest has only limited interest as illustrative of one current in intellectual history. Emile Durkheim's study of *Suicide* and a series of papers by Lewis Morgan and Edward Tylor brought statistical methods firmly into social science, especially as an aid to testing generalizations.

In the 1940s, a different kind of anthropological research was pioneered and the subject was alcohol. Donald Horton's (197) dissertation (one of the first in anthropology that was not based on intensive fieldwork by the author) was soon published (1943), and its importance is undiminished by the many methodological criticisms that have ensued. Not only had it served as a model for future studies in terms of selecting a sample, and designating specific data which are generally reported by ethnographers, to serve as indices of themes or motives which are rarely referred to explicitly in ethnographic monographs. It has also been cited consistently—whether in agreement or contradiction—as first of the few articles on alcohol to propose and systematically test a series of explicit and straightforward hypotheses about the functions of drinking. His sample was the 56 societies around the world for which data were adequate concerning alcohol use and various indices of anxiety. The source of his data was the Cross-Cultural Survey (subsequently renamed Human Relations Area Files), an ambitious compendium of world ethnography organized by George Murdock and his colleagues at Yale University.

Horton's article is so well-known and has been summarized so often that I will not do so again here, except to note that, on the basis of statistical correlations, he offered what has probably become the most frequently quoted generalization about drinking: " . . . *the primary function of alcoholic beverages in all societies is the reduction of anxiety*" (197, p. 223; italics in original). Horton's effort was an important milestone not only in alcoholic studies but also in anthropology. The methods of large-scale cross-cultural comparison were used subsequently, with considerable success, in the analysis of social structure, association between child training and personality, and for the testing of a wide variety of hypotheses.

The next such study to focus on alcohol was Field's 1962 reworking of the same data, with a new emphasis on social organization. Instead of examining in detail the correlates of drunkenness, Field paid more attention to the relatively rare phenomenon of communal sobriety, and found it to be significantly associated with corporate kin groups, patrilocal residence, bride price, and a village settlement pattern. In conclusion, he noted that " . . . drunkenness in primitive societies is determined less by the level of fear in a society than by the absence of corporate kin groups with stability, permanence, formal structure, and well-defined functions" (134).

A third cross-cultural study, using the large-scale correlational approach on 139 societies, provided a test of the previous efforts and also yielded significant support for the view that " . . . as a reaction to dependency conflict, alcohol has a triple function: it reduces anxiety and tension; it permits the satisfaction of desires for dependence; it permits uncritical indulgence of unrealistic fantasies of achievement" (21, p. 31). More details on this study are given in Section 9; see also Child (80, 81), Barry et al., (37), and Bacon (20).

During the 1970s, a new generation of statistically sophisticated anthropologists have paid special attention to methodological problems involved in the correlational approach to cross-cultural study (which they call "hologeistics") and a series of contributions to alcohol studies should be forthcoming soon (409).

But not all cross-cultural studies are on such a scale. Relatively simple, but theoretically significant, comparisons can be made between small numbers, or even pairs, of cultures which differ in terms of a few crucial variables.

In one sense, many of the "sociological" studies that were discussed in Section 4 ("Ethnic Groups" in Western Societies) appear to be comparisons in which attitudes and actions about alcohol are treated as dependent variables, and "ethnic group membership" is treated as the independent variable. Perhaps the major reason for dissatisfaction with such studies, on the part of some social scientists, is that distinguishing characteristics among those "ethnic groups" are not clearly delineated.

Less unequivocal as an example of controlled comparison is Bunzel's (69), classic study of alcoholism in two Middle American cultures. Although drinking and drunkenness play important roles in both Chamula and Chichicastenango, the forms, functions, and meanings of both drinking and drunkenness are very different in those nearby Indian communities. Her concern with unconscious as well as conscious behavior is evidenced in one of the earliest attempts at systematically relating cultural institutions (in this instance, those concerning drinking) to patterns of child rearing and personality development.

A number of studies have been made that focus on different ways in which populations of different communities drink, and relating these differences to differences in other aspects of culture: the Madsens (316) compare Indian and mestizo patterns in central Mexico; Viqueira and Palerm (452) relate Indian patterns of witchcraft and homicide to those of drinking in contrasting a Totonac and a mestizo village in eastern Mexico; Heath (178) compares changes in interethnic drinking patterns in two Bolivian communities; Geertz (143) looks at alcoholism and other problems in five neighboring but culturally distinct populations in New Mexico; a wide range of comparative studies on drinking in different communities is available for other areas.

A few studies have focused on contrasting drinking patterns among ethnic components of the same community: the Honigmanns looked at Indians, Eskimos, and whites in a couple of Alaskan towns (192–196), as did Clairmont (84, 85); Carstairs (76) compared castes in an Indian village; Whittaker (467), showed a wide range of variation in a Sioux community; Marconi (1969) did the same for a Mapuche group; Honigmann compared socioeconomic classes in an Eskimo village; and others are doing similar work elsewhere.

At a national level, a series of studies have compared drinking among various components of the populations of Norway, Sweden, Finland, and Denmark: teen-age boys (67), adult males (220), and others (7). Few epidemiological studies provide the kind of data that would be required to identify significant subgroups; the difficulties inherent in discussing "ethnic groups" in Western societies have been treated already (see Section 4).

An unusual kind of cross-cultural comparison is that of Csikszentmihalyi (98), in which he deals with the spatial context of drinking as expressive of national character. He contrasts the massed conviviality of the typical

German beer hall with the fluidly expanding and contracting cliques formed by small table groups in open-air cafes of the Mediterranean or Latin style, and also with the peer-oriented stance and mobility of Britons at a pub, or the stealthy privacy of North American couples in high-backed booths within dimly lit cocktail lounges. The article is by no means a rigorous effort at systematic correlation, but it is highly suggestive in a novel way.

Another kind of cross-cultural approach to drinking takes areal distribution of beverages, technology, modes of drinking, or other features as a focus of concern. On a continental scale, German anthropologists have made ambitious compilations of data garnered from ethnographic reports, Seekirchner (414) on Africa and Hartmann (168) on South America; recently, Marshall has reviewed the literature on Oceania (321), and Heath has done the same for Latin America (180). An unusual early study by Banks (32) showed variation among five tribes in Sarawak, along a virtual continuum in which degree of inebriety increased in proportion to isolation.

An interesting experiment in combining cultural geography and ethnology as an approach, and relying on historical sources for data, resulted in the delineation of "drink areas" in New Spain, a reconstruction of the distribution of various native alcoholic beverages in Mexico during the early colonial period (64).

Recognizing the similarities that sometimes underlie superficially different drinking patterns throughout broad regions, Mandelbaum (317) has suggested that it may be fruitful to look beyond communities, tribes, and sometimes even nations, with the aim of discerning widespread regional patterns.

8. "THE SCIENCE OF LEFTOVERS"

In one of the best books written by a professional scientist with the aim of explaining his academic discipline to the layman, Kluckhohn characterized anthropology as "the science of leftovers" (240). Far from denigrating the field, he was expressing a perverse pride many anthropologists share about the fact that in their grandiosely holistic concern for nothing less than "man and his works," anthropologists have long paid attention to archaeological materials that were of no interest to classicists, arts and literature (of primitive peoples) that were generally ignored by humanists, and aspects of culture in broad cross-cultural perspective that were rarely studied by other social scientists.

There is still enough truth to that characterization of the field, that it seems appropriate in this context to highlight those aspects of alcohol studies in which anthropologists are especially interested, and in which they could presumably contribute significant insights. In many instances, these interests and contributions remain potential—as noted earlier, few anthropologists have systematically or consistently focused on actions and attitudes associated with alcohol. Nevertheless, the range of subjects that have been treated from "an anthropological perspective" is considerable.

Human Biology

In the science of man, there is a division of labor whereby "physical anthropologists" attempt to understand the biological and physical aspects of the human animal, in relation to other animals, whereas "social anthropologists" focus on cultural aspects, including language and history as well as contemporary patterns of belief and behavior. Within the field of human biology, those topics to which anthropologists can probably contribute most are "race," nutrition, and health.

"Race"

During the first half of the twentieth century, classification of human populations on the basis of visible features was a major preoccupation of many physical anthropologists. The more recent view of races as breeding populations has shifted the focus of attention from phenotypic to genotypic characteristics. Nevertheless, a number of scientists working in other disciplines continue to use the terminology of "race" in the earlier and imprecise manner. For that reason, I will here use the term "race" (in quotation marks) to refer to groups that are considered as significantly different subspecies by some researchers. An excellent brief review of such studies will soon be published (116); in the meantime, it is appropriate here at least to indicate the recent developments that will probably make this topic a major area of concern during the next few years.

It has long been hypothesized that various "races" have, among other physical differences, differential susceptibility to the intoxicating effects of alcohol. In North America, the popular sterotypes of "the drunken Indian" occasionally has been reinforced by reviews of data on arrests (185, 429), epidemiology (e.g., 246) or other indices that are taken to imply lower tolerance than is typical of the general population, or of other "races." A few anthropological reports have supported the view (e.g., 103, 263); a few explicitly reject it (61, 194). The predominant trend among anthropologists for the past few decades, however, has been to stress the increasing fund of ethnographic data which illustrate the important role of ideological and other cultural variables in shaping the predisposition, frequency, intensity, and effects of drunkenness. Recognizing significant cultural variation on the other hand, and presuming virtual uniformity of physiological responses to alcohol among all human populations on the other hand, most anthropologists have tended to dismiss "the firewater myth" as an unfounded expression of social prejudice. In an apparent reaction against the implicit racism of the popular stereotype, cultural anthropologists were cited as authorities in an unusual source: see *Journal of the American Medical Association*, (221); for an historical review of the controversy, see Leland (260).

Not only were American Indians popularly thought to be inordinately susceptible to intoxication, but other "Mongoloid" populations were thought to share the weakness. Although alcohol was not present in Eskimo cultures before contact with Europeans, most Eskimo groups eagerly adopted it, and many observers remarked on the suddenness with which they became drunk, the extreme contrast between their normal and their drunken behavior, and the long time it takes for Eskimos to "sober up." Anecdotes and "folk wisdom" often refer to quick blushing and drunkenness among the Japanese, after the ingestion of only small amounts of alcohol.

During the 1970s, a few preliminary reports of physiological experiments have revived the issue, and the intellectual and political climate of the times is such that controversy presumably will be heated. Fenna and his colleagues (127) reported that Canadian Indians and Eskimos consistently metabolized alcohol at a significantly slower rate than a control group of Canadian "whites." Wolff (472) found that Japanese, Koreans, and Taiwanese all showed more facial flushing, increased pulse pressure, greater changes in optical density, and more extreme subjective reactions than Americans of European ancestry—and these reactions occurred faster, even with half the quantity of alcohol. Similar differences were found in a subsequent study (473) comparing Cree Indians, American-born Japanese and Chinese, and a range of hybrids.

A variety of questions have been raised concerning the methodology of those experiments (see e.g. 166, 276), but perhaps even more serious controversy is imminent with respect to the political implications of such studies. It appears that laymen in some Canadian provinces and the United States have been quick to cite these studies as grounds for discriminatory legislation, especially in attempts to control Indian or Eskimo access to alcoholic beverages. Reaction against this uncritical acceptance of such preliminary findings has been so strong among some academicians that they have—in a manner strikingly similar to that in the black-I.Q. controversy—raised questions about the relative priority of academic freedom and social ethics. In their concern to avoid prejudicial (sometimes called "irresponsible") uses of the "racist" implications of research, they disapprove of the "premature" release of such findings. It is likely that "the firewater myth" may again become a focal point in both native-white and liberal-conservative polemics, at least until better controlled experiments are undertaken on larger population samples, in an effort to identify what racial differences, if any, are pertinent with respect to the effects of alcohol on the human organism. Collard's (87) and Vallee's (443) expectation that such differences might be found seem to have been generally forgotten or ignored.

Although MacAndrew and Edgerton (292) did not introduce physiological data, they did muster an impressive body of ethnographic and historical case material that led them to " . . . conclude that drunken comportment is an essentially *learned* affair. . . . *Over the course of socialization, people learn about drunkenness what their society 'knows' about drunkenness; and, accepting and acting upon the understandings thus imparted to them, they become the living confirmation of their society's teachings*" (88; italics in original). This may not be an elegant solution to the question of possible differences in "racial" tolerance to alcohol, but it is sociologically sound, and deserves to be considered while such a sensitive issue is being reassessed.

Nutrition and Health

Nutrition and health are other realms of concern in which popular beliefs or "folk wisdom" about alcoholic beverages and the findings of biologists, physiologists, and other scientists have at some times and in some contexts been enormously discrepant, whereas in other times and contexts they have been remarkably similar. A recent review article provides a brief account of the history of medical knowledge about alcohol, and the uses of alcohol in medical treatment (230).

The nutritional value of fermented beverages is often presumed and extolled by people for whom beer or wine is a staple food; a few illustrative cases around the world include the Oraon of India (233), Balobedu (244) and others (274) of Africa, Quechua and Aymara Indians of South America (450), Austrian peasants (192), and others. In only a few instances is there the kind of detailed information that would allow one to evaluate the appropriateness of such a high estimation of food value; among those who do provide such data, however, are Jeffreys (209), Anderson et al. (16), Nelson et al. (345), and Platt (367).

Supporting data are also generally lacking in the works of authors who decry such drinking as injurious to the health: [e.g., (125), on the Philippines, I.L.O. (203), on South American indigenous populations, Sariola (406) on Colombian Indians, Graviere (158) and Gelfand (144) on sub-Saharan Africa, et al.]; a few do provide such details [as when Mears (327) implicates native beers in the differential occurrence of pellagra in three African tribes, McGlashan (299) links moonshine with cancer in central Africa, or Perisse et al. (358) document the significant loss of food value in the conversion of grains to alcoholic beverages]. By contrast, Collis et al. (88, 89) absolved home-brews of causing esophageal cancer in East Africa. An unusual instance is that of the Safwa of Tanganyika, in which an anthropologist focused on the *cultural context* of native beer as providing a positive adaptation against famine (170). Without judging the nutritional value of the beverage itself, he emphasized that beer selling is the best way in which poor people can get the cash required to buy food in times of scarcity.

A number of other studies reveal that people around the world often consider various alcoholic beverages to have other important medical properties apart from any nutritive value. St. Paul's praise of wine "for thy stomach's sake" is only the most famous among dozens of favorable biblical quotations that often are cited in response to ascetic Protestant pleas for total abstemiousness. Whether as a general tonic or as a specific (e.g., to stimulate a mother's lactation), positive medical value is attributed to alcohol by such diverse populations as Peruvian mestizos (419), villagers in northern India (171), Alaskan native peoples (348), the Amhara of Ethiopa (434), Orthodox Jews in urban United States (425), and many others. The medical importance of beer throughout Western history has been traced by Wright-St. Clair (476); other alcoholic beverages are discussed similarly by Strubing (430); Busch (70) summarizes medical uses of chicha in Andean America, and Ravi (381) traces such uses of alcohol in the ancient east Indian system of *ayurveda*. A recent volume even propounds and prescribes a number of uses of alcoholic beverages by modern Western clinicians (254). (For discussion of the epidemiology of alcoholism, see Section 10.)

An interesting sidelight in the discussion of alcohol and health is the question of the apparent absence of such reactions as hangovers, blackouts, and addiction among many populations, even where drunkenness is commonplace. Among groups where these outcomes are explicitly noted as being rare, or even incomprehensible, are the Quechua (318), Camba (175), Salish (261), Polynesians (264-266), and Tarahumara (232). It is not at all clear whether we are dealing, in this connection, with differences in thresholds to pain, with differences in physiological reactions to alcohol, with different attitudes and expectations about the effects of alcohol, or with other factors, biological and/or cultural.

In fact, it is apparent that there is considerable polarization of opinion on the nutritional and other physical effects of alcohol. Attitudes and values often color the observations and interpretations of authors who speak strongly for or against it without citing adequate objective evidence.

Aspects of Culture

In evaluating the anthropological contribution to alcohol studies, it is perhaps unfortunate but unquestionably obvious that relatively little systematic attention has been paid to documenting the chemical and physical properties and effects of alcohol in relation to human biology. Fortunately, the contribution of cultural anthropology is considerably more sizable and important, by which I refer to the relatively substantial literature devoted to illustrating and interpreting the many and diverse meanings and contexts of alcohol use.

In the companion article already cited, I have provided a detailed review of these contributions, under headings that relate to the interests and conceptual schemes of anthropologists (179). For this readership, it seems appropriate merely to provide a brief sampling of the kinds of information and interpretations that are available, especially those in sources that rarely come to the attention of those who are not social scientists.

Social organization is one of the major realms of concern on the part of cultural anthropologists, and a number of ethnographic studies reflect this (439). The functional importance of alcoholic beverages in fostering social integration has been emphasized in a wide range of societies throughout the world; among these are, for example, Finnish Lapps (356, 405), Bolivian Camba (175), Mexican Chamula (69), Peruvian Quechua (318), urban migrants among Canadian Indians (61), Papagos in Arizona (454), the Henga of Malawi (159), Soceity Islanders of Oceania (265), as well as most South African tribal societies and many other groups. A number of authors even go so far as to suggest that drinking is a significant act in terms of the delineation and maintenance of ethnic boundaries (see, e.g., 165, 253, 263, 389, 390, 457). In a large-scale cross-cultural study involving the correlation of a number of cultural variables for a sample of 62 societies, Field's " . . . most important single conclusion was that the degree of drunkenness at periodic communal drinking bouts is related to variables indicating a personal (or informal) rather than a corporate (or formal) organization, but is substantially unrelated to the level of anxiety in the society" (134).

It is a common mistake to assume that studies which emphasize social organization are necessarily synchronic; among those which deal with changes in drinking and in the structuring of relationships are Heath (177, 178) Dailey (103), Toit (437), and Honigmann and Honigmann (193, 196). One author even goes so far as to attribute a 30-year war between the Nama and Herero of southern Africa to increased demand for kaffir beer (451).

Realms of knowledge, both natural and supernatural, are other persistent interests of cultural anthropologists, and some links between such knowledge and alcohol deserve mention in this context. I have already noted some of the religious and medical beliefs and practices (see Sections 4, 5, and 7), but a few others should be cited if only to indicate the wide range of cultural usages relating to alcohol and of researches by ethnographers. In a number of societies, alcoholic beverages are thought to be highly esteemed by the gods, so that they constitute valuable offerings: for example, Sangree (402), Heath (178), Jellinek (214), Pozas (375), and others. In many other societies, alcoholic intoxication is construed as a valuable means of transcendence, an aid or accompaniment to religious experience: for example, Aztec (152), Iroquois (103), Tiriki (402), Zapotec (225), Turko-Mongolian nomads (50), and others; some authors have even gone so far as to propose general theories in which mystical and symbolic values are cardinal in accounting for the widespread distribution of alcohol and the peculiar emotional intensity that surrounds it (e.g., 124, 214, 238).

At a more mundane level, anthropologists are concerned also with the practical scientific knowledge of peoples around the world, and this interest is reflected in studies emphasizing technological aspects of beverage production (e.g., 2, 8, 44, 142, 168, 169, 341, 446), artifacts used in conjunction with drinking (e.g., 338, 218), and even the supposed influence of alcohol on art styles (360). Folk taxonomy is another realm of knowledge that has attracted the attention of anthropologists; studies that relate to alcohol include Everett (121, 122), Frake (137), Vanderyst (445), Hage (163), and Topper (438), among others; it has even been noted that alcohol relates to conceptions of time in a few societies (346, 406).

In their holistic concern with human behavior, cultural anthropologists deal not only with "leftovers" but also sometimes with topics that are addressed by scholars in other disciplines. Economics is one such realm of behavior; the role of alcohol in some primitive systems of exchange has been studied from a variety of points of view. The use of beer as a medium of exchange for paying fines or taxes, for gaining prestige, and so forth, is described for various societies in Africa by Platt (367), Parkin (353), Hutchinson (202), Umunna (441); in North America by R. Robbins (390) and Waddell (454); in South America by Rodriguez (391) and Vazquez (450). One particular economic use has received special attention because of its integral association with social structure, namely, the provision of beer by the landowner whenever teams of neighbors work jointly in the kind of reciprocal labor exchange that characterizes some activities of the Tarahumara (232, 462), Quechua (110), Bantu (202), Basuto (63), and other groups; Gregson went so far as to assert that "the beer work party is a relatively efficient means of mobilizing agricultural labor" (159).

A variety of ethnographic studies can be characterized broadly as relating alcohol to communication which, in anthropological terms, comprises much more than linguistic exchange. For example, when Hamer characterizes Potawatomi drinking as, in part, "attention seeking" behavior (165), or when Lemert notes that the Salish "act out the White stereotype of the 'drunken Indian'" (263), it seems fruitful to speak of what is happening as a process of communication as well as to speak of such an analytic perspective as a precursor of symbolic interactionism. Only in recent years have a few social scientists paid systematic attention to non-verbal aspects of communication, such as kinesics and proxemics. Occasional descriptive data in earlier detailed ethnographic studies of drinking situations may lend themselves to fresh analysis and interpretation in these terms; the most suggestive effort to date is Csikszentmihalyi's (98) comparison of the spatial characteristics of drinking contexts in various Western countries, as related to values, patterns of interpersonal relationship, and so forth.

Cultural anthropologists usually emphasize patterns of belief and behavior that are shared by at least some socially significant groups within societies, rather than focusing on idiosyncratic personal systems of ideas and action. Nevertheless, there is an obvious and continuous interplay between society, culture, and the individual in terms of motivations, attitudes, and the range of alternatives that are considered feasible or appropriate. For this reason, an important portion of the contribution that anthropology has made to alcohol studies is closely related to psychology and the individual.

It would be superfluous in this context even to outline the processes of enculturation, by which the human infant, relatively free of instincts, is taught to acept a certain range of beliefs and behaviors which are characteristic of his society (and to reject, or abhor, or esteem, or tolerate, or otherwise react to) beliefs and behaviors that lie beyond that range. Nevertheless, it is a generally recognized characteristic of the human animal that the major portion of our behavior is learned rather than inherited in the germ plasma, so that rewards and punishments from the point of view of the individual are important data, just as are "functions" at the level of the group or society. A number of these points are developed in considerably more detail in Sections 9 and 10, but it is appropriate here to indicate the range of topical concerns and methodological approaches in this connection.

In attempting to discern motivations for drinking in societies throughout the world, anthropologists have often applied psychological concepts—with a wide range of variation in the degree of sophistication and precision, to be sure. To illustrate, in many societies drinking is cited as a means of overcoming shyness or gaining courage (e.g., 265, 408, 485); in others, it is judged to be important as a symbol of social unity (e.g., 24, 30, 253, 317); in still others, anthropologists emphasize it as a way of relieving the specific anxieties and pressures that derive from conflict with a dominant alien culture (e.g., 111, 140, 484). The sacred symbolism of drinking is, in many contexts, interpreted as important to the individual (e.g., 316, 480); in other kinds of social ambience, alcohol use may enhance social status or prestige (e.g., 164, 201). Some authors discern or infer fairly specific and pointed personal motivations for drinking and/or drunkenness; as an aid in the religiously prescribed vision quest among the Iroquois (75), as a defense against witchcraft among the Tiriki (402), as a means of achieving mystical reunion with the past in Onitsha (441), or—just the opposite—as a means by which the Nasioi emulate the newly dominant European culture in Melanesia (349). A wide variety of other interpretations pertinent to psychology and the individual have been offered by anthropologists in relation to alcohol studies, as is indicated in excellent review articles by Barry (35), Reader (383), Blum and Blum (52), and others.

If we shift our attention again to social and cultural levels of analysis, we can fruitfully characterize another major thematic concern of anthropologists under the broad rubric of recreation and sexuality. Although it may seem in questionable taste to treat these topics jointly, there is considerable overlap in the literature, especially with reference to societies where casual sexual liaisons are not associated with emotional connotations or outcomes. For example, Deveraux (109) emphasizes the humorous intent of Mohave "gang bangs" and other ribaldry that many readers construe as sexual aggression. Navahos often speak of drinking as a pastime "because there's nothing else to do," and drinking very often results in illicit sex (176); the same is true of the Sioux (467) and the Salmon Indians (194). Cutter explicitly relates drinking to the general theory of games (101); drinking games are commonplace (e.g., 339, 471); and the remarkably consistent inverse association of drinking and gambling suggests the possibility of functional equivalence (3, 83).

It is with respect to change that I believe anthropology has heretofore made its major contribution to alcohol studies. Within that realm of concern, two principal topics should be distinguished: first, studies that deal with change in a population's patterns of belief and behavior concerning alcohol, and second, studies that deal with the impact of other cultural changes which appear to affect the drinking of that population.

We have already mentioned a number of books and articles that deal with the history of alcoholic beverages in various cultures (see Section 3); in recent years, anthropologists have been paying special attention to what might be labeled microhistory, the kinds of changes that occur within the lifetime of individuals. The following is only a partial sampling of the enormous and varied literature on the subject, chosen to illustrate the geographical and topical range.

Among the most obvious contexts in which a temporal perspective might illuminate alcohol studies is that where prohibition is imposed or repealed. The failure of the so-called "noble experiment" of total prohibition throughout the United States demonstrates the intensity of emotion that surrounds alcohol in some societies; it is the only occasion in which an amendment to the nearly 200-year-old constitution of that country was repealed. But it would be misleading to think of prohibition as applying only to complex Western cultures; it also often affects non-Western peoples, (examples are 176, 349, 447). Significant economic shifts also often have an impact on customary drinking; (see e.g., 390, 357).

Changes in the style of drinking within a given population may take many forms, and so can studies of change. Undoubtedly much can still be learned about how and why cheap gin became a brief but pervasive social problem in eighteenth-century England; certainly Hogarth's vivid portrayals fit with other historical data as accurately depicting an ambience that is probably unique in world history (cf. 86). Hutchinson (202) recounts how native drinking patterns changed in South Africa during the nineteenth century, and notes how meanings and contexts also changed, since traditional ideology was not applied to new beverages. Heath (178) shows how the interethnic composition of drinking groups changed, in diametrically contrasting ways, in two Bolivian communities. The Honigmanns (193) analyze "how Baffin Island Eskimo have learned to use alcohol." One of the recurrent themes throughout MacAndrew and Edgerton's (292) book on drunken comportment is that many North American Indian groups (and some other peoples) adopted alcoholic beverages with minimal social disruption during the early years of contact with Europeans, and that the extreme and violent drunken reactions that gave rise to "the firewater myth" developed later; they cite a rich variety of historical source materials that support their point. For one tribe in the southwestern United States, we can even identify the individual who introduced home brew (200), but it is probably already too late to try to reconstruct the channels of communication and exchange through which the technology was diffused. A sequence of phases in the history of drinking has been worked out for the Iroquois (104). If anyone should solve the historical component of "the great Jewish drink mystery" (231), we would be in a stronger position to evaluate conflicting sociological theories that are applied to contemporary Jewish patterns. In Polynesia, the acceptance of alcoholic beverages, unknown before the coming of European sailors, curiously occurred in approximately *inverse* relationship to the time of first contact (264). In a Moroccan city, Defer (108) found that alcohol displaced cannabis in direct proportion to the "modernity" of occupation among a representative sample of the population.

Studies on changing drinking patterns could be cited for most areas of the world; another kind of concern for cultural change has become increasingly significant with respect to alcohol studies, not only from the point of view of anthropology but also with significant implications for epidemiology and social action. I refer to the burgeoning interest in the relationship between acculturation and problem drinking. In the section on Theoretical Concerns (Section 9), I review the controversy over the importance of intrusive pressures from an alien cultural system, changes in norms or expectations, and other outcomes of contact between groups with differing cultures; in the present context, it is appropriate at least to sketch in broad terms the outline of work that focuses on acculturation and alcohol.

Two main threads run through this problem-oriented literature. The first takes entire societies or ethnic groups as the units of analysis, and deals with the impact that relations with another, dominant, sociocultural system may have in terms of reshaping the way of life of the subordinate group. Unusually concise formulations of this sort have been offered by Yawney (481): " . . . the integrative effects of drinking occur in the case of cultures in which . . . acculturation has not been severe," whereas " . . . the disruptive pattern occurs in the case of those societies undergoing severe acculturative processes, whether or not they had the use of alcoholic beverages historically." A second approach takes individual human beings as the unit of analysis, and deals with the impact that their relations with different, often conflicting, sociocultural systems may have in terms of disorienting them, with "escape," "protest," or other motivations being cited often as reactive "reasons" for widespread alcoholism among such persons. An early formulation of this sort typifies much of the writing during the 1950s and 1960s: drinking and drunkenness are interpreted as serving " . . . to furnish diversion and temporary escape from the anxieties arising from cultural conflict and community disintegration" (46). During the 1970s, a contrasing view has been expressed by a few authors, as exemplified in the findings of Levy and Kunitz (271) that, among Navaho Indians, " . . . the highest intensity of involvement with drinking and the greatest use of alcohol was found among the most traditional and least acculturated group, while the lowest use and involvement was found in the most acculturated off-reservation group." Implications of both the societal and the individual emphases on acculturation are discussed in more detail in Section 9, and in Heath (179).

9. THEORETICAL CONCERNS

As indicated in the introduction, I consider one of the principal functions of this kind of review article, in this kind of volume, to be the explication of what an anthropological perspective has to offer with respect to alcohol studies, for the benefit of scholars, social workers, epidemiologists, and others who bring a wide range of other fruitful and complementary perspectives to bear on the subject of alcohol and alcoholism. For this reason, the remaining portions of this chapter are organized in terms of categories that are more characteristic of nonethnographic writings on alcohol, and which, in many instances, have not systematically or frequently been investigated by anthropologists.

"Social Problems"

One of the reasons why anthropologists have generally remained on the fringes of much of the intensive public, international, and other nonacademic alcohol programs is that there is often an obvious—even if not explicit—preoccupation with alcohol*ism* (in a clearly problem-oriented or ameliorative sense) which takes precedence over attempting to understand alcohol in a normal, customary, and valuefree sense. It is obvious that many other scientists share similar reservations about the interrelations of "research" and "applications" of their disciplines (e.g. 23, 25, 78). It is equally obvious that many programs *are* broad enough to be concerned with alcohol and not just with alcoholism. Keller reviewed the vast literature (229) and offered a relatively brief operational definition that is still probably the most widely used; he called alcoholism " . . . a chronic disease manifested by repeated implicative drinking so as to cause injury to the drinker's health or to his social or economic functioning."

One of the most striking contrasts between the roles and meanings of alcohol in Western and non-Western cultures is the immense emphasis on "social problems" in the former, and a relative absence of such concerns in the latter. This does not necessarily mean that there is full consensus about drinking and its behavioral consequences in non-Western societies, nor does it mean that drunkenness does not sometimes result in social, psychological, economic, or other problems for individuals or groups in such societies. The evidence does, however, very strongly suggest—and, in many instances, explicitly affirm—that alcoholism, addiction, and other pathological manifestations are extremely rare in cross-cultural perspective.

Like Jellinek, I find it preferable to talk about "the problems of alcohol," and to regard "alcoholism" as one of those problems. The historical evolution of definitions of alcoholism was effectively reviewed by Jellinek (212), and subsequent approaches have been discussed and evaluated by Reader (383). For purposes of this review, it should be sufficient to cite only those definitions that seem to have had a major impact on the direction of systematic research, most of which has been undertaken only within the past few years. The first effort from W.H.O. (474) labeled as alcoholism " . . . any form of drinking which in its extent goes beyond the traditional and customary 'dietary' use, or the ordinary compliance with the social drinking customs of the whole community concerned." Only a year later, the focus was shifted and somewhat sharpened: "Alcoholics are those excessive drinkers whose dependence upon alcohol has attained such a degree that it shows a noticeable mental disturbance or an interference with their bodily or mental health, their interpersonal relations, and their smooth social and economic functioning; or who show the prodromal signs of such developments" (475). It is striking that, as S. Bacon (23) pointed out several years ago, the defining characteristics are basically sociological, although sociologists were not involved in drafting them. Although he did not say so, I feel confident that Bacon would accept my substituting (or adding, with an "or") the words "anthropological" and "anthropologists." The principal point in these definitions seems to have been an attempt to accommodate to the rich variety of cultural contexts that allow the label to be applied to strikingly different combinations of symptoms.

Perhaps a brief discussion of a few non-American patterns of "alcoholism" will clarify this point (cf. 115). France has long had an exceptionally high rate of mortality from liver cirrhosis (one of the key indices in Jellinek's formula for estimating the prevalence of alcoholism). Even more striking is the fact that many Frenchmen are "addicted to" or "dependent on" alcohol, in the sense that they suffer withdrawal symptoms when deprived of it for any reason. Both of these phenomena occur in a context where visible inebriation is rare, and many of the "addicts" are individuals whose blood-alcohol level rarely reaches that which would be considered "under the influence of alcohol," in a legal sense, in most of the United States.

Social and medical scientists collaborated in order to understand the phenomenon of *alcoolisation*: the state of the French peasant or townsman who drinks wine regularly throughout the day, consuming several liters and maintaining a low but constant blood-alcohol level during all his waking hours (255). In this way, damage to the liver and physiological dependence are commonplace, even among individuals whose drinking causes no psychological, social, or economic problems, who never drink alone, and who do not suffer the stigma of the North American alcoholic. Although it was principally on the basis of questionnaires and other "sociological" methods that this pattern was confirmed for the scientific community the pattern is clearly a cultural one and hence just as "anthropological" in its significance as it is "sociological" (15). In cross-cultural perspective, for example, one might look for similar kinds of alcoholism in areas with similar drinking patterns: Chile is clearly one such case (319);

parts of Italy appear to show the same situation (283); if adequate data were available for Portugal, it might well show the same characteristics.

In Finland, a different kind of "alcoholism" has long been a concern to administrators and to the public at large (10–12). Low rates of cirrhosis and rare cases of physiological addiction contrast with the French situation, and daily drinking is rare on the part of any individual. Infrequent drinking, however, occurs in the context of intensive sprees, in which men drink hard and fast. Fighting is a frequent outcome of such drinking sprees, and violent assault is commonplace. Finns emphasize the "social problem" aspect of alcoholism, focusing on behavior patterns that are virtually nonexistent in connection with French drinking.

Most anthropologists are uncomfortable in dealing with populations as large and as diverse as these, and rightly stress the fact that the nation-state is a political entity that rarely coincides with the kind of culture-sharing reference group that we prefer, whether it be called a "tribe," "society," "community," or "ethnic group." At the same time, I feel that it is worthwhile to indicate that the concern with cultural variables (such as who normally drinks how much of what beverage at what times of day) constitutes basically "an anthropological perspective."

One of Jellinek's pioneering efforts in attempting to bring some order to the largely anecdotal corpus of information on alcoholism that existed to that time (210) was his outlining of "phases," or developmental stages, of alcohol addiction (cf. 51). Jellinek did this originally on the basis of information supplied by members of Alcoholics Anonymous in the United States, and, although he did not explicitly anticipate it, I feel confident that he would be not at all surprised with Park's (352) finding that 686 Finns appear to have undergone a different sequence including mostly the same symptoms, or Almeida's (14) finding that 180 Peruvians more closely followed the U.S. pattern, but that the timing of their addiction careers was somewhat different.

One of the most important generalizations that does emerge from the ethnographic literature is the absolute rarity of the occurrence of alcoholism in non-Western societies, regardless of which of the previously cited "standard" definitions is used.

This is perhaps most striking when it occurs in societies in which virtually all adults of at least one sex drink regularly and where drunkenness is frequent and positively valued. Even in such contexts, which might be construed as constituting an ideal setting for "addiction," anthropologists often have explicitly indicated that there are no alcoholics in the community (see, e.g., 175, 261, 262, 324, 326). In other similar settings, investigators have expressed surprise at finding "very few" individuals who would be considered, by our standards, alcoholics (see, e.g., 46, 103, 110, 139, 191, 265, 420, 467).

In view of the relative rarity with which alcoholism is reported to occur among non-Western peoples, it might be assumed that there are few "social problems" associated with alcohol in those societies. In fact, this is one of the contexts in which the world view of the observer—even if he be a relatively "objective" social scientist—may color his reporting as well as his interpretation, identifying "problems" where native peoples, with a very different philosophy and cosmology, may not perceive any such (26). The discussion of "social problems" which follows must be recognized as reflecting my own attempt to fit data into categories that are meaningful to scholars and others interested in alcohol studies, and should not be construed as a classification of problem areas as they are perceived by members of the societies described.

Aggression and Criminality

One of the outcomes of drunkenness that has attracted special attention is the overt expression of aggression, whether in verbal or physical terms. Even before any psychological interpretations were attached to such behavior, it was often spectacular and/or dangerous enough to warrant special description on the part of observers. It is altogether probable that missionaries misinterpreted some social forms in a way that made the outcomes of drunkenness among non-Western peoples appear more socially disruptive than the natives themselves felt was the case, and it is also apparent that colonial administrators whose concern was largely with adjudication may have seen native drinking in terms primarily of its negative results. Even allowing for these selective distortions in reporting, there remains enough in the way of apparently "objective" reporting to convince us that—in some societies—one of the principal consequences of drinking is violence. It is important to stress that this is by no means a characteristic of non-Western drinking in general, and the ideas that primitive peoples are peculiarly susceptible to alcohol, or that they normally react violently when intoxicated, are not generally supported by either historical or ethnographic evidence (cf. Section 8).

Probably the most abundant and vivid corpus of literature that gave rise to "the firewater myth" is that on Indians of northern North America, especially during the eighteenth century. Accounts of atrocities committed by Indians upon their kinsmen are at least as common as those that deal with violence against whites, and, in a number of instances, no aggression other than internecine is reported. (In view of the fact that such reports usually comprise only small portions of sizable journals, accounts of travels, local histories, and similar sources that deal only in a tangential manner with drinking, I have not listed them in the bibliography of this chapter; MacAndrew and Edgerton (292) provide an excellent survey of the material.)

At least two major generalizations can be drawn from these data: first, that the aggression expressed by inebriated individuals, in whatever society, is not random or diffuse, but rather is patterned in the sense of being directed in a limited number of ways against a limited range of persons; and, second, that drinking and drunkenness were commonplace in a number of societies for several years before the pattern of aggression became usual (the Iroquois offer the most amply documented case).

A few illustrative data from various areas reflect the diversity of aggressive reactions connected with alcohol in non-Western cultures. Bunzel found wife beating, fighting, cursing, and other forms of aggression to be normal outcomes of drunkenness in Chichicastenango, although the normal ethical imperative was for nonaggression and strict adherence to an elaborate code of correctness in interpersonal relations. By contrast, in the same paper (69), she noted that aggression rarely got beyond the point of name calling in Chamula, where the people are generally considered "bad Indians" and permissive child-rearing practices are associated with relative independence and self-confidence among adults. The Honigmanns (194) found that the Salmon Indians became aggressive when drunk, although whites and other Indian groups in the same community did not. Brody (61) makes the point that Indians on skid row fight or argue with strangers or with policemen, but not with each other. Kaplan (224) makes much of what he calls "crazy violence" among drunken Navahos, and suggests that it reflects a counterculture ideology that is the obverse of ideal Navaho values; it is noteworthy, however, that the persons who are the objects of such violence are not a random sample of the population, nor are they even the people most near at hand when one gets drunk (174). A few of the groups who often fight when drunk are the Potawatomie (165) and Sioux (467) of North America, the Quechua (324, 326) in South America, Finns (66, 162) in Europe, Maria (116) and Bihar (140) in Asia, and Cook Islanders (265) and Tahitians (49) in Oceania. Among those who virtually never become aggressive are the Camba (175) and Lunahuana (420) of South America, the Tarahumara (232) and early Iroquois (75) of North America, the Kofyar (346) and Tiriki (402) of Africa, the Japanese (477) of Asia, and the Society Islanders (265) of Oceania. In noting the predominantly convivial use of alcohol in an East Indian community, Jay (208) offered a hypothesis of unusually broad scope: "This study of Hill Maria drinking, taken together with the literature as a whole, suggests a relationship between drinking and the general intensification of social interaction. Underlying conflict in societies is likely to be expressed by overt aggression during drinking. In societies where conflict is absent, overt friendliness will be expressed during drinking."

In a brief cross-cultural survey of drinking and violence, Rohrmann (392) found a strong association between the two in 20% of the 46 societies considered. He found violence to be unrelated to the type of beverage, rare in association with ceremonial or ritual drinking, and slightly associated with preadult drinking and with "degree of acculturation."

An unusual category of the literature on drinking among non-Western peoples is that having to do with "criminality"; I discuss it together with "aggression" because I have found that most people other than anthropologists presume that the major portion of criminality associated with alcohol is "logically" associated with physical violence, especially in colonial situations (e.g., 47, 145, 187). However, the association is not at all clear, especially in view of the long-standing legal restrictions on the sale of liquor to American Indians and to many other native peoples, as well as the prejudicial liability to a host of other nonviolent "crimes" in those areas for which information has been published.

Data could undoubtedly be searched out from archives throughout the world, but they have gone virtually unreported to date except with reference to North America and northern Europe. It is noteworthy that, within a few decades of contact with Europeans and their liquor, Indian leaders throughout the Americas were asking that the colonial governments restrict the sale of alcohol to their people. The use of alcohol as a tool of conquest and exploitation was widespread, whether in securing land from the Delawares, women from the Guarani in Paraguay, furs from the Iroquois in New England and Canada, food from the Cherokee of the southeast, gold from the Choco, or other goods and services from these and other groups (see, e.g., 138, 311, 361). As early as 1639, Archbishop Cardenas threatened to excommunicate anyone who sold alcoholic beverages to Indians in his episcopate within Peru (259); Jesuits in Canada (105) relayed the pleas of local Indians for prohibition from the early seventeenth century, and the first prohibition law in the history of the United States was enacted in 1802, in part in response to a plea to President Jefferson by Chief Little Turtle.

Such restrictions, even where enacted, were not strictly enforced. In the United States, for example, policies toward Indians have been notoriously inconsistent, to the point that the government itself issued liquor to Indians at least in the mid-nineteenth century. During the first half of the twentieth century, however, it was a federal offense to provide intoxicants to an Indian or to have them on Indian land; state laws to the same effect were widespread. In a context of prohibition, often combined with racial prejudice, it is not surprising that large numbers of Indians were arrested for drunkenness, drunk and disorderly conduct, drunken driving, loitering, and a number of other nonviolent crimes. However, federal prohibition for Indians was repealed in 1953, and many states followed; a provision for local option on reservations has resulted in a variety of responses, ranging from no restrictions, to tribal monopoly, to totally dry. Therefore, many of the criticisms that might be leveled against early studies of Indian criminality are not applicable to Stewart's (429) ambitious compilation which was based on data for 1960. He expressed concern that "The Indian arrests for all alcohol-related crimes is 12 times greater than the national average . . .," but furthermore, as an outspoken partisan of Indians, he was at a loss to explain why ". . . Indians also have a crime rate for non-alcohol connected crimes higher than the national average and higher than any other minority group in the nation." Baker (28), by contrast, came at the question from a wholly different direction; in reviewing the cases of all 36 Indians held in Leavenworth Federal Penitentiary for murder or manslaughter, he considered it noteworthy that in "every case alcohol seemed to be the triggering mechanism that released an acute outburst of hostile, aggressive, overwhelming impulses. . . ." In a more recent study among the Navaho, Levy and his colleagues (272) found that there is only a slight correlation between alcohol and crimes; their estimates suggest that the Navaho homicide rate has been remarkably constant throughout recorded history, with rates similar to those for the general population, although Navaho alcohol use has been increasing markedly in recent years.

In sum, the ethnographic record suggests that there is no clear and consistent relationship between the use of alcohol and expressions of aggression, or other criminal acts. Data on criminality among native peoples are distorted by the fact that drinking or drunkenness are often crimes in themselves. When aggression is a normal outcome of drinking or drunkenness, it tends to occur in stylized ways, and to be directed toward a limited range of target individuals. In this sense, violence as a form of drunken comportment is by no means random, any more than it is inevitable. Furthermore, in this connection, the role of culture in shaping individual behavior is dramatically highlighted—even in a context in which social constraints are generally thought to be largely ignored or overcome.

Familial and Group Disruption

In the literature on alcoholism in Western urban and industrial societies, there is often considerable concern with the social problems of interpersonal conflict and economic hardship within the family. It is a truism that the composition and meanings of that social unit called "the family" are enormously variable not only throughout history but also in cross-cultural perspective at any given time.

The most important fact in this connection, from an ethnographic point of view, is a simple bit of negative evidence—there are very few primitive or other non-Western societies in which habitual drinking in indigenous ways is a major cause of family problems. This does not mean that such problems are necessarily a monopoly of urban populations, or a product of the industrial revolution. Neither does it lend credence to the Rousseauan idealized image of "natural man." Nor does it imply a mystical primitive social solidarity that is immune against stress.

What it probably does mean is that *customary* patterns of drinking normally are integrated with other patterns of belief and behavior to a significant degree, and in ways that generally "fit" (that is, are compatible and complementary rather than discrepant) with the sexual division of labor, ideas and attitudes about behaviors appropriate to specific age groups, and other values and role expectations.

It is equally obvious, however, that habitual drinking in *other than* indigenous ways *is* often disruptive, both of the family and of other levels of social organization. In fact, much of what was written about the early impact of European liquors on native peoples around the world emphasizes this kind of problem. The same theme persists in recent studies, especially those dealing with Eskimos and with American Indians of whatever tribe, and especially those who have moved to cities or otherwise joined the national labor market.

Anxiety, Anomie, and Tension

In general, the abundant literature that deals with "social problems" in connection with alcohol in Western societies tends to focus on outcomes or results of drinking and/or drunkenness. As indicated above, some of this concern occurs also in ethnographic studies; however, the emphasis tends to be very different. In dealing with "social problems" in connection with alcohol in non-Western societies, the focus is more often on the aspects of the sociocultural context that predispose some members of those societies to "excessive" or "problem drinking." In grossly oversimplified terms, although social scientists sometimes look for the "causes" of problem drinking in their own societies, they more often look at the effects. By contrast, in looking at problem drinking in other societies, they more often emphasize "causes" than effects.

It is in this connection, more than other aspects of alcohol studies, that the ethnographic literature is especially rich in interpretative and evaluative statements, and that some attempt at theoretic integration of data and concepts is often attempted. The interpretations that are offered tend, in most instances, to emphasize the political and/or economic dominance of an alien society, and the disruptive impact that it has on native systems of belief and behavior. In part, this may appear to reflect "nativistic" bias on the part of anthropologists, but there is little doubt that it has been the predominant pattern throughout recent history.

Some authors tend to focus on cultural systems, so that their analyses seem to be based on an almost organic model, with problem drinking as one kind of pathology within the social organism. A smaller group draw on more general social science theories about individual behavior, and treat problem drinking as one kind of neurotic response to psychic stress (155–157, 275, 281). The differences between these approaches will become more readily apparent in a critical review of the literature that deals with anxiety, anomie, and tension as social problems associated with alcohol.

Probably the most famous single contribution to alcohol studies that is founded on ethnographic data is the early paper in which Horton (197) concluded, on the basis of statistical correlations of indices of anxiety and of insobriety, that " . . . *the primary function of alcoholic beverages in all societies is the reduction of anxiety*" (italicized in original). This article has been summarized and criticized so often that it is appropriate here only to note that he distinguished various types of anxieties ("anticipations of pain," related to subsistence, sorcery, acculturation, warfare, aggression, and sexual morality); he also paid attention to "counteranxiety" (elicited by painful experience during and after drinking). Using the few nonliterate cultures on which adequate data were then available, he found statistically significant support for his "theorems" that "The strength of the drinking response in any society tends to vary directly with the level of anxiety in that society [and] . . . to vary inversely with the strength of counteranxiety." Although subsequent cross-cultural studies have sometimes failed to confirm Horton's findings in detail, and have drawn attention to certain methodological weaknesses in his highly original effort (e.g., 20, 134, 410), the hypothesis that most people drink primarily in order to lessen anxiety is probably still the most popular and widely held view among laymen and professionals alike. One author even goes so far as to recommend "total alcohol consumption as [a direct] index of anxiety among urbanised Africans" (416), although several others have explicitly emphasized exceptions to Horton's generalization (e.g., 204, 208, 458).

A number of specific ethnographic studies make much of the role of anxiety as a factor predisposing individuals to excessive drinking or drunkenness. For example, this has been done with respect to recent changes in Japanese patterns (403), Mexicans who try to emulate Anglo culture (314), Kaska Indians (but not others in the same community, 313), well educated Navahos (130), aggressive Apache men (59), and many other groups around the world.

Although a few of the authors who use the terms are sometimes careful to distinguish between "anxiety" and "tension," much of the literature that is phrased in terms of either of these, whether as a problem or predisposing factor, could equally well be recast in terms of the other (74). Another chapter in this volume is entirely devoted entirely to a critical review of the abundant literature on the "tension reduction hypothesis" (TRH; see Chapter 5), it would be superfluous to devote much attention to it here. Nevertheless, it may be in order simply to illustrate, by means of a selective sampling, sources of anthropological importance that deal with TRH, even when they do not specifically use that term.

Among the many ethnographic sources that focus on tension as a primary motivating force for drinking, or for excessive drinking, the following are representative: Lemert (264), Park (351), Maynard (325), Lickliss (275), Heilizer (181), Kuttner and Lorincz 247, and Whittaker 467.

Needless to say, this is one of the topics on which it is extremely difficult to perform experiments in the laboratory, using human subjects. The classic studies were done on rodents (90, 91) and felines (323), although one of the pioneering experimenters in the field took special pains to disclaim that his work with rats might have any applicability to human beings (6).

A particular source of anxiety, or tension, is most often cited with reference to non-Western peoples, namely, the stress of cultural conflict or cultural change, usually in a context of acculturation but often in relation to urbanization, marginality, pauperism, or various cultural discontinuities that are sometimes called anomie.

It would be easy to dismiss this emphasis as reflecting a cultural bias on the part of anthropologists, if it were not similarly evident in much of the work by psychiatrists, psychologists, and others who use the individual as their unit of study. On the basis of work on Chilean patients with "meta-alcoholic psychoses," for example, Aguilar (5) articulated the broad conclusion that ". . . it is the conflict between traditional habits and the habits in force in countries in a period of technical evolution, which is reflected in the critical increase of psychotic disturbances amongst us." Another psychiatrist working with different non-Western populations (39) found differential rates of alcoholism "at variance with expectations of psychoanalytic theory," and concluded that "sociocultural deprivation which affects self-image and creates ego-need and inferiority feelings seems a likely explanation." In interpreting the "blitz drinking" of Mescalero Apache men, Curley (99) lends etiological weight to "the uncertainty of their role in society"; similarly, Sayres (408) attributed excessive compulsive drinking among the Zarzal mestizos to their insecurity over "the conflict between residual Indian traditions and new precepts."

The types of "conflict" or "sociocultural deprivation" cited in these studies are sometimes specified, or even differentiated, as including very different kinds of concerns. In some instances, the emphasis is on a dilemma of choice—new goals or values conflict with traditional ones. In other instances, the emphasis is on a dilemma of access—new goals or values have been chosen over old ones, but the new ones are difficult to achieve. One of the best studies of excessive drinking and other deviant behavior in different societies is that of Jessor et al. (215); while comparing Anglo-Americans, Spanish-Americans, and Indians in a small community, a significantly higher rate of deviance for Indians was related to a low degree of consensus on norms, stemming in large part from conflict between indigenous patterns and those of the dominant white culture. J. Levy and Kunitz (271) challenged the idea that social pathologies among American Indian tribes are recent outcomes of culture shock or anomie, and cited limited evidence suggesting constant and unexceptional rates of homicide and suicide among Navahos throughout the historical period; they also found that ". . . the highest intensity of involvement with drinking and the greatest use of alcohol was found among the most traditional and least acculturated group." Ferguson (133) also worked with Navaho alcoholics, but her emphasis is very different; the differential rates of success of different groups under similar therapy suggest that the etiological problems have less to do with "acculturation" than with "lack of a stake in society" or "lack of access to valued goals."

Similarly, in discussing the Sioux, Hurt and Brown (201) specify that ". . . although socioeconomic deprivation may be a major factor in the most general sense of social drinking, the particular types of drinking patterns among the Yankton Indians are the end result of various factors in their traditional culture that have reacted to two centuries with the dominant white society." Although it was formulated explicitly with reference to Western culture, Boalt's (53) sociological theory of alcoholism as an "escape to illness" when one cannot achieve a status to which he aspires might apply equally to interethnic situations where "marginal" individuals may reject the ways of a native group but not be accepted into another group. Norick's (348) account of Alaskan Eskimos seems to support that view; those who hold to the traditional ways rarely drink, whereas ". . . heavy drinking associated with deviant actions is characteristic of that segment of the native population *most* exposed to non-native influence," including aspirations which they have no means to attain; Ervin (119) makes much the same point, as does Vallee (444) in reference to Eskimos in Canada.

An unusual case is that of Society Islanders (273) in which drunkenness and associated violence appear to have diminished during recent years; however, this apparent reversal of a virtually universal pattern takes on different significance when we view it in historical perspective. The violent drunkenness dramatically reported a century ago was itself a reversal of earlier pacific patterns, involving a shift from home-brew to distilled liquor under pressure from white traders; this appears to be a return to earlier patterns, not only in terms of the beverage but also in terms of the context, meanings, and values associated with drinking.

In accounting for widespread problem drinking among American Indians, Dozier (111) emphasizes the role of sociocultural deprivation; alcohol is used to provide relief for "... the Indian's deep sense of inadequacy and inferiority." By contrast, Graves (157) argues strongly that "... the vast majority of Navaho drunkenness, at least in Denver, can be accounted for *without recourse to the fact that the subjects are Indians*" (italics in original), so that the problem lies not so much with Indians as with "the wider society within which Indians are trying to survive."

Symbolism

Apart from the descriptive approach in which ethnographers deal with the interrelations of religion and alcohol, a few authors have paid special attention to religious beliefs and practices as a rich field for interpretation. Perhaps the most influential of these has been Jellinek, in a posthumous paper (214). It is characteristic of the man that he casually offered suggestive insights frequently in lectures that drew on immense erudition, but that he never got around to publishing one of his most striking formulations—the version that is available was edited from tapes and notes, by Popham and Yawney (374).

In oversimplified form, his attempt to explain why people drink alcoholic beverages is built on the following points. The primal importance of fluids for the sustenance of life is universally recognized, so that the "stream of life" is widely equated with fertility as well as survival. Water and milk enjoy such importance in many cultures, and were even more exalted in ancient times. The special properties of alcohol and its physiological effects on the body (warming, relaxing, and giving a sense of power) make it a ritual symbol par excellence, and drinking jointly from the "stream of life" can promote a sense of identification, much as the merging of blood is often used to "create" brotherhood. (Patterns of toasting, and intensely strong moral imperative not to decline a proffered drink are taken as contemporary vestiges of this solidarity-enhancing quality of alcohol.) He also makes the point that "Drunkenness can be a kind of shortcut to the higher life, the achievement of a higher state without an emotional and intellectual effort." The "ritual" use of alcohol has, in many societies, been followed by a very different "utilitarian" kind of drinking, and Jellinek suggests that "It is when the utility of alcohol comes into the foreground that we begin to see individualized drinking."

Like most global theories, this has some of the qualities of a "just-so story," and may be unprovable, but it *is* as inclusive as any other to date and not only hangs together in terms of the material with which he dealt, but also "rings true" with relation to a wide range of data with which he was not familiar. The symbolism of blood and wine have been remarked on for centuries; the Christian ritual of communion perpetuates it explicitly; poets and playwrights recur to the theme: peasants are not the only ones who believe that red wine "builds" or replenishes the blood; and so forth.

In challenging the hypothesis put forth separately by Bales (30) and by Snyder (425) to the effect that there is an inverse correlation between the use of alcohol in ritual and heavy drinking, Klausner (238) made many of the same points as Jellinek; his paper is more readily accessible, but not much more methodologically rigorous. On the basis of data from 48 societies, he concludes that "the use of alcohol in conjunction with sacrifice suggests a link between its use and dealing with the problem of evil," and painstakingly musters evidence to support his view of alcohol as the "symbolic equivalent of blood." Unlike Jellinek, who was concerned with why people drink alcohol at all, Klausner was concerned with why people drink heavily, and he concluded that ". . . under strain, people turn to alcohol as the modern representative of the sacrificial cults for the riddance of evil."

The religions of classical antiquity have been analyzed in great detail, and wine was important to worshippers and to the gods as well. There are few deities in the Greek or Roman pantheons for which wine was not the ideal sacrifice, and individual gods and goddesses personified wine and its effects; a variety of general and detailed studies are available in McKinlay (300–310), Kircher (237), Crawley (95), and others.

A variety of other symbolic associations are alluded to in the literature—for example, the idea that heavy drinking connotes manliness, or that drinking together demonstrates friendship—but they are so highly variable in terms of intercultural differences that little theoretic weight can be given to them. Early Jewish symbolism is discussed by Goodenough (153); biblical and early Christian symbolism by Danielou (106), Fenasse (126), Raymond (382), and others. The symbolism of alcohol in ancient Japanese culture has been dealt with by Yamamuro (477–480), among South American tribes by Lenoir (270), and in east Indian culture by Mitra (334) and Ravi (381). Alcoholic beverages play symbolic roles with respect to religion in several primitive societies (459); some of the most thoroughly described cases are Ainu (245), Iroquois (442, 75), and Tiriki (402). One missionary went so far as to invite his colleagues to share his tolerant recognition of the sacred aspect of drunkenness (347); Fouquet (136) was considerably less sympathetic in deploring "fallacious references to a claimed sacred value," whereas Felice (124), also a clergyman, called alcoholics "devotees of a peculiar kind who unconsciously accomplish certain rituals effectively destined to give them access to another world, a supernatural world." Glover's (149) early psychoanalytic interpretation of alcoholic and other drug addictions is similar in theme. The idea of drunkenness as a transcendental state is clearly articulated among the Zapotecs (225), Haitian voodooists (55), the Rajputs (76), the Quechuas of Peru (320), and the early Senecas (105), among other groups.

Epidemiology

An excellent review article on this topic, emphasizing sociocultural perspectives, will soon be published (277), so that it seems appropriate in this context only to indicate briefly the kinds of mutual interests and complementary approaches that anthropologists and epidemiologists presumably bring to bear on studies of alcohol.

Ethnographers will contribute little in this connection unless they provide data on quantities of alcoholic beverages consumed, frequency of cirrhosis (e.g., 247), numbers of individuals who suffer various kinds of "problems" associated with their drinking, and other quantitative information that they rarely collect in detail. In the meantime, epidemiological formulations generally refer to situations where such statistics are available, together with other data on morbidity, mortality, economics, and so forth.

It is surprising, from an anthropological point of view, ". . . for a variety of populations that the distribution of consumption levels closely approximates a smooth skewed curve known as the logarithmic normal curve" (278). Although the data are all from groups within the mainstream of Western culture (Australia, Belgium, Canada, Finland, France, Netherlands, Sweden, and the United States), one might have expected that the strikingly different attitudes and uses of alcohol in those nations would be reflected in different distributions of alcohol consumption. With respect to patterns, it may also be significant that Lint and Schmidt's (279) epidemiological data (based on both consumption and cirrhosis) lend no support to the widely held views that Italians have a low rate of alcoholism, that the Irish have a high rate, or that distilled beverages lead to more alcoholism than do fermented ones. Each of these findings runs counter to simplistic (and often poorly documented) statements made by social scientists who use a vague functional or sociocultural model (466) and the discrepancy raises serious questions about the need to reexamine the largely anecdotal corpus of ethnographic data on alcohol, and to encourage more rigorous compilation and reporting on the part of field workers who deal with drinking in non-Western contexts.

Ambivalence

One of the earliest articles to appear in the *Quarterly Journal of Studies on Alcohol* was a brief review of the conflict between the thesis of hedonism and the antithesis of asceticism in Western history (342), and alcohol*ism* (in the sense of problems stemming from alcohol use) was interpreted as primarily a product of social ambivalence. An impressive portion of the abundant literature on alcohol since then has included reference to ambivalence, usually not in such general philosophic terms but rather in terms specifically of how various peoples estimate and evaluate the positive benefits and the dangers of alcohol; excellent review articles have appeared periodically (e.g., 48, 383, 440.)

There are many cultures in history which manifest ambivalence about beverage alcohol, in the sense of esteeming it as a healthful tonic, as a lubricant for sociability, as a good food, and so forth on the one hand, while on the other hand deploring the fact that excessive use often results in shameful behavior, causes physical injury, disrupts social relations, or is harmful in other ways.

Abundant sources from ancient history point out the dual quality of alcohol. A number of Egyptian papyri from the second millenium B.C. praise beer as a food but warn of the dangers of indiscretion when one drinks too much; the Roman Senate once cancelled the Bacchanalia festivities in the interests of public safety; classic Japanese and Indian writings, like the biblical scriptures of the same era, explicitly endorse temperate use of wines and beers but warn against the dangers of abuse (cf. Sections 3–5 and 7).

If we look at nonliterate societies around the world, we find that the same kind of ambivalence is not uncommon, although positive evaluation of alcohol is much more the norm. Bunzel (69) recognized the importance of this in the patterns of drunkenness among the Indians of Chichicastenango, especially in contrast with the Indians of Chamula, who do not share the sense of shame about the behavior of inebriates. In another comparative study, Yawney (482) found in Trinidad that East Indians are ambivalent about alcohol, but that Negroes are unequivocally positive in their attitude toward it. The Salish tribes of northwestern North America value drunkenness but fear the disruption that often follows it (261, 263); the same is true of the Lunahuaneno mestizos (418–420), the Frobisher Bay Eskimos (195), Mapuches (284–286), north Indian villagers (172), and Zapotecs (225), among others.

It is this dilemma that Horton (197) was addressing when he added a factor of "counter-anxiety" to his cross-cultural formulation that stressed various kinds of anxieties as the predominant factors in a society's inclination to "increased drinking response" (cf. Section 9).

Another of the few specific hypotheses that have been offered to account for cross-cultural differences in drinking and drunkenness takes ambivalence as its focus. "... *In any group or society in which the drinking customs, values, and sanctions—together with the attitudes of all segments of*

*the group or society—are well established, known to and agreed upon by
all, and are consistent with the rest of the culture, the rate of alcoholism
will be low*" (440; italics in original). A number of sociologists have found
the idea helpful, especially in dealing with complex or pluralistic societies in
which such a degree of consistency, or cultural integration, is unusual. In a
brief review of the literature addressed to nonspecialists, Knupfer (241)
used ambivalence as the central concept. E. Blacker (48) went even further
in another useful review article, offering an important additional qualifi-
cation by inserting, just prior to the final clause in Ullman's formulation,
the words: "*and are characterized by prescriptions for moderate drinking
and proscriptions against excessive drinking*" (italics in original). Neither
of these hypotheses has yet been subjected to systematic and rigorous
testing, but few exceptions come to mind, and the most recent and fairly
comprehensive review of the sociological literature on excessive drinking
(383) includes a well reasoned and substantial endorsement of them.

Blacker's (48) emphasis on prescriptions and proscriptions is an outgrowth of the work of Mizruchi and Perrucci (335) on norm qualities and
differential effects of deviant behavior. It fits well with the anomalous
situation of those members of ascetic Protestant sects who have become alcoholics even though abstinence is a cardinal article of faith in their
churches (cf. 242, 422, 435) and with the Pueblo Indian outcasts noted by
Kunitz et al. (247).

Another indirect kind of support comes from those instances, far more
common in the ethnographic literature, in which the consensus on drinking
is markedly favorable. An overwhelming majority of the societies for whom
attitudes about alcohol have been reported consider it unequivocally good
and useful, whether for religious, social, nutritional, symbolic, or other purposes; just a few of those groups for whom ambivalence is *explicitly*
reported to be absent are Aleuts (46), Camba (175), Sioux (337), Tarahumara (485), Giriama (353). In such societies, the rare individual who is ambivalent about alcohol is abnormal (in a statistical and a social sense), and
is subjected to considerable social pressures to drink and get drunk. Sometimes conversion to ascetic Protestantism serves as one of the few ways in
which a person who has reservations about culturally dominant patterns of
alcohol—whether for reasons of health, wealth, psychic welfare, or some
other factor—can escape the pressures (e.g., 225, 402). This is not to say
that such converts are able totally to escape social problems, but electing
that dramatic option changes the nature of the problems they face in social
relations.

The fact that anthropologists have not addressed themselves more to
testing the role of ambivalence should not be interpreted as meaning that
they are unaware of it or that they doubt it. There is a persistent strain

among professional anthropologists to emphasize the collection and analysis of "one's own" data, and—with occasional important exceptions—general propositions are rarely offered and perhaps even more rarely tested, except in the casual manner of mentioning the fact when an individual case does not conform to a widely known hypothesis. Even in the absence of cross-cultural testing, it appears that many anthropologists are providing the kinds of data that are immediately relevant to the Ullman-Blacker formulation. In terms of the global ethnographic picture, the preponderant tendency is clearly in the direction of confirmation: consensus and consistency are the rule, and rates of alcoholism are low. At the same time, it is clear that many of the questions raised by the findings of epidemiologists (cf. Section 9) call for more rigorous specification than "consensus," "consistency," "prescription," and similar variables that predominate in the sociocultural contributions to alcohol studies. This is especially true when relative weightings of attitudes are crucial to theory—as is the case with reference to ambivalence.

Functionalism

Since the 1930s, one of the predominant concerns in most ethnographic studies has been to go beyond descriptive reporting, and to delineate the functional relationships of society, culture, and the individual, in whatever conceptual or analytic categories were chosen for the description. For historical purposes, it is fruitful to distinguish at least two different emphases in functionalism. One approach focuses on the society or the culture as a sort of organism, and assays to spell out the functions that various institutions, beliefs, behaviors, or other component parts play with respect to facilitating, maintaining, adapting, or adjusting the societal and/or cultural organism as a whole. The other approach tends to focus on the individual as its unit of analysis, and tries to discern the functions that institutions, beliefs, behaviors, or other aspects of the sociocultural system play with respect to the adjustment and adaptation of the individual. The distinction is pertinent and often useful; however, many of the anthropologists who have written in any detail about alcohol and culture seem to consider the sociocultural and the individual approaches to functionalism to be complementary and use either or both, depending on what order of "fact" they are trying to "explain."

In many instances, writers appear to be using "the functionalist approach" even when they do not explicitly use any of the terms I have mentioned above. For example, I consider the emphasis on "group solidarity," or "positive social integration" frequently cited in the interpretation of drinking bouts to be a functionalist statement of the sociocultural type, in the same way that much of the writing on "motivation," "anxiety," "tension reduction," and so forth, appears to be functionalist with the emphasis on the individual. A number of the "functions" that drinking and drunkenness serve, for the group or for the individual, in various societies have already been cited throughout Sections 8 and 9 of this chapter; in this context it may still be worthwhile to list a few of the patterns that recur in the ethnographic literature.

With respect to non-Western and peasant cultures, the drinking of alcoholic beverages is probably most often cited as an act which has important value in promoting social cohesion or conviviality (e.g., 84, 159, 191, 192, 357, 403, 48). Somewhat more strongly phrased interpretations occasionally speak of group drinking as "symbolizing social unity" (e.g., 24, 30, 282, 317), and the unity theme is even more dramatic when a few authors refer to the importance of group solidarity vis-à-vis another reference group [e.g., distinguishing Indians or métis from whites (111, 290, 428, 437); cult members from outsiders (253); Zapotecs from Protestants (225); blacks from whites, (18); and Polynesians from elites (265)]. Sacred functions of alcohol have already been noted (see especially Section 9); related to these but often distinguishable from them are usages which emphasize alcohol as a means of achieving societal renewal, or a quasi-mystical link with a valued past, as reported by Lemert (263), Gallagher (140), Umunna (440), and others. Fallding (123) lists four types of uses, all of which serve different functions for "civilization." In this connection, the distinction between sociocultural functionalism and individual functionalism is far from being clear-cut; it becomes even more problematical when we consider the numerous sources that treat drinking or drunkenness as reactions to the pressures of acculturation or anomie (see especially Section 9) (also 197, 236, 437, 484).

A few of the interpretations of drinking and drunkenness offered by anthropologists do focus on the motivations of individuals. Drinking as a means of enhancing a man's social status or prestige is reported among the Potawatomi (164), Sioux (201), Chippewa (463), and many other groups; drinking to overcome shyness or to gain courage is cited for the Tarahumara (485), Zarzal mestizos (408), Society Islanders (265), and others; and members of some groups even mentioned the recreational value of drinking (see, e.g., 84, 140, 234, 235, 467). A general proposition is offered by Banay (31) who asserts that ". . . in the alcoholic fog one finds exactly what one seeks or boldly defies what one fears." One of the criticisms occasionally leveled at anthropologists is that, in their effort to discern the presumed logical consistency and functional integration of various traits within sociocultural systems, they sometimes overlook inconsistencies or *dys*functions. As has been indicated in Section 9, a number of "social problems" have been identified with respect to alcohol use, both customary and exceptional, in other cultures, although they tend to be less prevalent than in Western culture. A few of the dysfunctions not previously discussed are, for example, the excessive economic cost of drinking for the Malagaches (369) and Ubangis (350), factionalism between "wets" and "drys" among the Apaches (173), an apparent link between Pondomisi native beer and pellagra (327), gradual poisoning because of the accumulation of toxic substances in Quechua chicha (324), and so forth.

In recent years, functionalist interpretations have come increasingly under attack from a variety of perspectives. Some critics have expressed concern that, carried to its logical conclusion, sociocultural functionalism would result in a characterization of systems in terms of such precise integration that any change would be inexplicable. However, a number of studies of changes in drinking patterns are couched primarily in terms of changing functional interrelationships among aspects of culture. Although it may validly be argued that such diachronic analyses do not come to grips with the actual processes by which change comes about (424), it is apparent that a functional approach is no more ahistorical than other approaches to human behavior that are favored by such critics. For such discussions of change, see Section 8 above (also 258, 288, 388, 403, 413).

Another criticism of functionalism is that it is impressionistic, rarely based on replicable cases, and generally lacking in quantified or "objective" supporting data. At one level, this is certainly a limitation in comparison with the rigorous controlled experimentation conducted in some other kinds of alcohol studies; at another level, it is a limitation shared by the vast majority of other approaches to behavior, whether used by psychologists, sociologists, or anthropologists.

The value of functional interpretation is also being challenged by social scientists who consider it more fruitful to try to understand alien cultures in terms of native categories rather than in terms of Western analytic concepts. One such approach is that of "ethnoscience," which deals with the relations between words and concepts, but not with overt behavior or even with beliefs and attitudes. In this kind of study, folk taxonomies are used as keys to the "cognitive maps" of those who speak the language; examples are Frake (137) and Hage (163). A more recent elaboration moves in the direction of behavioral analysis at a relatively microscopic level; having elicited a typology of drinking situations or of drinkers, Topper (438) has attempted to elicit "verbal plans" relevant to each—that is, structured native descriptions of alternative planned activities in the language of the informant. An approach that attempts to combine native perspectives and those of the social scientist, to relate conceptualizations to behavior, and to interpret meanings in ways that would be acceptable both to the informant and the analyst, may have most of the strengths of all of these approaches as well as those of functionalism; a number of authors have tried to look at drinking among various North American Indian tribes in these terms, and their analyses have been brought together by Everett and Waddell (122).

It is interesting that one of the most broadly applicable propositions about why people drink was formulated by a psychiatrist and an anthropologist, in such a way as to combine functions from both the social and individual points of view. On the basis of ethnographic and historical sources dealing primarily with nonliterate societies, MacAndrew and Edgerton (292) emphasize that, in cross-cultural perspective, ". . . the state of drunkenness is accorded the status of at least a partial *time out* . . . [and] the option of drunken Time Out affords people the opportunity to 'get it out of their systems' with a minimum of adverse consequences."

In spite of the apparent value of some alternative approaches to the understanding of drinking and drunkenness, functional interpretations continue to predominante in the social science literature, often incorporating important aspects of perspectives that have been proposed as alternatives.

Dependence and Power

With respect to psychological motivations that, in social context, are thought to be primary motivations for drinking and drunkenness in a wide range of cultures, probably the best articulated are those that emphasize dependence and power. The former is best exemplified in the studies of McCord et al. (1960), and Barry, Bacon, and Child (21, 22, 37, 80, 81); and the latter in the work of McClelland and his colleagues (294, 295).

On the basis of studies among a local population in the United States, McCord et al. (298), criticized each of the major physiological, psychological, and sociological theories about alcoholism, and proposed as an alternative that conflict over dependency might be the crucial factor. Child and his colleagues provided dramatic cross-cultural support for such a view, using a worldwide sample of 139 societies and correlating variations in the use of alcohol with other traits. With a focus on child training and role expectations for adults, it was found that drinking and drunkenness tend to be more frequent in societies which produce a high degree of conflict about dependence and independence. Large-scale correlation and factor analysis led them to conclude that ". . . as a reaction to dependency conflict, alcohol has a triple function: it reduces anxiety and tension; it permits the satisfaction of desires for dependence; it permits uncritical indulgence of unrealistic fantasies of achievement" (21).

It is perhaps unfortunate that although the authors were careful to emphasize that *conflict* over dependency was a major covariant of heavy drinking in societies, many superficial discussions have referred to their findings as stressing *dependency* (the need itself) as a causal factor of heavy drinking in individuals (36). It had long been observed that dependency, as a personality trait, was commonplace among alcoholics (see 470), including Chileans (19), and some American Indians (59), but the idea of dependency as a causal factor seems to have stemmed in part from the Child, Bacon, and Barry studies (e.g., 219). [A number of other correlations that suggest a variety of other hypotheses about drinking and drunkenness were pointed out in the study, but have attracted considerably less attention (20).]

Just as the McCords' early statement on dependency conflict is rarely mentioned by writers who credit Child and his colleagues with having made a significant breakthrough, several observers remarked on the importance of power as a motivation for drinking long before McClelland and his associates compiled their studies in a book that many hail as a milestone.

Undoubtedly there are earlier explicit references to power in the literature of alcohol studies, but in cross-cultural perspective, Lemert's (264) interpretation of the way in which young Samoan men use drinking as a means of protesting the ceremonial and authoritarian traditions of the island is one of the most unequivocal; others include Hamer's (164) assertion that the Potawatomi use alcohol to create "a fantasy status of authority," or Jellinek's (214) interpretation of drinking as symbolic of power derived from the "stream of life."

The Drinking Man is a fascinating book, even if one does not find the power theory compelling, inasmuch as the authors have revised and brought together a number of papers that deal with specific limited experiments, using a wide variety of methods, in such a way that they seem to be letting the reader share with them the process of learning, by cumulative trial and error, what they experienced over the course of several years. This is not the context for a detailed critique or even a summary of the elaborate way in which the authors make vast leaps of logic in terms of devising indirect indices for psychological states, explaining away inconsistencies, and so forth.

The central thesis is succinctly stated: "Men drink primarily to feel stronger. Those for whom personalized power is a particular concern drink more heavily. Ingestion of alcohol cues off thoughts of strength and power in men everywhere, apparently for physiological reasons" (294, 334).

A distinction is made between power that is "socialized" and power that is "personal." "In normal settings, the physiological effects of drinking stimulate socialized power thoughts, which are here assumed to be pleasurable in the sense that men who are expected to be strong and assertive like to feel strong and assertive. This explains why people like to drink" (294, 137). But the theory is supposed to be equally applicable when contrasting conditions prevail: ". . . failure to gain social power, or recognition, may turn a man to drinking in order to gain a primitive and narcissistically gratifying sense of personal power. The action is self-defeating because it makes even less likely the support and recognition he needs, which again turns him to alcohol as a means of giving himself at least a temporary boost in his feelings of potency" (294, 197).

The work of McClelland and associates was based on a variety of approaches, including analysis of themes in folktales of various societies, role playing. Thematic Apperception Tests (TATs), and other projective analytic devices; it has been summarized effectively by Boyatzis (58). However, much of the apparent statistical preciseness of the summary statements derives from extremely crude indices, scalings, and extrapolations that progressively blur the primary data. Another severe criticism is the explicit exclusion of undistilled alcoholic beverages from the discussion of effects of drinking in Western society, although most of the nonliterate societies from which folktales were analyzed use only fermented drinks (222, 295). There has been little independent support offered for the basic proposition that men drink alcoholic beverages to attain or to regain a feeling of power (456), although a few authors have already offered conflicting evidence. For example, a subsequent study, using TATs, suggests that ". . . inhibition is more important than power in predicting drinking behavior when the subject can choose the amount he wants to drink" (102). What seems to be the only study of the effects of drinking on women's fantasies (468) suggests that power motivations do not obtain.

A number of observers have even suggested that power and dependence are two sides of the same coin, so that these approaches are similar rather than different (e.g., 107). According to this view, the conflict over dependency is an admission of powerlessness, so that the psychosocial dynamics of drinking are similar, whether one emphasizes the need for power or the strain of dependency conflict as motivations (122). Furthermore, the cross-cultural data suggest that such monotypic and psychologically reductionist theories may not be adequate to account for the wide range of motives and patterns of drinking and drunkenness that occur throughout the world. The heuristic value of either the dependency or the power approach is especially questionable when proponents are ready to demonstrate how either "theory" can equally well account for forms of belief and behavior that are themselves not only contradictory but diametrically contrastive.

10. CONCLUSIONS

In reviewing the abundant and immensely diverse ethnographic literature on nonliterate peoples, I have chosen not to focus on a few selected groups and summarize their patterns of belief and behavior concerning alcohol. A number of readily available sources do that in ways that should be not only comprehensible but even interesting to most readers of this volume (for example, 355, 363–366, 427, 458). What I have attempted to do instead is to provide a brief introduction to the abundant literature in a way that will help a person who is not already familiar with anthropology to find a few sources on each major world area, and also to appreciate the variety of topics and approaches represented, especially those which have been used by authors of other disciplines in writing about alcohol in general or in specific cultural contexts.

On the basis of such a review, one cannot help but be struck by several ways in which the ethnographic literature differs from other bodies of information on the subject.

The ethnographic work on alcohol has been extremely fragmented and uneven. By this I refer to the fact that there has been virtually no systematic attempt ever to do sustained investigation of a single population through time, nor to sample in an appropriate way the beliefs and behaviors of a given population in terms of age, sex, or other criteria that may be important in distinguishing significant subgroups in a given cultural context.

If the form of ethnographic reports is fragmentary and uneven, the content is even more so. Nevertheless, a number of significant propositions can be discerned even among the richly diverse reports on drinking. Perhaps some of these already have become generally accepted among those who study alcohol, but most of them are not known by nonspecialists, and some may even be surprising to a few readers of this volume.

Drinking is normally a social act, embedded in a context of (often implicit) values, attitudes, and conceptions of reality.

To a significant extent, the effects of drinking are shaped by those values, attitudes, and conceptions of reality, as well as by the social setting in which it takes place.

Drunkenness not only has different meanings and values in different cultures, but also involves significantly different kinds of behavior; drunken behavior is patterned to such a degree that it appears to be, in large part, the resultant of a learning process.

Alcoholism—even in the general sense of problems associated with drinking—is rare in the vast majority of the societies of the world. One might even go so far as to note that it is almost unknown outside the mainstream of Western culture, although it is becoming a widespread concomitant of acculturation which often accompanies the impact of modern industrial society.

Unfortunately, it is difficult to speak with any confidence about other orders of generalization. There is a vast gap between analyses of specific local case studies and global monocausal psychodynamic theories. Middle-range hypotheses are rare, largely because few of the reports provide the kind of data that lend themselves to confident cross-cultural comparison. It is not just that, as in many cross-cultural studies, frequent use of native terms makes it difficult to relate descriptions from one society to those of others. An even greater problem lies in the fact that many ethnographic studies of alcohol have been too narrowly focused in terms of discussing data within a given theoretic or methodological framework, sometimes to the point of omitting kinds of information that would be crucial to others who might want to analyze the situation in different terms. For example, such basic information as quantity, frequency, and alcoholic content of the beverage occur only rarely in such studies. In a sense, this is under-standable and even excusable when we recognize that most such studies are incidental by-products of research that was concerned primarily with other topics. Nevertheless, there is by now enough consensus on certain cate-gories of information that comprise an ideal (or at least a minimal) descrip-tion of beliefs and behaviors concerning alcohol, that a field guide would be useful (29). Such a "field guide," comprising a set of questions and cate-gories would by no means be a substitute for training in research methods nor could it anticipate what new kinds of information may be important in future years, but it could provide a set of flexible guidelines which would be helpful to a number of people with varying backgrounds (such as Peace Corps volunteers, missionaries, student anthropologists, and others) who would be interested and competent to collect data on drinking patterns among different populations. The value of such a tool has already been demonstrated with respect to socialization, sex beliefs and practices, kin-ship terminology, and a few other aspects of culture. Margaret Bacon and Dwight Heath are planning to compile such a guide, in the hope that it will help in providing more, and more comparable, data on drinking.

Another striking feature of the ethnographic literature on alcohol studies, in marked contrast with a major portion of the writings on alcohol in Western society, is the relative lack of concern with social problems, education, prevention, therapy, or even alcoholics and alcoholism as meaningful categories. As already discussed (Section 9), this is in large part a reflection of the fact that, in cross-cultural perspective, "problem drinking" is very rare, and alcoholism seems to be virtually absent even in many societies where drunkenness is frequent, highly esteemed, and ac-tively sought.

It seems appropriate in this context, however, to point to a few implica-tions for action that I believe can reasonably be inferred from the experience of the many societies around the world which have been reviewed for this article. It would be presumptuous, on the one hand, for an anthropologist to offer ready solutions to the many complex problems faced by therapists, social workers, and others who are actively engaged in attempting to deal with the many problems that stem from some uses of alcohol. It would be irresponsible, on the other hand, for a concerned research worker to neglect to point out what he takes to be some of the principal implications of his findings. The data summarized above are important as an introduction to the range of studies available for those who may wish to pursue further investigations; they also suggest some possibly fruitful avenues of action.

The fact that Jews, Cambas, Chinese, and many others drink distilled liquors often and yet have virtually no problems in connection with drinking suggests that one important measure for preventing alcoholism may well be socialization about where, when, and how to drink. The educational value of prescriptions as well as proscriptions may seem logically obvious, but it is often ignored in practice with respect to drinking.

One of the important gaps that has been revealed by this review is the virtual lack of information on drinking among important subgroups within populations. For example, there is almost no detailed discussion of drinking by women in any of the societies studied to date. In only a few instances are significant differences between age groups indicated (e.g., 264, 433) but it seems probable that both modes and motives in relation to alcohol contrast between generations more often; if that is the case, many of the ethnographic descriptions give an inaccurately unitary view which, in turn, can distort any hologeistic or cross-cultural studies that are done on the basis of speciously unrepresentative generalizations. There is an obvious need for more detailed studies of particular groups, and for substudies within societies.

Also lacking for all but a few countries are studies that trace the life histories of individuals, alcoholic or other. Until such data are more fully available, it is difficult to assess the accuracy or relevance of individual symptoms or of schematic sequences of developmental phases with respect to alcoholism (cf. 453).

With respect to therapy, the internationally famous high rate of "success" enjoyed by Alcoholics Anonymous has often been misinterpreted as proof of the universal efficacy of "the twelve steps." Such a view is not supported, however, when one recognizes that many institutions that share the name "Alcholics Anonymous" do not share "the twelve steps," or much else for that matter. Madsen's (315) study of AA as a religious movement aptly characterizes many of the strengths of the organizations in supporting white middle-class citizens of the United States, but at the same time underscores its irrelevance or even repugnance to many North American Indians; Littmann (280) made a similar point. Madsen earlier (314) showed how ineffective AA was in helping Mexican-American alcoholics. Beaubrun and Firth (41) showed clearly that AA was a very different institution in Trinidad and in London; Beaubrun (40) contrasted Trinidad's AA with that in Jamaica; Angrosino (18) described AA's value for East Indians and its irrelevance for blacks in Trinidad; and Podlewski and Catanzaro (368) pointed to the failure of AA in the Bahamas. Zentner (484) showed how the AA philosophy was rejected by Indians in eastern Canada, although Jilek-Aal (217) describes its worth among the Salish on Canada's west coast. Little else has been written on the subject, but these articles, together with informal discussion with colleagues, suggest that the meanings and values of Alcoholics Anonymous are highly variable around the world, in keeping with significant variations with respect to the view of the nature of man and of individual responsibility, as held by different populations. Further studies of AA and other therapeutic groups should be undertaken in the hope of learning the range of philosophical, moral, social, and psychological imperatives that are effective in providing the support that is needed by alcoholic individuals. Furthermore, a number of alternative institutional means of escaping alcoholism deserve to be analyzed in ways that may provide new insights: for example, Hippler's (186) interpretation of fundamentalist Christianity among Alaskan Athabascans, Dozier's (111) appeal for group-oriented programs (rather than personal and individual therapy) and his recognition of nativistic movements and evangelistic Christianity as ways of overcoming drinking problems among North American Indians.

In the same way that an anthropologist attempts to understand the inner logic of orgiastic, often violent, and sometimes even socially disruptive drinking in sociocultural context, the interests of social science also require that he appreciate that abstemiousness is not merely an aberrant pattern of a few frustrated puritanical misfits or compulsively "dry alcoholics." On the contrary, there is a small but theoretically important number of societies around the world in which alcoholic beverages are known but not used. Brief discussions by H.S (339) and Yawney (481) do not reveal any other clear-cut features that are shared by nondrinking cultures, or that distinguish them from others, but intensive investigation, incorporating a variety of disciplinary perspectives, might throw new light on this crucial sample.

One of the best documented programs for treating non-Western alcoholics is that among the Navaho Indians of the southwestern United States (128); three programs sponsored by various Amerindian groups are described by Shore and Fummetti (417), and an intertribal enterprise in California by Kline and Roberts (239). During the 1970s such efforts are being developed rapidly throughout the United States, as large-scale funding has been made available for the purpose. It is too early to judge the range or relative success of a number of experiments that are being undertaken, in many instances by members of local Indian communities, without direction from foreign "experts." Close study of such projects might be especially revealing, not only in terms of what they tell about folk theories of health, causality, and curing, but also for the new and unorthodox approaches that may prove effective among various populations (92).

The widespread association of initial drinking problems with the migration of peasant and tribal peoples to cities raises important questions about the social and psychological dynamics of migration, and about preventive measures that might be relevant in various contexts.

The basic sociocultural model that emphasizes norms and values concerning alcohol use obviously must be reconciled with the prospect that there may be physiological differences among populations that significantly affect their reactions to alcohol. At the same time, rigorously controlled experiments should be undertaken to test suggestive new hypotheses, however unorthodox or undemocratic they may be.

One important factor that has shaped ethnographic studies of alcohol to date is their almost uniformly incidental or casual conception. At a recent international conference on alcohol studies and anthropology, I got unequivocal confirmation of a long-term hunch—not a single one of the anthropologists in attendance who had published on drinking patterns had set out originally with that in mind. By that I do not mean that they had changed their focus of research during field work, but rather that they studied something else (e.g., cultural change, social organization, economics, etc.) and found, when analyzing their data *later*, that the relations between people and alcohol were important enough to deserve special discussion. In short, the extant ethnography of alcohol is, with very few exceptions, a by-product of broader studies of human behavior. It is striking that, at the same conference, almost as many young anthropologists were in attendance who see alcohol studies as a probable focus of their professional work; some of these people had already completed field work in which they set out to study alcohol and did so. This new generation are now writing books and articles that will presumably soon provide some sophisticated integration of theory with data, more replicability, and more comparability and cumulativeness among various studies, as well as a more systematic attempt to integrate their approaches with those of scientists working on the subject from different disciplinary perspectives.

REFERENCES

Titles are given in the original language only; place of publication is mentioned for those journals that might be confused with others of the same name, or that might be difficult to locate without such information. For historical purposes, books and articles are cited in their initial publication; in those instances where significant revision has been made, the most recent edition is also indicated. Unauthored articles are alphabetized under the name of the responsible source. A few unpublished sources are listed because they deal with topics or approaches that are not represented fully in the published literature.

In the great majority of cases, references were verified through examination of the original publication; in a few instances, I have seen only copies of the text of the article, so that bibliographic data on the inclusive source may be incomplete. This bibliography was closed in July, 1973; the author would welcome additional pertinent references.

1. Aalto, P., Alkoholens Ställning i Indiens Klassiska Kultur, *Alkoholpolitik*, **18**(2), 32–46 (1955).

2. Adandé, A., Le vin de palme chez les Diola de la Casamance, *Notes Afr.* (Dakar), **61**, 4–7 (1954).

3. Adler, N. and D. Goleman, Gambling and alcoholism; symptom substitution and functional equivalents, *Q. J. Stud. Alcohol*, **30**, 733–736 (1969).

4. Adriaens, S.-L. and F. Lozet, Contribution à l'étude des boissons fermentées indigenes au Ruanda, *Bull. Agric. Congo Belge*, **42**, 933–950 (1951).

5. Aguilar, G. Z., Suspension of control: a sociocultural study on specific drinking habits and their psychiatric consequences, *J. Existent. Psychiat.*, **4**, 245–252 (1964).

6. Ahlfors, U. G., *Alcohol and Conflict: A Qualitative and Quantitative Study on the Relationship between Alcohol Consumption and an Experimentally Induced Conflict Situation in Albino Rats*, Alcohol Research in Northern Countries 16, Finnish Foundation for Alcohol Studies, Helsinki, 1969.

7. Ahlström-Laakso, S., Review of European studies on drinking habits, In *Cross-Cultural Studies on Alcohol*, M. W. Everett, J. O. Waddell, and D. B. Heath (Eds.), Mouton, The Hague, expected 1974.

8. Alba, M. de, The maguey and pulque, *Mex. Folkways* **2**(4), 12–15 (1926).

9. *Alcohol, Science and Society*, Journal of Studies on Alcohol, New Haven, 1945.

10. Alhava, A., Väkijuomaolojen erikoisluonne Lapissa, *Alkohol. Aikak.* **12**, 35–37 (1949).

11. Allardt, E., Alkoholvanoran pa Landsbygden i Finland, *Alkoholpolitik*, **19**, 73–77 (1956).

12. Allardt, E., Drinking norms and drinking habits, in *Drinking and Drinkers*, E. Allardt et al., Finnish Foundation for Alcohol Studies Publication 6, Helsinki, 1957.

13. Allardt, E., et al., *Drinking and Drinkers*, Finnish Foundation for Alcohol Studies Publication 6, Helsinki, 1957.

14. Almeida V., M., Investigación clínica sobre la evolución del alcoholismo, *Rev. Neuropsiquiatr.* (Lima), **25**, 97–122 (1962).

15. Anderson, B. G., How French children learn to drink, *Trans-action*, **5**, 20–22 (1969).

16. Anderson, R. K., J. Calvo, G. Serrano, and G. Payne, A study of the nutritional status and food habits of Otomi Indians in the Mezquital Valley of Mexico, *Am. J. Public Health*, **36**, 883–903 (1946).

17. Ando, H. and E. Hasegawa, Drinking patterns and attitudes of alcoholics and nonalcoholics in Japan, *Q. J. Stud. Alcohol*, **31**, 153–161 (1970).

18. Angrosino, M. V., *Outside is Death: Alcoholism, Ideology and Community Organization among the East Indians of Trinidad*, Wake Forest University, Overseas Research Center, Medical Behavioral Science Monograph, Winston-Salem, N.C., expected 1974.

19. Auersperg, A. P. and A. Derwort, Beitrag zur vergleichenden Psychiatrie exogener Psychosen vom soziokulturellen Standpunkt, *Nervenarzt*, **33**, 22–27 (1962).

20. Bacon, M. K., Cross cultural studies of drinking, integrated drinking and sex differences in the use of alcoholic beverages, in *Cross-Cultural Studies on Alcohol*, M. W. Everett, J. O. Waddell, and D. B. Heath (Eds.), Mouton, The Hague, expected 1974.

21. Bacon, M. K., H. Barry, III, and I. L. Child, A cross-cultural study of drinking: II. relations to other features of culture, *Q. J. Stud. Alcohol Suppl.* **3**, 29–48 (1965).

22. Bacon, M. K., H. Barry, III, I. L. Child, and C. R. Synder, A cross-cultural study of drinking: V. detailed definitions and data, *Q. J. Stud. Alcohol Suppl.*, **3**, 78–111 (1965).

23. Bacon, S. D., Sociology and the problems of alcohol: foundations for a sociological study of drinking behavior, *Q. J. Stud. Alcohol*, **4**, 399–445 (1943).

24. Bacon, S. D., Alcohol and complex society, in *Alcohol, Science and Society*, Journal of Studies on Alcohol, New Haven, 1945 (revised, in Pittman and Snyder, 1962).

25. Bacon, S. D., Current research on alcoholism: V. report on the section on sociological research, *Q. J. Stud. Alcohol*, **16**, 551–564 (1955).

26. Bacon, S. D., The process of addiction to alcohol: social aspects, *Q. J. Stud. Alcohol*, **34**, 1–27 (1973).

27. Baird, E. G., The alcohol problem and the law, *Q. J. Stud. Alcohol* **4**, 535–556; **5**, 126–161; **6**, 335–383; **7**, 110–162, 271–296; **9**, 80–118 (1944–1948).

28. Baker, J. L., Indians, alcohol and homicide, *J. Soc. Ther.*, **5**, 270–275 (1959).

29. Baldus, H., Bebidas e narcóticos dos índios do Brasil: Sugestões para pesquisas etnográficas, *Sociologia* (São Paulo), **12**, 161–169 (1950).

30. Bales, R. F., Cultural differences in rates of alcoholism, *Q. J. Stud. Alcohol*, **6**, 480–499 (1946).

31. Banay, R. S., Cultural influences in alcoholism, *J. Nerv. Ment. Dis.*, **102**, 265–275 (1945).

32. Banks, E., Native drink in Sarawak, *Sarawak Mus. J.*, **4**, 439–447 (1937).

33. Barnett, M. L., Alcoholism in the Cantonese of New York City: an anthropological study, in *Etiology of Chronic Alcoholism*, O. Diethelm (Ed.), Charles C Thomas, Springfield, Ill., 1955.

34. Barrera Vásquez, A., *El pulque entre los Mayas*, Cuadernos Mayas 3, Mérida, Mexico, 1941.

35. Barry, H., III, Sociocultural aspects of addiction, *The Addictive States*, **46**, 455–471 (1968).

36. Barry, H. III, Cross-cultural evidence that dependency conflict motivates drunkenness, in *Cross-Cultural Studies on Alchol*, M. W. Everett, J. O. Waddell, and D. B. Heath (Eds.), Mouton, The Hague, expected 1974.

37. Barry, H., III, C. Buchwald, I. L. Child, and M. Bacon, A cross-cultural study of drinking: IV. comparisons with Horton ratings, *Q. J. Stud. Alcohol Suppl.* **3**, 62–77 (1965).

38. Beals, R. L., *The Comparative Ethnology of Northern Mexico before 1750*, University of California Press, Berkeley, 1932.

39. Beaubrun, M. H., Treatment of alcoholism in Trinidad and Tobago, 1956–1965, *Br. J. Psychiat.* **113**, 643–658 (1967).

40. Beaubrun, M. H., The influence of socio-cultural factors in the treatment of alcoholism in the West Indies, in *29th International Congress on Alcoholism and Drug Dependence*, L. G. Kiloh and D. S. Bell (Eds.), Butterworths, Sydney, 1971.

41. Beaubrun, M. H. and H. Firth, A transcultural analysis of Alcoholics Anonymous: Trinidad/London, Paper read at American Psychiatric Association meeting, Ocho Rios, Jamaica, 1969.

42. Beidelman, T. O., Beer drinking and cattle theft in Ukaguru: intertribal relations in a Tanganyika chiefdom, *Am. Anthropol.*, **63**, 534–549 (1961).

43. Bejarano, J. *La derrota de un vicio: Origen e historia de la chicha*, Editorial Iqueima, Bogotá, 1950.

44. Bellmann, H., Die Destillation bei den Naturvölkern, *Wiss. Z. Friedrich Schiller Univ.*, **3**, 179–185 (1954).

45. Belmont, F. V. de, *Histoire de l'Eau-de-Vie en Canada*, Société Litteraire de Quebec, Quebec, 1840.

46. Berreman, G. D., Drinking patterns of the Aleuts, *Q. J. Stud. Alcohol*, **17**, 503–514, (1956).

47. Bett, W. R. [et al.], Alcohol and crime in Ceylon: a preliminary communication [and discussion], *Br. J. Inebriety*, **43**, 57–60 (1946).

48. Blacker, E., Sociocultural factors in alcoholism, *Int. Psychiat. Clinics*, **3**(2), 51–80 (1966).

49. Blacker, H., Drinking practices and problems abroad: the Isle of Reunion; Tahiti, *J. Alcohol.*, **6**(2), 61–63 (1971).

50. Bleichsteiner, R., Zeremoniale Trinksitten und Raumordnung bei Turko-Mongolischen Nomader, *Arch. Völkerkunde*, **6–7**, 181–208 (1952).

51. Block, M. A., *Alcoholism: Its Facets and Phases*, John Day, New York, 1965.

52. Blum, R. H. and E. M. Blum, Drinking practices and controls in rural Greece, *Br. J. Addict.*, **60**, 93–108 (1964).

53. Boalt, G., *A Sociological Theory of Alcoholism*, International Bureau Against Alcoholism Selected Articles 4, Lausanne, 1961.

54. Bose, D. K., *Wine in Ancient India*, K. M. Connor, Calcutta, 1922.

55. Bourguignon, E. E., Comment on Leacock's "Ceremonial drinking in an Afro-Brazilian cult," *Am. Anthropol.*, **66**, 1393–1394 (1964).

56. Bourke, J. G., Primitive distillation among the Tarascoes, *Am. Anthropol.* (OS), **6**, 65–69 (1893).

57. Bourke, J. G., Distillation by Early American Indians, *Am. Anthropol. (OS)*, **7**, 297–299 (1894).

58. Boyatzis, R. E., Drinking as a manifestation of power concerns, in *Cross-Cultural Studies on Alcohol*, M. W. Everett, J. O. Waddell, and D. B. Heath (Eds.), Mouton, The Hague, expected 1974.

59. Boyer, L. B., Psychological problems of a group of Apaches: alcoholic hallucinosis and latent homosexuality among typical men, in *The Psychoanalytic Study of Society*, Vol. 3, W. Muensterberger and S. Axelrad (Eds.), International Universities Press, New York, 1964.

60. Braidwood, R. J., et al., Symposium: did man once live by beer alone? *Am. Anthropol.*, **55**, 515–526 (1953).

61. Brody, H., *Indians on Skid Row*, Northern Science Research Group, Department of Indian Affairs and Northern Development Publication 70-2, Ottawa, 1971.

62. Brown, W. L., Inebriety and its "cures" among the ancients, *Proc. Soc. Study Inebriety*, **55**, 1–15 (1898).

63. Brownlee, F., Native beer in South Africa, *Man* (OS), **33**, 75–76 (1933).

64. Bruman, H. J., Aboriginal drink areas in New Spain, Ph.D. dissertation (Geography), University of California, 1940.

65. Bruman, H. J., Asiastic origin of the Huichol still, *Geogr. Rev.*, **34**, 418–427 (1944).

66. Bruun, K., Significance of role and norms in the small group for individual behavioral changes while drinking, *Q. J. Stud. Alcohol*, **20**, 53–64 (1959).

67. Bruun, K. and R. Hange, *Drinking Habits among Northern Youths*, Finnish Foundation for Alcohol Studies Publication 12, Helsinki, 1963.

68. Buckland, A. W., Ethnological hints afforded by the stimulants in use among savages and among the ancients, *J. R. Anthropol. Inst.*, **8**, 239–254 (1878).

69. Bunzel, R., The role of alcoholism in two central American cultures, *Psychiatry*, **3**, 361–387 (1940).

70. Busch, C. E., Consideraciones médico-sociales sobre la chicha, *Excelsior* (Lima), **217**, 25–26 (1952).

71. Cagol, A., A note on Bapedi beverages, *Primitive Man*, **9**, 32 (1936).

72. Cahalan, D., I. H. Cisin, and H. M. Crossley, *American Drinking Practices: A National Study of Drinking Behavior and Attitudes*, Rutgers Center of Alcohol Studies Monograph 6, New Brunswick, N.J., 1969.

73. Calderón Narvaez, G., Consideraciones acerca del alcoholismo entre los pueblos prehispánicos de México, *Rev. Inst. Nac. Neurología*, **2**(3), 5–13 (1968).

74. Cappell, H. and C. P. Herman, Alcohol and tension reduction: a review, *Q. J. Stud. Alcohol*, **33**, 33–64 (1972).

75. Carpenter, E. S., Alcohol in the Iroquois dream quest, *Am. J. Psychiat*, **116**, 148–151 (1959).

76. Carstairs, G. M., Daru and bhang: cultural factors in the choice of intoxicant, *Q. J. Stud. Alcohol*, **15**, 220–237 (1954).

77. Chafetz, M. E., Consumption of alcohol in the Far and Middle East, *N. Eng. J. Med.*, **271**, 297–301 (1964).

78. Chafetz, M. E. and H. W. Demone, Jr., *Alcoholism and Society*, Oxford University Press, New York, 1962; (rev. ed., 1965).

79. Cherrington, E. H. (Ed.), *Standard Encyclopedia of the Alcohol Problem* (6 Vols.), American Issue Publishing Co., Westerville, Ohio, 1925–1930.

80. Child, I. L., M. K. Bacon, and H. Barry, III, A cross-cultural study of drinking: I. descriptive measurements of drinking customs, *Q. J. Stud. Alcohol Suppl.* **3**, 1–28 (1965).

81. Child, I. L., H. Barry, III, M. K. Bacon, A cross-cultural study of drinking: III. sex differences, *Q. J. Stud. Alcohol Suppl.* **3**, 49–61 (1965).

82. Chopra, R. N., G. S. Chopra, and J. C. Chopra, Alcoholic beverages in India, *Ind. Med. Gaz.*, **77**, 224–232, 290–296, 361–367 (1942).

83. Chu, G., Drinking patterns and attitudes of rooming-house Chinese in San Francisco, *Q. J. Stud. Alcohol Suppl.*, **6**, 58–68 (1972).

84. Clairmont, D. H., *Notes on the Drinking Behavior of the Eskimos and Indians in the Aklavik Area: A Preliminary Report*, Northern Coordination and Research Centre, Department of Northern Affairs and National Resources, Ottawa, 1962.

85. Clairmont, D. H. J., *Deviance among Indians and Eskimos in Aklavik*, Northern Coordination and Research Centre, Department of Northern Affairs and National Resources, Ottawa, 1963.

86. Coffey, T. G., Beer Street: Gin Lane; some views of 18th-century drinking, *Q. J. Stud. Alcohol*, **27**, 669–692 (1966).

87. Collard, J., Drug responses in different ethnic groups, *J. Neuropsychiat.*, **3**, 5114–5121 (1962).

88. Collis, C. H., P. J. Cook, J. K. Foreman and J. F. Palframan, A search for nitrosamines in East African spirit samples from areas of varying oesophageal cancer frequency, *Gut* (London), **12**, 1015–1018 (1971).

89. Collis, C. H., and P. J. Cook, J. K. Foreman, and J. F. Palframan, Cancer of the oesophagus and alcoholic drinks in East Africa, *Lancet*, **1**, 442 (1972).

90. Conger, J. J., The effects of alcohol on conflict behavior in the albino rat, *Q. J. Stud. Alcohol*, **12**, 1–29 (1951).

91. Conger, J. J., Reinforcement theory and dynamics of alcoholism, *Q. J. Stud. Alcohol*, **17**, 296–305 (1956).

92. Cooley, R., Indian alcohol program training needs, in *Alcohol, Drinking and Drunkenness among North American Indians*, M. W. Everett and J. O. Waddell (Eds.), expected 1974.

93. Cooper, J. M., Stimulants and narcotics, in *Handbook of South American Indians: 5. The Comparative Ethnology of South American Indians*, J. H. Steward (Ed.), Bureau of American Ethnology Bulletin 143, Washington, D.C., 1949.

94. Cornwall, E. E., Notes on the use of alcohol in ancient times, *Med. Times*, **67**, 379–380 (1939).

95. Crawley, A. E., Drinks, drinking, in *Encyclopaedia of Religion and Ethnics*, Vol. 5, J. Hastings (Ed.), Charles Scribner's Sons, New York, 1912.

96. Crawley, E., *Dress, Drink, and Drums*, Methuen, London, 1931.

97. Crothers, T. D., Inebriety in ancient Egypt and Chaldea, *Q. J. Inebriety*, **25**, 142–150 (1903).

98. Csikszentmihalyi, M., A cross-cultural comparison of some structural characteristics of group drinking, *Human Dev.* (Basel), **11**, 201–216 (1968).

99. Curley, R. T., Drinking patterns of the Mescalero Apache, *Q. J. Stud. Alcohol*, **28**, 116–131 (1967).

100. Cutler, H. C. and M. Cardenas, Chicha: a native South American beer, *Harvard Univ. Bot. Mus. Assoc. Leafl.*, **3**, 33–60 (1947).

101. Cutter, H. S. G., Conflict models, games, and drinking patterns, *J. Psychol.*, **58**, 361–367 (1964).

102. Cutter, H. S. G., J. C. Key, E. Rothstein, and W. C. Jones, Alcohol, power and inhibition, *Q. J. Stud. Alcohol*, **34**, 381–389 (1973).

103. Dailey, R. C., *Alcohol and the Indians of Ontario: Past and Present*, Addiction Research Foundation Substudy 1-20-64, 1964. Toronto.

104. Dailey, R. C., *Alcohol and the North American Indian: Implications for the Management of problems*, Addiction Research Foundation Substudy 2-20-66, Toronto, 1966.

105. Dailey, R. C., The role of alcohol among North American Indian tribes as reported in the Jesuit relations, *Anthropologica*, **10**, 45–59 (1968).

106. Danielou, J., *Les repas de la Bible el leur signification*, La Maison Dieu, Paris, 1949.

107. Davis, W. N., Drinking: a search for power or nurturance? in *The Drinking Man*, D. McClelland, W. Davis, R, Kalin, and E. Wanner, Free Press, New York, 1972.

108. Defer, B., Variations épidémiologiques de toxicomanies associées à des contacts de culture, *Toxicomanies* (Quebec), **2**, 9–18 (1969).

109. Devereux, G., The function of alcohol in Mohave society, *Q. J. Stud. Alcohol*, **9**, 207–251 (1948).

110. Doughty, P. L., The social uses of alcoholic beverages in a Peruvian community, *Human Organ.*, **30**, 187–197 (1971).

111. Dozier, E. P., Problem drinking among American Indians: the role of sociocultural deprivation, *Q. J. Stud. Alcohol*, **27**, 72–87 (1966).

112. Driver, H. E., *Indians of North America*, University of Chicago Press, 1961 (2nd ed., 1969).

113. Drower, E. S., *Water into Wine: A Study of Ritual Idiom in the Middle East*, John Murray, London, 1966.

114. Eddy, R., *Alcohol in History, An Account of Intemperance in All Ages: Together with a History of the Various Methods Employed for its Removal*, National Temperance Society and Publication House, New York, 1887.

115. Efron, V., Sociological and cultural factors in alcohol abuse, in *Alcohol and Alcoholism*, R. E. Popham (Ed.), University of Toronto Press, Toronto, 1970.

116. Elwin, V., *Maria Murder and Suicide*, Oxford University Press, Bombay, 1943.

117. Emerson, E. R., *Beverages Past and Present: An Historical Sketch of their Production, together with a Study of the Customs connected with their Use* (2 vols.), G. Putnam's Sons, New York, 1908.

118. Erlich, V. S., Comment on D. Mandelbaum's "Alcohol and culture," *Curr. Anthropol.*, **6**, 288–289 (1965).

119. Ervin, A. M., *New Northern Townsmen in Inuvik*, Department of Indian Affairs and Northern Development, Mackenzie Delta River Project 5, Ottawa [ca. 1971].

120. Everett, M. W., "Drinking" and "trouble": the Apachean experience, in *Alcohol, Drinking and Drunkenness among North American Indians*, M. W. Everett and J. O. Waddell (Eds.), expected 1974.

121. Everett, M. W. and J. O. Waddell (Eds.), *Alcohol, Drinking and Drunkenness among North American Indians: An Anthropological Perspective*, expected 1974.

122. Everett, M. W., J. O. Waddell, and D. B. Heath (eds.), *Cross-Cultural Studies on Alcohol: An Interdisciplinary Perspective*, Mouton, The Hague, expected 1974.

123. Fallding, H., The source and burden of civilization, illustrated in the use of alcohol, *Q. J. Stud. Alcohol*, **25**, 714–724 (1964).

124. Felice, Ph. de, *Poisons Sacrés, Ivresses Divines*, Albin Michel, Paris, 1936.

125. Feliciano, R. T., Illicit beverages, *Philip. J. Sci.*, **29**, 465–474 (1926).

126. Fenasse, J. M., La Bible et l'usage du vin, *Alcool ou Santé*, **63**, 17–28 (1964).

127. Fenna, D. L. Mix, O. Schaefer, and J. A. L. Gilbert, Ethanol metabolism in various racial groups, *Can. Med. Assoc. J.*, **105**, 472–475 (1971).

128. Ferguson, F. N., A community treatment plan for Navaho problem drinkers and a few words about the role of drinking in Navaho culture, Paper read at Southwestern Anthropological Association Meeting, Los Angeles, 1965.

129. Ferguson, F. N., The peer group and Navaho problem drinking, Paper read at Southern Anthropological Association Meeting, New Orleans, 1966.

130. Ferguson, F. N., Navaho drinking: some tentative hypotheses, *Human Organ.*, **27**, 159–167 (1968).

131. Ferguson, F. N., A treatment program for Navaho alcoholics: results after four years, *Q. J. Stud. Alcohol*, **31**, 898–919 (1970).

132. Ferguson, F. N., A "stake in society," deviance and conformity: an explanation of response to an alcoholism treatment program, Ph.D. dissertation (anthropology), University of North Carolina, 1972.

133. Ferguson, F. N., Similarities and differences among a heavily arrested group of 110 Navajo drinkers in a southwestern American town, in *Cross-Cultural Studies on Alcohol*, M. W. Everett, J. O. Waddell, and D. B. Heath (Eds.), Mouton, The Hague, expected 1974.

134. Field, P. B., A new cross-cultural study of drunkenness, in *Society, Culture and Drinking Patterns*, D. J. Pittman and C. R. Synder, (Eds.), John Wiley, New York, 1962.

135. Fort, J., Cultural aspects of alcohol (and drug) problems, in *Selected Papers presented at the 27th International Congress on Alcohol and Alcoholism*, Vol. 1, International Bureau against Alcoholism, Lausanne, 1965.

136. Fouquet, P., Alcool et religions, *Rev. Alcoolisme*, **11**, 81–92 (1965).

137. Frake, C. O., How to ask for a drink in Subanun, *Am. Anthropol.*, **66**,(No 6, pt.2), 127–132 (1964).

138. Frederikson, O. F., *The Liquor Question among the Indian Tribes in Kansas, 1804–1881*, Bulletin of the University of Kansas, Vol. 33, No. 8, Lawrence, 1932.

139. Frølund, B., Drinking patterns in Zambiza (Pichincha), in *Drinking Patterns in Highland Ecuador*, E. Maynard et al., Ithaca, N.Y., 1965.

140. Gallagher, O. R., Drinking problems of the tribal Bihar, *Q. J. Stud. Alcohol*, **26**, 617–628 (1965).

141. Gandhi, M. K., *Drink, Drugs and Gambling*, Navajivan, Ahmedabad, 1952.

142. García Alcaraz, A., El maguey y el pulque en Tepetlaoxtoc, *Comunidad* (México) 7(38), 461–474 (1972).

143. Geertz, C., Drought, death and alcohol in five southwestern cultures, Department of Social Relations, Harvard University, manuscript, 1951.

144. Gelfand, M., Alcoholism in contemporary African society, *Cent. Afr. J. Med.*, **12**, 12–13 (1966).

145. Gelfand, M., The extent of alcohol consumption by Africans: the significance of the weapons at beer drinks, *J. Forensic Med.*, **18**, 53–64 (1971).

146. Gilder, D. D., Drink in the scriptures of the nations, *Anthropol. Soc. Bombay*, **12**, 172–189 (1921).

147. Glad, D. D., Attitudes and experiences of American-Jewish and American-Irish male

youth as related to differences in adult rates of inebriety, *Q. J. Stud. Alcohol,* **8,** 406–472 (1947).

148. Glatt, M. M., Hashish and Alcohol "scenes" in France and Great Britain 120 years ago, *Br. J. Addict.,* **64,** 99–108 (1969).

149. Glover, E., Common problems in psycho-analysis and anthropology: drug ritual and addiction, *Br. J. Med. Psychol.,* **12,** 109–131 (1932).

150. Gómez Huamán, N., Importancia social de la chicha como bebida popular en Huamanga, *Wamani,* **1**(1), 33–57 (1966).

151. Gómez, J., Chichismo: Estudio general, clínico y anatomopatológico de los efectos de la chicha en la clase obrera de Bogotá, *Repert. Med. Cir.* (Bogotá), **5,** 302–320, 366–379, 424–440, 483–497, 540–559, 588; 652–667; **6,** 179– (1914–1915).

152. Gonçalves de Lima, O., *El maguey y el pulque en los códices mexicanos,* Fondo de Cultura Económica, México [ca. 1956].

153. Goodenough, E. R., *Jewish Symbols in the Greco-Roman Period, 5-6: Fish, Bread, and Wine,* Bollingen Series 37, Pantheon Books, New York, 1956.

154. Gorer, G., *Himalayan Village: An Account of the Lepchas of Sikkim,* 2nd ed., Basic Books, New York, 1967.

155. Graves, T., Acculturation, access, and alcohol in a tri-ethnic community, *Am. Anthropol.,* **69,** 306–321 (1967).

156. Graves, T. The personal adjustment of Navajo Indian migrants to Denver, Colorado, *Am. Anthropol.,* **72,** 35–54 (1970).

157. Graves, T., Drinking and drunkenness among urban Indians, in *The American Indian in Urban Society,* J. O. Waddell and O. M. Watson (Eds.), Little, Brown, Boston, 1971.

158. Gravière, E. la, The problem of alcoholism in the countries and territories south of the Sahara, *Int. Rev. Missions,* **46**(183), 290–298 (1957).

159. Gregson, R. E., Beer, leadership, and the efficiency of communal labor, Paper read at American Anthropological Association Meeting, New Orleans, 1969.

160. Gremek, M. D., Opojna piča i otrovi antiknih Ilira, *Farm. Glas.* (Zagreb), **6,** 33–38 (1950).

161. Gunson, N., On the incidence of alcoholism and intemperance in early Pacific missions, *J. Pacific Hist.,* **1,** 43–62 (1966).

162. Haavio-Mannila, E., Alkoholens Roll vid Byslagsmålen i Finland, *Alkoholpolitik,* **22,** 16–18 (1959).

163. Hage, P., A structural analysis of Munchnerian beer categories and beer drinking, in *Culture and Cognition: Rules, Maps and Plans,* J. P. Spradley (Ed.), Chandler, San Francisco, 1972.

164. Hamer, J. H., Acculturation stress and the functions of alcohol among the forest Potawatomi, *Q. J. Stud. Alcohol,* **26,** 285–302 (1965).

165. Hamer, J. H., Guardian spirits, alcohol, and cultural defense mechanisms, *Anthropologica,* **11,** 215–241 (1969).

166. Hanna, J. M., Ethnic groups, human variation and alcohol use, in *Cross-Cultural Studies on Alcohol,* M. W. Everett, J. O. Waddell, and D. B. Heath (Eds.), Mouton, The Hague, expected 1974.

167. Hartman, L. F. and A. L. Oppenheim, *On Beer and Brewing Techniques in Ancient Mesopotamia,* American Oriental Society, Baltimore, 1950.

168. Hartmann, G., *Alkoholische Getränke bei den Naturvölkern Südamerikas*, Freien Universität Berlin, Berlin, 1958.

169. Hartmann, G., Destillieranlagen bei südamerikanischen Naturvölkern, *Z. Ethnol.*, 93, 225-232 (1968).

170. Harwood, A., Beer drinking and famine in a Safwa village: a case of adaptation in a time of crisis, Paper read at East African Institute of Social Research Conference, Kampala, 1964.

171. Hasan, K. A., Drinks, drugs and disease in a North Indian village, *East. Anthropol.*, 17, 1-9 (1964).

172. Hasan, K., Comment on D. Mandelbaum's "Alcohol and culture," *Curr. Anthropol.*, 6, 289 (1965).

173. Hays, T. E., San Carlos Apache drinking groups: institutional deviance as a factor in community disorganization, Paper read at American Anthropological Association Meeting, Seattle, 1968.

174. Heath, D. B., Alcohol in a Navaho community, A.B. thesis (social relations), Harvard College, 1952.

175. Heath, D. B., Drinking patterns of the Bolivian Camba, *Q. J. Stud. Alcohol*, 19, 491-508 (1958); (revised version in Pittman and Snyder, 1962).

176. Heath, D. B., Prohibition and post-repeal drinking patterns among the Navaho, *Q. J. Stud. Alcohol*, 25, 119-135 (1964).

177. Heath, D. B., Comment on D. Mandelbaum's "Alcohol and culture," *Curr. Anthropol.*, 6, 289-290 (1965).

178. Heath, D. B., Peasants, revolution, and drinking: interethnic drinking patterns in two Bolivian communities, *Human Organ.*, 30, 179-186 (1971).

179. Heath, D. B., Anthropological perspectives on alcohol: a review, in *Cross-Cultural Studies on Alcohol*, M. W. Everett, J. O. Waddell, and D. B. Heath (Eds.), Mouton, The Hague, expected 1974.

180. Heath, D. B., Anthropological studies of alcohol in Latin America: a review, *Acta Psiquiátr. Psicol. América Latina* (expected 1974).

181. Heilizer, F., Conflict models, alcohol, and drinking patterns, *J. Psychol.*, 57, 457-473 (1964).

182. Hellmann, E., The importance of beer-brewing in an urban native yard, *Bantu Stud.*, 8, 38-60 (1934).

183. Henderson, N. B., Cross-cultural action research: some limitations, advantages and problems, *J. Soc. Psychol.*, 73, 61-70 (1967).

184. Henderson, N. B., Indian problem drinking: stereotype or reality? a study of Navajo problem drinking, Paper read at American Psychological Association Meeting, Honolulu, 1972.

185. Hentig, H. von, The delinquency of the American Indian, *J. Criminal Law Criminol.*, 36, 75-84 (1945).

186. Hippler, A. E., Fundamentalist Christianity: an Alaskan Athabascan technique for overcoming alcohol abuse, *Transcult. Psychiat. Rev.*, 10, 173-179 (1973).

187. Hirsh, J., Historical perspectives on the problem of alcoholism, *Bull. N.Y. Acad. Med.*, 29, 961-971 (1953).

188. Hirvonen, K., Antiikin alkoholijuomat, *Alkoholipolitiikka*, 34, 138-142, 191-194, 244-248, 300-305 (1969).

189. Hocking, R. B., Problems arising from alcohol in the New Hebrides, *Med. J. Aust.,* **2,** 908–910 (1970).

190. Hoffman, M., *5000 Jahre Bier,* Alfred Metzner, Berlin, 1956.

191. Holmberg, A. R., The rhythms of drinking in a Peruvian coastal mestizo community, *Human Organ.,* **30,** 198–202 (1971).

192. Honigmann, J. J., Dynamics of drinking in an Austrian village, *Ethnology* **2,** 157–169 (1963).

193. Honigmann, J. J., Comment on D. Mandelbaum's "Alcohol and culture," *Curr. Anthropol.* **6,** 290–291 (1965).

194. Honigmann, J. and I. Honigmann, Drinking in an Indian-White community, *Q. J. Stud. Alcohol,* **5,** 575–619 (1945).

195. Honigmann, J. and I. Honigmann, How Baffin Island Eskimo have learned to drink, *Soc. Forces,* **44,** 73–83 (1965).

196. Honigmann, J. and I. Honigmann, Alcohol in a Canadian northern town, Institute for Research in Social Science, University of North Carolina, Chapel Hill, multigraphed, 1968.

197. Horton, D. J., The functions of alcohol in primitive societies: a cross-cultural study, *Q. J. Stud. Alcohol,* **4,** 199–320 (1943).

198. Horwitz, J., J. Marconi, and G. Adis-Castro (Eds.), *Bases para una epidemiología del alcoholismo en America latina,* Fondo para la Salud Mental, Buenos Aires, 1967.

199. Howay, F. W., The introduction of intoxicating liquors amongst the Indians of the Northwest Coast, *Brit. Columbia Hist. Quart.,* **6,** 157–169 (1942).

200. Hrdlička, A., Method of preparing tesvino among the White River Apaches, *Am. Anthropol.* **6,** 190–191 (1904).

201. Hurt, W. R. and R. M. Brown, Social drinking patterns of the Yankton Sioux, *Human Organ.,* **24,** 222–230 (1965).

202. Hutchinson, B., Alcohol as a contributing factor in social disorganization: the South African Bantu in the nineteenth century, *Rev. Antropol.* (São Paulo), **9,** 1–13 (1961).

203. International Labor Office, Alcoholism and the mastication of coca in South America, in *Indigenous Populations,* I.L.O., Geneva, 1953.

204. Irgens-Jensen, O., The use of alcohol in an isolated area of Norway, *B. J. Addict.,* **65,** 181–185 (1970).

205. Jacobs, W. R., *Diplomacy and Indian Gifts: Anglo and French Rivalry along the Ohio and Northwest Frontiers, 1748–63,* Stanford University Press, Stanford, 1950.

206. Jacobsen, E., Alkohol als soziales Problem, in *Rauschgifte und Genussmittel,* K. O. Møller (Ed.), Benno Schwabe, Basel, 1951.

207. Jastrow, M., Jr., Wine in the pentateuchal codes, *J. Am. Orient. Soc.,* **33,** 180–192 (1913).

208. Jay, E. J., Religious and convivial uses of alcohol in a Gond village of middle India, *Q. J. Stud. Alcohol,* **27,** 88–96 (1966).

209. Jeffreys, M. D. W., Palm wine among the Ibibio, *Niger. Field,* **22,** 40–45 (1937).

210. Jellinek, E. M., Alkoholbruket såsom en Folksed, *Alkoholpolitik,* **15,** 36–40 (1952).

211. Jellinek, E. M., Phases of alcohol addiction, *Q. J. Stud. Alcohol,* **13,** 673–684 (1952); (revised version in Pittman and Snyder, 1962).

212. Jellinek, E. M., *The Disease Concept of Alcoholism,* Hillhouse Press, New Haven, Conn., 1960.

213. Jellinek, E. M., *Drinkers and Alcoholics in Ancient Rome*, Addiction Research Foundation Substudy 2-J-61, Toronto, 1961.

214. Jellinek, E. M., *The Symbolism of Drinking: A Culture-Historical Approach*, Addiction Research Foundation Substudy 3-2 & Y-65, Toronto [1965].

215. Jessor, R., T. D. Graves, R. C. Hanson, and S. L. Jessor, *Society, Personality and Deviant Behavior: A Study of a Tri-Ethnic Community*, Holt, Rinehart and Winston, New York, 1968.

216. Jessor, R., H. B. Young, E. B. Young, and G. Tesi, Perceived opportunity, alienation, and drinking behavior among Italian and American youth, *J. Pers. Soc. Psychol.*, **15**, 215–222 (1970).

217. Jilek-Aal, L., Alcohol and the Indian-White relationship: the function of Alcoholics Anonymous in coast Salish society, M.A. thesis, University of British Columbia, Vancouver, 1972.

218. Jochelson, W., Kumiss festivals of the Yakut and the decoration of kumiss vessels. in *Boas Anniversary Volume*, B. Laufer (Ed.), Stechert, New York, 1906.

219. Jones, M. C., Personality correlates and antecedents of drinking patterns in adult males, *J. Consult. Clin. Psychol.*, **32**, 2–12 (1968).

220. Jonsson, E. and T. Nilsson, *Samnordisk undersökning av vuxna mäns alkoholvanor*, Centralförbundet för alkohol- och narkotikaupplysning, Stockholm, 1974.

221. *Journal of American Medical Association*, Alcohol intoxication in Indians, *J. Am. Med. Assoc.*, **156**, 1375 (1954).

222. Kalin, R., W. N. Davis, and D. C. McClelland, The relationship between use of alcohol and thematic content of folktales in primitive societies, in *The General Inquirer*, P. J. Stone et al., (Eds.), M.I.T. Press, Cambridge, Mass., 1966; (revised version in McClelland et al., 1972).

223. Kant, I., *Anthropologie in pragmatischer Hinsicht*, F. Nicolovius, Königsberg, 1798.

224. Kaplan, B., The social functions of Navaho "heavy drinking," Paper read at Society for Applied Anthropology Meeting, Kansas City, 1962.

225. Kearney, M., Drunkenness and religious conversion in a Mexican village, *Q. J. Stud. Alcohol*, **31**, 132–152 (1970).

226. Keehn, J. D., Reinforcement of alcoholism: schedule control of solitary drinking, *Q. J. Stud. Alcohol*, **31**, 28–39 (1970).

227. Kelbert, M. and L. Hale, *The Introduction of Alcohol into Iroquois Society*, Addiction Research Foundation Substudy 1-K and H-65, Toronto [1965].

228. Keller, M., Beer and wine in ancient medicine, *Q. J. Stud. Alcohol*, **29**, 153–154 (1958).

229. Keller, M., Definition of alcoholism, *Q. J. Stud. Alcohol*, **21**, 125–134 (1960) (revised version in Pittman and Snyder, 1962).

230. Keller, M., Alcohol in health and disease: some historical perspectives, *Ann. N.Y. Acad. Sci.*, **113**, 820–827 (1966).

231. Keller, M., The great Jewish drink mystery, *Br. J. Addict.*, **64**, 287–296 (1970).

232. Kennedy, J. G., Tesguino complex: the role of beer in Tarahumara culture, *Am. Anthropol.*, **65**, 620–640 (1963).

233. Kerketta, K., Rice beer and the Oraon culture: a preliminary observation, *J. Soc. Res.* (Ranchi), **3**, 62–67 (1960).

234. Kermorgant, A., L'alcoolisme dans les colonies françaises, *Bull. Soc. Pathol. Exot. Ses Fil.*, **2**, 330–340 (1909).

235. Kim, Y. C., *A Study of Alcohol Consumption and Alcoholism among Saskatchewan Indians: Social and Cultural Viewpoints*, The Research Division, Alcoholism Commission of Saskatchewan, Regina, 1972.

236. Kinsey, B. A. and L. Phillips, Evaluation of anomy as a predisposing or developmental factor in alcohol addiction, *Q. J. Stud. Alcohol*, **29**, 892–898 (1968).

237. Kircher, K., Die sakrale Bedeutung des Weines im Alterum, *Religionsgesch. Vers. Vorarb.*, **9**, 2 (1910).

238. Klausner, S. Z., Sacred and profane meanings of blood and alcohol, *J. Soc. Psychol.*, **64**, 27–43 (1964).

239. Kline, J. A. and A. C. Roberts, A residential treatment program for American Indian alcoholics, *Q. J. Stud. Alcohol* (expected 1974).

240. Kluckhohn, C., *Mirror for Man*, McGraw-Hill, New York, 1949.

241. Knupfer, G., Use of alcoholic beverages by society and its cultural implications, *Calif. Health*, **18**, 9–13 (1960).

242. Knupfer, G. and R. Room, Drinking patterns and attitudes of Irish, Jewish and white Protestant American men, *Q. J. Stud. Alcohol*, **28**, 676–699 (1967).

243. Koplowitz, I., *Midrash Yayin Veshechor: Talmudic and Midrashic Exegetics on Wine and Strong Drink* [no publisher], Detroit, 1923.

244. Krige, E. J., The social significance of beer among the Balobedu, *Bantu Stud.*, **6**, 343–357 (1932).

245. Kubodera, I., Ainu no Kozoku, Sake no Jōzō Oyobi sono saigi, *Minozokugaku Kenkyū*, **1**, 501–532 (1935).

246. Kunitz, S. J., J. E. Levy, and M. W. Everett, Alcoholic cirrhosis among the Navaho, *Q. J. Stud. Alcohol*, **30**, 672–685 (1969).

247. Kunitz, S. J., J. E. Levy, C. L. Odoroff, and J. Bollinger, The epidemiology of alcoholic cirrhosis in two southwestern Indian tribes, *Q. J. Stud. Alcohol*, **32**, 706–720 (1971).

248. Kuttner, R. E. and A. B. Lorincz, Alcoholism and addiction in urbanized Sioux Indians, *Ment. Hyg.*, **51**, 530–542 (1967).

249. La Barre, W., Native american beers, *Am. Anthropol.*, **40**, 224–234 (1938).

250. La Barre, W., Some observations on character structure in the Orient: I. The Chinese, Part 2, *Psychiatry*, **9**, 375–395 (1946).

251. Lane, E. W., *Arabian Society in the Middle Ages*, Chatto and Windus, London, 1883.

252. Larni, M., Kinesiska Dryckesseder, *Alkoholpolitik*, **23**, 116–118 (1960).

253. Leacock, S., Ceremonial drinking in an Afro-Brazilian cult, *Am. Anthropol.*, **66**, 344–354 (1964).

254. Leake, C. and M. Silverman, *Alcoholic Beverages in Clinical Medicine*, World, Cleveland, 1966.

255. Ledermann, S. (Ed.), *Alcool, Alcoolisme—Alcoolisation* (2 vols.), Institut National d'Etudes Demographiques, Travaux et Documents Cahiers 29 and 41, Presses Universitaires de France, Paris, 1956–1964.

256. Lee, R. H. and E. Mizruchi, A study of drinking behavior and attitudes toward alcohol of the Chinese in the United States, manuscript [ca. 1960].

257. Leibowitz, J. O., Acute alcoholism in ancient Greek and Roman medicine, *Br. J. Addict.*, **62**, 83–86 (1967).

258. Leis, P. E., Palm oil, illicit gin, and the moral order of the Ijaw, *Am. Anthropol.*, **66**, 828–838 (1964).

259. Lejarza, F. de, Las borracheras y el problema de las conversiones en Indias, *Arch. Ibero-Americano,* **1,** 111–142, 229–269 (1941).

260. Leland, J., *The Firewater Myth: Alcohol Addiction among North American Indians,* Rutgers Center of Alcohol Studies Monograph, New Brunswick, N.J., expected 1974.

261. Lemert, E. M., Alcohol and the Northwest Coast Indians, *Univ. Calif. Publ. Cult. Soc.,* **2,** 303–406 (1954).

262. Lemert, E. M., Alcoholism and the sociocultural situation, *Q. J. Stud. Alcohol,* **17,** 306–317 (1956).

263. Lemert, E. M., The use of alcohol in three salish tribes, *Q. J. Stud. Alcohol,* **19,** 90–107 (1958).

264. Lemert, E. M., Alcohol use in Polynesia, *Trop. Geogr. Med.,* **14,** 183–191 (1962).

265. Lemert, E. M., Forms and pathology of drinking in three Polynesian societies, *Am. Anthropol.,* **66,** 361–374 (1964).

266. Lemert, E. M., Drinking in Hawaiian plantation society, *Q. J. Stud. Alcohol,* **25,** 689–713 (1964).

267. Lemert, E. M., Comment on D. Mandelbaum's "Alcohol and culture," *Curr. Anthropol.* **6,** 291 (1965).

268. Lemert, E. M., Socio-cultural research on drinking, in *28th International Congress on Alcohol and Alcoholism,* vol. 2, M. Keller and T. Coffey (Eds.), Hillhouse Press, Highland Park, N.J., 1969.

269. Lender, M., Drunkenness as an offense in early New England: a study of "Puritan" attitudes, *Q. J. Stud. Alcohol,* **34,** 353–366 (1973).

270. Lenoir, R., Les fêtes de boisson, in *Compte-Rendu de la XXIe Session, Deuxième Partie,* Congrès Internationale des Américanistes, Museum, Göteborg, 1925.

271. Levy, J. E. and S. J. Kunitz, Indian reservations, anomie, and social pathologies, *Southwest. J. Anthropol.,* **27,** 97–128 (1971).

272. Levy, J. E., S. J. Kunitz, and M. Everett, Navajo criminal homicide, *Southwest. J. Anthropol.,* **25,** 124–152 (1969).

273. Levy, R. I., Ma'ohi drinking patterns in the Society Islands, *J. Polynesian Soc.,* **75,** 304–320 (1966).

274. Leyburn, J. G., Native farm labor in South Africa, *Soc. Forces,* **23,** 133–140 (1944).

275. Lickiss, J. N., Alcohol and aborigines in cross-cultural situations, *Aust. J. Soc. Issues,* **6,** 210–216 (1971).

276. Lieber, C. S., Metabolism of ethanol and alcoholism: racial and acquired factors, *Ann. Int. Med.,* **76,** 326–327 (1972).

277. Lint, J. de, The epidemiology of alcoholism with specific reference to socio-cultural factors, in *Cross-Cultural Studies on Alcohol,* M. W. Everett, J. O. Waddell, and D. B. Heath (Eds.), Mouton, The Hague, expected 1974.

278. Lint, J. de and W. Schmidt, *The Epidemiology of Alcoholism,* Addiction Research Foundation Substudy 12-20 and 4-70, Toronto [1970].

279. Lint, J. de and W. Schmidt, Consumption averages and alcoholism prevalence: a brief review of epidemiological investigations, *Br. J. Addict.,* **66,** 97–107 (1971).

280. Littmann, G., Some observations on drinking among American Indians in Chicago, in *Selected Papers Presented at 27th International Congress on Alcohol and Alcoholism,* Vol. 1, International Bureau against Alcoholism, Lausanne, 1965.

281. Littmann, G., Alcoholism, illness and social pathology among American Indians in transition, *Am. J. Publ. Health,* **60,** 1769–1787 (1970).

282. Loeb, E. M., Primitive intoxicants, *Q. J. Stud. Alcohol,* **4,** 387–398 (1943).

283. Lolli, G., E. Serriani, G. M. Golder, and P. Luzzatto-Fegiz, *Alcohol in Italian Culture: Food and Wine in Relation to Sobriety among Italians and Italian Americans,* Yale Center of Alcohol Studies Monograph 3, New Haven, 1958.

284. Lomnitz, L., Patrones de ingestión de alcohol entre migrantes mapuches en Santiago, *Am. Indíg.,* **29,** 43–71 (1969).

285. Lomnitz, L., Función del alcohol en la sociedad mapuche, *Acta Psiquiátr. Psicol. Am. Latina,* **15,** 157–167 (1969).

286. Lomnitz, L., Patterns of alcohol consumption among the Mapuche, *Human Organ.,* **28,** 287–296 (1969).

287. Lomnitz, L., Influencia de los cambios políticos y económicos en la ingestión del alcohol: el caso mapuche, *Am. Indíg.,* **33,** 133–150 (1973).

288. Lomnitz, L., Alcohol and culture: the historical evolution of drinking patterns among the Mapuche, in *Cross-Cultural Studies on Alcohol,* M. W. Everett, J. O. Waddell and D. B. Heath (Eds.), Mouton, The Hague, expected 1974.

289. Lucia, S. P. (Ed.), *Alcohol and Civilization,* McGraw-Hill, New York, 1963.

290. Lurie, N. O., The world's oldest on-going protest demonstration: North American Indian drinking patterns, *Pacific Hist. Rev.,* **40,** 311–332 (1971).

291. Lutz, H. F., *Viticulture and Brewing in the Ancient Orient,* J. C. Heinrichs, Leipzig, 1922.

292. MacAndrew, C. and R. B. Edgerton, *Drunken Comportment: A Social Explanation,* Aldine, Chicago, 1969.

293. McCarthy, R. G. (Ed.), *Drinking and Intoxication: Selected Readings in Social Attitudes and Controls,* Free Press, Glencoe, Ill., 1959.

294. McClelland, D. C., W. N. Davis, R. Kalin, and E. Wanner, *The Drinking Man,* Free Press, New York, 1972.

295. McClelland, D. C., W. Davis, E. Wanner, and R. Kalin, A cross-cultural study of folktale content and drinking, *Sociometry* **29,** 308–333 (1966) (revised version in McClelland et al., *The Drinking Man,* 1972).

296. Maccoby, M., El alcoholismo en una comunidad campesina, *Rev. Psicoanál., Psiquiatr. Psicol.* **1,** 38–64 (1965).

297. Maccoby, M., Alcoholism in a Mexican village, in *The Drinking Man,* D. McClelland, W. Davis, R. Kalin, and E. Wanner, Free Press, New York, 1972.

298. McCord, W. and J. McCord with J. Gudeman, *Origins of Alcoholism,* Stanford University Press, Stanford, 1960.

299. McGlashan, N. D., Oesophageal cancer and alcoholic spirits in Central Africa, *Gut,* **10,** 643–650 (1969).

300. McKinlay, A. P., The "indulgent" Dionysius, *Trans. Am. Philos. Assoc.,* **70,** 51–61 (1939).

301. McKinlay, A. P., How the Athenians handled the drink problem among their slaves, *Cl. Weekly,* **37,** 127–128 (1944).

302. McKinlay, A. P., The Roman attitude toward women's drinking, *Cl. Bull.,* **22,** 14–15 (1945).

303. McKinlay, A. P., Temperate Romans, *Cl. Weekly,* **41,** 146–149 (1948).

304. McKinlay, A. P., Early Roman sobriety, *Cl. Bull.,* **24,** 52 (1948).

305. McKinlay, A. P., Ancient experience with intoxicating drinks: non-classical peoples; non-Attic Greek states, *Q. J. Stud. Alcohol,* **9,** 388–414; **10,** 289–315 (1948–1949).

306. McKinlay, A. P., Roman sobriety in the later Republic, *Cl. Bull.*, **25**, 27–28 (1949).

307. McKinlay, A. P., Bacchus as health-giver, *Q. J. Stud. Alcohol*, **11**, 230–246 (1950).

308. McKinlay, A. P., Roman sobriety in the early Empire, *Cl. Bull.*, **26**, 31–36 (1950).

309. McKinlay, A. P., Attic temperance, *Q. J. Stud. Alcohol*, **12**, 61–102 (1951).

310. McKinlay, A. P., New light on the question of Homeric temperance, *Q. J. Stud. Alcohol*, **14**, 78–93 (1953).

311. MacLeod, W. C., *The American Indian Frontier*, Alfred A. Knopf, New York, 1928.

312. MacLeod, W. C., Alcohol: historical aspects, in *Encyclopaedia of the Social Sciences*, Vol. 1, E. R. A. Seligman and A. Johnson (Eds.), Macmillan, New York, 1930.

313. McNair, C. N., *Drinking Patterns and Deviance in a Multi-Racial Community in Northern Canada*, Addiction Research Foundation Clinical Division Substudy 32-1969, Toronto, [1969].

314. Madsen, W., The alcoholic Agringado, *Am. Anthropol.*, **66**, 355–361 (1964).

315. Madsen, W., *The American Alcoholic: The Nature-Nurture Controversy in Alcoholic Research and Therapy*, Charles C Thomas, Springfield, Ill., 1973.

316. Madsen, W. and C. Madsen, The cultural structure of Mexican drinking behavior, *Q. J. Stud. Alcohol*, **30**, 701–718 (1969).

317. Mandelbaum, D. G. et al., Alcohol and culture [with comments], *Curr. Anthropol.*, **6**, 281–294 (1965).

318. Mangin, W., Drinking among Andean Indians, *Q. J. Stud. Alcohol*, **18**, 55–66 (1957).

319. Marconi, J., Chile, in *Bases para una epidemiología del alcoholismo en América latina*, J. Horwitz, J. Marconi, and G. Adis (Eds.), Fondo para la Salud Mental, Buenos Aires, 1967.

320. Marroquín, J., Alcoholismo entre los aborígenes peruanos, *Crón. Méd.* (Lima), **60**, 226–231 (1943).

321. Marshall, M., A review and appraisal of alcohol and kava studies in Oceania, in *Cross-Cultural Studies on Alcohol*, M. W. Everett, J. O. Waddell and D. B. Heath (Eds.), Mouton, The Hague, expected 1974.

322. Martín del Campo, R., El pulque en México precortesiano, *Univ. Nac. Autón. México, Anal. Inst. Biol.*, **9**, 5–23 (1938).

323. Masserman, J. H. and K. S. Yum, An analysis of the influence of alcohol on experimental neurosis in cats, *Psychosom. Med.*, **8**, 36–52 (1946).

324. Maynard, E., Drinking patterns in the Colta Lake Zone (Chimborazo), in *Drinking Patterns in Highland Ecuador*, E. Maynard, B. Frøland, and C. Rasmussen, Department of Anthropology, Cornell University, 1965.

325. Maynard, E., Drinking as part of an adjustment syndrome among the Oglala Sioux, *Pine Ridge Res. Bull.*, **9**, 35–51 (1969).

326. Maynard, E., B. Frøland, and C. Rasmussen, *Drinking Patterns in Highland Ecuador*, Andean Indian Community Research and Development Program, Department of Anthropology, Cornell University (multigraphed), 1965.

327. Mears, A. R. R., Pellagra in Tsolo District, *South Afr. Med. J.*, **16**, 385–387 (1942).

328. Medical Practitioner, A, *Notices respecting Drunkenness, and of the Various Means which have been Employed in Different Countries for restraining the Progress of that Evil*, William Collins, Glasgow, 1830.

329. Medina, C., E. and J. Marconi, Prevalencia de distintos tipos de bebedores en adultos mapuches de zona rural en Cautín, *Acta Psiquiátr. Psicol. Am. Latina*, **16**, 273–285 (1970).

330. Mesa y P., S. A., Historia del alcohol y el alcoholismo en Europa y en América, *Orientac. Méd.* (Medellín), **8,** 107 (1959).

331. Metzger, D. G., Interpretations of drinking performances in Aguacatenango, Ph.D. dissertation (anthropology), University of Chicago, 1964.

332. Midgley, J., Drinking and attitude toward drink in a Muslim community, *Q. J. Stud. Alcohol* **32,** 148–158 (1971).

333. Miles, J. D., The Drinking Patterns of Bantu in South Africa, National Bureau of Educational and Social Research Series 18, Department of Education, Arts and Sciences [Johannesburg], 1965.

334. Mitra, B. R., Spirituous drinks in ancient India, *J. Asiat. Soc,.* (Bengal), **43,** 1–23, (1873).

335. Mizruchi, E. H. and R. Perucci, Norm qualities and differential effects of deviant behavior: an exploratory analysis, *Am. Soc. Rev.,* **27,** 391–399 (1962).

336. Modi, J. J., *Wine among the Ancient Persians*, Bombay Gazette Steam Press, Bombay, 1888.

337. Mohatt, G., The sacred water: the quest for personal power through drinking among the Teton Sioux, in *The Drinking Man*, D. McClelland, W. Davis, R. Kalin, and E. Wanner, Free Press, New York, 1972.

338. Montell, G., Distilling in Mongolia, *Ethnos,* **2,** 321–332 (1937).

339. Moore, M., Chinese wine: some notes on its social use, *Q. J. Stud. Alcohol,* **9,** 270–279 (1948).

340. Morewood, S., *A Philosophical and Statistical History of the Invention and Customs of Ancient and Modern Nations in the Manufacture and Use of Inebriating Liquors*, William Curry, Jr., and William Carson, Dublin, 1838.

341. Muelle, J. C., La chicha en el distrito de San Sebastian, *Rev. Mus. Nac.* (Lima), **14,** 144–152 (1945).

342. Myerson, A., Alcohol: a study of social ambivalence, *Q. J. Stud. Alcohol,* **1,** 13–20 (1940).

343. Myerson, A., The social psychology of alcoholism, *Dis. Nerv. Syst.,* **1,** 43–50 (1940b).

344. Negrete, J. C., Les attitudes envers le comportement des alcooliques: étude comparative dans trois sous-cultures québécoises, *Toxicomanies* (Québec), **3,** 193–212 (1970).

345. Nelson, G. K., L. Novellie, D. H. Reader, H. Reuning, and H. Sachs, Psychological, nutritional and sociological studies of kaffir beer, Johannesburg Kaffir Beer Research Project, South African Council for Scientific and Industrial Research, Pretoria (multigraphed), 1964.

346. Netting, R. McC., Beer as a locus of value among the West African Kofyar, *Am. Anthropol.,* **66,** 375–384 (1964).

347. Nida, E. A., Drunkenness in indigenous religious rites, *Pract. Anthropol.,* **6,** 20–23 (1959).

348. Norick, F. A., Acculturation and drinking in Alaska, *Rehabil. Rec.,* **11,**(5) 13–17 (1970).

349. Ogan, E., Drinking behavior and race relations, *Am. Anthropol.,* **68,** 181–187 (1966).

350. Otele, A., Les boissons fermentées de L'Oubangui-Chari, *Liaison* (Brazzaville), **67,** 34–42 (1959).

351. Park, P., Problem drinking and role deviation: a study of incipient alcoholism, in *Society, Culture and Drinking Patterns*, D. J. Pittman and C. R. Snyder, (Eds.), John Wiley, New York, 1962.

352. Park, P., Developmental ordering of experiences in alcoholism, *Q. J. Stud. Alcohol*, **34**, 473–488 (1973).

353. Parkin, D. J., *Palms, Wine, and Witnesses: Public Spirit and Private Gain in an African Farming Community*, Chandler, San Francisco, 1972.

354. Patnaik, N., Outcasting among oilmen for drinking wine, *Man in India*, **40**, 1–7 (1960).

355. Patrick, C. H., *Alcohol, Culture, and Society*, Duke University Sociological Series 8, Durham, N.C., 1952.

356. Pelto, P. J., Alcohol use in Skolt Lapp society, Paper read at American Ethnological Society Meeting, Stanford, Calif., 1960.

357. Pelto, P. J., Alcohol use and dyadic interaction, Paper read at Northeastern Anthropological Association Meeting, Ithaca, N.Y., 1963.

358. Perisse, J., J. Adrian, A. Rerat, and S. Le Berre, Bilan nutritif de la transformation du sorgho en bière: preparation, composition, consommation d'une bière du Togo, *Ann. Nutr. Aliment.*, **13**, 1–15 (1959).

359. Pertold, O., The liturgical base of mahuda liquor by Bhils, *Archiv Orientalni (Prague)*, **3**, 400–407 (1931).

360. Piga Pascual, A., Influencia del uso de las bebidas fermentadas en la primitiva civilización egipcia, *Acta Mem. Soc. Esp. Antropol. Etnograf. Prehist.*, **17**, 61–86 (1942).

361. Piga Pascual, A., La lucha antialcohólica de los españoles en la época colonial, *Rev. Indias*, **3**, 711–742 (1942).

362. Pitt, P., Alcoholism in Nepal, *J. Alcohol.* (London), **6**, 15–19 (1971).

363. Pittman, D. J., Social and cultural factors in drinking patterns, pathological and nonpathological, in *Selected Papers Presented at 27th International Congress on Alcohol and Alcoholism*, Vol. 1, International Bureau against Alcoholism, Lausanne, 1965.

364. Pittman, D. J. (Ed.), *Alcoholism*, Harper and Row, New York, 1967.

365. Pittman, D. J., Transcultural aspects of drinking and drug usage, in *29th International Congress on Alcoholism and Drug Dependence*, L. G. Kiloh and D. S. Bell (Eds.), Butterworths, Australia, 1971.

366. Pittman, D. J. and C. R. Snyder (Eds.), *Society, Culture, and Drinking Patterns*, John Wiley, New York, 1962.

367. Platt, B. S., Some traditional alcoholic beverages and their importance in indigenous African communities, *Proc. Nutr. Soc.*, **14**, 115–124 (1955).

368. Podlewski, H. and R. J. Catanzaro, Treatment of alcoholism in the Bahama Islands, in *Alcoholism: The Total Treatment Approach*, R. J. Catanzaro (Ed.), Charles C Thomas, Springfield, Ill., 1968.

369. Poirier, J., L'alcoolisme a Madagascar: données statistiques et problèmes psycho-sociologiques, *Toxicomanies* (Québec), **2**, 57–77 (1969).

370. Popham, R. E., Some problems of alcohol research from a social anthropologist's point of view, *Alcoholism*, **6**(2), 19–24 (1959).

371. Popham, R. E., Some social and cultural aspects of alcoholism, *Can. Psychiatr. Assoc. J.*, **4**, 222–229 (1959).

372. Popham, R. E., *The Practical Relevance of Transcultural Studies*, Addiction Research Foundation Substudy 9-2-70, Toronto [1968].

373. Popham, R. E. (Ed.), *Alcohol and Alcoholism*, University of Toronto Press, Toronto, 1970.

374. Popham, R. E. and C. D. Yawney (comps.), *Culture and Alcohol Use: A Bibliography of Anthropological Studies*, Addiction Research Foundation, Toronto, 1966 (2nd ed., 1967).

375. Pozas Arciniegas, R., El alcoholismo y la organización social, *La Palabra y el Hombre*, **1**, 19–26 (1957).

376. Poznanski, A., Our drinking heritage, *McGill Med. J.*, **25**, 35–41 (1956).

377. Prakash, O., *Food and Drinks in Ancient India: From Earliest Times to c. 1200 A.D.*, Munshi Ram Manohar Lal, Delhi, 1961.

378. Quichaud, J., Problèmes médico-sociaux d'outre-mer: l'alcoolisme en Guinée, *Sem. Méd. Prof. Méd. Soc.*, **31**, 574–575 (1955).

379. Raman, A. C., Cultural factors in alcoholism, Paper read at International Congress of Mental Health, London, 1968.

380. Rao, M. S. A., A religious temperance movement and its impact on a toddy-tapping caste in Kerala, in preparation.

381. Ravi Varma, L. A., Alcoholism in Ayurveda, *Q. J. Stud. Alcohol*, **11**, 484–491 (1950).

382. Raymond, I. W., *The Teaching of the Early Church on the Use of Wine and Strong Drink*, Columbia University Studies in History, Economics, and Public Law 286, New York, 1927.

383. Reader, D. H., Alcoholism and excessive drinking: a sociological review, *Psychol. Afri. Monogr. Suppl.*, **3**, National Institute for Personnnel Research, [Johannesburg] 1967.

384. Redding, C., *A History and Description of Modern Wines*, 3rd ed., Henry G. Bohn, London, 1860.

385. Reiche, C., C. E., Estudio sobre el patrón de embriaguez en la región rural altaverapacense, *Guatemala Indig.*, **5**, 103–127 (1970).

386. Reichel-Dolmatoff, G. and A. Reichel-Dolmatoff, *The People of Aritama: The Cultural Personality of a Colombian Mestizo Village*, University of Chicago Press, Chicago, 1961.

387. Riley, J. W., Jr. and C. F. Marden, The social pattern of alcoholic drinking, *Q. J. Stud. Alcohol*, **8**, 265–273 (1947).

388. Robbins, M. C. and R. B. Pollnac, Drinking patterns and acculturation in rural Buganda, *Am. Anthropol.*, **71**, 276–284 (1969).

389. Robbins, R. H., Role reinforcement and ritual deprivation: drinking behavior in a Naskapi village, *Pap. Soc. Sci.*, **1**, 1–7 (1969).

390. Robbins, R. H., Alcohol and the identity struggle: some effects of economic change on interpersonal relations, *Am. Anthropol.*, **75**, 99–122 (1973).

391. Rodríguez Sandoval, L., Drinking motivations among the Indians of the Ecuadorean Sierra, *Primitive Man*, **18**, 39–46 (1945).

392. Rohrmann, C. A., Drinking and violence: a cross cultural survey, manuscript [ca. 1972].

393. Rojas, U. (comp.), La lucha contra las bebidas alcohólicas en la época de la colonia, *Repert. Boyacense*, **46**, 877 (1960).

394. Rolleston, J. D., Alcoholism in classical antiquity, *Br. J. Inebriety*, **24**, 101–120 (1927).

395. Rolleston, J. D., Alcoholism in mediaeval England, *Br. J. Inebriety*, **31**, 33–49 (1933).

396. Rolleston, J. D., The folklore of alcoholism, *Br. J. Inebriety*, **39**, 30–36 (1941).

397. Room R., Cultural contingencies of alcoholism: variations between and within nineteenth-century urban ethnic groups in alcohol-related death rates, *J. Health Soc. Behav.*, **9**, 99–113 (1968).

398. Ruiz Moreno, A., La lucha antialcohólica de los Jesuitas en la época colonial, *Estudios* (Buenos Aires), **62**, 339–352, 423–446 (1939).

399. S., H., Non-drinking Societies, [Institute for the Study of Human Problems?] ms. 46, Stanford (multigraphed), 1963.

400. Sadoun, R., Giorgio L., and M. Silverman, *Drinking in French Culture*, Rutgers Center of Alcohol Studies Monograph 5, New Brunswick, N.J., 1965.

401. Salonen, A., Dryckesseder före och efter Muhammed, *Alkoholpolitik*, **20**, 50–52, 81–83, 107–109 (1957–1958).

402. Sangree, W. H., The social functions of beer drinking in Bantu Tiriki, in *Society, Culture, and Drinking Patterns*, D. J. Pittman and C. R. Synder, (Eds.), John Wiley, New York, 1962.

403. Sargent, M. J., Changes in Japanese drinking patterns, *Quart. J. Stud. Alcohol*, **28**, 709–722 (1967).

404. Sargent, M. J., A cross-cultural study of attitudes and behaviour towards alcohol and drugs, *Br. J. Sociol.*, **22**, 83–96 (1971).

405. Sariola, S., *Lappi ja Väkijuomat*, Vakijuomaksmyksen Tutkimussäätiö, Helsingfors, 1954 (English translation, 1956).

406. Sariola, S., Drinking customs in rural Colombia, *Alkoholpolitik*, **24**, 127–131 (1961).

407. Savard, R. J., Effects of disulfiram therapy on relationships within the Navaho drinking group, *Q. J. Stud. Alcohol*, **29**, 909–916 (1968).

408. Sayres, W. C., Ritual drinking, ethnic status and inebriety in rural Colombia, *Q. J. Stud. Alcohol*, **17**, 53–62 (1956).

409. Schaefer, J. M., Galton's problem in a hologeistic study of drunkenness, *Behav. Sci. Notes* (expected 1974).

410. Schaefer, J. M., *Drunkenness: A Hologeistic Treatise*, H.F.A.F. Press, New Haven, expected 1974.

411. Schaefer, J. M., Drunkenness and culture stress: a holocultural test, in *Cross-Cultural Studies on Alcohol*, M. W. Everett, J. O. Waddell, and D. B. Heath (Eds.), Mouton, The Hague, expected 1974.

412. Schreiber, G., Der Wein und die Volkstumsforschung: zur Sakralkultur und zum Genossenrecht, *Rhein. Jahrb. Volkskunde*, **9**, 207–243 (1958).

413. Sears, W. F. and E. L. Mariani, Community treatment plan for Navajo problem drinkers, New Mexico Department of Public Health, Santa Fe (multigraphed), 1964.

414. Seekirchner, A., Der Alkohol in Afrika, in *Atlas Africanus*, Vol. 8, L. Frobenius and R. von Wilm (Eds.), W. de Gruyter, Berlin, 1931.

415. Seltman, C., *Wine in the Ancient World*, Routledge and Kegan Paul, London, 1957.

416. Serebro, B., Total alcohol consumption as an index of anxiety among urbanized Africans, *Br. J. Addict.*, **67**, 251–254 (1972).

417. Shore, J. H. and B. Von Fumetti, Three alcohol programs for American Indians, *Am. J. Psychiatry*, **128**, 1450–1454 (1972).

418. Simmons, O. G., Drinking patterns and interpersonal performance in a Peruvian mestizo community, *Q. J. Stud. Alcohol*, **20**, 103–111 (1959).

419. Simmons, O. G., Ambivalence and the learning of drinking behavior in a Peruvian community, *Am. Anthropol.*, **68**, 1018–1027 (1960).

420. Simmons, O. G., The sociocultural integration of alcohol use: a peruvian study, *Q. J. Stud. Alcohol*, **29**, 152–171 (1968).

421. Singer, K., Drinking patterns and alcoholism in the Chinese, *Br. J. Addict.*, **67**, 3–14 (1972).

422. Skolnik, J. H., Religious affiliation and drinking behavior, *Q. J. Stud. Alcohol*, **19**, 453–470 (1958).

423. Slotkin, J. S., Fermented drinks in Mexico, *Am. Anthropol.*, **56**, 1089–1090 (1954).

424. Smythe, D. W., Alcohol as a symptom of social disorder: an ecological view, *Social Psychiatry* (Berlin), **1**, 144–151 (1966).

425. Snyder, C. R., *Alcohol and the Jews: A Cultural Study of Drinking and Sobriety*, Yale Center of Alcohol Studies Monograph 1, Free Press, Glencoe, Ill., 1958.

426. Snyder, C. R., Culture and Jewish sobriety: the ingroup-outgroup factor, in *The Jews: Social Patterns of an American Group*, M. Sklare (Ed.), Free Press, Glencoe, Ill., 1958.

427. Snyder, C. R. and D. J. Pittman, Drinking and alcoholism: social aspects, in *International Encyclopedia of the Social Sciences*, Vol. 4, Macmillan and Free Press, New York, 1968.

428. Spaulding, P., The social integration of a northern community: white mythology and metis reality, in *A Northern Dilemna: Reference Papers*, A. K. Davis (Ed.), Western Washington State College, Bellingham, 1966.

429. Stewart, O. C., Questions regarding American Indian criminality, *Human Organ.*, **23**, 61–66 (1964).

430. Strübing, E., Vom Wein als Genuss- und Heilmittel im Alterum mit Plinius und Asklepiades, *Ernährungsforschung*, **5**, 572–594 (1960).

431. Suolahti, J., Alkoholmissbruket under Antiken, *Alkoholpolitik*, **18**, 77–78 (1955).

432. Suolahti, J., Statlig Alkoholpolitik i Rom under Kejsartidens Slutskede, *Alkoholpolitik*, **19**, 5–12 (1956).

433. Swanson, D. W., A. P. Bratrude, and E. M. Brown, Alcohol abuse in a population of Indian children, *Dis. Nerv. Syst.*, **32**, 835–842 (1971).

434. Tadesse, E., Preparation of Täg among the Amhara of Šäwa, *Bull. Addis Ababa Univ. Coll. Ethnol. Sociol.*, **8**, 101–109 (1958).

435. Thorner, J., Ascetic Protestantism and alcoholism, *Psychiatry* **16**, 167–176 (1953).

436. Tillhagen, C.-H., Food and drink among the Swedish Kalderaša Gypsies, *J. Gypsy Lore Soc.*, **36**, 25–52 (1957).

437. Toit, B. M. du, Substitution: a process in culture change, *Human Organ.*, **23**, 16–23 (1964).

438. Topper, M., Alcohol and the young Navajo male, in *Alcohol, Drinking and Drunkenness among North American Indians*, M. W. Everett and J. O. Waddell (Eds.), expected 1974.

439. Trice, H. M. and D. J. Pittman, Social organization and alcoholism: a review of significant research since 1940, *Soc. Prob.*, **5**, 294–306 (1958).

440. Ullman, A. D., Sociocultural backgrounds of alcoholism, *Ann. Am. Acad. Polit. Soc. Sci.*, **315**, 48–54 (1958).

441. Umunna, I., The drinking culture of a Nigerian community: Onitsha, *Q. J. Stud. Alcohol*, **28**, 529–537 (1967).

442. Vachon, A., L'eau-de-vie dans la société indienne, *Can. Hist. Assoc. Ann. Rep.*, 22–32 (1960).

443. Vallee, B. L., Alcohol metabolism and metalloenzymes, *Ther. Notes*, **14**, 71–74 (1966).

444. Vallee, F. G., Stresses of change and mental health among the Canadian Eskimos, *Arch. Environ. Health*, **17**, 565–570 (1968).

445. Vanderyst, H., Le vin de palm ou malafu, *Bull. Agric. Congo Belge*, **8**(11), 219–224 (1920).

446. Varlet, F., Fabrication et composition de l'alcool de Bangui, *Notes Afr.*, **71**, 74–75 (1956).

447. Varma, S. C., Problem of drinking in the primitive tribes, *East. Anthropol.*, **12**, 252–256 (1959).

448. Vasev, C. and V. Milosavčević, Alkoholizam kod Cigana, *Alkoholizam* (Beograd), **10**, 47–57 (1970).

449. Vatuk, V. P. and S. Vatuk, Chatorpan: a culturally defined form of addiction (manuscript), 1967.

450. Vázquez, M. C., La chicha en los países andinos, *Am. Indig.*, **27**, 265–282 (1967).

451. Vedder, H., Notes on the brewing of kaffir beer in South West Africa, *South West Africa Sci. Soc. J.*, **8**, 41–43 (1951).

452. Viqueira, C. and A. Palerm, Alcoholismo, brujería y homicidio en dos comunidades rurales de México, *Am. Indig.*, **14**, 7–36 (1954).

453. Vogel-Sprott, M. D., Alcoholism as learned behavior: some hypotheses and research, in *Alcoholism: Behavioral Research Therapeutic Approaches*, R. Fox (Ed.), Springer, New York, 1967.

454. Waddell, J. O., For individual power and social credit: the use of alcohol among Tucson Papagos, Paper read at Society for Applied Anthropology Meeting, Tucson, 1973.

455. Wang, R. P., A study of alcoholism in Chinatown, *Int. J. Soc. Psychiatry*, **14**, 260–267 (1968).

456. Wanner, E., Power and inhibition: a revision of the magical potency theory, in *The Drinking Man*, D. McClelland, W. Davis, R. Kalin, and E. Wanner, Free Press, New York, 1972.

457. Washburne, C., Alcohol, self and the group, *Q. J. Stud. Alcohol*, **17**, 108–123 (1956).

458. Washburne, C., *Primitive Drinking: A Study of the Uses and Functions of Alcohol in Preliterate Societies*, College and University Press, New York, 1961.

459. Washburne, C., Primitive religion and alcohol, *Int. J. Comp. Sociol.*, **9**, 97–105 (1968).

460. Weaver, D. G. (Ed.), Alcoholism Workshop Report, Dec. 1–2, 1962, Window Rock, Arizona, Gallup Indian Community Center, Gallup, N.M., (multigraphed) 1962.

461. Wechsler, H., H. W. Demone, Jr., D. Thum, and E. H. Kasey, Religious-ethnic differences in alcohol consumption, *J. Health Soc. Behav.*, **11**, 21–29 (1970).

462. West, L. J., A cross-cultural approach to alcoholism, *Ann. N.Y. Acad. Sci.*, **197**, 214–216 (1972).

463. Westermeyer, J. J., Options regarding alcohol use among the Chippewa, *Am. J. Orthopsychiat.*, **42**, 398–403 (1972).

464. Westermeyer, J. J., Cross cultural studies of alcoholism in the clinical setting, in *Cross-Cultural Studies on Alcohol*, M. W. Everett, J. O. Waddell, and D. B. Heath (Eds.), Mouton, The Hague, expected 1974.

465. Wheeler, D., *Effects of the Introduction of Ardent Spirits and Implements of War among the Natives of the South Sea Islands and New South Wales*, Harvey and Darton, London, 1839.

466. Whitehead, P. C., Toward a new programmatic approach to the prevention of alcoholism: a reconciliation of the socio-cultural and distribution of consumption approaches, in *30th International Congress on Alcoholism and Drug Dependence*, E. Tongue and Z. Adler (Eds.), Lausanne, 1972.

467. Whittaker, J. O., Alcohol and the Standing Rock Sioux Tribe: I. The pattern of drinking; II. Psychodynamic and cultural factors in drinking, *Q. J. Stud. Alcohol*, **23**, 468–479; **24**, 80–90 (1962–1963).

468. Wilsnack, S. C., Psychological factors in female drinking, Ph.D. dissertation (social relations), Harvard University, 1972.

469. Wilson, G. C., Drinking and drinking customs in a Mayan community, Cornell-Columbia-Harvard-Illinois Summer Field Studies Program in Mexico, Harvard University, (multigraphed) 1963.

470. Witkin, H. A., S. A. Karp, and D. Goodenough, Dependence in Alcoholics, *Quart. J. Stud. Alcohol*, **20**, 493–504 (1959).

471. Wolcott, H. F., *The African Beer Gardens of Bulawayo: Integrated Drinking in a Segregated Society*, Rutgers Center of Alcohol Studies Monograph, New Brunswick, N.J., expected 1974.

472. Wolff, P. H., Ethnic differences in alcohol sensitivity, *Science*, **175**(4020), 449–450 (1972).

473. Wolff, P. H., Vasomotor sensitivity to alcohol in diverse Mongoloid populations, *Am. J. Human Genet.*, **25**, 193–199 (1973).

474. World Health Organization, Expert Committee on Mental Health, *Report of the First Session of the Alcoholism Subcommittee*. W.H.O. Technical Report Series 42, Geneva, 1951.

475. World Health Organization, Expert Committee on Mental Health, *Second Report of the Alcoholism Subcommittee*, W.H.O. Technical Report Series 48, Geneva, 1952.

476. Wright-St. Clair, R. E., Beer in therapeutics: an historical annotation, *N.Z. Med. J.*, **61**, 512–513 (1962).

477. Yamamuro, B., Notes on drinking in Japan, *Q. J. Stud. Alcohol*, **15**, 491–498 (1954).

478. Yamamuro, B., Japanese drinking patterns: alcoholic beverages in legend, history and contemporary religions, *Q. J. Stud. Alcohol*, **19**, 482–490 (1958).

479. Yamamuro, B., Further notes on Japanese drinking, *Q. J. Stud. Alcohol*, **25**, 150–153 (1964).

480. Yamamuro, B., Origins of some Japanese drinking customs, *Q. J. Stud. Alcohol*, **29**, 979–982 (1968).

481. Yawney, C. D., *The Comparative Study of Drinking Patterns in Primitive Cultures*, Addiction Research Foundation Substudy 1-Y-67, Toronto, [1967].

482. Yawney, C. D., Drinking patterns and alcoholism in Trinidad, *McGill Stud. Caribb. Anthropol. Occas. Pap.*, **5**, 34–48 (1969).

483. Younger, W., *Gods, Men and Wine*, World, New York, 1966.

484. Zentner, H., Factors in the social pathology of a North American Indian society, *Anthropologica*, **5**, 119–130 (1963).

485. Zingg, R. M., The genuine and spurious values in Tarahumara culture, *Am. Anthropol.*, **44**, 78–92 (1942).

APPENDIX: SUPPLEMENTARY BIBLIOGRAPHY

In a review of this nature and scope, it seems appropriate to indicate a number of works that were sought out and considered relevant to the topic, even though they were not specifically discussed in the text. The organization and intention of this supplementary bibliography is similar to that of the list of references cited.

Ablon, J., Responses of the American middle-class family to "alcoholism," in preparation.

Aiyappan, A. [Alcohol and Anxiety in Orissa, India], in preparation.

América Indígena, El alcohol y el indio, *Am. Indig.,* **14,** 283–285 (1954).

American Medical Association, *Manual on Alcoholism*, A.M.A., Chicago, 1956 (rev. ed., 1967).

Amouak, R., Alcoholism/Cultural Heritage Program [among Alaskan native peoples], research in progress.

Arriola, J. L., Introducción al estudio [del] alcoholismo como problema social, in *Primera Reunión Regional Centroamericana sobre Alcoholismo*, Patronato Antialcohólico de Guatemala, Guatemala, 1962.

Bacon, S. D. (Ed.), *Understanding Alcoholism*, Annals of the Academy of Political and Social Science 315, Philadelphia, 1958.

Baddeley, F. J., African beerhalls, thesis (architecture), University of Cape Town, Cape Town, 1966.

Bard, J., C. Mare, C. Williams, and I. Wolpaw, Effect of intra-group competition on alcohol consumption in primitive cultures, manuscript [ca. 1955].

Beaubrun, M. H., Alcoholism and drinking practices in a Jamaican suburb, *Alcoholism, ,* **4,** 21–37 (1968).

Bernier, G. and A. Lambrecht, Étude sur les boissons fermentées indigènes du Katanga, *Probl. Soc. Congolais,* **48,** 5–41 (1960).

Bismuth, H. and C. Menage, Alcoolisation du Niger; . . . du Senegal; . . . d'Haut Volta; . . . des Etats de Langue Française de l'Afrique Occidentale; Aspects de l'alcoolisation du Dahomey; Aperçu de l'Alcoolisation de la Guinée, Haut Comité d'Étude et d'Information sur l'Alcoolisme, Paris, (multigraphed) 1960.

Blevans, S. A., A. critical review of the anthropological literature on drinking, drunkenness, and alcoholism, M.A. thesis (anthropology), University of Washington, 1967.

Blom, F., On Slotkin's "Fermented drinks in Mexico," *Am. Anthropol.,* **58,** 185–186 (1956).

Bloom, J. D., Socio-cultural aspects of alcoholism, *Alaska Med.,* **12,** 65–67 (1970).

Blyth, W., Transcultural studies in alcoholism in a rural catchment area as pertaining to three cultures: White Americans, American Negroes, American Indians, (multigraphed) 1972.

Brown, D. N., Patterns of heavy drinking at Taos Pueblo, New Mexico, Paper read at Southwestern and Rocky Mountain Division, American Association for the Advancement of Science Meeting, Tucson, 1967.

Bruun, K., Den Sociokulturella Backgrunden till Alkoholismen, *Alkoholpolitik,* **22,** 54–58 (1959).

Buckley, J. P., A. P. Furgiule, and M. J. O'Hare, The pharmacology of kava, *J. Polynesian Soc.,* **76,** 101–102 (1967).

Cahalan, D., Observations on methodological considerations for cross-cultural studies, in *Cross-Cultural Studies on Alcohol*, M. W. Everett, J. O. Waddell, and D. B. Heath (Eds.), Mouton, The Hague, expected 1974.

Carpenter, J. A. and N. P. Armenti, Some behavioral effects of alcohol on man, in *The Biology of Alcoholism*, Vol. 2, B. Kissin and H. Begleiter (Eds.), Plenum Press, New York, 1972.

Cavan, S., *Liquor License: An Ethnography of Bar Behavior*, Aldine, Chicago, 1966.

Central African Journal of Medicine, Native liquors in southern Rhodesia, *Cent. Afr. J. Med.*, 4, 558–559 (1958).

Chassoul M., C. and D. B. Heath, [research on drinking patterns in several communities of Costa Rica], in progress.

Chattopadhyay, A., The ancient Indian practice of drinking wine with reference to Kathasaritsagara, *J. Orient. Inst.* (Baroda), 18, 145–152 (1969).

Cheinisse, L., La race juive, jouit-elle d'une immunité a l'égard de l'alcoolisme? *Sem. Med.*, 28, 613–615 (1908).

Cinquemani, D. K., [research on drinking and alcoholism in Middle America], in preparation.

Claudian, J., History of the usage of alcohol, in *International Encyclopedia of Pharmacology and Therapeutics* Vol. 2, sec. 20, J. Tremolières (Ed.), Pergamon Press, Oxford, 1970.

Collins, T., Economic change and the use of alcohol among American Indians, Paper read at American Anthropological Association Meeting, San Diego, 1970.

Collins, T., Variance in northern Ute drinking, in *Alcohol, Drinking, and Drunkenness among North American Indians*, M. W. Everett and J. O. Waddell (Eds.), expected 1974.

Collins, T. and J. Dodson, Arapahoe, Shoshone and Ute drinking behavior: a comparative analysis, Paper read at American Anthropological Association Meeting, Toronto, 1972.

Collocott, E. V., Kava ceremonial in Tonga, *J. Polynesian Soc.* 36, 21–47 (1927).

Commission to Study Alcoholism among Indians, *Report* [to U.S., Department of Interior, Bureau of Indian Affairs], (multigraphed) 1956.

Connell, K. H., Illicit distillation: an Irish peasant industry, *Hist. Stud.*, 3, 58–91 ( ).

Davis, W., Sociocultural factors in black alcoholism, manuscript, ca. 1972.

Deihl, J. R., Kava and kava drinking, *Primitive Man*, 5, 61–68 (1922).

Desai, A. V., An exploratory survey of drinking in Suraf and Bulsar community, Department of Psychology, S.B. Garda College, Navsari, India, manuscript, 1965.

Devenyi, *Sociocultural Factors in Drinking and Alcoholism, Alcoholism and Drug Addiction Research Foundation of Ontario*, Clinical Division Substudy 17-1967, Toronto, 1967.

Dobyns, H. F., Drinking patterns in Latin America: a review, Paper read at American Association for the Advancement of Science Meeting, Berkeley, Cal., 1965.

Douyon, E., Alcoolisme et toxicomanie en Haïti, *Toxicomanies* (Québec), 2, 31–38 (1969).

Doxat, J., *Drinks and Drinking: An International Distillation*, Ward Lock, London, 1971.

Dube, K. C., Drug abuse in northern India, *Bull. Narc.*, 24, 49–53 (1972).

Dummett, R. E., The social impact of the European liquor trade on the Akan of Ghana: an interdisciplinary study, Paper read at the International Congress of Anthropological and Ethnological Sciences, Chicago, 1973.

Eis, G., Altdeutsche Hausmittel gegen Trunkenheit und Trunksucht, *Med. Monatsschr.* (Stuttgart), 15, 269–271 (1961).

Eriksson, K. and K. Käkkäinen, Pullo-ja tölkkijatteen Kasaantriminen luontoon Suomessa uvonna 1970, *Alkoholipolitiika*, 36, 175–186 (1971).

Escalante, F., Yaqui drinking groups, in *Alcohol, Drinking and Drunkenness among North American Indians*, M. W. Everett and J. O. Waddell (Eds.), expected 1974.

Everett, M. W., C. J. Baha, E. Declay, M. R. Endfield and K. Selby, Anthropological Expertise and the "Realities" of White Mountain Apache Adolescent Drinking, Paper read at Society for Applied Anthropology meeting, Tucson, 1973.

Ezell, P. H., A comparison of drinking patterns in three Hispanic cities, Paper read at American Association for the Advancement of Science meeting, Berkeley, 1965.

F., H., Chikaranga cocktails, *Nada* (Salisbury), **11**, 116–117 (1933).

Feldman, W. M., Racial aspects of alcoholism, *Br. J. Inebriety*, **21**, 1–15 (1923).

Ferguson, F. N., Navajo drinking: an aspect of culture conflict (research in progress).

Galang, R. C., Pangasi: the Bukidnon wine, *Philipp. Mag.*, **31**, 540 (1934).

Gearing, F., Toward an adequate therapy for alcoholism in non-Western cultures: an exploratory study of American Indian drinking, Department of Anthropology, University of Washington, (manuscript) 1960.

Génin, A. M.A., *La cerveza entre los antiguos mexicanos y en la actualidad*, [no publisher] México, 1924.

Ghosh, S. K., Alcohol and alcoholism in the North-East Frontier Area, Paper read at International Congress of Anthropological and Ethnological Sciences, Chicago, 1973.

Goldman, I., *The Cubeo: Indians of the Northwest Amazon*, Illinois Studies in Anthropology 2, Urbana, 1963.

Górski, J., Alkohol u kulturze i obyczaju, *Probl. Alkohol.*, **17**(7–8), 10–11 (1969).

Grace, V., Wine jars, *Cl. J.*, **42**, 443–452 (1957).

Gracia, M. F., Analysis of incidence of alcoholic intake by Indian population in one state of U.S.A. (Montana), Paper read at International Congress of Anthropological and Ethnological Sciences, Chicago, 1973.

Grant, A. P., Some observations on alcohol consumption and its results in Northern Ireland, *Ulster Med. J.*, **32**, 186–191 (1963).

Guiart, J., *Un siècle et demi de contacts culturels à Tanna, Nouvelles Hébrides*, Publications de la Société des Océanistes 5, Paris, 1956.

Haas, S. J. de and C. Jonker, Horton's hypothese getoetst, manuscript, 1965.

Hansen, E. C., From political association to public tavern: two phases of urbanization in rural Catalonia, manuscript [ca. 1971].

Harford, C. F., Drinking habits of uncivilized and semi-civilized races, *Br. J. Inebriety*, **2**, 92–103 (1905).

Harrison, B. H. and B. Trinder, Drink and sobriety in an early Victorian country town: Banbury 1830–1869, *Engl. Hist. Rev. Suppl.*, **4**, 1–72 (1969).

Hartocollis, P., Alcoholism in contemporary Greece, *Q. J. Stud. Alcohol*, **27**, 721–727 (1966).

Havard, V., Drink plants of the North American Indians, *Bull. Torrey Bot. Club*, **23**, 33–46 (1896).

Hawthorn, H. B., C. S. Belshaw, and S. M. Jamieson, The Indians of British Columbia and alcohol, *Alcohol. Rev.*, **2**(3), 10–14 (1957).

Helgason, T., Rapport från Island: Alkoholismens Epidemiologi, *Alkoholfrågån*, **62**, 219–230 (1968).

Herrero, M., Las viñas y los vinos del Perú, *Rev. Indias*, **1**(2), 111–116 (1940).

Hes, J. P., Drinking in a Yemenite rural settlement in Israel, *Br. J. Addict.*, **65**, 293–296 (1970).

Hickman, R. C., Demonstration Tri-Cultural Alcoholism Treatment Program in Santa Fe (research in progress).

Hoff, E. C., *Cultural Aspects of the Use of Alcoholic Beverages,* New Hampshire State Department of Health, Division on Alcoholism Publication 22, Concord, 1958.

Holloway, R., *Drinking among Indian Youth: A Study of the Drinking Behaviour, Attitudes and Beliefs of Indian and Metis Young People in Manitoba,* Alcohol Education Service, Winnipeg, 1966.

Honigmann, J. J., Alcohol in its cultural context, Paper read at Interdisciplinary Symposium on Alcoholism, Washington, 1971.

Irish National Council on Alcoholism [Research on endogenous depression and alcoholism in Ireland], in progress.

Jackson, C., Some situational and psychological correlates of drinking behaviour in Dominica, W.I., Paper read at American Anthropological Association Meeting, San Diego, 1970.

Jarvis, D. H., *Report of the Cruise of the U.S. Revenue Cutter* Bear, *and the Overland Expedition for the Relief of the Whalers in the Arctic Ocean.* House Document 511 (56th Cong., 2nd Sess., Vol. 93), U.S. Government Printing Office, Washington, D.C., 1899.

Jay, M., L'Évolution de l'alcoolisme à la Reunion, *Alcool ou Santé,* **104,** 32–38 (1971).

Jellinek, E. M., The world and its bottle, *World Health,* **10**(4), 4–6 (1957).

Johnston, T. F., Musical instruments and practices of the Tsonga beer-drink, *Behav. Sci. Notes,* **8,** 5–34 (1973).

Joseph, A., R. Spicer, and J. Chesky, *The Desert People,* University of Chicago Press, Chicago, 1949.

Juhaz, P. and R. Frater, Alcohol consumption and alcoholism in a rural [Hungarian] community, *Alcoholism* (Zagreb), **7,** 93–95 (1971).

Jupp, G. A., Social-cultural influences on drinking practices, *Brewers Digest,* **46,** 76 ff. (1971).

Kalant, H., Problems of alcohol and drugs: relationships and non-relationships from the point of view of research, in *Proceedings of 28th International Congress on Alcohol and Alcoholism,* Vol. 2, M. Keller and T. G. Coffey (Eds.), Hillhouse Press, Highland Park, N.J., 1969.

Keehn, J. D., Translating behavioral research into practical terms for alcoholism, *Can. Psychol.* **10,** 438–446 (1969).

Keirn, S. E., Urban African biculturalism: stress and adaptation (research in progress).

Keller, M., Bibliography and documentation on alcohol: resources for the anthropologist, in *Cross-Cultural Studies on Alcohol,* M. W. Everett, J. O. Waddell, and D. B. Heath (Eds.), Mouton, The Hague, expected 1974.

Keller, M. (Ed.), *International Bibliography of Studies on Alcohol* (3+ vols.), Rutgers Center of Alcohol Studies, New Brunswick, N.J., 1966–.

Kline, J. A., V. V. Rozynko, G. Flint, and A. C. Roberts, Personality characteristics of male native American alcoholic patients, *Int. J. Addict.,* (expected 1974).

La Barre, W., Professor Widjojo goes to a koktel parti, *N.Y. Times Mag.,* December 9, 1956; 17 ff.

Langness, L. L. and L. Herrigh, American Indian drinking; alcoholism or insobriety, Paper read at Mental Health Research Meeting, Fort Steilacoom, Wash., 1964.

Lanu, K. E., *Control of Deviating Behavior: An Experimental Study on the Effect of Formal Control over Drinking Behavior,* Finnish Foundation for Alcohol Studies Publication 2, Helsinki, 1956.

LeBlanc, A. E. and W. Schmidt, Deconfounding of natural variables present in human alcohol drinking patterns by the use of animal experimentation, in *Cross-Cultural Studies on Alcohol*, M. W. Everett, J. O. Waddell and D. B. Heath (Eds.), Mouton, The Hague, expected 1974.

Leland, J., Indian alcohol users: an insiders' view (in preparation).

Lemert, E. M., Secular use of kava in Tonga, *Q. J. Stud. Alcohol*, **28**, 328–341 (1967).

Levy, R. I., [drinking among the Newars of Nepal] in preparation.

Lindner, P., El secreto del "Soma", bebida de los antiguos indios y persas, *Invest. Progr.*, **7**, 272–274 (1933).

Lines, J. A., Chicha in aboriginal Costa Rica: historical references and sketches, in preparation.

Little, M. A., Effects of alcohol and coca on foot temperature responses of highland Peruvians during a localized cold exposure, *Am. J. Phys. Anthropol.*, **32**, 233–242 (1970).

Lobban, M. C., Cultural problems and drunkenness in an Arctic population, *Brit. Med. J.*, **1**, 344 (1971).

Loeb, E. M., Wine, women, and song: root planting and head-hunting in Southeast Asia, in *Culture and History*, S. Diamond (Ed.), Columbia University Press, New York, 1960.

Lolli, G., Alcoholism as a medical problem, *Bull. N.Y. Acad. Med.*, **31**, 876–885 (1955).

Long, J. K., [drinking and witchcraft as indices of tension in Latin America] in preparation.

Lubart, J. M., Field study of the problems of adaptation of Mackenzie Delta Eskimos to social and economic change, *Psychiatry*, **32**, 447–458 (1969).

Lundberg, G., Sociocultural change and drinking patterns in British Honduras, in preparation.

McCall, G., [Drinking patterns of Basques in Europe] in preparation.

McCloy, S. G., [Drinking patterns and religion in the Outer Hebrides] in preparation.

McFarland, R. A. and W. H. Forbes, The metabolism of alcohol in man at high altitudes, *Human Biol.*, **8**, 387–398 (1936).

McGuire, M. T., S. Stein, and J. H. Mendelson, Comparative psychosocial studies of alcoholic and nonalcoholic subjects undergoing experimentally induced ethanol intoxication, *Psychosom. Med.* **28**, 13–25 (1966).

Madsen, W., Comment on D. Mandelbaum's "Alcohol and culture," *Curr. Anthropol.*, **6**, 291–292 (1965).

Madsen, W., Alcoholics Anonymous as a crisis cult, Paper read at National Institute on Alcoholism and Alcohol Abuse Conference, Washington, 1973.

Maha Patra, S. S. K., [Alcohol and alcoholism among the tribal communities in Orissa, India] in preparation.

Mail, P. D., The prevalence of problem drinking in the San Carlos Apache, M.P.H. thesis, Yale University Medical School, New Haven, 1967.

Malen, V. D., [Value orientation and alcoholism on the Pine Ridge Sioux Reservation] in preparation.

Martindale, D. and E. Martindale, *The Social Dimensions of Mental Illness, Alcoholism, and Drug Dependence*, Greenwood, Westport, Conn., 1971.

Medical Tribune and Medical News, Unusual intoxication laid to GI fermentation, *Med. Trib. Med. News*, **13**(43), 23 (1972).

Merry, J., The "loss of control" myth, *Lancet*, **1966**(1; 7449), 1257–1258 (1966).

Metzger, D. G. and G. Williams, Drinking patterns in Aguacatenango: code and content, manuscript [ca. 1963].

Montoya y F., J. B., El alcoholismo entre los aborígenes de Antioquia, *Anal. Acad. Med.* (Medellín), **12**, 132 (1903).

Mora, C. F., Problemas psicológicos peculiares al aborígen Guatemalteco, in *Primera Reunión Regional Centroamericana sobre Alcoholismo*, Patronato Antialcohólico de Guatemala, Guatemala, 1962.

Morote Best, E., Chicha, *Impulso,* **1**(3), 1-6 (1952).

Mossman, B. M. and M. D. Zamora, Culture-specific treatment for alcoholism, Paper read at International Congress of Anthropological and Ethnological Sciences, Chicago, 1973.

Nagler, M., *Indians in the City: A Study of the Urbanization of Indians in Toronto*, Canadian Research Centre for Anthropology, Saint Paul University, Ottawa, 1970.

Negrete, J. C., Factores socio-culturales en el alcoholismo, Paper read at Curso Internacional sobre Alcoholismo, San José, Costa Rica, 1973.

Negrete, J. C., Cultural influences on social performance of chronic alcoholics: a comparative study, *Q. J. Stud. Alcohol* (expected 1974).

Newell, W. H., The kava ceremony in Tonga, *J. Polynesian Soc.,* **56**, 364-417 (1947).

New Mexico Association on Indian Affairs Newsletter, The liquor problem among Indians of the Southwest, *New Mexico Association on Indian Affairs Newsletter* (July 1956).

Newsletter of Southwestern Association on Indian Affairs, Drinking and Indian problems, *Newsletter of Southwestern Association on Indian Affairs* (Jan. 1959).

Nissly, C. M., [chicha in Peru] in preparation.

Norelle-Lickiss, J., Social deviance in aboriginal boys, *Med. J. Aust.,* **58**, 460-470 (1971).

Obayemi, A. M. U., Alcohol usage in an African society, in *Cross-Cultural Studies on Alcohol*, M. W. Everett, J. O. Waddell, and D. B. Heath (Eds.), Mouton, The Hague, expected 1974.

O'Laughlin, B., Mbum beer-parties and structures of production and exchange in an African social formation, Ph.D. dissertation (anthropology), Yale University, 1973.

Owen, R. C., [Alcohol consumption and use in several Brazilian population segments: an evolutionary approach] in preparation.

Pacheco e Silva, A. C., Intoxicación crónica en América latina, *Rev. Psiquiátr. Peruana,* **2**, 159-181 (1959).

Paredes, A., L. J. West, and C. C. Snow, Biosocial adaptation and correlates of acculturation in the Tarahumara ecosystem, *Int. J. Soc. Psychiatry* (London), **16**, 163-174 (1970).

Pascal, G. R. and W. O. Jenkins, On the relationship between alcoholism and environmental satisfactions, *Southern Med. J.,* **59**, 698-702 (1966).

Pendered, A., Kubika Wawa: beer making, *Nada* (Salisbury), **9**, 30 (1931).

Piedade, J. da, H. Ayats, and H. Collomb, Aspects socio-culturels de l'alcoolisme au Senegal, *Alcoholism* (Zagreb), **7**, 104-108 (1971).

Plaut, T. F., *Alcohol Problems: A Report to the Nation by the Cooperative Commission on the Study of Alcoholism*, Oxford University Press, New York, 1967.

Poirer, J., Les problèmes de la consommation du chanvre Indien a Madagascar, *Toxicomanies* (Québec), **3**, 65-88 (1970).

Polacsek, E., T. Barnes, N. Turner, R. Hall, and C. Weise (comps.), *Interaction of Alcohol and Other Drugs*, Addiction Research Foundation Bibliography Series 3, Toronto, 1972.

Poot, A., Le "munkoyo" boisson des indigenes Bapende (Katanga), *Bull. Séances Inst. R. Colon. Belge,* **25,** 386–389 (1954).

Preuss, K. Th. Das Fest des Erwachens (Weinfest) bei den Cora-Indianern, in *Verhandlungen des XVI Internationalen Amerikanisten-Kongresses,* Vol. 2, A. Hartleben, Wien, 1910.

Prince, R., R. Greenfield, and J. Marriott, Cannabis or alcohol? Observations on their use in Jamica, *Bull. Narc.,* **24,** 1–9 (1972).

Quarcoo, A. K., [Alcohol and tradition religions in Ghana] in preparation.

Radović, B., Pechenje Rakije v Nashem Narodu, *Glas. Ethnograf. Muz.,* **55,** 69–112 (1937).

Rasmussen, C., Drinking patterns in Peguche (Imbabura), in *Drinking Patterns in Highland Ecuador,* E. Maynard, et al., Department of Anthropology, Cornell University, 1965.

Ray, R. B. J.-C., Hindu method of manufacturing spirit from rice, *J. Asiat. Soc. Bengal* (NS), **2,** 4 (1906).

Reader, D. H. and J. May, *Drinking Patterns in Rhodesia: Highfield African Township, Salisbury,* University of Rhodesia, Department of Sociology Occasional Paper 5, Salisbury, 1971.

Reddy, G. P., Where liquor decides everything: drinking subculture among tribes of Andhra, *Soc. Welfare* (New Delhi), **17**(11), 4–5 (1971).

Resnik, H. L. P., and L. H. Dizmang, Observations on suicidal behavior among American Indians, *Am. J. Psychiatry,* **127,** 882–887 (1971).

Ribstein, M., A. Certhoux, and A. Lavenaire, Alcoolisme au rhum: étude de la symptomatologie et analyse de la personalité de l'homme martiniquais alcoolique au rhum, *Ann. Méd.-Psychol.,* **125,** 537–548 (1967).

Richards, A. I., *Land, Labour and Diet in Northern Rhodesia: An Economic Study of the Bemba Tribe,* Oxford University Press, London, 1939.

Riffenberg, A. S., Cultural influences and crime among Indian-Americans of the Southwest, *Fed. Probation,* **10,** 38–41 (1956).

Riley, J. W., Jr., Sociological factors in the alcohol problem, *Sci. Temperance J.,* **54,** 67–74 (1946).

Robarts, E., Distilling liquor in Tahiti in 1806, *J. Pacific Hist.,* **1,** 62 (1966).

Roca, W., D., Apuntes sobre la chicha, *La Verdad,* **42**(2004), 3 (1953).

Roebuck, J. B. and R. G. Kessler, *The Etiology of Alcoholism: Constitutional, Psychological and Sociological Approaches,* Charles C Thomas, Springfield, Ill., 1972.

Rojas González, F., Estudio histórico-etnográfico del alcoholismo entre los indios de México, *Rev. Mex. Soc.,* **4,** 111–125 (1942).

Roth, W. E., On the native drinks of the Guianese Indian, *Timehri Demerara* (Ser. 3), **2,** 128–134 (1912).

Rotter, H., Die Bedeutung des alkoholischen Milieus für den Alkoholismus, *Wiener Med. Wochenschr.,* **107,** 236–239 (1957).

Roueché, B., *The Neutral Spirit: A Portrait of Alcohol,* Little, Brown, Boston, 1960.

Roufs, T. G. and J. M. Bregenzer, Some aspects of the production of pulque, in *Social and Cultural Aspects of Modernization in Mexico,* F. Miller and P. Pelto (Eds.), Department of Anthropology, University of Minnesota, Minneapolis, (multigraphed) 1968.

Rubington, E., The bottle gang, *Q. J. Stud. Alcohol,* **29,** 943–955 (1968).

Rubington, E., The language of "drunks," *Q. J. Stud. Alcohol,* **32,** 721–740 (1971).

Rüden, E., Der alkohol in Lebensprozess der Rasse, *Int. Monatsschr. Erforsch. Alkohol. Bekaemp. Trinksitten,* **13,** 374–379 (1903).

Salone, E., Les sauvages du Canada et les maladies importées de France au xviie et au xviiie siècle: la picote et l'alcoolisme, *J. Soc. Am. Paris* (NS), **4**, 7–20 (1907).

Sanders, A., [Alcohol and alienation: the Amerindians of the Corentyne River Valley] in preparation.

Sargent, M. J., Theory in alcohol studies, in *Cross-Cultural Studies on Alcohol*, M. W. Everett, J. O. Waddell, and D. B. Heath (Eds.), Mouton, The Hague, expected 1974.

Savard, R. J., Cultural stress and alcoholism: a study of their relationship among Navaho alcoholic men, Ph.D. dissertation (sociology), University of Minnesota, 1968.

Schaefer, J. M., A methodological review of holocultural studies in drunkenness, Paper read at 9th International Congress of Anthropological and Ethnological Sciences, Chicago, 1973.

Schmidt, K. E., *Some Preliminary Observations on Excessive Alcohol Consumption in Port Vila*, Report to the Resident Commissioners, New Hebrides Condominium, 1969.

Schmidt, K. E., Excessive alcohol consumption (E.A.C.) in the New Hebrides and recommendations for its management, South Pacific Commission, (multigraphed) 1970.

Schmidt, K. E., The present state of alcohol and drug consumption in the South Pacific, Paper read at the 29th International Congress on Alcohol and Drug Dependence, Sydney, Australia, 1970.

Schmidt, W. and R. E. Popham, *Some Hypotheses and Preliminary Observations concerning Alcoholism among Jews*, Addiction Research Foundation Substudy 1-4 and 2-61, Toronto, 1961.

Shalloo, J. P., Some cultural factors in the etiology of alcoholism, *Q. J. Stud. Alcohol*, **2**, 464–478 (1941).

Sievers, M. L., Cigarette and alcohol usage by southwestern American Indians, *Am. J. Publ. Health*, **58**, 71–82 (1968).

Siliceo Pauer, P., El pulque, *Ethnos*, **2**, 60–63 (1920).

Singh, S., Preparation of beer by the Loi-Manipuris of Sekami, *Man in India*, **17**, 80 (1937).

Siverts, H., Drinking patterns in highland Chiapas, in *A Teamwork Approach to the Study of Semantics through Ethnography*, H. Siverts (Ed.), Universitetsforlaget, Bergen, Norway, 1972.

Solms, H., Sozio-kulturelle und wirtschaftliche Bedingungen der Giftsuchten, des Medikamentenmissbrauches und des chronischen Alkoholismus, *Hippokrates*, **37**, 184–192 (1966).

Sommer, R., *Personal Space: The Behavioral Basis of Design*, Prentice-Hall, Englewood Cliffs, N.J., 1969.

Spradley, J. P., *You Owe Yourself a Drunk: Ethnography of Urban Nomads*, Little, Brown, Boston, 1970.

Spindler, G. D., Alcohol symposium: editorial preview, *Am. Anthropol.*, **66**, 341–343 (1964).

Steiner, C., *Games Alcoholics Play: The Analysis of Life Scripts*, Grove Press, New York, 1971.

Stewart, O. C., Theory for understanding the use of alcoholic beverages, Paper read at American Anthropological Association Meeting, Minneapolis, 1960.

Straus, R. and R. G. McCarthy, Nonaddictive pathological drinking patterns of homeless men, *Q. J. Stud. Alcohol*, **12**, 601–611 (1951).

Szwed, J. F., Gossip, drinking and social control; consensus and communication in a Newfoundland parish, *Ethnology*, **5**, 343–441 (1966).

Tapia, P., I., J. Gaete A., C. Muñoz, I., S. Sescovitch, I. Miranda, J. Minguell I., G. Pérez P., and G. Orellana A., Patrones socio-culturales de la ingestión de alcohol en Chiloé; informe preliminar: algunos problemas metodológicos, *Acta Psiquiátr. Psicol. Am. Latina*, **12**, 232–240 (1966).

Taylor, W. B., [research on Indian drunkenness in colonial Mexico], in progress.

Titcomb, M., Kava in Hawaii, *J. Polynesian Soc.*, **57**, 105–169 (1948).

Topper, M. D., Navajo culture, "social pathology," and alcohol abuse: a broad interpretation, Paper read at Society for Applied Anthropology Meeting, Tucson, 1973.

Udvalget for Samfundsforskning i Grønland, *Alkoholsituation i Vestgrønland*, Dansk Bibliografisk Kontor, København, 1961.

United States, Department of Health, Education and Welfare, Indian Health Service, *Alcoholism—A High Priority Health Problem: A Report of the Indian Health Service Task Force on Alcoholism*, U.S. Govt. Printing Office, Washington, 1970.

United States, Department of the Interior, Bureau of Indian Affairs, *Report of the Commission to Study Alcoholism among Indians*, (multigraphed) 1956.

Valenzuela Rojas, B., Apuntes breves de comidas y bebidas de la región de Carahue, *Arch. Folklórico*, **8**, 90–105 (1957).

Velapatiño Ortega, A. and A. García Bonilla, [alcohol and drugs in eastern Peru] in preparation.

Viñas Tello, E., La composición química de las diferentes variedades de chicha que se consumen en el Perú, Ministerio de Salud Pública y Asistencia Social, Departamento de Nutrición, Lima, (multigraphed) 1951.

Voss, H. L., *Alcoholism in Hawaii*, Economic Research Center, Honolulu, 1961.

Waddell, J. O., "Drink, friend!" Social contexts of convivial drinking and drunkenness among Papago Indians in an urban setting, in *Proceedings of 1st Annual Institute on Alcohol Abuse and Alcoholism* (expected 1973).

Waddell, J. O., Social and pathological dimensions of Papago drinking behavior, in *Drinking, Drunkenness, and Alcoholism among North American Indians*, M. W. Everett and J. O. Waddell (Eds.), expected 1974.

Webe, G., [a distributional study of drinking among South American Indians] in preparation.

Westermeyer, J. J., Use of alcohol and opium by the Meo of Laos, *Am. J. Psychiatry*, **127**, 1019–1023 (1971).

Westermeyer, J. J., Chippewa and majority alcoholism in the twin cities: a comparison, *J. Nerv. Ment. Dis.*, **155**, 322–327 (1972).

Westermeyer, J. and J. Brantner, Violent death and alcohol use among the Chippewa in Minnesota, *Minn. Med.*, **55**, 749–752 (1972).

White, M. F., Drinking behavior as symbolic interaction, Ph.D. dissertation (sociology), University of Kentucky, 1971.

Whitehead, P. C., C. F. Grindstaff, and C. L. Boydell (Eds.), *Alcohol and Other Drugs: Perspectives on Use, Abuse, Treatment and Prevention*, Holt, Rinehart and Winston, New York, 1973.

Whittaker, J. O., The problem of alcoholism among American reservation Indians, *Alcoholism* (Zagreb), **2**, 141–146 (1966).

Whittet, M. M., An approach to the epidemiology of alcoholism: studies in the highlands and islands of Scotland, *Br. J. Addict.*, **65**, 325–339 (1970).

Wilkinson, R., *The Prevention of Drinking Problems: Alcohol Control and Cultural Influences*, Oxford University Press, New York, 1970.

Williams, A. F., Social drinking, anxiety, and depression, *J. Pers. Soc. Psychol.*, **3**, 689–693 (1966).

Wolcott, H. F., Feedback influences on fieldwork, or, a funny thing happened on the way to the beer garden, in *Urban Man in Southern Africa*, C. Kileff and W. Pendleton (Eds.), expected 1974.

ACKNOWLEDGMENTS

In a very real sense this review is an unforeseen outgrowth of several years' interest in the subject; it is not the outcome of any specific research project and no funding agency provided financial support at any stage of the work. Obviously this was possible only because Brown University has provided a liberal and supportive general ambience for teaching and research for several years.

It was Mark Keller who originally sparked my interest in comparative studies on drinking patterns while I was a graduate student at Yale, and Charles R. Snyder and Floyd Lounsbury sharpened my awareness of the craft of writing. Clyde Kluckhohn and George P. Murdock taught "the anthropological perspective" in the most effective way—by example.

Robert Popham and the Addiction Research Foundation provided generous hospitality during a crucial last-minute review of the literature; Ron Hall and his staff made our stay at the library pleasant as well as fruitful.

At the invitation of Sol Tax, I planned a Conference on Alcohol Studies and Anthropology, held in August 1973, in conjunction with the Ninth International Congress of Anthropological and Ethnological Sciences. Bela Maday at the National Institute of Mental Health and Mie Caudill at the National Institute on Alcohol Abuse and Alcoholism were helpful in securing a grant which provided administrative support through Center for the Study of Man at Smithsonian Institution. Sam Stanley, William Douglass, and Valerie Aschenfelter did an excellent job at every stage of the work. When illness interfered with my efficiency, Michael W. Everett and Jack O. Waddell volunteered as co-organizers. In a very real sense, the proceedings of that conference constitute an extension of this chapter; they will be published as *Cross-Cultural Studies on Alcohol: An Interdisciplinary Perspective*, edited by Michael W. Everett, Jack O. Waddell, and Dwight B. Heath, Mouton, The Hague, expected 1974.

Chapter Two

AN APPRAISAL
OF DRUG EDUCATION
PROGRAMS

GERALD GLOBETTI, *University of Alabama, University, Alabama*

1. INTRODUCTION

Researchers who undertake the evaluation of social action programs are beset with numerous conceptual, methodological, and practical problems (59). Consequently, evaluation is one of those program objectives that is widely praised but sadly practiced. Nowhere is this situation more evident than in the field of alcohol and drug education. There has been little research on who has been saying what about mood modifiers, to whom, and with what effect. Thus the kinds of critical evaluation which lead to generalizations about effective methods for transmitting information about alcohol and drugs are almost nonexistent.*

Evaluation studies of the educational enterprise are difficult for two major reasons. First, there is a general inability to obtain widespread agreement on what should be the ultimate aims of alcohol and drug education. Goals range from an emphasis on abstinence to a stress on decision making and the formation of values. This lack of consensus has led to a kind of immobilization of evaluation studies, where by default nothing is done because no one is sure what is to be accomplished. Second, the methodological considerations required to detect changes in behavior and attitudes are difficult to approximate in real life situations. An adequate evaluation procedure would have to be longitudinal in nature and would have to measure attitudes and behavior not only at the point of departure but also at subsequent periods in time. Moreover, random assignments into programs and nonprogram groups would have to be made along with the

---

* For example, a partial review of more than 100 drug education programs by Fejer and Smart revealed that only six had received any sort of evaluation, primarily short-term attitude change. The situation is even worse in the field of alcohol education (48).

control of the research population's exposure to consequential variables extraneous to the educational system (28, 29). Up to this time, such evaluation has been too costly in terms of effort, time, and funding. As a result, the determination of the effects of any given educational endeavor or innovation in the fields of alcohol and drug education, except in rare instances, has usually been impressionistic or anecdotal in nature. In viewing the current situation one is reminded of Spencer's old dictum recorded in 1872, but applicable today:

> The data for forming scientific judgments are not to be had: most of them are unrecorded, and those which are recorded are difficult to find as well as doubtful when found. . . . Life is too short, and the demands upon our energies too great to permit such elaborate study as seems required. We must, therefore, guide ourselves by common sense as best we may [cited by Baumgartiver (5)].

Given these limitations, the purpose of this chapter is to examine several critical issues which confront the educational effort to teach about alcohol and drugs and to digest what is known about progress toward generally accepted goals. For organization of effort, attention is directed primarily to education in the schools. In addition, because of several significant differences in historical background, degree of community concern, and legal status, alcohol and drug education are treated separately.

2. ALCOHOL EDUCATION IN THE SCHOOL

Introduction

Historically, whenever a problem affecting a large segment of society has been recognized, Americans customarily have turned to the schools for its solution (14). Yet the subject of alcohol education elicits a curious ambivalence on the part of the citizens of most communities. To be sure, faith in education as the primary preventive agent of undesirable conditions receives almost universal endorsement. Virtually all the states require, by legal mandate, some instruction about alcohol in the public school curriculum. However, sharp emotional disagreements concerning overall goals and plans of action have resulted in a neglect of instructional programs or at best superficial coverage (57).

It has long been the contention of action workers in the field that one of the major reasons for this state of affairs is the outmoded concept that alcohol education, especially among the young, must be instruction against alcohol (10). Thus to fully understand the incongruence between the public's verbal ratification of the need for alcohol education and the paucity of programming in the school system, it is essential to describe the conditions which led to the educational approach.

History of the Educational Response to Alcohol Problems

Alcohol education in American society, like the custom of drinking, has both a historical content and a contemporary character (34). Early in the colonial period, the moderate use of nondistilled beverages, such as ales, beers, and wines, was expected and generally accepted. Alcohol was called the "good creature of God" and was considered a prime necessity and an indispensable part of colonial life. There was no condemnation of alcoholic beverages as such nor was there an attitude of hostility toward intoxicants on the part of moral or religious forces (2).

This conception of alcohol as an integral element of society with no intrinsic evil attached to it prevailed until the late eighteenth century. However, during this period a significant development occurred which altered American drinking practices and attitudes toward alcohol; for when distilled spirits gained in prominence as the country's preferred alcoholic beverage, drinking became increasingly an all-male, outside-the-home-activity. Imbibing developed as essentially a separate pursuit from religious, family, and ceremonial functions. Loud, boisterous, and unrestrained drinking styles emerged notably on the western frontier and in the expanding urban centers of the country. Such a pattern of use was considered to be a definite threat to the social order and to the values of self-reliance and individual achievement. Gradually, a stigma toward all forms of alcohol intake emerged which, in turn, provided an impetus to the temperance movement (4).

For generations temperance material dominated people's attitudes and knowledge about drinking in this country. This movement, properly interpreted as the abstinence period, was based on the assumption that all forms of alcohol intake led to personal tragedy and social ills and, as a result, had catastrophic consequences for the individual and society. The aim was to excise the custom of drinking from the national and the cultural scene by legal decree. A series of organizations and activities emerged for this purpose. Prominent among these were various educational efforts. It was felt early in the movement that education and indoctrination of the young would be of more significance in eliminating the drinking custom than attempts to reform the inebriate.

The most effective organization in giving scope and purpose to alcohol education during this period was the Woman's Christian Temperance Union. In 1874, its members made this pledge:

I hereby solemnly promise, God helping me, to abstain from all distilled, fermented and malt liquors including wine, beer and cider and to employ all proper means to discourage the use of and traffic in the same. To confirm and enforce the rationale of this pledge we declare our purpose to educate the young, to form a better public sentiment; to reform so far as possible by religious, ethical and scientific means, the drinking classes, to seek the transforming power of divine grace for ourselves and for all whom we work.

To achieve this objective, the Union established a Department of Scientific Temperance whose purpose was to develop literature and teaching material (26). The message was somewhat simplistic and included the belief that in order to get people to think or act against alcohol, one had only to tell enough people enough times in sufficiently striking terms about the evils of drink. The tone was to stress that all alcohol was poison, and that its use was degrading, unpatriotic, and criminal. The aim was to get all people, especially youth, to loathe and fear alcohol (4).

Efforts were also directed toward making the "teaching of scientific temperance" a compulsory part of the public school curriculum. In 1882, Vermont passed the first statute requiring instruction about alcohol and narcotics as units of physiology and hygiene courses. Within 20 years all the states had a similar law. In addition to the time allotted in the schools, the Union nurtured other channels of communication with the young. Special antialcohol youth groups were developed, some for those under 7 years, some for 8–12 years old, and some for adolescents. The staff of the Department of Scientific Temperance wrote, published, and distributed a mass of material for the public schools and often sent their representatives into the schools to present lectures.

Other organizations, though not as influential as the W.C.T.U., joined the drive to educate the youth to the dysfunctional effects of drink. The Anti-Saloon Leagues, established 1895, had as their slogan "Education, Legislation and Law Enforcement." In 1919, the World League Against Alcoholism declared its intentiion to achieve the total suppression of alcohol use and abuse through both legislation and education. But it remained for the W.C.T.U. to provide the leadership and primary force for alcohol education.

Despite the temperance forces' concerted drive and success, however, not everyone was pleased with what they were trying to accomplish. About 1890, a group of professionals and laymen, known as the Committee of Fifty to Investigate the Liquor Problem, was organized to make a comprehensive study of the issues surrounding alcohol use. Out of this Committee's six volumes of published material came a critical evaluation of the instruction given in the schools and the community. Consequently, the confidence of educators in the material prepared by the W.C.T.U. was reduced. The information was criticized as being distorted and based upon a strategy of fear.

With these changes the W.C.T.U. concentrated on preparing new outlines, pamphlets, and films for classroom use. One outline, Alcohol and Other Narcotics, was prepared and distributed as part of a joint report of the American Medical Association and the National Education Association. With such prestigious endorsement this outline was widely accepted by school officials.

During the prohibition period, the educational activities of the W.C.T.U. and other temperance groups were sharply curtailed since it was felt that the law had eliminated alcohol problems (15). This confidence in a legal solution to alcohol use and misuse was soon shaken as the unsuccesses of national prohibition began to multiply. With the repeal of prohibition, the strength of the abstinence message naturally began to wane. A study commissioned by John D. Rockefeller made the following recommendation concerning education in the mid-1930s:*

Not only do we need research so that facts can displace opinion and superstition but we need clear unprejudiced dissemination of facts. This requires a tolerant spirit, and tolerance in education, free from the bias of preconceived objectives, is perhaps difficult to achieve. But it is distinctly within the range of possibility to promote understanding of facts to a point where common knowedge supports a steadily improving national ideal. Whatever line temperance instruction may take, its chief emphasis, if it is to capture this younger generation, should be on life and health and not on disease and death. It should be constructive and not negative. The necessity of keeping fit for work and sport is a far more effective appeal than moral homilies. Our young people cannot be brow-beaten into righteousness or frightened into good behavior. They are alert to detect exaggeration and they are not moved by sanctimonious exhortation. It is this kind of approach which too often made temperance teaching in the past what one well known educator called a "pedagogical monstrosity." The only effective appeal today is an appeal not to fear or prejudice but to intelligence.

Into the decades of the forties and the fifties the old monolithic message of the temperance forces, its tenets and methods, began to deteriorate. Yet no satisfactory message has emerged to take its place. Faced with this situation educators with few exceptions have reacted in one of several ways. First they have attempted to avoid the subject of alcohol education altogether. If this is not possible they have delegated the responsibility to someone else, usually an expert who represents a particular point of view which in most cases is an abstinence one (4). Finally, there are some educators who recognize the value of teaching about alcohol but strain to avoid offending community groups who have differing attitudes about alcohol. As a consequence, they respond with the "individualization" approach in which an attempt is made to present the facts about alcohol in a dispassionate manner in order to assist young people to form acceptable standards of conduct regarding alcohol. This response, although more educa-

* From R. G. McCarthy (Ed.), *Alcohol Education for Classroom and Society*, 1964. Used with permission of McGraw-Hill Book Company.

tionally sound, is much less common than the other two. Moreover, it is beset by several difficulties, some of which will be explored (16).

Youth and Alcohol Education

It is apparent then that much of our so-called alcohol education of the young is either ignored or still carries with it the imprint of the prohibitionist voice of the past. Children continue to be warned, although under somewhat more sophisticated guises, of the dire results and tragic consequences of alcohol use in ways which make them appear inevitable if a person begins to drink. This negative kind of teaching runs counter to the experiences of a great many young people and has the adverse consequence of substantially reducing the credibility of adults on other matters vital to youth behavior.

Teaching about alcohol has failed in the main because it has focused on what the older generation thinks younger people should be told rather than finding out what young people themselves feel about alcohol and its use (44). For this reason, it is relevant to report and interpret here the findings of a survey concerned with the perception of alcohol education among a group of junior and senior high school students who were preparing to enter an alcohol instructional program for the first time. Two major areas were studied. First the students were asked to report their exposure to what they recognized as alcohol education. They were then asked to indicate something of what they had learned about beverage alcohol as well as thier opinions regarding the teaching about it.*

The data showed that the students were eager to learn about alcohol and felt there was a need for instruction regarding it in their schools. Approximately 9 in 10 replied that they should have an opportunity to learn about the nature of alcohol and its use. A similar proportion said that it was a responsibility and function of the school to establish programs of this type.

When asked what they wanted to know about intoxicants, two dominant themes emerged: 41% said that young people should be taught to realize the dysfunctional aspects of drinking, whereas 36% indicated that teen-agers should be presented the objective facts, with the purpose of letting them make their own decision about whether or not to drink.

The findings suggest, therefore, little reason to doubt the adolescent's motivation to learn about intoxicants. However, they also point out that young people, like adults, have a variety of interests in the subject of al-

---

* This section is adapted from G. Globetti, Alcohol education in the school, *J. Drug Educ.* (1971). Reprinted by permission of Baywood Publishing Company.

cohol use. Subsequently, educators should realize that an initial assessment of the student's attitude toward drinking and his pattern of alcohol intake is an almost mandatory prerequisite to effective instruction.

Despite their desire to learn more about alcohol, it was found that the students were actually receiving little formal, organized information regarding it. This is not surprising in the light that most school systems lack any meaningful or articulate program of instruction about alcohol. To school officials, alcohol education implies something more than the transmission of information, namely, the teaching of morality, an issue not yet resolved by the educational enterprise (3). Until this issue is resolved, administrators feel the school has little responsibility in this area and see it as a function of the home or church.

However, more than half of the students replied that they never discussed *any* aspect of drinking with their parents, which suggests that many parents are also reluctant to accept the responsibility of teaching their children about the use of alcohol. This finding was further demonstrated by an accompanying survey among parents which showed that only 11% felt that the child should be taught about alcohol *only* in the home and church. Approximately 9 in 10 felt that the school was the logical place for such instruction. To be effective it appears that both the home and the school must realize that they have a part to play in alcohol instruction. No single agency is adequate for the task. Effective alcohol education seems to be, of necessity, a community responsibility.

Further analysis revealed that in the absence of instruction about alcohol in the home and school, the students relied on informal discussion with their age peers. Of those questioned, 7 in 10 said the use of intoxicants was a major topic of conversation with their friends. One can hardly fail to draw a parallel between alcohol education and sex education in this respect. In the absence of proper instruction concerning vital teen-age problems, the young person must depend on inadequate information from his contemporaries. Friends are normally poor sources because their alcohol education has usually been just as poorly handled.

Questions also were asked concerning from whom a teen-ager would seek objective information regarding alcohol. More than half of the students said they would use reference materials from such agencies as Alcoholic Anonymous and the public library. School as a source was not mentioned and only 2% indicated the church. When asked to what person they would turn, only 5% mentioned a school official or minister.

Moreover, the students said they would seek advice from a particular adult concerning drinking only if he were understanding and trustworthy. This finding illustrates that the subject of drinking is a sensitive topic for teen-agers and that adults should avoid any inclination to ridicule or to be

unsympathetic toward a young person's desire to learn more about alcohol
(18).

Some Program Considerations for Effective Alcohol Education

The purpose of this section is to extrapolate some apparent implications
from the preceding analysis and other conceptual reports which are
germane to the implementation of an alcohol education program within the
school. This study, along with others, shows that the student wants to learn
more about alcohol and its use. However, it points out that young people,
like adults, reflect a certain ambiquity in the overall goals of education,
some aiming toward total abstinence, others favoring moderate and controlled drinking.

It is this lack of consensus regarding the ultimate objectives of alcohol
education which has led to an immobilization of most school programs. Is
the preferred state of affairs total and permanent abstinence, or abstinence
during the adolescent period with the option of free choice with approaching adulthood, or the development of responsible patterns of use for
the adolescent years? Teachers traditionally have avoided the subject because of their discomfort in introducing material which has the strong
possibility of antagonizing one segment of the community or the other.
Furthermore, schools are basically conservative institutions, which means
its officials are reluctant to resolve societal problems which are
characterized by community dissensus. Moreover, if the challenge of special interest groups is accepted there is always an administrative price to
pay in the forms of specialization of teachers and new demands on an already crowded curriculum. Subsequently, every school system faced with
requests for new programs has to determine the place of instruction about
alcohol in the hierarchy of other educational needs facing the community.
It is obvious that alcohol education today is not high on the priority list
(28).

But given the acceptance by the school to teach about alcohol, the
question then becomes one of which model, abstinence or moderate
drinking, has the best hopes for success in terms of the type of society the
young graduate will enter. America is a drinking society, but education in
the schools up to this time, with few exceptions, has been basically toward
abstinence (45). This approach has not reduced either the incidence of
drinking or alcohol neglected problems. Some have cautioned that this approach may exacerbate the situation by making alcohol use a forbidden
item and, therefore, more attractive as a symbol for those who wish to
demonstrate a contempt for authority. Moreover, studies show that a
teaching which implants a repugnance to drinking tends to identify the

drinking act with personal and social disorganization. It may, therefore, suggest an inebriety pattern for drinking and may actually encourage behavior it most deplores.

Evidence would suggest that the moderate drinking model offers the best hope for success. This approach maintains that problems related to alcohol arise when abusive drinking takes place and that moderate drinking is both acceptable and distinguishable from other styles of alcohol use (11). The aim is not to promote or prevent use but rather to encourage responsible drinking habits if one makes the choice to drink. This should be achieved without impinging upon the individual's freedom to abstain or drink as long as both behaviors are done in a responsible and tolerant manner. This appears to be the direction in which expert opinion in the field of alcohol education is headed (39).

Yet even if the moderate drinking model appears the most realistic in terms of our society's definition of alcohol, the closely related issue of whether to focus on programs to prepare the adolescent for his adult drinking behavior or on his relation to alcohol while a youth still remains (16). The implied message of most education programs, which employ the moderate drinking model, is to give young people the scientific facts so they can make up their own minds not to drink—at least until they are legally entitled to do so or are adults (46). Evidence, however, would suggest many legitimate reasons to focus on current adolescent use rather than projected adult drinking styles (16). For example, three-fourths of our young people will use alcohol before they are legally entitled to do so, one-third on a somewhat regular basis, and 5–10% will experience serious complications as a result of drinking (17). In addition, although the data are not conclusive, several studies suggest that problem drinking among adults can be traced to incipient teen-age problems (16). Then there is the relationship of teen-age drinking and driving. On the other hand, there are several complicating problems to consider when emphasizing preparation for teen-age drinking. Prominent among these is that this focus advocates a program contrary to legal codes. Furthermore, there is considerable disagreement on a minimum age below which persons should not drink or what norms would constitute appropriate teen-age drinking. Community reaction is especially sensitive to any program which even indirectly alludes to teaching young people how to drink. As a result alcohol educators have been especially reluctant to come to grips with the question of alcohol use among adolescents. It is assumed that by focusing on preparation for the adult decision to drink or to abstain, the questions and concerns that young people have about their own drinking or that of their peers will be allayed (16).

Another issue related to aims is that there is no single message of alcohol education which is applicable to all students who compose the typical classroom. Students have a variety of interests and needs insofar as alcohol education is concerned. Yet there are few indications that alcohol educators have been particularly sensitive to identifying the needs of the audience they wish to address. Young people are treated as a single entity who will respond to the same message in the same way. This seems especially unrealistic when we realize that numerous influences outside of the school shape and influence a young person's attitude toward alcohol use and nonuse. Our approaches and methods must be adapted to the characteristics of specific subgroups of adolescents, a prerequisite called for by McCarthy and Douglas over 30 years ago (23, 29). There is no general alcohol education program to be used uniformly in all schools or even with all children in the same class. Instead, the various influences that condition a child's behavior in respect to alcohol must be studied, analyzed into major configurations, and used as guidelines for separate specific approaches. It is evident that such an objective presents extremely difficult and involved problems. Yet to be successful, program content should be dictated by the needs of young people rather than the opinions and professional biases of alcohol education experts (23).

A second set of issues, besides the goals of alcohol education, has to do with the methods of communication. Currently, the emphasis in instructional programs is on autonomy and decision making. The aim is to convey information from which we assume young people will make a more deliberate and constructive decision about alcohol use. This approach assumes man to be a rational being who orders his life according to his understanding of the best information available to him. We all question this assumption, yet the notion persists in educational programs. Man is shaped by numerous and subtle influences, many of which are in conflict with what our intellect tells us we should do. Facts alone are not enough; no matter how convincing they appear to us, they often fail to impress young people. Information is certainly a prerequisite for intelligent action but it is usually not sufficient to produce the desired effect or action. Other conditions must be met, especially the motivation of the learner to accept the information as a guide to his behavior. This acceptance is usually dependent on the learner's perception of how relevant the material is to his real life situation. Educational programs should strive to relate what the child learns in school to his life outside the school, not an easy task. How little alcohol educators do this, and how difficult it is, is reflected in the arguments used in the field today. Many of our appeals are based on typical adult values, as mentioned elsewhere. For example, much of our educational effort is devoted to the possible long-range consequences which are related to alcohol misuse. But it is the nature of adolescents to be more concerned with immediate affairs rather than with possible results of a distant future (23).

Finally, there has been little research on the efficacy of the techniques of transmitting information about alcohol to young people. Among the methods employed have been the usual lectures, discussions, conferences, and visits from outside experts. Some evidence would suggest that the best framework for the instructional program is the informal discussion group with the teacher's role primarily nondirective (11). His task is to provide a nonthreatening environment in which young people can explore, examine, and discuss their own attitudes and behavior concerning alcohol (58). In addition, teachers should realize that to teen-agers the use of alcohol is a sensitive topic. If one seeks his advice he should be understanding rather than judgmental. It is only within the frame of feeling that the subject of drinking should be interpreted to the young person. Consequently, intensive teacher education is essential and crucial to a program's success. The instructor must equip himself with the best current information in the area of alcohol usage. He must understand the wide differences in the motivational and attitudinal makeup of his students. The communicator must examine his own biases and feelings about alcohol. All too often teachers are hampered by the same misconceptions and fears which afflict the lay public. He is often considered by students as another spoiling member of a censorious older society (11). Effective communication is a function of the prestige, respect, and credibility of the communicator. As the students of the reviewed study stated, "the educator should be understanding, trustworthy and knowledgeable."

Unfortunately, systematic evaluation of the outcome of the few alcohol education programs which operate in our schools is rare. Programs are usually judged on the basis of subjective testimonials, or input (e.g., "we distributed blank number of pamphlets," or "blank number of students were exposed"). In some instances, there is a one group measure of the level of knowledge retained after exposure to instruction. Only one study has employed any controls, random assignment, and before-after measures to determine attitude and behavior change. But as these researchers themselves concluded, there is little evidence of the long-term effects of alcohol education. Thus one is left in the position of reiterating the usual recommendation that a demonstration project with proper measures and controls be designed and implemented (1).

Conclusions

In American society the prevention and the reduction of undesirable conditions have always centered around education. However, the field of education about alcohol is unfortunately in a rudimentary stage with no clear-cut philosophy. Instructional programs, as a result, are nonexistent or sparse and fragmentary, usually consisting of an occasional visit from individuals who often represent a particular view. Traditionally, this viewpoint has been limited to admonishing young people about the hazards of drinking (11). Educational programs have had limited value. Currently, there is an abundance of data regarding beverage alcohol. It is time that we design more realistic and effective ways to transmit this information to our young.

DRUG EDUCATION IN THE SCHOOL

Introduction and Background

Few issues in American society command as much attention or generate more discussion than the use and misuse of drugs, especially among young people. Out of this concern has emerged a vast bureaucratic system to provide programs which will ameliorate or reduce drug use and its attendant problems (32). Prominent in this "drug industrial complex" is a large and significant investment in various educational activities by federal, state, and local agencies. For unlike the dearth of programming in alcohol education, the American public has been inundated by a flurry of drug education strategies which differ significantly in format and content.

It is difficult to identify the beginnings of the process which has brought the nation to its present level of awareness and educational response to the use of drugs in society (32). Drug problems, which appear so characteristic of this age and time, are not new or unique. Drugs were imported to this country during colonial times and by the late 1800s the use of opium was quite common. Miracle medicines which contained narcotics mixed with alcohol were sold everywhere. Further abuse of narcotics resulted with the invention of the hypodermic needle immediately prior to the War Between the States. Physicians encouraged their patients to buy this device and to administer drugs on a "do it yourself" basis. Of the many substances injected, morphine was found to be an effective pain killer and was valued for its soporific effects.

The Civil War witnessed the indiscriminate use of morphine to relieve the pain of wounds. Consequently, many soldiers, on both sides, became addicted. After the war, the unregulated use of patent medicine again became widely popular, reaching its peak in the late nineteenth century (25). At the turn of the century, the number of Americans addicted to one of the opiates was probably higher than at any other period, past or present. Reports from the Federal Government estimated a total of 1,000,000 addicts in the United States at this time. More recently, several authorities have put the figure dependent on drugs at no less than 1% of the population of the country in the early part of this century (41).

However, opiates constituted only a small part of the American reform movement during this time (36). Moreover, except for sporadic activity, the public in the main was rather indifferent toward the user of narcotics (43). The addict was outside the mainstream of American life and, as a result, was ignored or punished for his behavior. This attitude, except in a few instances, prevailed until the decade of the sixties when to the public's dismay and alarm the characteristics of the drug-using population began to change. The use of drugs broke from its class and ethnic structures and infiltrated every sector of American life including white middle-class youth. Reports from all sections of the country revealed an increasing rate of use, with a large part of this increase occurring among younger age groups from the more advantaged social classes (41).

With this changing scene came the realization that drugs could become a problem for anyone in the general population, even those with whom we hoped to entrust the nation. Rhetoric, emotion, and urgency for solutions became the theme during the decade of the 1960s.

In response to this state of affairs, the public reacted in a reasonably predictable manner. At first, the prevention of use was to be accomplished by the deterrent force of the law (14, 33). Under the terms of the legal model, primary efforts to reduce and eliminate drug use were to threaten the user with criminalization, imprisonment, and other forms of social punishment.

Yet use continued to increase and youth, as a result of the harshness of the law, became even more alienated from the American value system. To counter this reaction, prestigious groups called for decriminalization and revival of the medical model which defines drug abuse as an illness requiring treatment rather than punishment. Under the terms of this approach, it was assumed that the prospect of serious complications resulting from the abuse of drugs would serve as an effective deterrent to the initiation of drug use and the progression of abuse.

These models, although valid for some individuals, have proved to be inadequate with respect to their ability to influence a large number of those who have become involved with drugs (33). Invariably, the educational enterprise was called upon once again to help remedy an undesirable social condition. The response to this urgent call has been prodigious in the variety and the number of stratagems, programs, and techniques (43).

Levels of the Educational Response

In order to appreciate this large outpouring of drug education activities, it may be helpful to look at the scope of the various programs which currently operate at the national, state, and local levels.

Programs at the National Level

As the public became more cognizant of the changing nature of drug abuse in this country, federal agencies intensified their efforts in the area of prevention and education. Initially, the programs of the different federal agencies operated in isolation. However, as the problem of drug abuse became more acute and complex, the need to coordinate energies and resources became apparent. As a result, the Interagency Coordinating Committee was established in 1970 to bring the various federal programs together for review and coordination (22). Through the action of 92nd Congress which enacted Public Law 92-255, The Drug Abuse Office and Treatment Act of 1972, the Special Action Office for Drug Abuse Prevention was formed to mobilize the resources of the nation against the problems related to drug use and misuse. In short, the director of this office was charged with the immediate objective to significantly reduce the incidence of drug abuse within the shortest time possible and to develop and activate a comprehensive, coordinated federal strategy to combat the problem (32).

Federal programs which have relevance to drug education in the school include, among others, those of the United States Office of Education. It was started in March, 1970 when the President announced the creation of the National Drug Education Program and released approximately $4,000,000 for its operation. The program provides for grants to all states and territories and is delegated to state departments of education. Emphasis is on provision for the training of local teams composed of school personnel, youth, and community representatives.

The Drug Abuse Education Act (Public Law 91-527) was signed into law in December, 1970 and formalized the aforementioned program of the U.S. Office of Education. The training program which began in that year has continued although at reduced funding. In addition, two new programs were activated by this bill, namely, pilot programs on college campuses and a limited number of locally based and comprehensive community drug education programs. The thrust of this act acknowledges the complex nature of the drug problem which necessitates a coordinated community-wide approach to solution, including the schools.

The emphasis planned by the U.S. Office of Education for 1973 stresses community programs but continues to provide for the involvement of the school. Included in the plan is the establishment of several training centers located in various areas of the country. These centers are designed to prepare local community teams for effective and comprehensive action against drug abuse.

In addition to the programs supported by the Drug Abuse Education Act, the U.S. Office of Education, in 1971–1972, funded 11 comprehensive drug education programs which were submitted by local school districts or county education agencies under provisions of the Elementary and Secondary Education Act. A major prerequisite to the consideration of these proposals was the involvement of the community in the education effort.

Other educational efforts at the federal level include the National Cleaninghouse for Drug Abuse Information which was created in 1970 to serve as a focal point for public inquiries. This program is operated by the National Institute of Mental Health and includes three basic services: publication distribution, computer-based information storage, and retrieval and referrals. Numerous educational materials such as curricula, bibliographies, film guides, and catalogs are available for distribution and use. Another service of the National Institute of Mental Health is a series of films for teacher and parent education entitled "The Social Seminar." In addition, the Federal Bureau of Narcotics and Dangerous Drugs of the Department of Justice periodically develops and distributes drug education materials. (See, for example, Louise G. Richards and John H. Langer, *Drug Taking in Youth*, Office of Scientific Support, Bureau of Narcotics and Dangerous Drugs, U.S. Government Printing Office, Washington, D.C., 1971). In other instances the National Institute of Mental Health, the Office of Economic Opportunity, and the Law Enforcement Assistance Agency have funded local school-community drug education programs.

Another service at the federal level is the National Coordinating Council on Drug Abuse Education, a private nonprofit organization formed in 1968. The stated purposes of the Council are to coordinate educational and informational efforts of organizations in the area of drug abuse; to evaluate drug abuse education programs; to give visibility to effective programs; to evaluate and develop the role of professional and public information in drug abuse education; to stimulate regional, state, and local involvement in drug abuse education by establishing interdisciplinary committees to respond to area needs; and to provide leadership in the area of drug abuse information and education (22).

Federal outlays for education, information, and training have increased from $15.9 million in the fiscal year 1970 to an estimated $67.6 million in 1972. As shown in Table 1, this effort is administered by 10 separate federal agencies. Approximately three-fifths of these funds are spent directly on information production and dissemination of materials and the remainder is channeled into training programs (14).

Such activity points to the faith that the American society has in its schools as a vanguard for prevention. One Congressional Committee has tentatively proposed spending $5 billion in 5 years on school drug programs, a proposal made even without any assurance of what the money will buy or has brought (14).

TABLE 1   FEDERAL DRUG EDUCATION, INFORMATION, AND TRAINING PROGRAMS

Agency	Estimated Obligations (Millions of Dollars)				
	1969	1970	1971	1972	1973
Education/information					
SAODAP	0	0	0	0	0
HEW					
NIMH	1.2	4.2	4.2	6.5	7.9[a]
OE	.2	0	3.4	9.5	7.9[a]
SRS	0	0	0	.1	0
DOD	.1	.1	.2	10.9	9.6
Justice					
LEAA	0	2.6	13.2	8.3	6.0
BNDD	.5	1.3	.7	1.2	1.1
HUD	.7	2.1	2.4	7.2[b]	8.0[c]
Education/information total	2.7	10.3	24.1	43.7	40.5
Training					
SAODAP	0	0	0	0	0
HEW					
NIMH	[d]	[d]	2.5	9.9	12.7
OE	0	3.4	2.0	2.1	2.0
SRS	0	0	.4	.4	0
OEO	0	.4	.7	1.4	0
VA	0	0	0	.2	.4
DOD	[e]	[e]	[e]	1.5	2.8
Justice					
BOP	[f]	[f]	[f]	[f]	[f]
LEAA	[d]	1.8	10.8	8.4	6.0
Training total	0	5.6	16.4	23.9	23.9

[a] HEW is operating under a contingent resolution for fiscal year 1973; obligations are confined to fiscal year 1972 level.
[b] Includes 0.3 from DOT and 0.4 from USDA.
[c] Includes 0.4 from DOT and 0.5 from USDA.
[d] Included in Education/information.
[e] DOD includes training as part of treatment/rehabilitation; cannot be broken out.
[f] Less than $100,000.

Source: *Drug Use in America: Problems in Perspective*, Second Report of the National Commission on Marihuana and Drug Abuse, U.S. Government Printing Office, Washington, D.C., March, 1973, p. 348.

Programs at the State Level

As one would expect, there is an array of educational activities at the state level, all at different stages of development. Consequently, it is not possible to give an accurate or comprehensive portrayal of what is occurring in state drug education programs. Perhaps the only common feature is the previously mentioned Drug Education Training Program funded by the U.S. Office of Education. But even here the approach employed differs from state to state (22).

Few attempts have been made to sort through individual descriptions of state programs in order to find common elements. However, the Commission on Marihuana and Drug Abuse, in its first inquiry, did succeed in developing an overall understanding of what the states had undertaken in drug education (30). Early in July, 1971, Commission investigators asked the chief state school officer by questionnaire to respond to the following points:

1.   The role of the State Departments of Education in initiating teacher-training programs and other state programs in drug education.
2.   Whether the State Departments of Education had developed special drug education curricula or were in planning stages.
3.   Whether the public and private colleges and universities were offering professional training for teachers in drug education at the undergraduate and postbaccalaureate levels.
4.   Whether the states were requiring the teaching of drug education programs at the elementary and secondary grades, or permitting the local school districts to make that determination.
5.   The kinds of resource materials which the states had developed and made available to the local school districts.
6.   The concerns, attitudes, or philosophies which the State Departments of Education had adopted or might want to convey to the Commission related to students' use of drugs.

Findings revealed considerable variation by the states to each of the six points of interest. A number of the school officials viewed the increasing use of drugs among the young with seeming detachment whereas others reacted with perplexity and concern. A few states appeared committed to a well developed program of instruction by directing some of their professional and financial resources toward a specific course of action. They had produced and distributed curriculum guides, provided in-service training for teachers, and assumed a position of leadership in developing materials and coordination of activities. On the other hand, some of the Departments had made virtually no progress in these points.

In general, it was found that the State Departments had little support from their state legislatures. As a result, programs have developed slowly and more often than not operate with insufficient funding and programming. This is reflected in several ways. The Commission found, for example, that only 24 states require drug education as a part of the curriculum or as a part of health and physical education classes. Thus less than half of the states have taken an official position that drug education should be incorporated into regular classroom instructions. Moreover, at the time of the survey, only 17 states had developed drug education curricula which were available to all school districts. In 20 states, the development of materials was centered in the local school district. The remaining states were in the process of preparing curriculum guides or had plans to do so. However, although ostensibly providing curricula guidelines, many of the state Departments of Education were in actuality only expanding already existing physical and health education curricula. Half of the states provided resource materials for their school districts. Some of these materials were evaluated by the Commission as being well done, carefully written and edited. Yet there was an abundance of extremely poor materials being distributed.

The review of the in-service drug training program revealed that it existed to some extent in every state, a finding attributed to the availability of federal funds. Yet few states added any monies to the federal base and as a result, according to the Commission's report, had suffered from several handicaps. It was found that the selection of many teachers for the program was based on factors other than those which would make him an effective coordinator and instructor of drug education. Moreover, it was found that in many cases, the trained teachers failed to receive any support from their supervisors for implementing a drug program when they returned to their school system. In short, the Commission, while favoring the intent of the teacher training program, evaluated it to have fallen far short of its objective (14).

This situation at the state level reflects, in general, the fragmentary nature of drug education in this country. There is little uniformity in purpose, design, and stage of development.

Programs at the Local School Level

As the preceding suggests, many state education officials appear to take the position that drug education is a local responsibility and act accordingly. Consequently, the urgency of an increasing rate of substance use and abuse among young people has created strong community pressure that the local school reverse the trend.

Thus many of the 17,200 school districts in this country have initiated some form of instructional program regarding drugs (14). However, about the only thing that can be said with any degree of certainty is that drug education goes under a variety of names, which implies that it is handled in a variety of ways. In some school systems it may be called value training, in others drug abuse education. It may be handled as a separate course or as an integrated part of the curriculum. Time allotments may range from a 1 hour assembly program to a 2 week unit. In short, an infinite number of strategies and techniques have been subsumed under its rubric. Basically, however, all these efforts may be grouped loosely into three major types of programs, namely, the Scare Approach, the Information-Transmission Approach, and the Value Training Approach.

The Scare Approach stresses the sordid and frightening aspects of drug use in order to convince young people that they should not use drugs. The assumption is that young people are willing to accept ready-made decisions from others about how they should behave regarding drugs and, by implication, how they should choose their values and order their lives. This approach has been regarded as especially ineffectual and has been singled out as perhaps stimulating rather than deterring drug use (42).

The Information-Transmission Approach stresses the cognitive domain and assumes that the knowledge transferred and absorbed by young people will be utilized to make a healthy and wise choice about drugs. It is usually assumed that given adequate knowledge of the facts concerning the effects, risks, and harms of drug taking, the user or potential user will decide to discontinue or not to engage in this behavior. This approach typically has not allowed for an adequate consideration of the affective or the noncognitive elements such as attitudes, values, and developmental needs which influence drug use. Subsequently, the major emphasis commonly has been on the pharmacology of drugs with little reference to the noncognitive domain. Although evaluation of this approach has seldom been attempted, it is quite likely that facts as a means to change and modify behavior, as previously mentioned, are inadequate. Some studies have shown that informational level has not acted in a dominant way among the factors related to the different forms of drug use (20). Moreover, it has been suggested that an approach which emphasizes the cognitive only may lead to the conclusion that chemical substances produce pleasure and can be used with little risk (14). Researchers at Pennsylvania State University, for example, found an actual increase and more tolerance toward drugs after exposure to this type of program.

Although the Information-Transmission Approach has been exceedingly popular, a trend toward an increasingly noncognitive and affective approach is becoming more evident. This model, referred to here as the Value Training Approach, is predicted upon the recognition that an individual's behavioral choices, such as drug taking, are influenced by his fundamental needs, aspirations, wants, and desires. Subsequently, the aim is to sharpen the perspective of the causes of use, what needs such behavior fulfills, and how constructive alternatives may be employed which serve the same ends as drug use but expose the user to less risk. Value input, the development of value awareness, and the classification of how an individual's personal values are actualized into behavior are the vehicles for reaching this goal (33). Simply stated, values are assumed to be based on needs. Thus a person places value on those things he feels he must have, and in so doing, these values become the basis for his decision (35). The aim of this model is to become conversant with a student's value profile, to remediate where there are felt deprivations, and to substitute more constructive alternatives to enhance self worth (35, 42).

Among the advantages cited by proponents of this model are that it avoids the weakness of the strictly informational strategy by making knowledge about drugs more relevant to needs. It further proposes the direct involvement of the individual for whom the program is aimed in the planning, implementation, and evaluation process (33). Such involvement increases relevancy between program objectives and subsequent activities. It also precludes the imposition of the values and biases upon young people of those administering the program (33). One reason cited for the failure of other approaches is the lack of student involvement in the planning and carrying out of the program. Research suggests that a person is much more receptive to a presentation if he is involved in its operation (27). Finally, the most salient feature of this model is that it focuses upon the causes of drug abuse rather than the resulting symptoms or consequences, a point often ignored in other approaches (33).

This model, of course, presents many more difficulties than the other two. In the first place it requires an agreement upon the values that should be taught, a touchy issue in any community. Moreover, it requires the need for constructive alternatives which can be controversial or too costly to implement (14).

Evaluation of Drug Education

The preceding descriptions, although far from complete, reflect something of the effort being mounted to dispense information about the drug phenomenon in this country. Presently, however, there is no adequate appraisal of the impact of this effort on behavior. Evaluation studies are in short supply, a situation which results from several sources. First, it is difficult to actually know what is going on since there is no central exchange to which independent programs report. Furthermore, there is no way to check on the accuracy of the information being dispensed nor how it may be reaching its intended audience (14). Then there are complex methodological problems involved in attempting to test the efficacy of specific ap-proaches in drug education (42). For example, the problems involved in employing the experimental model in evaluation research, which remains the ideal, are numerous in large-scale social programs. Random assign-ments, control groups, and the perseverance required to measure long-term efforts are rare amenities. Moreover, it is not exactly clear if the experi-mental model is always the most relevant for measuring the effectiveness of drug education. It may indicate if goals are accomplished but rarely why the observed results occur or what processes may intervene to influence outcomes. This model is especially difficult to apply to programs where goals and emphases may change in mid-course (59). Furthermore, the quasi-experimental design, which frees the evaluator from some of the ex-periment's restrictive conditions, especially randomization, suffers from similar limitation in uncovering the process of changes in attitudes and be-havior. There is also the added difficulty of matching groups so as to con-trol for differences prior to the introduction of the experimental variable (49).

These limitations are not intrinsic to the experimental or the quasi-ex-perimental models, but they do pose some critical problems of design (59). Because of these and other methodological difficulties, the few evaluative studies which exist consist of posttest designs in which measures of a group are made after exposure to a drug program or the pretest-posttest design in which the same subjects are measured prior to and after exposure to a program. These designs are most often employed in programs of an in-formation-transmission type and assume short-term changes in attitudes and knowledge about drugs. In both of these designs it is difficult to specify the role of drug education on behavior and attitudes. An even more inade-quate technique which is often employed to determine efficacy is one in which the evaluator collects subjective appraisals from participants on the impact of a program on their feelings and behavior (49).

Added to these methodological difficulties is the situation where the evaluation of a social program has become increasingly political. This is especially the case in drug education where programs have been launched with much fanfare regarding their value as deterrents of drug use. Adminis-trators, therefore, have a vested interest in their programs, and do not relish careful evaluation. They look for positive results and seek evaluation studies which are least likely to be damaging (49). It must be quite dis-maying to many drug educators that careful and competent studies in the past have been shown few positive effects from a variety of other social programs (59).

Thus despite a substantial investment in drug education activities, we are just beginning to think about evaluation and strategy (42). However, even without adequate and comprehensive evaluations, there is increasing evidence that the effort up to this time has been a failure, especially if the major aim has been to stop all use of illegal drugs.* For example, in 1972 The National Education Association after a year-long study reported (20):

> ... the greater percentage of existing drug education programs are superficial and educationally poor. Some of the programs because of the false statements made by the misinformed educators could very well have contributed to the increase in drug usage in this society. . . .

In a similar vein, the Second Report of the Commission on Marihuana and Drug Abuse (14)critically observed:

> ... In spite of many and varied efforts made thus far, the incidence of drug use for self-defined purposes, has continued to rise. This raises the troubling possibility that something basic is wrong with our pedagogy.

The Commission went on to recommend that a moratorium on all drug education programs in the schools be declared at least until they are soundly evaluated. Others have called the effort useless, counterproductive, or a miserable failure (20).

Although it is difficult to specify the reasons for the limited effectiveness of drug education, at least two common conclusions have emerged from the isolated and scattered studies of different investigators: (1) much of the material now in use is scientifically inaccurate and (2) most programs operate in total disregard of basic communication theory (14).

There is little question that many drug programs, reacting to the urgency of the moment, have been ill conceived, rapidly established, and based on false and judgemental material (42). For example, the Task Force on Drug Education of the National Education Association has this to say about the caliber and the quality of drug education information currently in use in our schools (14):

> ... Much false material has been produced for and used in drug education with widespread indiscretion in schools across the nation. Commercial agencies have taken advantage of the concern caused by the emergence of the drug problem and have produced and sold much material without thought of quality. The Task Force feels that use of false, poor, emotionally oriented and judgmental materials is more harmful than no materials and is not indicative of the N.E.A.'s desire for high level educational materials.

Studies of the National Coordinating Council on Drug Education also have

---

* An analysis of program objectives reveals such aims as the prevention of dysfunctional drug use, irrational decisions due to lack of information, drug dependence, irresponsible behavior, inadequate coping, and drug abuse. Yet it is obvious that the implicit objective of almost all existing drug education programs is to stop all use of currently illegal drugs (14).

pointed out the inaccurate and distorted nature of drug education materials. One rating of more than 500 drug abuse education films showed 80% to contain misleading scientific and medical statements about drugs and their effects. One-third were conceptually unsound and included so many errors as to be classified as scientifically unacceptable, and 53% were placed in a restricted category, which meant they were not suitable for general audiences. Only 16% of the films were recommended by the Council. Further content analyses and ratings revealed an even more dismal picture of various posters, charts, pamphlets, and other similar types of literature. Only 30 items of more than 800 pieces of literature reviewed met acceptable standards (20).

All this sensationalization, journalistic exaggeration, and nefariousness in drug education, so it appears, has done little more than to lead young people to a basic mistrust of the total effort. Young people can quickly detect bias whatever its source and direction. They, therefore, are aware of the hoax being perpetrated on them by innumerable groups who sense the commercial and political attractiveness of the drug issue. For example, many young people who appeared before the Le Dain Commission, which inquired into the nonmedical use of drugs in Canada, were highly critical of the exhortation and propaganda to which they had been exposed. Specifically, they said the attempts to use scare techniques had backfired and destroyed the credibility of sound information (8).

Drug education currently suffers from the excesses of a rapid proliferation of programs founded on sources of information in a state of flux and change (7). It is unfortunate that there is no agency empowered to test the accuracy of facts and to expunge the misinformation which exists. Until this is done, the credibility of drug education will continue to be suspect among young people.

So much then for the quality of the material being transmitted to students. Consideration is now given to the communication process and what research has to suggest about the failure of drug education in this respect.

The familiar rubric of communication research is who says what to whom. Although much has been studied regarding this process, little has been applied to the development of drug education programs. For example, research has consistently shown a positive relationship between the credibility of a communicator and his ability to persuade an audience to alter its attitudes and behavior. Credibility, as defined by young people, consists of two dimensions, expertness and trustworthiness (17, 4S). In addition, those communicators who are seen as similar to their audience are more effective than those perceived as dissimilar (48). Although the characteristics of the effective drug education teacher are not yet known, it appears that the choice of those assigned to instruct about drugs has usually been made on other than these factors. In many cases, teachers of drug education have been selected on the basis of their subject matter area alone, such as health or physical education, rather than on such characteristics as knowledge of drugs, ability to relate to young people to the point of gaining their confidence, and motivation to be involved in a drug problem. Although it is unwise to generalize, it appears safe to say that many teachers who were called upon to implement an education program were untrained and uncertain about their own feelings about drugs (14). Most felt their charge was to dissuade their students from using drugs; thus they became insensitive to opinions and facts antiethical to their own position. Students came to view teachers as representing a bias toward their own general life styles and, therefore, refused to accept what was being taught (12).

Thus one reason for the failure of drug education has been the inability to establish the credibility and trust of those charged to instruct on drugs. There are many indications that any teacher has more than an ordinary problem in gaining the confidence of young people in his ability to teach objectively about drugs (37). It is because of this that other communicators, such as the peer group, the ombudsman, and the counselor, have been suggested as the more effective teachers of drug education (12, 40, 56, 58).

Another area of special interest in communication and the evaluation of drug education has to do with the relation of knowledge to behavior. Much of the present effort to teach about drugs rests on the assumption that a causal relationship exists between the presentation of facts and changes in attitude and behavior. It is generally believed that if students are given the facts about drugs they will choose not to use or abuse them. Yet studies reveal that information alone is not enough to modify behavior and in fact may lead to experimentation (7). For example, Swisher and his associates in three studies of drug use among young people found a significant relationship between level of knowledge and a prodrug attitude (51, 53, 54). Smart, in a study of young people in Canada, found a similar relationship (48). These data suggest several conclusions. Swisher et al. (52) interpreted their findings as follows:

> One [interpretation] is that the drug users in these samples have learned about drugs through their experience and that this is not the same kind of knowledge that would be included in a drug education program. A second interpretation might be that drug users would tend to score on the liberal end of an attitude scale in order to justify their behavior. Yet another interpretation might be that drug education efforts of a factual nature may de-sensitize youngsters' fears of drugs which in turn could lead to greater experimentation and use. . . . It is also possible that emphasis on drug education may heighten curiosity and consequently lead to greater experimentation.

This latter interpretation is a concern that has been expressed quite often in the past regarding various subjects vital to teen-age behavior such as sex, alcohol, and drugs (42). It is this interpretation that led the Commission on Marihuana and Drug Abuse (14) to state*:

> ... It is possible to speculate that the avalanche of drug education in recent years has been counterproductive and that it may have stimulated rebellion, or simply raised interest in the forbidden. Historically, this nation has vacillated on the notion that information about potential harm will have a beneficial impact on behavior. Periodically preventive education has been re-discovered and revived with a great outpouring of public funds only to be shelved again in the belief that such information serves only to arouse curiosity.

However, whether such informational programs encourage experimentation or serve to reduce the problem remains a matter of conjecture and calls for systematic research.

Such findings as those mentioned have inspired a search for possible explanations of why facts seem to fail to confer immunity to drug use. Some investigators have suggested that one reason may be a person's tendency to avoid dissonance producing situations. That is, users may actively avoid information which emphasizes the harmful effects of drugs. However, there is little evidence to support this particular explanation (48).

Another explanation has to do with the content of the message which is being transmitted and whether or not young people weigh it in the same manner as those who provide it. For example, the position of the Information-Transmission Approach is that young people will respond to a balanced presentation of the facts, without an overtone of authority, and then make up their own minds (53). This statement implies that through the accurate knowledge of drugs, their benefits and liabilities, young people will decide not to abuse them. In actuality, however, most drug education programs are weighed to emphasize the harmful effects of drugs to the neglect of a consideration of any advantages which may result from their use. Instructional programs may proclaim aims which stress such aspects as the prevention of high-risk drug use, drug dependence, or the use of particular drugs, or the development of decision making skills, but in practice they attempt to curtail all illicit drug use. Any program which only expressly emphasizes the harm of certain patterns of use by implication seems to suggest that other patterns are relatively harmless and thus to tacitly condone them. This is an unacceptable goal since it runs counter to community sentiment, program sponsorship, and the law. Thus the emphasis, by default, becomes one that all use is wrong. The problem with this

---

* For example, the onset of opium smoking in the 1870s led to multistate legislation inserting anti-opium classes in the school curriculum. They were abandoned a short time afterward, however, because it was felt that they had heightened curiosity in the drug. A similar case resulted 50 years later with marihuana (14).

approach is that it assumes that those who receive the information correspondingly see all drug use as wrong or in the same way as the transmitters. As is obvious, young people view drugs from a different perspective than do adults. They see some advantages in certain types of use, primarily marihuana. Thus the "all use is equally dangerous" approach undermines the credibility of the total program since it fails to coincide with the experiences of many occasional and experimental uses of certain drugs at low and moderate dosage levels (20).

It is because of this dilemma that some educators are calling for programs oriented away from drugs and toward responsible decision making (42). For example, the Commission on Marihuana and Drug Abuse (14) calls for a shift from a negative to a more positive preventive approach. It recommends:

> ... That drug use prevention strategies, rather than concentrating resources and efforts in persuading or educating people not to use drugs, emphasize alternative means of obtaining what users seek from drugs; means that are better for the user and better for society. The aim of prevention policies should be to foster and instill the necessary skills for coping with the problems of living, particularly the life concerns of adolescents. Information about drugs and the disadvantages of their use should be incorporated into more general programs, stressing benefits with which drug consumption is largely inconsistent.

This approach recognizes that drugs very often have positive results for the user, which probably outweigh any warnings of potential harm. It aims to uncover some of the underlying causes for use and attempts to assist young people to discover alternatives which compete with drugs in offering these positive results (9, 13).

Although attractive, this approach is admittedly not any easy task. Drugs are used by the young for a variety of reasons including enjoyment, recreation, temporary mood alteration, escape, and protest, among others. In order to turn young users away from drugs, more satisying and constructive alternatives for these needs must be found and implemented. However, this challenge will involve broad institutional and structural changes in society.

Finally, drug education programs have in most cases ignored the person for whom they have been designed. Similar to alcohol education, drug education has been based upon what the older generation feels the young person should be told about drugs. Most programs have been developed and activated with little or no regard for the differing needs, attitudes, and perceptions of the audience to whom the instruction is directed. Young people in the classroom are treated as a single audience who respond in the same way to the same message about drugs. This seems particularly myopic when we realize that there are various user types in any classroom. Drug educators, like alcohol educators, need to develop a sense for the diversity of audiences in the alcohol and to undertake research to acquaint themselves with important differences in needs.

Conclusion

Since evaluation of drug education has just begun, no definite conclusion can be drawn about its overall efficiency. It appears unrealistic to assume that programs can reverse a force that has been gathering momentum for years. As Richards (42) has observed:

> . . . That momentum may still be strong enough to soften or neutralize the best planned education effort. Some of the opposing forces encouraging illicit drug use today are famililar to all—the influence of youth culture and peer groups, the pill using ethos, the secularization of values, affluence, psychological conditions of alienation, apathy and boredom. It would be naive to expect struggling new education projects to make heavy inroads on these problems so soon.

What data we have reveal that our approaches up to this time have not been very effective. But before the effort is totally abandoned, perhaps it would be wise to seek new methods and content of programming (7). Negative findings need not lead to abject pessimism. They simply remind us that human behavior is extremely complex and that our methods of studying it are still developing. The negative results pertaining to drug education may simply reflect gaps in the basic social science knowledge necessary to bring about change in behavior. As the scientific information accumulates regarding drug use, the educational enterprise with its abundant resources should do better than it has done to design effective programs of drug education. At least we now have some idea about what does not appear to work. In the long run perhaps the increasing demand for systematic research and evaluation will assure us of a more effective educational effort.

REFERENCES

1. Ackers, R. L., Teenage drinking: A survey of action programs and research, *J. Alcohol Educ.*, **13**, 1–9 (1968).

2. Asbury, H., *The Great Illusion*, Doubleday, Garden City, N.Y., 1950.

3. Bacon, M. and M. B. Jones, *Teenage Drinking*, Thomas Y. Crowell, 1968.

4. Bacon, S. D., Education of alcohol: a background statement, in *Conference Proceedings on Alcohol Education*, U.S. Department of Health, Education and Welfare, U.S. Government Printing Office, Washington, D.C., 1966.

5. Baumgartiver, L., Crisis in school health, Paper presented at the Centennial Meeting of the American Public Health Association, Atlantic City, N.J., November, 1972.

6. Bland, H. B., Problems related to teaching about drugs, *J. School Health*, 30 (1969).

7. Boe, S., Philosophy and objectives for a drug education program, *J. School. Health* (Jan. 1971).

8. *Cannabis: A Report of the Commission of Inquiry into the Non-Medical Use of Drugs*, Information Canada, Ottawa, 1972.

9. Cohen, A. Y., Psychedelic drugs and the student: educational strategies, *J. Coll. Stud. Pers.* (March 1969).

10. Daniel, R., To your health?, *Mich. Health*, **54**, 7–13 (1966).

11. Davies, J. and B. Stacey, Alcohol and health education in schools, *Health Bull.*, 29 (1971).

12. Elkin, A. R., One psychiatrist's view of drug education, *J. Drug Educ.*, **1** (1971).

13. *Doing Drug Education*, Southern Regional Education Board, Atlanta, November, 1972.

14. *Drug Use In America: Problems in Perspective, Second Report of the National Commission on Marihuana and Drug Abuse*, National Commission on Marihuana and Drug Abuse, U.S. Government Printing Office, Washington, D.C., March, 1973.

15. Ferrier, K., Alcohol education in the public school curriculum, in *Alcohol Education For Classroom and Community*, R. G. McCarthy (Ed.), McGraw-Hill, N.Y. 1964, Chapter 3.

16. Freeman, H. E. and J. F. Scott, A critical review of alcohol education for adolescents, *Community Ment. Health J.*, 2 (1966).

17. Globetti, G., Young people and alcohol education: abstinence or moderate drinking?, *Drug Forum*, 1 (1972).

18. Globetti, G. and D. E. Harrison, Attitudes of high school students toward alcohol education, *J. School Health* **40**, (1970).

19. Goode, E., *Drugs in American Society*, Alfrea A. Knopf, New York, 1972.

20. Hammond, P. G., Why drug abuse education is failing in America, Paper presented at the 30th International Congress on Alcoholism and Drug Dependence, Amsterdam, September, 1972.

21. Harrison, D. E., W. H. Bennett, and G. Globetti, Factors related to alcohol use among pre-adolescents, *J. Alcohol Educ.*, 15 (1970).

22. Hill, P., Programs for drug education, in *Children and Drugs*, Association for Childhood Education International, Washington, D.C.

23. Hochbaum, G. M., How can we teach adolescents about smoking, drinking and drug abuse?, *J. Health, Phys. Educ. Recreation*, 39 (1968).

24. Hochbaum, G. M., Learning and behavior—alcohol education for what? in *Conference Proceedings on Alcohol Education*, U.S. Department of Health, Education and Welfare, U.S. Government Printing Office, Washington, D.C., 1966.

25. Jones, K. L., L. Shainsberg, and C. O. Byer, *Drugs and Alcohol*, Harper and Row, New York, 1973.

26. Kelley, N. L., Social and legal programs of control in the United States, in *Alcohol Education For Classroom and Community*, R. G. McCarthy, (Ed.), McGraw-Hill, New York, 1964, Chap. 1.

27. Lawler, J. T., Peer group approach to drug education, *J. Drug Educ.*, 1 (1971).

28. Maddox, G. L., Alcohol education: clues from research, in *Conference Proceedings on Alcohol Education*, U.S. Department of Health, Education and Welfare, U.S. Government Printing Office, Washington, D.C., 1966.

29. Maddox, G. L., Research relating to alcohol education: a review and some suggestions, in *Selected Papers of the 15th Annual Meeting of the North American Association of Alcoholism Programs*, Portland, 1964.

30. *Marihuana: A Signal of Misunderstanding, The Technical Papers of the First Report of the National Commission on Marihuana and Drug Abuse*, Vol. II, U.S. Government Printing Office, Washington, D.C., March, 1972.

31. McConnell, J. T., Issues in alcohol education, *Int. J. Health Educ.,* 12 (1969).

32. McCune, D. A., An analysis of the role of the state in drug education, unpublished paper, 1973.

33. McCune, D. A., The new generation drug education programs, Paper presented at meeting on Education in More Developed Countries to Prevent Drug Abuse, United Nations Educational, Scientific and Cultural Organizations, Paris, 1972.

34. Monroe, M. E. and J. Stewart, *Alcohol Education For the Layman*, Rutgers University Press, New Brunswick, 1959.

35. Murphy, M. L., Values and health problems, *J. School Health,* 43 (1973).

36. Musto, D. F., *The American Disease, Origins of Narcotic Control*, Yale University Press, New Haven, Conn., 1973.

37. New York State Department of Education, A position paper, *J. Drug Educ.,* 1 (1971).

38. Pethel, D. L., Comparison of two approaches to instruction on drug abuse, *School Health Rev.,* 2 (1971).

39. Plaut, T. F., *Alcohol Problems: A Report to the Nation*, Oxford University Press, New York, 1967.

40. Pollack, B., Decision making—a key to prevention of drug abuse, *J. Drug Educ.,* 2 (1972).

41. Ray, Oakley, *Drugs, Society and Human Behavior*, C. V. Mosley, St. Louis, 1972.

42. Richards, L. G., Evaluation in drug education, *School Health Rev.,* 2 (1971).

43. Richards, L. G. and J. H. Langer, *Drug Taking in Youth*, U.S. Government Printing Office, Washington, D.C., 1971.

44. Robinson, R., The prospects of alcohol education about alcohol and alcoholism, *J. Alcohol Educ.,* 14 (1968).

45. Russell, R. D., Education About alcohol—for real American youth, Paper presented at International Congress on Alcohol and Alcoholism, Washington, D.C., September, 1968.

46. Russell, R. D., What do you mean—alcohol education? *J. School Health*, 35 (1965).

47. Russell, R. D., Why teachers don't jump at the chance to teach about alcohol, *Michigan Alcohol Educ. J.,* 1 (1964).

48. Smart, R. G., Factors in the effectiveness of drug education, Paper presented at 30th International Congress on Alcoholism and Drug Dependence, Amsterdam, September, 1972.

49. Smart, R. G., Trapped administrators and evaluation of social and community development programs, *Addictions*, 19 (1972).

50. Straus, R. and S. Bacon, *Drinking in College*, Yale University Press, New Haven, 1953.

51. Swishen, J. D. and J. L. Crawford, Jr., An evaluation of a short term drug education program, *The School Couns.* (March 1971).

52. Swisher, J. D., J. Crawford, R. Goldstein, and M. Yura, Drug education: pushing or preventive? *Peabody J. Educ.* (Oct. 1971).

53. Swisher, J. D. and R. E. Horman, Drug abuse prevention, *J. Coll. Stud. Pers.,* (Sept. 1970).

54. Swisher, J. D., R. W. Warner, and E. L. Herr, Experimental comparison of four approaches to drug abuse prevention among ninth and eleventh graders, *J. Couns. Psychol.,* 19 (1972).

55. Ungerleider, J. T., Drugs and the educational process, *Am. Biol. Teach.,* 30 (1968).

56. Ungerleider, J. T. and H. L. Brown, Drug abuse and the schools, *Am. J. Psychiat.,* 125 (1969).

57. Unterberger, H. and L. DiCicco, Alcohol education re-evaluated, *Bull. Natl. Assoc. Secondary School Princ.,* 52 (1968).

58. Unterberger, H. and L. DiCicco, Alcohol education through small group discussion, *J. Alcohol Educ.,* 14 (1968).

59. Weiss, C. H., The politicization of evaluation research, *J. Soc. Issues,* 26 (1970).

Chapter Three

THE DRINKING DRIVER AND THE LAW: LEGAL COUNTERMEASURES IN THE PREVENTION OF ALCOHOL-RELATED ROAD TRAFFIC ACCIDENTS

J. D. J. HAVARD, *British Medical Association, London, England*

1. PERSPECTIVE

The Importance of Road Accident Prevention

The success achieved by public health authorities in controlling mortality and morbidity from the traditional scourges of infectious and parasitic diseases and malnutrition has led to the emergence of accidental injury as a major cause of mortality and morbidity in technically developed countries. Road traffic accidents are now the most important cause of accidental mortality and morbidity in such countries, and they are increasing both in numbers and in severity in nearly all of them. The relatively high incidence of road traffic accidents in the lower age groups has increased their importance in relation to loss of expectation of life. Nearly one-half, and in some technically developed countries more than one-half, of all male deaths in the 15–24 age group are now caused by road traffic accidents. Less well appreciated is the importance of morbidity from road traffic accidents in terms of long-term residual disability, and it is becoming increasingly clear that road accidents are now a major cause of permanent incapacity in the community. The economic consequences of road accidents are enormous. In the United Kingdom, which has one of the best road accident records in Europe, the cost is approaching £500 million annually (12). The burden on accident and emergency services is considerable as the demands made by road accident casualties are unpredictable and often occur at irregular hours requiring the immediate attention of highly qualified staff. It follows that the prevention and control of road accidents must occupy high priority in legislative programs, and the purpose of this chapter is to review recent developments in the legislation introduced by different countries to deal with one of the leading causes of road accidents—the drinking driver. In doing so it is important not to overlook the role of the drinking pedestrian, if only to observe that a number of studies from different countries have drawn attention to the high proportion of adult pedestrian casualties found to be intoxicated at certain times of the day.

The Changing Picture of Road Accidents

The rapidly increasing numbers of motor vehicles on the roads has led to a change in the distribution of casualties among different categories of road user. Whereas far more pedestrians used to be killed than car users, the position has now changed dramatically in that more people are now being killed in motor cars than by them. Furthermore, as will be seen from Table 1, the increase in the numbers of car occupants killed during the last decade has been far greater than is the case with pedestrians, so that factors influencing the risk of injury to car occupants, and to drivers in particular, have assumed increasing importance. Although improvements in first aid, emergency treatment, and rehabilitative services may be expected to lead to

TABLE 1   PERCENTAGE INCREASE IN ROAD USERS KILLED IN 1970 AS COMPARED WITH 1961 IN EIGHT EUROPEAN COUNTRIES

Country	All Road Users	Pedestrians	Private Car Users	Increase in Private Cars (%)
France	65	54	150	99
Netherlands	59	29	241	306
Belgium	44	29	135	137
Austria	36	33	136	152
Germany	32	25	116	161
Switzerland	19	21	90	139
Italy	15	19	114	318
United Kingdom	9	8	86	90

Source: European Conference of Ministers of Transport, 1972, Annex 1, p. 49, Table 1, p. 29.

some improvement, even the most expensive and sophisticated measures are unlikely to make a significant impression on increases in casualty rates of this magnitude. Far more success is likely to be achieved by modifications of the vehicle and by the introduction of restraint systems such as safety belts, together with improvements in highway design and the removal of the more lethal aspects of roadside furniture, but even these measures, important as they are, must not be allowed to detract from the basic problem, which is to reduce the risk of a road accident occurring, and in particular a road accident causing death or serious personal injury.

The Epidemiological Approach

The most important development in road accident prevention in recent years has been the introduction of epidemiological techniques in identifying and assessing the human and environmental factors which influence the risk of an accident occurring. The ad hoc approach to the problem of road safety so long adopted by transport authorities, and summed up by Baker (1) in the phrase "anything that sounds reasonable will be effective," has led to huge sums of money being expended with very little to show in terms of casualty savings. On the other hand, epidemiological techniques such as the case control method first introduced in the field of road accident prevention by Holcomb (26), on a budget reputed to be as low as £500, has yielded extremely valuable information on which it has been possible to base effective countermeasures. No better example of this exists than the Grand Rapids survey (4) in which the incidence of several variables in large samples of accident-involved and accident-free drivers was compared. The results of this very carefully controlled survey have been discussed extensively in the literature and are still being analyzed. The survey established beyond doubt the importance of alcohol in determining the risk of accident involvement and provided important information on the extent of the risk at different blood alcohol concentrations (BAC). This survey together with both earlier and later surveys from other countries have established that as the BAC approaches 50 mg* the majority of drivers incur increased risk of

* Blood alcohol concentration (BAC) is expressed in different ways in the legislation of various countries. In continental Europe the notation is promille or permille (grams per liter on a weight/volume basis) and in North America percentage values are given, usually on a weight/weight basis. In the United Kingdom and its former dominions and colonies BAC is expressed in mg/100 ml. In order to save confusion and to facilitate comparisons all values given in this chapter have been expressed in mg/100 ml, a method which has the advantage of avoiding the use of decimal points. Exact conversion is not possible unless it is known whether the relevant law prescribes weight/weight or weight/volume, but for the purposes of this chapter a simple conversion can be carried out by shifting the decimal point; for example, 0.08% equals 0.8 promille, which equals 80 mg/100 ml. In order to save endless repetition the latter notation (which is used in this chapter) is expressed simply as "mg."

accident involvement, and that at 80 mg alcohol emerges as the dominant factor in determining the extent of the increased risk of accident-involved drivers. The practical application of these findings has been made possible by the development of increasingly reliable qualitative (screening) and quantitative methods of determining the BAC of drivers. Screening breath tests are now used extensively by the police at the roadside in many countries, and in nearly all countries highly specific methods of estimating BAC are available in laboratories to which samples of blood can be sent for analysis. Although breath tests are used mainly for screening purposes very reliable quantitative breath methods have become available and already are accepted by the courts as evidence of BAC in some jurisdictions. Meanwhile, the development of even newer methods involving fuel cells holds promise of the appearance before long of an entirely accurate and portable roadside quantitative breath method.

2. TYPES OF LEGISLATION

A review of the effectiveness of legislation to deal with the drinking driver not only must take account of the existence and nature of the laws concerned with driving under the influence of alcohol, but also must consider the means available for the enforcement of the law and for the disposal of drivers who are convicted under it. These considerations are interdependent in determining the effectiveness of the legislation as a whole, but perhaps the most important consideration is the extent to which the existence and enforcement of the law deters drivers from driving under the influence of alcohol. The point is made in order to draw attention to the need for legislation to be associated with an effective program of education of the driving population. Legislation can reinforce such a program but it can never replace it.

The Legal Significance of Blood Alcohol Concentration

Nearly all countries have introduced a specific offense of driving under the influence of alcohol, distinct from other offenses involving alcohol, and distinct from other offenses involving impairment of driving. Exceptions to this rule include West Germany, where the offense is prosecuted as part of a general offense relating to driving while impaired from any cause, although at the time of writing an important amendment to the law in relation to driving while impaired by alcohol has been approved by the Bundestag (25a).

It is convenient to study those countries that have introduced a specific offense under two headings, those which have incorporated BAC as a constituent element of the substantive law and those which accept BAC only insofar as it provides evidence of impairment under procedural law along with other evidence. The advantage of introducing BAC as a constituent of the substantive law lies in its superiority over other evidence of alcoholic impairment of driving ability. The alternative methods of proof, which are limited virtually to observation of the driver's behavior by police officers and clinical examination by a doctor, are grossly inferior. Unless the BAC is written into the substantive law these other methods of proof remain acceptable as evidence and can either establish or exclude alcoholic impairment of driving ability irrespective of the BAC.

Introduction of an offense based on BAC does not always lead to repeal of previous legislation relating to the drinking driver. In the United Kingdom it has been found that powers of arrest under previous legislation are rarely ever used by the police if the screening breath test is positive, because a conviction is far more likely to be secured under the new Act. If the breath test is negative the chances of conviction under the previous legislation are so remote that the driver is detained only in exceptional circumstances such as cases in which impairment by other drugs is suspected. However, most cases known to the police of impairment caused by abuse of alcohol in combination with other drugs are associated with a relatively high BAC and may be expected to give a positive screening breath test.

The problems encountered by the police in detecting alcoholic impairment by observation are dealt with later in this chapter (Section 3). Insofar as clinical examination is concerned the literature contains many studies of the unreliability and nonspecific nature of clinical tests for alcoholic impairment of driving ability. It has also been pointed out many times that by the time the driver comes under examination by the police doctor a psychological and physiological alarm reaction to his predicament may have occurred, enabling him or her to perform clinical tests satisfactorily in spite of being intoxicated. This reaction does not affect the BAC. Conversely, cases have occurred in which the doctor has decided the driver was impaired by alcohol although there was no alcohol present in the blood, so that evidence based on BAC provides a valuable safeguard.

These studies are now only of academic interest in those countries which have introduced offenses based on BAC, but they continue to occupy the time of research workers in countries which have not yet taken this step, as they form part of the process of persuading the legislature that the existing law should be changed and placed on a scientific footing. Recent studies have only confirmed what was found in previous studies and should be regarded as wasteful and unnecessary. An example is provided by the situation in Finland where the Road Traffic Act provides that the results of clinical examination and other relevant factors may be taken into account by the Court in reaching judgment. Complicated and sophisticated tests have been carried out in Finland using advanced computer techniques to analyze the results of clinical examination (31). The examinations were carried out by specially trained doctors with long experience in examining intoxicated drivers, but even under these conditions serious defects in the system were found to exist, particularly at low concentrations of alcohol. The reluctance of the courts and of the legislature in some countries to accept the evidence based on BAC as a constituent part of the substantive law is fairly characteristic of legal attitudes to expert scientific evidence. It is basic to legal philosophy that it is the function of the expert to offer advice and of the court (including the jury) to reach a decision based on the expert advice and such other evidence as it chooses to receive. The introduction of BAC into the substantive law makes inroads on this precept by fettering the discretion of the court, and it is therefore resented. It was probably for these reasons that as late as 1931, decades after evidence based on X rays had become available to provide incontrovertible evidence of the presence of a fetus *in utero*, the issue of pregnancy in a condemned woman prisoner was still being decided in England by a jury of 12 matrons, especially impaneled for the purpose, under the medieval writ *de ventre inspiciendo*.

Blood Alcohol Concentration as Evidence of Impairment

The extent to which courts pay attention to evidence based on BAC in circumstances where it is not an element of the substantive offense varies considerably. In accusatorial systems based on common law precepts the situation offers full scope for the "battle of the experts" so that it is often very difficult to prove "beyond reasonable doubt" that the driver was impaired by alcohol. Reference has already been made to the nonspecific nature, unreliability, and insensitivity of the alternative methods of proof, such as evidence based on clinical examination and observation by the police, and it is relatively easy for an astute defense lawyer to discredit expert evidence based on these methods in the eyes of juries which are not trained to assess expert evidence, and whose sympathies may often rest with the driver. In the United Kingdom, shortly before the introduction of a statutory offense based on a fixed BAC, it was noted that one-third of the drivers committed for trial and shown to have a BAC in excess of 200 mg were being acquitted and nearly half of those with a BAC of 150–200 mg (28).

In countries with inquisitorial systems based on civil law precepts the arrangements for receiving expert evidence are generally much more satisfactory and considerably more attention is paid by judges to evidence based on BAC. Indeed, in many such countries conviction is almost automatic at certain concentrations of alcohol as a result of established court practice even though no fixed concentration is stated in the substantive offense. The courts nearly always convict at 150 mg in Belgium, at 130 mg in West Germany, and at 100 mg in Denmark, although it is often necessary for the prosecution to take the case to appeal in order to get a conviction in Denmark. Below these concentrations the practice varies. In Belgium a conviction is highly unlikely below 150 mg. In Denmark the offense of second degree intoxication is recognized, and convictions for that offense can be obtained at about 80 mg, provided the case is supported by convincing evidence from other sources such as police observation and clinical tests. However, a recent survey in Denmark showed that only 45% of drivers with a BAC between 50 and 80 mg were found to be under the influence of alcohol by police doctors (32). Convictions may also be obtained in West Germany at concentrations below 130 mg provided there is sufficient supporting evidence and the concentration is in excess of 80 mg. The Uniform State Model Vehicle law in the United States recommended that impairment should be presumed at 150 mg and excluded below 50 mg. In between these concentrations it was recommended that the presumption that the driver was impaired by alcohol could be rebutted by other evidence. More recently the National Highway Traffic Safety Administration (14) has recommended the introduction into legislation of an offense based on a BAC of 100 mg. In the meantime a number of states had already adopted such a law in favor of previous legislation based on the presumptions in the model law. The position at the time Farmer (23) reviewed the law in 1973 was that two states had adopted a BAC of 80 mg, 32 states 100 mg, one state 120 mg, and the remaining nine states were still operating the model code at 150 mg. The fact that BAC is not an inherent part of the substantive offense allows the courts considerable latitude in dealing with these cases, and the prospects of conviction inevitably influence the prosecution in deciding whether to bring the case to court. Attitudes may vary not only between different countries but within the same country. Philips (32) reports one federal judge in Schleswig (West Germany) as stating that he had to remit about 75% of cases to the lower courts for retrial because of failure to convict. The Belgian courts so rarely convict drivers at a BAC lower than 150 mg that it is the practice not to prosecute below that level. In Denmark it is alleged that the police will present cases for prosecution only where there is substantial evidence of intoxication and that the prosecuting authorities, which are independent of the police, scrutinize the cases presented by the police with great care before deciding to prosecute (34).

Although the introduction of a substantive offense based on a fixed BAC resolves many of these difficulties, the resistance of the courts may still be considerable, particularly in common law countries adopting the accusatorial system. In the UK the courts were prepared to go to extraordinary lengths to avoid convicting drivers, even those with two or three times the statutory limit. For a time almost any technical defect in the procedure was held by the lower courts to provide an excuse for not returning a conviction. It was necessary to go to the Court of Appeal to prove that a driver could not insist on blood being taken from his penis and to the highest appeal court in the land (House of Lords) to decide that a driver could not elect for his big toe. In one case a driver was acquitted on the fiction that there are only four gas chromatographs (necessary for analyzing microsamples) in the UK.

In concluding this section it is important to emphasize that the opinions expressed about the value of clinical examination apply only to its use as a method of determining alcoholic impairment of driving ability. It must not be assumed that it has no place at all in the medicolegal procedure for dealing with drivers suspected of the offense. Many clinical conditions mimic alocholic intoxication, particularly head injuries, which are a common sequel of road accidents. Abnormal behavior may be caused by conditions other than alcoholic intoxication and the need to exclude illness, injury, or the effects of drugs other than alcohol must always be borne in mind when a driver presents abnormal behavior, so that the necessary medical treatment can be given. Indeed, it would appear from the very high BACs recorded in some cases that the driver may sometimes be in need of treatment for alcoholic toxemia. It follows that in those countries which incorporate BAC as part of the substantive offense, it is still necessary to provide arrangements for clinical examination in appropriate cases and for the examination to be carried out by doctors experienced in medicolegal procedures.

Blood Alcohol Concentration as a Constituent of the Offense

In 1967 the European Conference of Ministers of Transport (21) recommended that member countries introduce a statutory offense based on a BAC not exceeding 80 mg. This recommendation was made on the advice of OECD Expert Group on the Effects of Alcohol and Other Drugs on Driver Behaviour as set out in the report of the Group's consultants (25). A number of European countries have followed this recommendation. Some

European countries had introduced legislation based on a fixed BAC at a very much earlier date. Norway introduced an offense based on a level of 50 mg in 1927 long before any evidence based on epidemiological studies was available as to the extent of the risk of accident involvement at that concentration, although evidence of impairment from laboratory studies on skills resembling driving was available at that time. Sweden followed suit soon afterward. Austria introduced an offense based on a level of 80 mg in 1961 and has since been followed by Switzerland, the United Kingdom, Netherlands, France, and West Germany. The Republic of Ireland has introduced an offense based on a level of 125 mg.

In some countries the offense or offenses are linked to two different concentrations carrying different penalties on conviction. In Sweden the first degree offense set at 150 mg is punishable by imprisonment up to 1 year with the option in extenuating circumstances of not less than 25 "day fines" (one "day fine" is the equivalent of 1/1000 of the annual income of the driver). A second degree offense set at 50 mg (but not exceeding 150 mg) is punishable by not less than 10 "day fines" or imprisonment up to 6 months. Withdrawal of the license for varying periods is automatic in both cases. In France the first degree offense set at 120 mg carries imprisonment for a period of 1–12 months and a fine of 500–5000 francs. The second degree offense fixed at 80 mg carries imprisonment for 10 days to a month and a fine of 400–1000 francs. Iceland also has two degrees of offense set at 120 mg and 50 mg, respectively. The Australian states have introduced offenses based on a BAC of 80 mg, with the exception of Victoria where the level is fixed at 50 mg. In New Zealand the statutory offense is based on a BAC of 100 mg. There is a wide variety of offense in the United States but the National Highway Traffic Safety administration (14) has recommended that states introduce offenses based on a statutory BAC of 100 mg; this recommendation has already been anticipated in several states. Canada has introduced an offense based on a BAC of 80 mg. The situation varies in East European countries, but most of them have introduced laws making it an offense to drive after taking any alcohol whatsoever. In most cases this is interpreted by the courts as requiring conviction if the BAC is in excess of 30 mg, for example, Czechoslovakia and East Germany, which is regarded as a generous allowance for errors in the analytical method.

3. PROBLEMS OF ENFORCEMENT

The Provision of Samples for the Courts

Though the introduction of a fixed BAC into the substantive law will solve most of the problems of proving alcoholic impairment, the effectiveness of the law will depend on the legal powers that are available for its enforcement. It would be pointless to introduce a substantive offense based on a fixed BAC in Italy so long as the constitutional position in that country prevents the police from obtaining a sample of blood from a living driver in any circumstances. In many countries with fixed constitutions the powers that can be exercised by the police in detecting drivers who are impaired by alcohol and in obtaining the necessary proof are severely limited. In the United States the introduction of effective legislation was handicapped in many states by the constitutional position over self-incrimination (Fifth and Fourteenth Amendments), the right of privacy, and other legal problems (19). A series of cases in the courts was necessary to clear the way, and devices such as the "implied consent law," whereby a driving license is issued only on condition that the driver provides a sample of blood upon a reasonable request by a police officer, themselves ran into constitutional difficulties (41). The National Highway Traffic Safety Administration (15) has recommended that states introduce legislation requiring drivers (in cases where a breath test indicates that the driver is impaired by alcohol) to provide the necessary sample on pain of the license being revoked for 6 months, specific protection being provided for those drivers who object "on valid religious or medical grounds" (16).

In some European countries such as West Germany, Sweden, and Denmark there is no need for such a provision since the police have powers, on reasonable suspicion of alcoholic impairment, to obtain samples of blood from drivers against their will, using physical force if necessary. In other European countries, where the police do not have such powers, various factors come into play to ensure that drivers gain no advantage by refusing to provide a sample. In the UK a driver who refuses to provide a sample of blood or urine is automatically found guilty of the offense of exceeding the 80 mg limit, and is punished accordingly. However, he cannot legally be required to provide a specimen unless at least two positive readings have been obtained by a qualitative (screening) breath method. In the Netherlands there is no statutory obligation to provide a sample and as many as 40% of drivers detained by the police are said to refuse, but the courts are allowed to take the fact of refusal into consideration and nearly always convict the uncooperative driver of the offense (35).

Screening Procedures

Even though powers may exist to obtain samples from drivers suspected of the offense there still remains the problem of detecting those drivers who should properly be regarded as providing grounds for suspicion. The most valuable aid in this connection is the qualitative (screening) breath test. Although the existing instruments, as compared with the quantitative breath methods, are unreliable and relatively crude, they are cheap, portable, and far more efficient than relying on the police officer's own powers of observation. As a result they are used increasingly by police officers, and the procedure by which drivers can be required to take screening breath tests is set out in most of the recent legislation.

The Swedish Government Committee (42) set up to review legislation on the drinking driver conducted a number of studies at simulated roadblocks to assess the reliability of police observation in detecting alcoholic impairment of driving ability and concluded that the chances of a police officer detecting the smell of alcoholic liquor and other signs of intoxication were remarkably low. The majority of drivers with a BAC between 50 and 150 mg, and nearly half of those with concentrations in excess of 150 mg, aroused no suspicion on the part of the police.

It follows that screening procedures are unlikely to be effective if the legal powers of the police to obtain a breath test are limited to drivers who they have reason to believe are impaired by alcohol, and it is therefore necessary to extend those powers beyond such cases. The political controversy which has been engendered by such proposals is commonly, but wrongly, labeled as "random testing." A procedure based on random tests would require the tests to be carried out in accordance with a predetermined randomly selected procedure entirely free of bias, so that a grossly intoxicated driver who was not included in the sampling method would have to be ignored and allowed to go free. What is meant by "random" testing in the context of the present controversy is the free exercise of selective testing by the police, so that the police may require a test to be taken in circumstances where they believe there is a good chance of the driver being intoxicated even though they have no positive evidence to suggest the driver is impaired by alcohol, that is, the opposite of random in the scientific sense of the term. Selective testing of this kind carried out at particular times of the day, on particular days of the week, and on particular roads, in circumstances where drivers impaired by alcohol are most likely to be found, would be far more effective than random testing.

An interesting example of selective testing which has been highly effective can be found in the recent United Kingdom legislation which empowers a police officer to require a driver, under pain of a fine for refusal, to take a screening breath test in cases where he has been involved in an accident or where he has committed a traffic offense while the vehicle is moving, irrespective of the presence or absence of signs of intoxication. Similar provisions exist in some other European laws, including Norway, where the police also have powers to set up roadblocks for the purpose of conducting tests. According to Bø (3) roadblocks are used widely in

Norway, especially in urban areas where between 500 and 700 drivers may be tested at a time. An opportunity is taken to check any mechanical faults in the vehicle at the same time. In France a breath test may be required from any driver involved in an accident and from drivers involved in offenses against the traffic regulations, but not on other grounds. Farmer (24) has attributed the relative failure of the new Canadian law (based on a BAC of 80 mg) to the lack of provision of adequate screening procedures. Whereas it was estimated that an increase in arrests of about 500% would have occurred following the introduction of the 80 mg level an increase of only 59% was recorded. But most recent legislation requires the police to have reasonable grounds to believe the driver has been drinking before a screening breath test or a sample of blood can be obtained. The Motor Car (Driving Offenses) Act 1971 in the Australian State of Victoria requires the police officer to satisfy himself that the driver has consumed alcohol within the previous 2 hours and that the driving ability is impaired thereby. The Transport Act of New Zealand requires the police "to have good cause to suspect" that a driver is in breach of the law before requiring the driver to take a breath test, but the Government Road Safety Committee (29) declined by a majority to recommend any extension of these powers after they had been told by the police that the existing powers did not limit their enforcement powers to any serious extent. The Committee pointed out that the police had powers "on reasonable grounds" to impound ignition keys, immobilize vehicles, and prohibit drivers from driving, and expressed the view that it was more important to extend this preventive activity than to permit such drivers to drive and then to carry out a breath test. The Belgian law specifically permits the police to do just this if the screening breath test indicates the BAC is in excess of 80 mg. The driver is allowed to request a repeat of the breath test at intervals not exceeding 2 hours and his vehicle is returned to him as soon as the screening breath test indicates a level below 80 mg (9, 36). However this assumes that the driver is safe to drive as soon as the BAC is below 80 mg, and it also relies on the accuracy of the breath test. Neither of these assumptions can be accepted. The Swedish Government Committee took a different view from the New Zealand Road Safety Committee and recommended that the police be authorized to take "routine" breath tests in association with prearranged roadblocks (43).

The "implied consent" law adopted in most of the United States does not become effective until an arrest has occurred and the constitutional position requires the police officer to have "probable cause" before he can effect an arrest. The recent "stop and frisk" case decided by the U.S. Supreme Court suggests that an officer might be within the law if he requires a breath test in circumstances where he suspects a traffic violation to have occurred, and that grounds not amounting to "probable cause" such as involvement in an accident might also be permitted (20).

Hospital Cases

In many countries the driver escapes the enforcement net if he is admitted to hospital and it is interesting to note the way in which this was dealt with under the recent UK legislation. Early versions of the Act made no provision for samples of breath or of blood to be taken from drivers admitted to hospital, and as involvement in an accident is one of the three statutory criteria on which a breath test can be obtained it was clear that the absence of any legal provision in hospital cases provided an important loophole. It was the medical profession itself which suggested that the necessary provision should be included in the Act, subject only to two conditions. First, the doctor in charge of the case should give his permission, and secondly, samples for analysis on which the prosecution would rely must be taken by independent doctors, preferably a police surgeon, who has no responsibility for the treatment of the patient (5). In practice the provision has given rise to no difficulties and the hospitals in UK are no longer a haven of refuge for the intoxicated driver.

It would appear that the medical profession in New Zealand has been less cooperative because the Government Road Safety Committee (30) has complained that some hospital doctors were refusing to allow samples to be taken from patients for purposes of law enforcement. The European Conference of Ministers of Transport attribute the underestimate of alcohol-related accidents in its survey almost entirely to drivers escaping detection by necessary (or deliberately unnecessary) recourse to medical treatment (22).

4. DISPOSAL

Penalties on Conviction

The three main penalties attached to the offense of driving while impaired by alcohol are imprisonment, fines, and disqualification from driving by suspension of the driving license. Some indication of the extent to which these are involved in different countries has been given in an earlier part of the chapter (Section 2), where it was noted that in some cases the penalties are graded according to the severity of the offense. Penalties may also be graded according to the history of previous offenses. In the United States the National Highway Traffic Safety Administration (17) has recommended that, on a second conviction within 10 years, registration of the vehicle(s) owned by the driver should be suspended as well as the driving license. It has already been noted that in Sweden the penalty of a fine is made more effective by relating the fine to the annual income of the driver ("day fines"). In most countries suspension of a driving license for varying periods is automatic on conviction for the offense of driving under the influence of alcohol. In some countries the offense forms part of a "points" system in which repeated offenses are taken into consideration. This system was commended by the Council of Europe, although the Council's Committee of Ministers was only prepared to consider suspension as appropriate for the alcohol offense if the driver had been proved to have been a "real danger" (konkrete Gefährdung) in traffic, and was unwilling to recommend automatic suspension in other cases, even at concentrations in excess of 120 mg, on the curious ground that it might operate where the driver drives his car from the garage premises into his garage (8).

Recidivism

One of the problems associated with legislation against the drinking driver is that it so often fails to take into account the idiosyncrasies of the convicted driver. The amount of alcohol required to reach a BAC of 80 mg under conditions of ordinary social drinking is quite considerable and would be regarded as excessive in ordinary social circles. Reference to the literature will confirm that at around 80 mg ordinary subjects participating in experiments on the effects of alcohol become subjectively affected to an uncomfortable degree and are reluctant to continue drinking. Workers in many countries have noted that drivers convicted above this level frequently have alcohol problems. Bjerver (2) noted that of 804 persons convicted for driving under the influence of alcohol in Sweden in 1964, 64% were already known by the authorities for alcohol offenses not connected with driving. Without entering into the controversy over the definition of alcoholism it may be stated that many convicted drivers will be likely to repeat the offense if their licenses are restored without their alcohol problems being resolved by treatment, and very few countries require treatment as a condition of restoring the license.

40% of all prison sentences in Sweden each year are for driving under the influence of alcohol, and drivers convicted of this offense constitute 10% of the prison population (44). The Government Committee appointed in Sweden to review the legislation on the drinking-driving offense drew attention to the need for such sentences to be combined with treatment of the alcohol problems of the inmates, and emphasized that the prospects of satisfactory treatment are good insofar as the driver convicted fo the offense is often in an early stage of the disease (45). The National Highway Safety Administration of the United States has recommended that courts should be given powers to commit medically diagnosed alcoholic drivers to a hospital or clinic rather than to prison, on conviction of the offense (18). A number of workers in other countries have noted that conviction of a drinking driving offense is frequently an early symptom of alcoholism.

This has been confirmed in a recent survey carried out in Ireland where the histories of 100 male alcoholic drivers of cars were compared with matched controls (7a). Whereas the average alcoholic received his first formal treatment for alcoholism about the age of 38, he had been involved in his first road accident involving alcohol at least 6 years previously. Over a third of the alcoholic sample has been admitted to hospital for treatment of physical conditions related to or associated with alcoholism, and were recognizably suffering from alcoholism. Nevertheless, many of them received no formal treatment for their alcoholism for 4 years or more after discharge from hospital, during which period they were involved in road accidents associated with alcohol. The authors conclude that the diagnosis of alcoholism is still being missed because those who come into contact with the patient, including doctors, nurses, social workers, and law officers, are not alert to the problem and may often assume that the average alcoholic conforms to the stereotypic "skid-row" down-and-out. The fact that the majority of alcoholics are well-dressed and healthy looking for the most of their drinking careers is not generally appreciated.

Failure to treat the underlying condition in drivers with alcohol problems is one of the main causes of the high recidivist rate attached to the offense. Raymond (37) has reported that at least 25% of drivers convicted of the offense in Melbourne repeat the offense, some of them as many as four or five times. More still may repeat the offense without being apprehended or may escape altogether through being killed or injured in an accident. A Select Committee of the State Parliament in Victoria (Australia) recommended that all drivers convicted of the offense with a BAC of more than 150 mg should be assessed medically in order to see whether treatment of the alcoholic condition was necessary (38).

Buikhuisen has carried out a detailed survey of the problem. In a review of the literature he mentions 11 references to studies in different countries showing the high frequency of recidivism among drivers convicted of the offense (6). In his own study of the criminal records in the Netherlands he found that there was no inverse relationship between the severity of the sentence and prospect of recidivism. What he did find was that there was a positive relationship. The longer the prison sentence, the more likely the driver is to repeat the offense (7).

5. EVALUATION

Criteria for Evaluation

Scientific evaluation of countermeasures against road traffic accidents is a very difficult exercise, and very few examples exist which will satisfy the necessary tests of credibility. The main reason for this is the lack of adequate base line data against which the performance of a new countermeasure can be assessed.

Law enforcement agencies, transport authorities, and public health authorities have different criteria for assessing the results of countermeasures, but the ultimate test as far as the community is concerned is always the effect on the rate of mortality and morbidity from road traffic accidents. In the case of alcohol-related offenses this test is particularly important because surveys have repeatedly shown that where alcohol is a factor an accident is far more likely to be serious in terms of the severity of injuries received by the casualties.

The first requirement of a scientific method of evaluation is a reliable system of reporting road accident mortality and morbidity. The most recent developments in this connection have been a series of surveys which have shown gross discrepancies between the police returns of road accident casualties, on which transport authorities depend for purposes of evaluation and the numbers of persons actually injured in road accidents and treated in hospitals and clinics. Both the World Health Organization (46) and the Council of Europe (10, 11) have drawn attention to the highly unsatisfactory nature of the official returns of morbidity from road traffic accidents, and the Economic Commission for Europe (ECE), which publishes an annual volume of statistics of road traffic accidents in Europe, recently has called a series of meetings of the Group of Experts with a view to improving the position. If the total returns of road accident mortality and morbidity are so unreliable it cannot be expected that the detailed returns will be any less unreliable, and the point is made by the information given in the ECE annual statistical volumes since 1968 on road accidents in which drivers involved are found to be under the influence of alcohol (Table 2).

The discrepancies between the countries are far too great to be explained by the variable factors prevailing in different countries. It cannot be accepted that a major wine producing country like Italy, with one of the largest pools of motor vehicles in Europe, had only 182 road accidents in which the driver was under the influence of alcohol. Even when special survey techniques are applied it is highly doubtful whether any credence

TABLE 2   DRIVERS INVOLVED IN ROAD ACCIDENTS WHILE UNDER THE INFLUENCE OF ALCOHOL IN 13 EUROPEAN COUNTRIES, 1968–1972

Country	Total No. of Registered Private Cars (in Tens of Thousands) 1970	Number of Drivers				
		1968	1969	1970	1971	1972
West Germany	110.16	35765	36276	42188	42894	44926
United Kingdom	103.18	—	4176	5738	7614	9376
Italy	73.11	—	—	—	186	317
Sweden	19.67	—	1004	1054	—	1180
Netherlands	17.25	—	2231	2624	2689	2944
Spain	13.35	235	241	264	262	291
Switzerland	9.79	3016	3432	3747	4385	—
Austria	9.65	2145	2252	2503	2724	—
Denmark	8.88	1009	1074	1410	1345	1719
Finland	5.51	766	539	592	685	757
Czeckoslovakia	5.21	1824	—	—	—	—
Yugoslavia	3.56	1648	1754	—	3539	3815
Poland	3.32	—	—	—	377	816

Source: Economic Commission for Europe, *Statistics of Road Traffic Accidents* in Europe, United Nations, Geneva (publications for years concerned).

can be attached to the results. The survey conducted by ECMT into accidents involving bodily injuries in which alcohol was a factor produced the results given in Table 3.

The comment attached to the table is that the proportions "seem far short of the actual facts" and the conclusion was reached "that the seriousness of the problem of drunken driving might be minimised if judged in the light of the calculated average figure (9.9%)". The shortfall in the figures was attributed almost entirely to drivers escaping detection by being admitted to hospital following the accident, although no facts are given in support of this supposition (22).

TABLE 3 ACCIDENTS INVOLVING
BODILY INJURIES IN WHICH THE
DRIVER WAS UNDER THE INFLUENCE
OF ALCOHOL

Country	Accidents Involving Bodily Injuries (%)
Germany	15.0
Austria	6.9
Belgium	5.0
Spain	35.0 (estimate)
France	—
Italy	0.6
Luxembourg	6.6
Switzerland	6.6
Yugoslavia	19.3
Average rate:	8.4

Source: European Conference of Ministers of
Transport, 1972, p. 23.

Methods of Evaluation

Time Series Studies on Casualty Savings

In spite of the qualifications which must be attached to the official returns
of road accident casualties it is sometimes possible to attempt a scientifically based evaluation of countermeasures by reference to the effects on
overall road accident mortality and morbidity. Ross (39) subjected the
recent United Kingdom legislation to a searching examination in this
respect, employing a time series analysis. The methods he adopted, which
repay careful study, showed conclusively that the Act "did produce a sharp
and important decline in traffic casualties although this effect may have
been partly the result of the accompanying publicity campaign" (40). If the
record of previous publicity campaigns is anything to go by, the decline
must have been almost entirely due to the Act.

Level of Blood Alcohol Concentration in the Driving Population

Another method of evaluation is to compare the distribution of BAC
among drivers before and after the counter-measure has been introduced in
order to determine whether the measure has had any effect on drinking

habits in relation to driving. This is very rarely possible in practice as legal problems usually prevent fully representative sampling of drivers. The development of roadside screening surveys is under way as part of the international collaborative program administered jointly by OECD and by the Committee on Challenges in a Modern Society (CCMS) of NATO.

A selective variation of this method of evaluation was carried out in the UK where the BACs of all drivers killed in road accidents were recorded for a period of 9 months before the Act became effective in October, 1967, and it is possible to compare the changes which occurred subsequently. As might have been expected the proportion of drivers killed at higher concentrations, representing predominantly alcoholics or compulsive drinkers, has now returned to the pre-1967 value (13), but the effects of the Act can still be seen in the proportions at lower concentrations representing moderate or social drinkers (Table 4).

The "Shock" Effect

As with most legislation aimed at influencing the behavior of road users, a "shock" effect is very often noticeable immediately after the legislation has been introduced and this has been a fairly constant feature in the case of legislation on alcohol and road traffic. It was noticeable in Austria following the introduction in 1961 of the offense based on a BAC of 80 mg (27), and it was very marked in the UK during the period immediately following the Road Safety Act 1967, when the casualty savings were far greater than could have been expected even if the Act had been fully ef-

TABLE 4 MOTOR VEHICLE RIDERS AND DRIVERS DYING IN ENGLAND AND WALES WITHIN 12 HOURS OF AN ACCIDENT

	Number of Deaths	Percentage with Blood Alcohol Exceeding (mg/100 ml)					
		9	50	80	100	150	200
Before Road Safety Act							
Dec. 1966–Sept. 1967	544	37	29	25	22	13	6
After Road Safety Act							
Dec. 1967–Sept. 1968	389	26	17	15	14	10	4
Dec. 1968–Sept. 1969	454	29	22	19	17	11	5
Dec. 1969–Sept. 1970	449	29	23	20	16	12	6

fective in preventing drivers from taking the road at BACs in excess of 80 mg. The probable explanation is that drivers knew they could be required to take a breath test if they had been involved in an accident or a moving traffic offense and were therefore driving more carefully whether or not they had been drinking. As the "shock" effect wears off the drinking-driving population begins to assess the risk of being detected while driving after drinking so that any falling off of the effectiveness of legislation becomes closely related to the level of enforcement. The casualty savings following the Act can, however, be shown to have continued over a long period by the chart in Table 1.

6. CONCLUSION

The limited review in this chapter of recent trends in legal countermeasures against the drinking driver suggests that the following principles are important in the introduction of effective legislation.

Detection

Drivers should be required to take a screening breath test whether or not they exhibit signs or symptoms of alcoholic intoxication and law enforcement officers should be given powers to stop traffic for the purpose of taking such tests. These powers should be exercised in a highly selective manner at times and places where persons are most likely to be found driving under the influence of alcohol. Subject to suitable safeguards, drivers receiving treatment in hospitals and clinics following road accidents should also be required to take a screening breath test.

Confirmation

Drivers suspected of driving under the influence of alcohol as a result of the screening breath test should be required to provide a sample of blood for quantitative estimation of the concentration of alcohol in the blood. Subject to suitable safeguards this requirement should also apply to drivers attending hospitals or clinics following road accidents.

Conviction

Driving with a blood alcohol concentration in excess of a statutory limit should be regarded as a separate offense, distinct from other offenses involving driving while impaired. Conviction of the offense should be mandatory if the blood alcohol concentration is proved to have been in excess of the statutory limit, which should not exceed 80 mg.

Disposal

Suspension of the driving license for a period of at least 1 year should be mandatory in all cases where persons have been convicted of the offense, and courts should have powers to place conditions on the return of the license at the end of this period, for example, completion of treatment for an alcohol condition or satisfactory performance of a driving test. Courts should have powers to remand drivers for medical examination before sentence and should have discretion to order a period of medical treatment in lieu of imprisonment or fines in appropriate cases.

Evaluation

Authorities responsible for the prevention and control of road accidents should ensure that adequate base line data are collected before the introduction of any changes in legislation so that their effects can be evaluated by scientific methods and the need for any further changes fully assessed.

It appears from the review in this chapter that whereas nearly all technically developed countries have adopted one or more of the above principles in legislation, none has adopted all of them. If the mortality and morbidity caused by drivers under the influence of alcohol is to be reduced effectively legislation must ensure not only that the drinking driver is detected and convicted, but that the case is disposed of in such a way that the risk of the offense being repeated is also reduced.

REFERENCES

1. Baker, S. P., Injury control—accident prevention and other approaches to reduction of injury, in *Preventive Medicine and Public Health,* 10th ed., Appleton Century Crofts, New York, 1973.

2. Bjerver, K. B., Punishment or treatment for intoxicated drivers, *Blutalkohol,* **9,** 59 (1972).

3. Bø, O., Norwegian countermeasures to driving under the influence of alcohol and other drugs, Paper read at the International Symposium on Countermeasures to Driver Behaviour under the Influence of Alcohol and other Drugs, Sept. 22–23, 1971, British Medical Association, London.

4. Borkenstein, R. F., R. F., Crowther, R. P., Shumate, W. B., Zill, and R. Zylam, *The Role of the Drinking Driver in Traffic Accidents,* Department of Police Administration, Indiana University, Bloomington, Ind., 1964.

5. British Medical Association, *The Drinking Driver*, London, 1965, p. 36.

6. Buikhuisen, W., *Criminological and Psychological Aspects of Drunken Drivers*, Criminological Institute, State University of Croningen, Netherlands, 1969, p. 3.

7. Buikhuisen, W., *Criminological and Psychological Aspects of Drunken Drivers*, Criminological Institute, State University of Croningen, Netherlands, 1969, p. 29.

7a. Clare, A. W. and J. G. Cooney, Alcoholism and road accidents, *J. Irish Med. Assoc.*, **66**, 281 (1973).

8. Council of Europe, *Explanatory Memorandum on the Resolution on the Deprivation of the Right to Drive a Motor Vehicle* (adopted by the Committee of Ministers) B(71) 102 Annex II Strasbourg, France, 1971, pp. 3–4.

9. Council of Europe, *Report on Action Taken by Member States* [Resolution (68)31 on Road Accident Prevention CESP(73) 20], Strasbourg, France, 1973.

10. Council of Europe, *Structure and Organisation of Road Accident Prevention*, Strasbourg, France, 1970, p. 93.

11. Council of Europe, *Accidents in Childhood as a Public Health Problem*, Strasbourg, France 1972, p. 29.

12. Department of the Environment, *Road Accidents in Great Britain in 1971*, HMSO, London, 1973, para. 23, p. xvi.

13. *Ibid.*, para. 15, p. xii.

14. Department of Transportation, *Safety Administration Highway Safety Program Standards*, para. 242.6.(a), *Federal Register* 37 (No. 150), Part II, Washington, D.C., 1972, pp. 15602–15621.

15. *Ibid.*, para. 242.6(c)(2).

16. *Ibid.*, para. 242.6(d).

17. *Ibid.*, para. 242.6(i)(2).

18. *Ibid.*, para. 242.6(j)(1).

19. Department of Transportation, *1968 Alcohol and Highway Safety Report*, Committee on Public Works Paper 90-34 90th Congress, 2nd Session, U.S. Government Printing Office, Washington, 1968, Chapter 7, pp. 100–124.

20. *Ibid.*, p. 123.

21. European Conference of Ministers of Transport, *Resolution No. 21 passed by 17th meeting of the Council of Ministers*, 14 June 1967, Organisation for Economic Co-operation and Development, Paris, France, 1967.

22. European Conference of Ministers of Transport, *Report on Recent Trends in Road Accidents*, C.M. (72)10, Paris, France, 1972, pp. 23–24.

23. Farmer, P. J., Review and evaluation of legislation and evaluation of legislative and enforcement programs related to the use of alcohol and other drugs, in *Proceedings of the Conference on Medical, Human and Related Factors Causing Traffic Accidents including Alcohol and Other Drugs*. Traffic Injury Research Foundation of Canada, Ottawa, Ontario, Canada, 1973, pp. 55–64.

24. *The Role of Legislation and Community Education in the Prevention of Alcohol Related Traffic Accidents*, Symposium on Alcohol, Drugs and Traffic Safety, 8th Annual Conference of Canadian Foundation on Alcohol and Drug Dependencies.

25. Goldberg, L. and J. D. J. Havard, *Research on the Effects of Alcohol and Drugs on Driver Behaviour*, Organisation for Economic Co-operation and Development, Paris, France, 1968.

25a. Handel, K., Anwendung and Auswirkungen des 0,8-Promille-Gesetzes, *Blutalkohol,* **10,** 353 (1973).

26. Holcomb, R. L., Alcohol in relation to traffic accidents, *J. Am. Med. Assoc.,* **3,** 12 (1938).

27. Maurer, H., Report of the working party on efficacy of general deterrents and individual sanctions, in *Proceedings of the Fifth International Conference on Alcohol and Traffic Safety.* Freiburg, Br., Germany, 1970, Section VI, p. 18.

28. Ministry of Transport, *Road Safety Legislation 1965-6*, HMSO London, 1965, para. 20.

29. *New Zealand Road Safety Committee 1972*, Paper L.17, Government Printer, Wellington, New Zealand, 1972, para. 38, p. 24.

30. *Ibid.*, p. 4.

31. Penttila, A., M. Tenhu, and M. Kataja, *Clinical Examination in Cases of Suspected Drunken Driving*, Reports From Talja Vol. 11. Central Organisation for Traffic Safety in Finland, Helsinki, Finland, 1971.

32. Philips, P., *Alcohol and Road Safety*, Report of Investigations and Observations into these matters in Europe during 1969 to the Honourable the Minister of Health of the State of Victoria, Melboure, Australia, 1970, p. 43.

33. *Ibid.*, p. 28.

34. *Ibid.*, p. 42.

35. *Ibid.*, p. 36.

36. *Ibid.*, p. 32.

37. Raymond, A., Characteristics of drivers breathalysed in Melbourne in 1967, *Proc. Fifth Conf. Aust. Road Res. Board,* **5,** 209–228 (1970).

38. Raymond, A., *Alcohol in Relation to Road Safety*, Australian Road Research Board Doc. NR/3, Melbourne, Australia, 1972, p. 41.

39. Ross, H. L., Law, Science and Accidents, The British Road Safety Act of 1967, *J. Legal Stud.* (University of Chicago Law School), **2,** 1–78 (1973).

40. *Ibid.*, p. 35.

41. Schaeffer, S. L., Constitutionality of "implied consent" statutes, in *The Enforcement of Traffic Laws—Some Current Legal Problems*, Highway Safety Research Institute, University of Michigan, Ann Arbor, 1967, pp. 35–43.

42. Swedish Government Committee to Review Legislation on Driving under the Influence of Alcohol (SOU. 1970:61) Stockholm, Sweden, 1970, summary para. 20, p. 373.

43. *Ibid.*, para. 20, p. 374.

44. *Ibid.*, para. 19, pp. 370–371.

45. *Ibid.*, para. 19, p. 372.

46. World Health Organization, Availability of Accident Statistics, *World Health Stat. Rept.,* **25,** 756–758 (1972).

Chapter Four

ACUTE EFFECTS OF ETHANOL AND OPIATES ON THE NERVOUS SYSTEM

EDUARDO EIDELBERG, *Division of Neurobiology, Barrow Neurological Institute of St. Joseph's Hospital and Medical Center, Phoenix, Arizona*

1. INTRODUCTION

Probably the least explored area in neuropharmacology is that which lies between biochemical and behavioral pharmacology and deals with the cellular and integrative events mediating the transformation of a set of biochemical changes into alterations of behavioral performance, emotionality, etc. The key reason for this neglect is a combination of technical difficulties and uncertainties of interpretation of the data, added to the fact that neurophysiologists have tended to use drugs to analyze physiological mechanisms rather than use well-defined physiological preparations to investigate the dynamics of drug action.

I have chosen to discuss the "acute" neurophysiology of ethanol and opiate effects for a number of reasons: (*a*) there is very little material available on the long-term as opposed to the immediate neurophysiological effects of these agents. This tends to deemphasize phenomena such as tolerance and dependence which have been thought—probably wrongly—to be induced only by long-term repeated or sustained administration of alcohol and opiates. (*b*) My own work has centered upon "acute" effects and I am, therefore, more familiar with the relevant literature in the field; (*c*) I have joined together two superficially unrelated kinds of drugs because it may be that their physiological mechanisms of action are more closely related than we usually suppose. I am not referring to the recent suggestion that alcohol metabolites may become structural components of opiate-like substances in brain, but rather to the possibility that both ethanol and opiates may produce their effects through alterations in Ca^{2+} regulation of

147

membrane transport and synaptic mechanisms. Even if crucial differences in pharmacodynamic action are demonstrated, the emphasis placed on possible commonalities of action for broader and broader groups of drugs of abuse is at least of heuristic value in suggesting new experiments.

2. ACUTE EFFECTS OF ETHANOL ON THE NERVOUS SYSTEM

The Cerebral Cortex

Loomis, Harvey, and Hobart (40) were the first to seek electroencephalographic correlates of ethanol intoxication by giving an adult subject a rather large dose of gin, causing a decrease in the amount of alpha rhythm of the EEG and the appearance of high-voltage slow waves. Gibbs et al. (19) found that low doses of alcohol produced an increase in the amplitude of components in the 20 Hz range and a decrease in the 10 Hz band, the EEG being "slowed down" after higher doses. Davis et al. (8) reproduced these findings, in a series of studies correlating behavioral and blood alcohol measurements with the EEG tracings. They showed a dissociation between a return to near control performance in psychometric tests while the EEG was still abnormal and the blood alcohol level high, 4–5 hours after alcohol ingestion. The rate of entry of alcohol into the circulation was found by Mirsky et al. (43) to be an important variable, emphasizing the presence of acute "adaptation" or "tolerance" to alcohol as well. Other, later studies have fully confirmed these findings (13, 20, 21).

Sauerland and Harper (48) studied the effects of alcohol on the EEG in cats maintained under Flaxedil® immobilization, recording the electrocorticogram and analyzing it by Fourier transformation. They found that medium (>1.0 g/kg) doses of intravenous alcohol produced a characteristic shift to the left of the frequency spectrum, that is, an increase in the slower and a decrease in the higher-frequency components of the EEG. A qualitatively similar effect was noted in preparations where the midbrain had been previously transected, so that ascending brain stem tegmental influences were excluded. Return to preinjection characteristics occurred within 2 hours, at which time one should have expected significant residual levels of ethanol to remain in blood and brain (17, 33, 52, 53).

The results of studies on animals where evoked potential techniques were used for investigating changes in cortical activity induced by ethanol yielded essentially the same conclusions reached with EEG methods: alcohol at doses of 0.1–0.4 g/kg or higher produced a dose dependent decrease in the amplitude of cortical responses to sensory stimuli or their surrogates (such as electrical stimulation of the optic tract, peripheral nerves, or thalamic relay nuclei) (9, 10, 46, 52). Again, the cortical responses tended to recover sooner than did the blood alcohol levels (52). In one study it was found that sensory evoked responses were depressed, but the responses to direct cortical stimulation (direct cortical response, transcallosal response) were not (52). This has not been reinvestigated in spite of its possible relevance to the mechanisms of cortical depression by ethanol. If we accept that there are different synaptic arrangements for transcallosal versus sensory inputs to cortical cells, as was proposed originally by Chang, then those differences are clearly dissected out by alcohol.

It appears from this evidence that it is very likely that the cerebral cortex is affected by ethanol directly, although this does not exclude the possibility that some effects may be due additionally to its actions upon subcortical—and even peripheral structures (46). It appears, further, that certain classes of cortical neurones and/or synapses may be more sensitive than others. The presence of acute tolerance or adaptation ["Mellanby effect," (33)] has been demonstrated repeatedly in these testing situations.

The Hypothalamus

Some clinical actions of alcohol suggest the possibility that hypothalamic neurones are affected directly by it. One such action is diuresis exceeding the actual fluid intake, which may be mediated by alterations in hypothalamic-hypophyseal function in addition to direct actions upon nephron (34). The only systematic and direct test of this possibility is described in a recent report by Wayner (54) in which the activity of single lateral hypothalamic units was studied in rats subjected to acute alcohol intoxication. Wayner found that neurones which responded to hypertonic sodium chloride solutions (injected intranvenously) also responded to very low doses of alcohol (threshold: 40 mg/kg) by changes in their mean firing rate or subtler alterations in their firing pattern. Wayner also found relatively long lasting (up to 48 hr) cellular effects after the last of a series of alcohol doses. He concluded that the particular sensitivity to alcohol of lateral hypothalamic Na^+ sensitive neurones might be related to a specialized organization of Na^+ channels in their membrane.

The Brain Stem

Caspers (6) first proposed that alcohol may produce its effects upon the central nervous system via a selective action on the reticular formation of the brain stem. This suggestion was based on the conception, current at the time, of a reticular activating system with efferents projecting both in cephalad and caudad directions and regulating or modulating such states as wakefulness or sleep, and muscular tone. The conceptual strength of this basic scheme of the central nervous system organization offered a good deal of simplification in interpreting drug effects. Over the past 20 years, the original concept of the reticular activating system has been refined and modified by the identification of a series of nearly independent subsystems within it, each with apparently specific roles. The attribution of the central actions of alcohol to this single mechanism has been weakened considerably by the accumulation of experimental data showing that alcohol acts upon a great variety of sites in the nervous system, regardless of whether or not these sites were surgically disconnected from the brain stem. Since most of this material is discussed in other sections of this review, no repetition is needed here.

A more restricted model of a brain stem reticular system is still viable (30) and it is quite reasonable to suggest that alcohol narcosis may involve significant interference with the function of reticular systems controlling sleep levels and arousal, but no direct experimental proof of this is yet available. A suggestive series of experiments comes from Feldstein's studies (14) in which alcohol produced a reduction in brain serotonin (5HT) levels possibly by increasing the conversion of 5HT to a reductive pathway leading to 5-hydroxytryptophol. This, together with the finding that ethanol modifies the ratio of REM to non-REM sleep [probably controlled by an ascending serotonergic pathway issuing from the raphe nuclei of the brain stem (30)], could be taken as support for the possibility that alcohol-induced sleep is mediated via brain stem mechanisms.

Cerebello-Vestibular Function

The most obvious effect of alcohol intoxication is the presence of astasia, ataxia, dysmetria, and adiadochokinesis, that is, a full constellation of "cerebellar" symptoms, upon which the usual police tests for intoxication are based. As early as 1831, Flourens (16) suggested that the cerebellum must be an important site for the acute central actions of alcohol. I will not discuss the neuropathology of chronic alcoholism but only mention the report by Romano et al. (47) on the presence of severe degenerative changes in the cerebellum of chronic alcoholic humans and the studies by Jarlstedt and Hultborn in rats (28), which bear on this particular area.

Nystagmus—the presence of rhythmic pendular movement of the eyeballs upon fixation outside central position, and even within it—is also a well studied acute effect of alcohol. The first systematic study of alcoholic nystagmus was carried out by Aschan (3), who described two separate types of alcohol-induced nystagmus in man. In one of them (AGN), the eyes jerk in the direction of the gaze, independently of head position. The other, positional alcohol nystagmus (PAN), changes direction with head position and is closely associated with vertiginous sensations, nausea, etc., whereas the AGN is not. Most interestingly, the two types of nystagmus appear at different times and have a different course with respect to the time of alcohol intake. AGN appears with the shortest delay, peaks after a blood alcohol level threshold has been passed, and disappears after the blood alcohol descends below that level. PAN shows two phases, with the direction of the nystagmic jerks reversing as time passes, and outlasts, even by several hours, the presence of detectable blood alcohol. Aschan suggested that PAN is of vestibular origin, but did not speculate upon the mechanisms of AGN. Fregly et al. (17) confirmed these findings and emphasized the fact that "acute tolerance" or "adaptation" could be demonstrated in this test situation.

Eidelberg, Bond, and Kelter (11) restudied this problem using decerebrate cats, with microelectrodes inserted in the cerebellar cortex and vestibular (Deiters') nuclei. They found that intoxicating doses of alcohol severely, but transiently, modified the spontaneous activity and responsiveness of vestibular neurons to dc polarization of the labyrinth, whether or not the cerebellum was intact or had been removed. This indicated that alcohol affects the vestibular system directly, apart from effects mediated by the cerebellum. Cerebellar Purkinje cell firing uniformly depressed by intravenous alcohol, but cerebellar cortical interneurones were affected variably (some were depressed and some highly excited). This established that, indeed, the cerebellum is sensitive to alcohol as predicted by Flourens, and that not all neurones are depressed by it, in agreement with the finding by Meyer-Lohmann et al. (42) that similar doses of alcohol cause marked acceleration of Renshaw cell firing in the spinal cord. Again, a Mellanby effect could be clearly demonstrated with these techniques.

The Spinal Cord

The classic work on the effects of alcohol on the spinal cord was done by Kolmodin (36), who studied cord reflex activity in cats following graded doses of alcohol. Using a decapitate (high cervical section) standard "Lloyd preparation" he recorded the L_7 and S_1 ventral root discharges elicited by single stimuli to a muscle nerve (gastrocnemius) and to a skin nerve (sural). Responses to the first he regarded as monosynaptic and those to the second as polysynaptic, following standard criteria of latency, etc. In about half the animals, both reflex responses were reduced following relatively low doses of intravenous alcohol solutions (100–200 mg/kg). In the other half of the animals, polysynaptic responses were depressed more than monosynaptics. The N_1 cord dorsum potentials, signaling early postsynaptic responses in the cord, were essentially unchanged. Kolmodin interpreted this as indicating a relatively greater sensitivity of interneurones to alcohol, although both motoneurones and interneurones must be affected. A nearly identical series of experiments was reported by Ishido (23) with the same results. Eidelberg and Wooley (12) also recently confirmed this, with the added observation that those techniques which presumably measure the excitability of cord sensory afferents (dorsal root reflex and antidromic responses recorded in a peripheral nerve to direct stimulation of afferent terminals) showed essentially no changes following alcohol injection, even at rather high doses. These results were in disagreement with experiments reported by Miyahara et al. (44) as well as those of Banna (4), who found that alcohol increased presynaptic inhibition, if it is true that presynaptic depolarization and presynaptic inhibition are closely related causally. Sauerland et al. (49, 50) also found that alcohol produced afferent depolarization in the trigeminal nerve nucleus in neuraxially intact cats but not in animals where the brain stem has been transected at the collicular level. These authors concluded that, in their experiments, alcohol affects presynaptic endings of cortical origin. The contradiction between the results of Miyahara et al.(44) and those of Eidelberg and Wooley (12) may reflect differences in methodology and measured variables, but the issue of whether alcohol acts presynaptically or not is crucial only if one makes the assumption that presynaptic inhibition is monosynaptic. If, however, presynaptic inhibition involves at least one interneurone, then the precision with which one may localize the effects to a specific synaptic mode of organization is greatly reduced. Davidoff (7) has shown very recently that in the isolated spinal cord of the frog, alcohol in fairly high concentrations does increase primary afferent depolarization, dorsal root potentials, and terminal excitability, potentiating the effects of gamma-aminobutyric acid which may act as the presynaptic inhibitory transmitter. Davidoff's experiments will, we hope, be followed up later by pharmacological blockade experiments with bicuculline and picrotoxin (to block GABA-mediated presynaptic inhibition), as well as by additional experiments in mammalian preparations, but using lower alcohol concentrations.

There is direct evidence that, regardless of the controversial nature of the presynaptic effects, alcohol affects the "resting" discharge and membrane properties of cord neurones. As predicted by Kolmodin, interneurones were found to be relatively more sensitive than ventral horn motoneurones, although both types of cells were affected. Intracellular records from motoneurones indicated that alterations in membrane conductance are probably of greater importance than resting potential changes in determining the depressant actions of alcohol upon cell firing (12). Meyer-Lohmann et al. (42) have shown recently that the interneurones of the recurrent inhibitory system controlling motoneurone firing (Renshaw elements) respond differently to alcohol than sensory interneurones in the dorsal horn; the latter are consistently depressed, but the former increase their firing activity. This is in close agreement with the findings of others (11) in the cerebellum showing that some interneurones are depressed whereas others accelerate their firing rate. The effects of alcohol on motoneurones may be explained as being due in part to increased recurrent inhibition, in part to depression of excitatory inputs, and in part to the direct action of alcohol upon the postsynaptic membrane. More interestingly, these findings suggest that different synaptic organizations, with possibly different transmitters, are affected in opposite ways by alcohol. This may allow a precise dissection of the mechanism of alcohol action at this level.

Neuromuscular Transmission

Knutsson and Katz (35) have shown that alcohol in vitro increases the sodium permeability of muscle fibers, and possibly also the permeability to chloride but not to potassium. As long ago as 1941, Feng and Li (15) showed that alcohol increased the twitch tension in muscles stimulated via their nerve. Gage (18) restudied and clarified this phenomenon in the isolated phrenic nerve-diaphragm preparation from rats. Alcohol in concentrations above 8 mM caused an increase in the release of transmitter, whether spontaneous or driven by nerve stimulation. This effect appeared to add to another, an increase in the depolarizing action of the transmitter upon the postsynaptic membrane, which may have been related to a decrease in postsynaptic membrane electrical conductance or, perhaps, to the increase in sodium permeability described by Knutsson and Katz.

Peripheral Receptors and Nerve Fibers

Little is known about the actions of alcohol on peripheral receptors. Bernhard and Skoglund (5) found that intravenously injected ethanol selectively reduced a late negative component of the cat's electroretinogram, presumably reflecting changes produced by it in retinal neurones. McNichol and Benolken (41) used an invertebrate eye as the experimental material (Limulus) and found that dilute alcohol solution selectively depressed synaptic actions mediating lateral inhibition. Liljestrand (39) and Landgren et al. (38) found that ethanol depressed carotid baroceptor responses while enhancing the responsiveness of the carotid body chemoceptors. Recently, Kucera and Smith (37) studied its effects on the rat caudal muscle spindles and Golgi tendon organs. At low alcohol concentrations the receptors (spindle primaries and secondaries and Golgi organs) fired at higher rates than normal, this effect being dose related. Higher levels of alcohol (above 417 mM) resulted in cessation of firing. These effects, they concluded, are due to direct action of the drug at the sites where the generator and/or action potentials are produced, not at the intra- or extrafusal end plates.

Israel et al. have reviewed very recently (27) the effects of alcohol on axonal conduction and ionic transport mechanisms, to which review the reader is referred. Their conclusion is that alcohol affects the mechanisms maintaining the resting membrane potential by inhibiting the active transport of Na^+ and K^+, but not the diffusional permeability to these ions in the direction of equilibrium. Since an adenosinetriphosphatase, activated by Na^+, K^+, and Mg^{2+} and inactivated by Ca^{2+}, is very likely the critical element in active ionic transport, Kalant, Israel, and their colleagues studied the effects of ethanol on the ATPase activity of brain microsomal fractions. As they expected, relatively low concentrations of alcohol did depress it in a dose-related manner (24, 25, 26, 31). The role of Ca^{2+} in this story is not so clearly understood, however. Shanes (51) classified Ca^{2+} ions, alcohol, and local anesthetics as membrane stabilizers, that is, substances which prevent the rapid changes in membrane permeability which are the substrate of the action potential, but do not cause significant changes in resting membrane potential. There is evidence that alcohol may act upon ionic transport and permeability changes by somehow interacting with Ca^{2+} or its sites of attachment (1, 2, 22, 45). If the effects of alcohol depend upon this interaction—perhaps of a competitive displacement nature—with Ca^{2+} control of ionic transport, then the actual tissue or plasma levels of ethanol may not necessarily correlate with the membrane events, and this could be at the root of "adaptation" (Mellanby) effect.

3. ACUTE EFFECTS OF OPIATES ON THE NERVOUS SYSTEM

The Cerebral Cortex

Berger, in 1933, was the first to record the effects of morphine injection upon the EEG, as a generalized flattening of the record. Later on Gibbs et al. (84) and Andrews (57) described a situation in which a subject under the influence of a dose of morphine appears behaviorally awake, while his scalp EEG shows patterns comparable to those of slow wave sleep. This dissociation was investigated further by Wikler (66, 149–151), who showed that morphine shared this same property with atropine and subsequently followed up these findings by showing that EEG effects of morphine in dogs were antagonized by n-allylnormorphine (nalorphine), this being confirmed by Gangloff and Monnier in 1955 (82). Soulairac et al. (136) later found fast seizurelike waves in the cortex of rats after high doses of morphine, in addition to the slow wave bursts, in agreement with its well-known convulsant action (123).

The first attempt to quantify the relationship between the EEG effects of low doses of morphine and the partial antagonist nalorphine was made by Goldstein and Aldunate in 1960 (85). They used an integrating device designed by Drohocki, which measures the area under the EEG by voltage integration. Nalorphine alone produced similar effects to morphine, whereas it antagonized them when the two drugs were given together.

Khazan et al. (40, 41, 59, 95, 96, 114) attempted to correlate the EEG and the behavior of rats in an intravenous self-administration experiment. Morphine initially suppressed the appearance of paradoxical (REM, deep, desynchronized) sleep, which reappeared gradually as tolerance to the narcotic developed. Withdrawal of the drug resulted in a complex series of alternating sequences of EEG patterns, during which slow wave and paradoxical sleep were reduced proportionately for several days and then returned to base line levels.

Navarro and Elliott, in 1971 (116), reported a series of experiments in cats and rabbits in which electrodes in cortical and subcortical areas were used for recording. In cats, at the dose range which elicits "feline mania," morphine produced seizurelike discharges in the hippocampus. Morphinone and thebaine, two naturally occurring morphine antagonists, produced similar discharges in the cortex. In rabbits, all three opiates produced cortical and hippocampal "spiking." We have confirmed the findings of Navarro and Elliott with morphine in cats, using animals with chronically implanted electrodes, but have failed to obtain the same effects in monkeys where, curiously enough, seizurelike discharges do appear in the hippocampus and amygdala during precipitated abstinence in dependent animals (Eidelberg, Barstow, and Woodbury, unpublished).

An alternative to EEG recording is to activate inputs to the cortex, either via stimuli addressed to peripheral sense organs or by electrical stimulation of peripheral or central neural pathways, measuring the changes in the EEG which follow each stimulus within a period of ≤ 1 sec after the stimulus. These "evoked potentials" are of such small magnitude (unless rather unnatural stimuli or heroic pharmacological tricks are used to enhance the ratio between the evoked activity and the "background" EEG) that averaging techniques are often required to extract them, based upon the assumption that the background signal, being randomly related to the stimuli, will average out by superposing successive post-stimulus epochs. Sinitsin (134) used this method to study the effects of morphine upon cortical responses to visual, auditory, and somatosensory stimuli in acute experiments in immobilized cats. Low doses of the drug (< 5 mg/kg) did not produce any changes in the responses in the primary receiving areas, while modality-specific changes were found in the associational and motor cortex responses to the same stimuli. Higher doses (5–10 mg/kg) caused a marked enhancement of responses in primary receptive and motor cortical areas. These findings were replicated in Jurna's laboratory (94). Chin and Domino (68) also reported similar results in dogs, except that evoked responses were enhanced by morphinization in "associational" and "non-specific" thalamic nuclei.

Low-frequency repetitive electrical stimulation of certain thalamic nuclear groups (*N. Centre median*, intralaminar group, and *N. ventralis anterior*) gives rise to a peculiar sequence of cyclically waxing and waning "recruiting" responses in certain cortical areas. These are supposed to indicate a peculiar diffuse distribution for the cortical projection of this system, as well as different synaptic endings, as opposed to the thalamocortical systems relaying modality-specific information. Mizoguchi and Mitchell (113) studied the effects of morphine upon recruiting responses in dogs, and found that, contrary to the effects reported by Sinitsin, Jurna, Chin, and Domino upon specific cortical responses to sensory stimulation, recruiting responses were often depressed, even by doses of morphine under 5 mg/kg.

No coherent picture can yet be extracted from the available data involving the actions of opiates upon the cerebral cortex. It seems reasonable to suppose that morphine affects cortical function directly, in addition to effects mediated by subcortical structures, but there is no direct proof of this as yet. Jhamandas et al. and Matthews et al. (92, 110) have shown that opiate narcotics reduce the outflux of acetylcholine from regionally perfused cortex, and this suggests a possible synaptic mechanism of action, but without specifying whether purely cortical events are involved.

Limbic Structures

It is generally agreed that the limbic system comprises the following structures: the hippocampus and the adjacent allocortex and their connexions, the amygdaloid complex, septum, mammillary bodies, cingulate gyrus, and the primary olfactory cortex and its inputs.

The paper that focused attention upon this system as being involved specifically in opiate dependence was that of Foltz and White (75), who showed that the signs of precipitated abstinence in monkeys who were morphine dependent were attenuated following lesions of the cingulum bundle and adjacent cingulate cortex. A series of patients suffering from chronic pain and iatrogenic opiate dependence were subjected by Foltz and White to bilateral cingulum lesions, and the withdrawal distress and physical signs were reported by them to be attenuated by the surgery. Together with C. Loschiavo, I attempted to replicate Foltz and White's monkey experiments. Although the animals reacted less strongly to the setting in which they had been subjected to episodes of precipitated abstinence previously, the visceral and somatic manifestations elicited by antagonist challenge were unchanged (unpublished). A more systematic study in rats, by Wikler, Norrell, and Miller (154) on the same problem, also failed to confirm the Foltz and White findings. By contrast, Trafton and Marques (139) reported that ablations of the cingulate cortex reduced opiate seeking behavior (drinking in a preferred choice situation) and relapse drinking of drug solutions. It would appear that choice of animal species and strains, lesion parameters, and, particularly, degree of dependence (which is highly time-dependent) may all be critical variables in these discrepancies.

Basal Ganglia and Thalamus

Morphine produces remarkably powerful effects on locomotor activity in all species tested so far. The direction of the changes is dose dependent and species related so that, for example, doses below 4 mg/kg in albino rats produce increased motor activity whereas doses above 4 mg/kg produce locomotor depression (usually referred to as catatonia or catalepsy) (65, 71). In the mouse low doses (under 10 mg/kg) produce diminished locomotion, whereas higher doses sharply increase it. Manipulation of brain monoamine levels or blockade of monoaminergic synapses strongly modifies these actions (65, 67, 71).

It is well-known that striatal lesions produce hyperkinesia in several species (67), which leads to the possibility that the striatum may be a key site of action of morphine. Fuxe and Ungerstedt (81) have shown that unilateral caudate lesions produce rotational behavior in rats, which is modified by morphine in a manner which they interpret as due to a dopaminergic blocking action. This view is shared by Puri et al. (124, 125) on the basis of experiments in nonlesioned rats where aggressive and stereotyped behavior—induced by other agents—was blocked by morphine or haloperidol (a dopaminergic blocking agent). Ahtee and Kääriäinen (55) have provided some supporting evidence for this by showing that morphine increased the level of a catecholamine metabolite (HVA) in the striatum. High (60 mg/kg) doses of morphine also resulted in a marked in vivo increase in dopamine turnover in rat striatum (83), an effect which may be expected of an agent blocking the entry of dopamine into postsynaptic receptors (86, 124, 126).

Dependent rats respond to antagonist administration by developing a precipitated abstinence syndrome, consisting of hypothermia, wet-dog shakes, diarrhea, weight loss, etc. Injection of very small doses of an antagonist (naloxone) in the medial thalamus resulted in some signs of precipitated abstinence (wet-dog shakes and escape attempts) in dependent rats, but injections elsewhere in the brain (hippocampus, neocortex, hypothalamus, or midbrain tegmentum) were ineffective (147). This suggests that the medial thalamus or its areas of projection, which include primarily the striatum, may be importantly involved in this phenomenon.

Hypothalamus

Intimately related to the limbic system, the hypothalamus contains a set of key regulatory centers for a number of visceral and endocrine functions. It is well established that opiates depress eating and drinking, and modify thermoregulation, gonadal function, thyroid and adrenal hormone production, etc., all of which involve control by the hypothalamus. Barraclough and Sawyer (59) first called attention to this area by showing that morphine suppresses ovulation in female rats by interfering with hypothalamic control of anterior pituitary gonadotropin release. Lotti, Lomax, and George (101–103), in a systematic series of experiments in rats with implanted intracerebral cannulae, demonstrated that intrahypothalamic morphine is several hundredfold more effective than the same drug given intravenously in producing hypothermia, that this effect shows tolerance, and that it is antagonized by intrahypothalamic or systemic injection of nalorphine (see 147, however). Curiously, nalorphine did not antagonize the hypothermia produced by morphine in tolerant rats. To what degree these drug effects may involve learning is shown by Holtzman and Villarreal (91), who reported that chair restraint alone caused hypothermia in morphine tolerant monkeys, an effect which could be reversed by morphine.

Since the hypothalamic region is exceptionally rich in serotonin and catecholamines it is interesting to note here that Haubrich and Blake (88) have shown that serotonin depletion prevented morphine-induced hypothermia, whereas catecholamine depletion potentiated it.

Electrical stimulation of the lateral hypothalamus and septal region can act as a behavioral reinforcer, as has been known since Olds and Milner's classic work on the subject (117). Olds and Travis (118) found that intracranial electrical self-stimulation was blocked by morphine injection (8 mg/kg, subcutaneous) if the stimulating electrodes were placed in the septal region, but not when midbrain tegmental placements were employed. This was confirmed by others later (60) and suggested the presence of a dual reinforcing mechanism, a possibility supported by histochemical work indicating discrete pathways, which contain serotonin and catecholamines, joining the midbrain and basal forebrain (107). Harvey and Lints (87) found that lesions which destroyed primarily 5HT-containing pathways caused significant hyperalgesia, which reversed upon administration of 5-hydroxytryptophan. Samanin, Gumulka, and Valzelli (128, 129) also found that morphine was less effective as an analgesic in the presence of lesions of the 5-HT pathway, its potency being enhanced when the main source of this pathway, the N. raphe dorsalis, was electrically stimulated. A closely related series of experiments performed in Liebeskind's laboratory (112) also showed that analgesia was produced by electrical stimulation of certain mesencephalic tegmentum sites. This effect was antagonized by naloxone injection.

That morphine produces marked aphagia and adipsia is well known to clinicians. Conceivably this effect also could be mediated directly upon the hypothalamic regulatory nuclei for eating and drinking in addition to the hyperglycemia, also produced by morphine, which could depress eating. Kerr and Pozuelo found that bilateral lesions of the ventromedial hypothalamic nuclei grossly modify the signs of precipitated morphine abstinence in dependent rats, while markedly reducing their tolerance to the drug (97). This remarkable series of experiments has not yet been replicated in other laboratories.

Together with M. Bond, I studied the effects of morphine and naloxone upon anterior hypothalamic cell electrical activity (73). We selected neurones that showed osmosensitive responses to hypertonic saline intravenously and found that morphine depressed neuronal firing, in drug-naive rats, that the same doses (< 5 mg/kg) speeded up mean firing rate, with a bursting pattern, and naloxone—which was ineffective in naive animals—induced an increase in mean firing rate but without a bursting pattern, in morphine dependent animals.

All this evidence, taken together, indicates a remarkable sensitivity of hypothalamic centers to the actions of opiates, which agrees with the gross modifications induced by morphine on the output of the target organs of hypothalamic regulation. It is, therefore, reasonable to suggest that this region is a very good place to look for the neurophysiological mechanisms of action of opiates at the cellular level. The properties of intracranial self-stimulation of certain basal forebrain sites, a behavior which bears some outward resemblance to narcotic self-administration, suggest a commonality of mechanisms well worth exploring experimentally.

Brain Stem

A great deal of interest developed some 20 years ago in the possibility that opiates, as well as general anesthetics, tranquilizers, etc., might act directly on the brain stem reticular system and, through it, indirectly upon a multi-

plicity of sites in the central nervous system. This was the logical consequence of the now classical work of Ranson, Hess, Magoun, Moruzzi,
Bremer, and their students (79, 108) on the presence of central forebrain
systems controlling relatively nonspecific functional states such as sleep,
arousal, attention, etc. Eva King Killam (98) has reviewed thoroughly the
evidence upon which "reticular pharmacology" was based, much of which
came from her own excellent work. Although the reticular activating
system concept has lost some of its functional attributes, the evidence for
reticular sites of action for opiates has gained considerable direct support in
several laboratories. I have referred already to the role of ascending and
descending systems issuing from the raphe nuclei in the possible mediation
of morphine analgesia. McKenzie and Beechey (105, 106) reported that
both morphine and meperidine selectively depressed responses evoked in
the midbrain tegmentum and hippocampus by tibial nerve electrical
stimulation. T'sou and Jang (140) used a microinjection technique in rabbits and found that analgesia was produced by very small quantities of
morphine injected in the mesencephalic or posterior hypothalamic periven-
tricular gray matter. Herz and his group have used rabbits, first injecting a
waxy compound so as to selectively block the cerebral ventricular
pathways. Analgesia and changes of hind limb flexor reflexes were
produced when morphine (injected in the ventricles) reached the gray matter surrounding the fossa rhomboidea of the fourth ventricle (56, 90, 138,
143). In close relationship to this work are the reports from Liebeskind's
laboratory referred to previously (112), which show that unresponsiveness
to nociceptive stimuli is produced by electrical stimulation of the midbrain
tegmentum near the periaqueductal gray. Samanin, Gumulka, and Valzelli
(128, 129) whose work is discussed above, showed that electrical
stimulation of the midbrain raphe nuclei potentiates morphine analgesia
while lesions of the same area diminish it.

Two questions are raised by the work just mentioned: the first is whether
pain can be dissected pharmacologically away from all other sensory modalities, in other words, whether "opiate analgesia" is separable from attenuation of other sensory inputs (80, 115). The evidence that would answer
this question is lacking, for some of the classical tests of analgesic action of
opiates measure, in fact, the reactivity of local spinal cord mechanisms,
some are clearly contaminated by changes in locomotor activity (such as
the various hot plate tests), whereas others measure escape or avoidance
responses to what one presumes may be painful stimuli. Thus we have no
assurance, on one side, that what we call pain in human terms is measured
objectively by tests in animals, nor do we have, on the other side, reliable
measurements of disturbances in other sensory modalities that have been
applied to the study of narcotic opiate effects, although the evidence from

experiments using cortical evoked potentials suggests that they probably exist.

The second question is: what are the mechanisms of action involved in opiate analgesia? It is one thing to demonstrate that "analgesia" is produced when the drug is put in contact with a specific set of brain stem structures and quite another to specify whether these structures serve as "pain centers" by themselves, or that their neurones project to other forebrain structures concerned with the perception of, or the responsiveness to, painful stimuli, or that they project downstream to those cord and lower brain stem neurones which first relay nociceptive data. Obviously more work is needed to be sure of the answers.

It has been known for a long time that opium and its derivatives are potent emetic agents. In fact, it is a source of some puzzlement to many researchers that early opiate experience in humans, which often includes vomiting, does not discourage many would-be addicts. One of the few things we really know about the central actions of opiates is the localization of the structures mediating emesis, thanks to the work of Borison and Wang and their students, which established beyond reasonable doubt that a medullary chemoreceptor zone in the area postrema is the site of action for opiate-induced emesis (62, 145, 146).

Morphine also produces hyperglycemia, an effect which is absent during barbiturate anesthesia and which is dependent on intact adrenal and hepatic sympathetic innervation. It is produced, with high effectiveness, by intraventricular injection of morphine and is partially prevented by previous lesioning of the subfornical organ, although it can still be elicited in attenuated form in midbrain decerebrate cats (62–64). It would appear, from this evidence, that although the hypothalamic region is involved, lower brain stem structures are still capable of mediating the phenomenon through descending projections, eventually reaching the sympathetic ganglionic chain.

Respiratory depression is a prominent effect of opiate narcotics. Borison recently has summarized the experimental evidence bearing on the possible mechanisms involved, so that I will not go over the same territory. He concludes that opiates probably act via the CO_2 detection system, by raising its set point (62).

Spinal Cord

Opiates affect spinal cord reflex and sensory relay mechanisms, most likely acting both directly and indirectly: directly through actions upon intrinsic cord elements and indirectly via supraspinal descending pathways. Schemes of possible sites of action of opiates on the spinal cord are presented in

Figures 1–3. The first systematic study of localized cord actions was reported by Wikler and Frank (153), who used chronically spinalized dogs (low thoracic section) and classic Sherringtonian methods to study the effects of acute and chronic morphinization and withdrawal upon segmental hind limb reflexes. Single doses of morphine or methadone (between 2 and 5 mg/kg) produced gross depression of flexor and crossed extensor reflexes, no consistent changes in knee jerks, and enhancement of extensor thrusts. Chronic morphinization resulted in tolerance development to the effects upon the flexor and crossed extensor reflexes but not upon the enhancement of extensor thrust. Withdrawal of morphine then resulted in increased flexor and crossed extensor reflexes and reduction of the extensor thrust, progressing to "spontaneous" repetitive stepping movements of the hind limbs. In a later paper Wikler and Carter (152) showed that an opiate antagonist, nalorphine, blocked the above described single dose effects of morphine and, in dependent animals, precipitated the same changes which resulted from withdrawing the narcotic. Later on Martin and his associates made extensive use of this methodology to compare the effects of opioid agonists, partial agonists, and antagonists (104, 109, 111). The importance of these studies cannot be overstressed. They show unequivocally that opiates act at many levels of the CNS, not only on the forebrain, and that tolerance and dependence can be demonstrated even in the humble lumbar

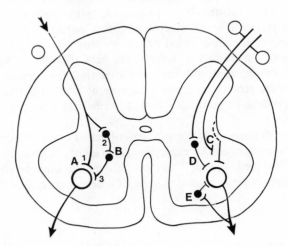

Fig. 1. Segmental connections of the cord. Left side of figure excitatory, right side inhibitory. A, Monosynaptic reflex arc; B, polysynaptic reflex arc; C, presynaptic inhibitory connection onto monosynaptic excitatory afferent; D, postsynaptic (reciprocal and flexor reflex afferent) inhibitory input to motoneurone; E, recurrent inhibitory connection (Renshaw).

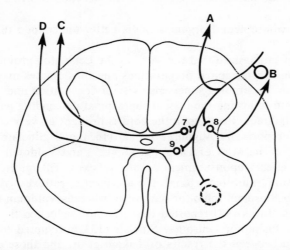

Fig. 2. Ascending pathways from segmental cord levels. A, Dorsal column; B, uncrossed spinocere-bellar; C, crossed spinocerebellar; D, spinothalamic and spinoreticular; others (spino-olivary, etc.) not diagrammed.

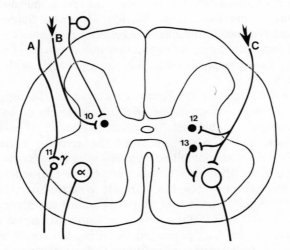

Fig. 3. Descending pathways into segmental cord levels. A, Brain stem to fusimotor (gamma) neurones (11); B, forebrain and brain stem to sensory relay interneurones (10); C, corticospinal to sensory (12) and motor (12) interneurones and to ventral horn alpha motoneurones.

spinal cord, whose neural organization is better understood than of higher structures.

It must be emphasized that the work of the Lexington group was carried out mostly in chronic spinal preparations and thus opiates may have acted upon neurones undergoing supersensitivity of denervation and/or collateral reafferentation following the loss of supraspinal descending pathways. The question of indirect effects upon the cord is brought up very clearly by the very recent reports by Vigouret et al. (143) and Sinclair (133), who followed up on the work of Takagi et al. (137) and Valdman (142) on the supraspinal effects upon segmental cord reflexes. Takagi et al. reported that morphine inhibited spinal monosynaptic reflexes by activating descending bulbospinal inhibitor pathways, whereas Valdman reported opposite effects. Jurna (93) reported that morphine blocked the bulbospinal inhibition of fusimotor neurones. Sinclair (133) attempted to resolve the contradiction between the results of Takagi et al. and those of Valdman, and came out on the side of the latter. By using a method of localized intraventricular injection in rabbits, Vigouret et al. (143) and Teschemacher et al. (138) concluded that morphine acts upon descending pathways to the cord originating in rhombencephalic structures (pons and medulla). These pathways may be monoaminergic (58, 69). However, Satoh et al. (130) have presented evidence for interactions between antagonists and morphine at the spinal segmental level, indicating that not all effects of morphine can be attributed to supraspinal mediation, in agreement with Wikler and Frank's studies.

With respect to cellular mechanisms involved at the segmental level, Kruglov (100) found that morphine, in 5–10 mg/kg doses, in acute spinal cats, reduced recurrent but not antagonist inhibition of motorneurones. Felpel, Sinclair, and Yim (74) recorded the activity of Renshaw cells (which mediate recurrent inhibition) and found that intravenous morphine did not modify their firing rate. Duggan and Curtis (72) repeated these experiments, but also injected the narcotic electrophoretically next to Renshaw cells. Again, they found that intravenous morphine (10 mg/kg) did not modify the firing of these cells in response to ventral root stimuli. Local injection of the drug prolonged the firing latency of these cells to ventral root stimuli, but without modifying their response to acetylcholine. Duggan and Curtis concluded that morphine acts upon recurrent inhibition by interfering with synaptic cholinergic driving of Renshaw cells by motoneuron recurrent collaterals.

A good deal can still be learned about the neurophysiological effects of opiates at the spinal level, particularly in terms of their synaptic or nonsynaptic mechanisms of action with newer, high-resolution, techniques of electrophysiological analysis that were not available at the time of

Wikler's pioneering work. The paucity of morphine effects upon Renshaw elements suggests that the profound alterations in reflexes in spinalized animals that Wikler described cannot be explained on the basis of actions upon the recurrent control of motoneurone firing alone. Jurna has shown that morphine accelerates the firing of spindle afferents to the cord, if the ventral roots are intact (93). This indicates that changes in the excitability of the fusimotor system are produced by morphine, but it remains to be seen whether this is a sufficient explanation for Wikler and Frank's findings.

Nerve, Muscle, and Peripheral Autonomic System

Nerve Fibers

Kosterlitz and Wallis (99) and Ritchie and Armett (127) sought possible local anesthetic properties for morphine and its agonists in mammalian peripheral nerves. With morphine concentrations up to 4×10^{-5} M Kosterlitz and Wallis found no such effects, and with higher concentrations of the same drug ($1\text{--}5 \times 10^{-3}$ M) Ritchie and Armett found only minimal changes, where the narcotic antagonized acetylcholine depolarization of fine vagal axons.

In the isolated squid giant axon, however, morphine and levorphanol have been shown to behave as mild local anesthetic agents (76, 77, 132), when tested at concentrations between 1×10^{-3} to 5×10^{-4} M. This effect was evidenced by reduction or abolition of action potentials without change of the membrane potential. The ionic currents for Na^+ and K^+ were grossly reduced, indicating this to be the cause of the action potential block. Simon and Rosenberg (132) observed that the blocking action of levorphanol on spontaneous axonal firing was strongly enhanced when the axons were immersed in seawater low in Ca^{2+} and Mg^{2+} and noted the possible connection between their findings and the antagonism of morphine analgesia by Ca^{2+} and its potentiation by Ca^{2+} chelators. Their suggestion that levorphanol may act upon Ca^{2+} binding sites of the membrane is of particular interest now in view of the demonstration by Pert and Synder (121) of the dependence on divalent ions of the uptake of opioid agonists and antagonists into the membrane proteolipids which may act as opiate receptors in neural tissue.

Frazier et al. (77) also compared the relative effects of one potent morphine agonist, etorphine, and two antagonists, M5050 and naloxone, as local anesthetics in squid nerve. They were disappointed to find that all these agents had the same properties and relative potency, and concluded that the local anesthetic effect could not be responsible for centrally mediated analgesia in mammals. Unfortunately, neither Simon and Rosenberg nor Frazier et al. tested stereo pairs of opioids, so that the possible stereospecificity of the presumed receptor inside the axon membrane was not established. This would have been much more important, had it proved to be present, than potency ratios, which depend too much upon permeability and uptake mechanisms to be a clear indication of differences in receptor affinity in brain. The lack of opposition of effects between agonists and antagonists in this test situation does not prove that their actions upon the axonal membrane are unrelated to analgesia, since there is no proof that they compete for the same receptor sites under all circumstances. The situation in the CNS is complex enough to allow for subsidiary hypotheses when it comes to explaining analgesia.

Finally, it may be much more than coincidental than ethanol, cocaine, and the opiate narcotics are all local anesthetics that appear to act (exclusive of synaptic mediation effects) as membrane stabilizers acting on Ca^{2+} binding sites.

Neuromuscular Junction

Whether or not the neuromuscular effects of morphine are pharmacologically important is unclear at the present time. Hebb and Konzett (89) found that morphine did not act as a blocking curare in the frog rectus abdominis preparation. Pinsky and Frederickson (122) and Frederickson and Pinsky (78) found that morphine reduced acetylcholine release in the rat diaphragm and frog sartorius neuromuscular junctions, and at the same time it increased the sensitivity of the end plate to extrinsic acetylcholine. The same effect was produced by morphine as by the partial antagonist nalorphine.

Soteropulos and Standaert (135), using a cat neuromuscular preparation (soleus), found that both morphine and an antagonist, naloxone, produced a sharp reduction in the tetanic and posttetanic contraction of the muscle, naloxone being some 10 times more potent than morphine. They noted also a second effect, the delayed potentiation of twitch tension. Taking these results together with those of Pinsky and Frederickson one may safely conclude that the neuromuscular effects are related to prejunctional stabilization, with consequent decrease in ACh release.

Peripheral Autonomic Function

The oldest known use of opium was apparently as an antidiarrheic, in ancient China. It is interesting to notice that this effect, based upon the inhibition by morphine and its congeners of the peristaltic reflex is still very useful in studying the mechanism of action of the opiates and their antagonists, or as a highly efficient drug-screening test. Schaumann (131) and Paton (119) found that the antiperistaltic effect was related to a decrease in the release of acetylcholine in the parasympathetic input to the gut. This appears to be the case also in the superior cervical ganglion (120, 141). A similar mechanism might be involved in the alterations in tonus of other visceral smooth muscle structures also endowed with muscarinic cholinergic innervation. The role of serotonergic or catecholaminergic cells which are interposed between the afferent parasympathetic input and the effector glands or smooth muscle in the action of opioid drugs remains to be established.

4. CONCLUSIONS

It appears to this reviewer that there is overwhelming evidence in the literature to support the conclusion that alcohol and opiate narcotics act upon many sites in the nervous system. The overt clinical or behavioral changes they produce reflect, in this view, the involvement of multiple functional systems and one may suspect that the differences seen in the time course of their acute effects and the development, tolerance, and dependence reflect this heterogeneity of sites and perhaps also heterogeneity of mechanisms of action. This conclusion runs counter to the desire to generalize from restricted experimental data. The same may apply to identification of the receptor for opiates, where it may be necessary to prove that the same substance is present at multiple sites in the CNS before one can postulate that the same cellular mechanisms are involved everywhere, even within the same species.

Though the oculomotor and equilibrium alterations in intoxication are probably due to its actions upon the cerebello-vestibular system, and the thermoregulatory action of morphine probably involves the hypothalamus in a crucial manner, other drug actions are less obviously attributable to specific systems. This, I believe, is particularly the case with opiate analgesia, where entirely different mechanisms may be involved depending on the operations involved in measuring "analgesia."

Finally, we have tended to assume implicitly an equivalence between neuropharmacology and synaptic pharmacology, which may be less real than we think. Neuronal excitability is under the influence of many mechanisms—such as ionic transport, to mention only the best known one—not all of which depend on synaptic activation, so that we are not compelled to invoke neurotransmitters every time we consider the mechanisms of drug action. Thus the actions of alcohol and opiates on axonal membranes, where they may interfere with the regulation by divalent ions of the permeability of the membrane to monovalent ions, may provide models of central actions where synaptic elements are excluded.

A very great deal remains to be learned about these drugs, in spite of man's close association with them for thousands of years. It would appear that application of the more sophisticated techniques of neurophysiology, almost unused by most neuropharmacologists, should help push forward our understanding of drug actions and our ability to deal intelligently with drug abuse.

ACKNOWLEDGMENTS

The author's own work in the field was supported by the National Institute of Mental Health. Mrs. Joy Harvey lent considerable assistance in the literature search and made many valuable suggestions as to the format and style of this review.

REFERENCES

Ethanol

1. Aceves, J. and X. Machne, The action of calcium and local anesthetics on nerve cells, and their interaction during excitation, *J. Pharmacol. Exp. Ther.*, **140**, 138–148 (1963).

2. Armstrong, C. M. and L. Binstock, The effects of several alcohols on the properties of the squid giant axon, *J. Gen. Physiol.* **48**, 265–277 (1964).

3. Aschan, G., Different types of alcohol nystagmus, *Acta OtoLaryngol. Suppl.*, **140**, 69–78 (1968).

4. Banna, N. R., Potentiation of cutaneous inhibition by alcohol, *Experientia,* **25,** 619–620 (1969).

5. Bernhard, C. G. and C. R. Skoglund, Selective suppression with ethyl alcohol of inhibition in the optic nerve and in the negative component pII of the electroretinogram, *Acta Physiol. Scand.*, **2**, 10 (1941).

6. Caspers, H. H., Die Beeinflussung der Corticalen Krampferregbarkeit durch das Aufsteigende Reticulärsystem des Hirnstammes. II Narkosewirkungen, *Z. Gesamte Exp. Med.*, **129**, 582–600 (1958).

7. Davidoff, R. A., Alcohol and presynaptic inhibition in an isolated spinal cord preparation, *Arch. Neurol.*, **28**, 60–63 (1973).

8. Davis, P. A., F. A. Gibbs, H. Davis, W. W. Jetter, and L. S. Trowbridge, The effects of alcohol upon the electroencephalogram (brainwaves), *Q. J. Stud. Alcohol,* **1**, 626–637 (1941).

9. DiPerri, R., A. Dravid, A. Schweigerdt, and H. E. Himwich, Effects of alcohol on evoked potentials of various parts of the central nervous system of cats, *Q. J. Stud. Alcohol* **29**, 20–37 (1968).

10. Dravid, A. R., R. DiPerri, A. Morillo, and H. E. Himwich, Alcohol and evoked potentials in the cat, *Nature*, **200**, 1328–1329 (1963).

11. Eidelberg, E., M. L. Bond, and A. Kelter, Effects of alcohol on cerebellar and vestibular neurones, *Arch. Int. Pharmacol. Ther.*, **192**, 213–219 (1972).

12. Eidelberg, E. and D. F. Wooley, Effect of ethyl alcohol on spinal cord neurones, *Arch. Int. Pharmacodyn. Ther.*, **185**, 388–396 (1970).

13. Engle, G. L. and M. Rosenbaum, Delirium III. Electroencephalographic changes associated with acute alcoholic intoxication, *Arch. Neurol. Psychiat.*, **53**, 44–45 (1945).

14. Feldstein, A., Ethanol-induced sleep in relation to serotonin turnover and conversion to 5-hydroxyindoleacetaldehyde, 5-hydroxytryptophol and 5-hydroxyindoleacetic acid, *Ann. N.Y. Acad. Sci.*, **215**, 71–76 (1973).

15. Feng, T. P. and T. H. Li, Studies on the neuromuscular junction XXV. Eserine-like actions of aliphatic alcohols & ketones, *Chin. J. Physiol.*, **16**, 317–340 (1941).

16. Flourens, P., Action Exercée par Certaines Substances Immediatement Appliquées sur les Differentes Parties du Cerveau, *Mem. Acad. R. Sci.* (Feb. 7, 1831).

17. Fregly. A. R., M. Bergstedt, and A. Graybiel, Relationships between blood alcohol, positional alcohol nystagmus and postural equilibrium, *Q. J. Stud. Alcohol*, **28**, 11–21 (1967).

18. Gage, P. W. The effect of methyl, ethyl and n-propyl alcohol on neuromuscular transmission in the rat, *J. Pharmacol. Exp. Ther.*, **150**, 236–243 (1965).

19. Gibbs, F. A., E. L. Gibbs, and W. G. Lennox, Effect on the electroencephalogram of certain drugs which influence nervous activity, *Arch. Int. Med.*, **60**, 154–166 (1937).

20. Hedenström, I. V. and O. Schmidt, Electroencephalographische Untersuchungen nach Alkoholgabe, *Deutsche Z. Ges. Gerichtl. Med.*, **40**, 234–251 (1951).

21. Horsey, W. J. and K. Akert, The influence of ethyl alcohol on the spontaneous electrical activity of the cerebral cortex and subcortical structures of the cat, *Q. J. Stud. Alcohol*, **14**, 363–377 (1953).

22. Hurwitz, L., F. Battle, and G. B. Weiss, Action of the calcium antagonists cocaine and ethanol on contraction and potassium efflux of smooth muscle, *J. Gen. Physiol.*, **46**, 315–332 (1962).

23. Ishido, T., The effect of alcohol on the spinal reflex of the cat, *EEG Clin. Neurophysiol.*, **18**, 98 (1959).

24. Israel-Jacard, Y. and H. Kalant, Effect of ethanol on electrolyte transport and electrogenesis in animal tissues, *J. Cell. Comp. Physiol.* **65**, 127–132 (1965).

25. Israel, Y., H. Kalant, E. LeBlanc, J. C. Bernstein, and I. Salazar, Changes in cation transport and $(Na^+ K^+)$-activated adenosine tri-phosphate produced by chronic administration of ethanol, *J. Pharmacol. Exp. Ther.*, **174**, 330–336 (1970).

26. Israel, Y., H. Kalant, and I. Laufer, Effects of ethanol on Na^+, K^+ Mg^{++}-stimulated microsomal ATPase activity, *Biochem. Pharmacol.*, **14**, 1803–1814 (1965).

27. Israel, Y., E. Rosenmann, S. Hein, G. Colombo, and M. Canessa-Fischer, Effects of alcohol on the nerve cell, Chapter II in *Biological Basis of Alcoholism*, J. Mardones and Y. Israel (Eds.), Wiley, New York, 1971.

28. Jarlstedt, J., Experimental alcoholism in rats: protein synthesis in subcellular fractions from cerebellum, cerebral cortex and liver after long term treatment, *J. Neurochem.*, **19**, 603–608 (1972).

29. Jarlstedt, J. and R. Hultborn, Experimental alcoholism in rats: RNA content and com-

position in isolated cerebellar Purkinje cells after long term treatment, *J. Neuropath. Exp. Neurol.*, **31**, 346–351 (1972).

30. Jouvet, M., Recherches sur les Structures Nerveuses et les Mechanismes Responsables des Differentes Phases du Sommeil Physiologique, *Arch. Ital. Biol.*, **100**, 125–206 (1962).

31. Kalant, H. and Y. Israel, Effects of ethanol on active transport of cations, in *Biochemical Factors in Alcoholism*, Pergamon Press, Oxford, 1966.

32. Kalant, H., Y. Israel, and M. A. Mahon, The effect of ethanol on acetylcholine synthesis release, and degradation in the brain, *Can. J. Physiol. Pharmacol.*, **45**, 172–176 (1967).

33. Kalant, H., A. E. LeBlanc, and R. J. Gibbins, Tolerance to, and dependence on, some non-opiate psychotropic drugs, *Pharmacol. Rev.*, **23**, 135–191 (1971).

34. Kleeman, C. R., M. E. Rubini, E. Lamdin, and F. H. Epstein, Studies on alcohol diuresis II: the evaluation of ethyl alcohol as an inhibitor of neurohypophysis, *J. Clin. Invest.*, **134**, 448–455 (1955).

35. Knuttson, E. and S. Katz, Studies of the effect of ethanol on ionic permeability of muscle fiber membranes, *Acta Physiol. Scand.*, **68**, 109 (1966).

36. Kolmodin, G. M., The action of ethyl alcohol on the monosynaptic extensor reflex and the multisynaptic reflex, *Acta. Physiol. Scand. (Suppl. 106)*, **29**, 530–537 (1953).

37. Kucera, J. and C. M. Smith, Excitation by ethanol of rat muscle spindles, *J. Pharmacol. Exp. Ther.*, **179**, 301–311 (1971).

38. Landgren, S., G. Liljestrand, and Y. Zotterman, Wirkung von Alkohol, Aceton, Aether und Chloroform auf die Chemorezeptoren des Glomus Caroticum, *Naunyn-Schmiedebergs Arch. Pharmakol.*, **219**, 185–191 (1953).

39. Liljestrand, G., The effects of ethyl alcohol and some related substances on baroreceptor and chemoreceptor activity, *Acta Physiol. Scand.*, **29**, 74–82 (1973).

40. Loomis, A. L., E. N. Harvey, and G. Hobart, Electrical potentials of the human brain, *J. Exp. Psychol.*, **19**, 249–279 (1936).

41. McNichol, E. F., and R. Benolken, Blocking effect of ethyl alcohol on inhibitory synapses in the eye of Limulus, *Science*, **124**, 681 (1956).

42. Meyer-Lohmann, J., R. Hagenah, C. Hellweg, and R. Benecke, The action of ethyl alcohol on the activity of individual Renshaw cells, *Arch. Pharmacol.*, **272**, 131–142 (1972).

43. Mirsky, I. A., P. Piker, M. Rosenbaum, and K. Lederer, Adaptation of the central nervous system to varying concentrations of alcohol in the blood, *Q. J. Stud. Alchol*, **2**, 35–45 (1941).

44. Miyahara, J. T., D. W. Esplin, and B. Zablocka, Differential effect of depressant drugs on presynaptic inhibition, *J. Pharmacol. Exp. Ther.*, **154**, 118–127 (1966).

45. Moore, J. W., W. Ulbricht, and M. Takata, Effect of ethanol on the sodium and potassium conductances of the squid axon membrane, *J. Gen. Physiol.*, **48**, 279–295 (1964).

46. Nakai, Y., Y. Takeda, and S. Takaori, Effects of ethanol on the afferent transmission in the central visual pathway of cats, *Eur. J. Pharmacol*, **21**, 318–322 (1973).

47. Romano, J., M. Michael, and H. H. Merritt, Alcoholic cerebellar degeneration, *Arch. Neurol. Psychiat.*, **44**, 1230–1236 (1940).

48. Sauerland, E. K. and R. M. Harper, Effects of ethanol on EEG spectra of the intact brain and isolated forebrain, *Exp. Neurol.*, **27**, 490–496 (1970).

49. Sauerland, E. K., T. Knauss, and C. D. Clemente, Effect of ethyl alcohol on orbital-cortically induced reflex inhibition in the cat, *Brain Res.*, **6**, 181–183 (1967).

50. Sauerland, E. K., N. Mizuno, and R. M. Harper, Presynaptic depolarization of trigeminal cutaneous afferent fibers induced by ethanol, *Exp. Neurol.*, **27**, 476–489 (1970).

51. Shanes, A. M., Electrochemical aspects of physiological and pharmacological action in excitable cells, Part II. The action potential and excitation, *Pharmacol. Rev.*, **10**, 165–273 (1958).

52. Story, J. L., E. Eidelberg, and J. D. French, Electrographic changes induced in cats by ethanol intoxication, *Arch. Neurol.*, **5**, 565–570 (1961).

53. Wallgren, H., Effects of alcohol on biochemical processes in the central nervous system, *Psychosom. Med.*, **28**, 421–442 (1966).

54. Wayner, M. J., Effects of ethyl alcohol on lateral hypothalamic neurons, *Ann. N.Y. Acad. Sci.*, **215**, 13–37 (1973).

Opiates

55. Ahtee, L. and I. Kääriäinen, The effect of narcotic analgesics on the homovanillic acid content of rat nucleus caudatus, *Eur. J. Pharmacol.*, **22**, 206–208 (1973).

56. Albus, K., M. Schott, and A. Hertz, Interaction between morphine and morphine antagonists after systemic and intraventricular application, *Eur. J. Pharmacol.*, **12**, 53–64 (970).

57. Andrews, H. L., Brain potentials and morphine addiction, *Psychom. Med.*, **3**, 399–409 (1941).

58. Barasi, S. and M. H. T. Roberts, The Modification of bulbospinal facilitation of the monosynaptic reflex by 5-hydroxytryptamine precursors and antagonists, *J. Physiol.*, **229**(1), 33P (1973).

59. Barraclough, C. A. and C. H. Sawyer, Inhibition of the release of pituitary ovulatory hormone in the rat by morphine, *Endocrinology*, **57**, 329–337 (1955).

60. Beleslin, D. and L. Polak, Depression by morphine and chloralose of acetylcholine release from the cat's brain, *J. Physiol.*, **117**, 411–419 (1965).

61. Blake, P. H. and L. M. Halpern, The effects of morphine on intracranial self-stimulation behavior in rats, *The Pharmacologist*, **13**, 280 (1971).

62. Borison, H. L., The nervous system, in *Narcotic Drugs; Biochemical Pharmacology*, D. H. Clouet (Ed.), Plenum Press, New York, 1971.

63. Borison, H. L., B. R. Fishburn, and L. E. McCarthy, A possible receptor role of the subfornical organ in morphine-induced hyperglycemia, *Neurology*, **14**, 1049–1053 (1964).

64. Brooks, C. M., R. A. Goodwin, and H. N. Willard, The effects of various brain lesions in morphine-induced hyperglycemia and excitement in the cat, *Am. J. Physiol.*, **133**, 226–227 (1941).

65. Buxbaum, D. M., G. G., Yarbrough, and M. E. Carter, Biogenic amines and narcotic effects. I. Modification of morphine-induced analgesia and motor activity after alteration of cerebral amine levels, *J. Pharmacol. Exp. Therap.*, **185**, 317–327, (1973).

66. Cahen, R. L. and A. Wikler, Effects of morphine on cortical electrical activity of the rat, *Yale J. Biol. Med.*, **16**, 239–245 (1944).

67. Carroll, B. J. and P. T. Sharp, Monoamine mediation of the morphine-induced activation of mice, *Br. J. Pharm.*, **46**, 124–139 (1972).

68. Chin, J. H. and E. F. Domino, Effects of morphine on brain potentials evoked by stimulation of the tooth pulp of the dog, *J. Pharmacol. Exp. Therap.,* **132**, 74–86 (1960).

69. Clineschmidt, B. V. and E. G. Anderson, The blockade of bulbo-spinal inhibition by 5-hydroxytryptamine antagonists, *Exp. Brain Res.,* **11**, 175–186 (1970).

70. Collier, H. O. J. Tolerance, physical dependence and receptors, *Adv. Drug. Res.,* **3**, 171–188 (1966).

71. Davis, W. M., M. Babbini, and J. H. Khalsa, Antagonism by alpha-methyltyrosine of morphine-induced motility in non-tolerant and tolerant rats, *Res. Comm. Chem. Path. Pharmacol.,* **4**, 267–279 (1972).

72. Duggan, A. W. and D. R. Curtis, Morphine and the synaptic activation of Renshaw cells, *Neuropharmacology,* **11**, 189–196 (1972).

73. Eidelberg, E. and M. L. Bond, Effects of morphine and antagonists on hypothalamic cell activity, *Arch. Int. Pharmacodyn. Therap.,* **196**, 16–24 (1972).

74. Felpel, L. P., J. G. Sinclair, and G. K. W. Yim, Effects of morphine on Renshaw cell activity, *Neuropharmacology,* **9**, 203–210 (1970).

75. Foltz, E. L. and L. E. White, Experimental cingulumotomy and modification of morphine withdrawal, *J. Neurosurg.,* **14**, 655–673 (1957).

76. Frazier, D. T., K. Murayama, N. J. Abbott, and T. Narahashi, Effects of morphine on internally perfused squid giant axons, *Proc. Soc. Exp. Biol. Med.,* **139**, 434–438 (1972).

77. Frazier, D. T., M. Ohta, and T. Narahashi, Nature of the morphine receptor present in the squid axon, *Proc. Soc. Exp. Med.,* **142**, 1209–1214 (1973).

78. Frederickson, R. C. A. and C. Pinsky, Morphine impaires acetylcholine release but facilitates acetylcholine action at a skeletal neuromuscular junction, *Nature; New Biol.,* **231**, 93–94 (1971).

79. French, J. D. and E. E. King, Mechanisms involved in the anesthetic state, *Surgery,* **38**, 228–238 (1955).

80. Fujita, S., M. Yasuhara, and K. Ogiu, Studies on sites of action of analgesics. 2. The effect of analgesics on afferent pathways of pain, *Jap. J. Pharmacol.,* **4**, 41–51 (1954).

81. Fuxe, K. and U. Ungerstedt, Histochemical, biochemical and functional studies on central monoamine neurons after acute and chronic amphetamine administration, in *Amphetamine and Related Compounds*, A. Garattini and E. Costa (Eds.), Raven Press, New York, 1970, pp. 257–288.

82. Gangloff, H. and M. Monnier, Demonstration de l'impact des analgesiques morphiniques et d'une substance antimorphinique sur le cortex et le subcortex du lapin, *Helv. Physiol. Pharmacol. Acta,* **13**, c47–c48 (1955).

83. Gauchy, C., Y. Agid, J. Glowinski, and A. Cheramy, Acute effects of morphine on dopamine synthesis and release and tyrosine metabolism in the rat striatum, *Eur. J. Pharmacol.,* **22**, 311–319 (1973).

84. Gibbs, F. A., E. L. Gibbs, and W. G. Lennox, Effect on the electroencephalogram of certain drugs which influence nervous activity, *Arch. Int. Med.,* **60**, 154–166 (1937).

85. Goldstein, L. and J. Aldunate, Quantitative encephalographic studies on the effects of morphine and nalorphine on rabbit-brain, *J. Pharmacol. Exp. Ther.,* **130**, 204–211 (1960).

86. Goldstein, M., B. Anagnoste, and C. Shirron, The effect of trivastal, haloperidol and dibutyryl cyclic AMP on ^{14}C dopamine synthesis in rat striatum, *J. Pharm. Pharmacol.,* **25**, 348–351 (1973).

87. Harvey, J. A. and C. E. Lints, Lesions in the medial forebrain bundle: relationship between pain sensitivity and telencephalic content of serotonin, *J. Comp. Physiol. Psych.*, **74**, 28–36 (1971).

88. Haubrich, D. R. and D. E. Blake, Modification of the hypothermic action of morphine after depletion of brain serotonin and catecholamines, *Life Sci.*, **10**, 175–180 (1971).

89. Hebb, C. O. and H. Konzett, Difference between morphine and synthetic analgesics in their actions on ganglionic transmission, *Nature*, **163**, 720–721 (1949).

90. Herz, A., K. Albus, J. Metys, P. Schubert, and H. J. Teschemacher, On the central sites for the antinociceptive action of morphine and fentanyl, *Neuropharmacology*, **9**, 539–551 (1970).

91. Holtzman, S. G. and J. E. Villarreal, Morphine dependence and body temperature in rhesus monkeys, *J. Pharmacol. Exp. Ther.*, **166**, 125–133 (1969).

92. Jhamandas, K., J. W. Phillis, and C. Pinsky, Effects of narcotics analgesics and antagonists on the *in vitro* release of acetylcholine from cerebral cortex of the cat, *Br. J. Pharmacol.*, **43**, 53–66 (1971).

93. Jurna, I. The effect of morphine on the discharge of muscle spindles with intact motor innervation, *Int. J. Neuropharmacol.*, **4**, 177–183 (1965).

94. Jurna, I., W. R. Schlue, and U. Tamm, The effect of morphine on primary somatosensory evoked responses in the rat cerebral cortex, *Neuropharmacology*, **11**, 409–415 (1972).

95. Khazan, N., J. R. Weeks, and L. A. Schroeder, Electroencephalographic, electromyographic and behavioral correlates during a cycle of self-maintained morphine addiction in the rat, *J. Pharmacol. Exp. Ther.*, **155**, 521–531 (167).

96. Khazan, N. and J. R. Weeks, The electroencephalogram and electromyogram of self-maintained morphine addicted rats in relation to injections, *The Pharmacologist*, **10**, 189 (1968).

97. Kerr, F. W. L. and J. Pozuelo, Suppression of physical dependence and induction of hypersensitivity to morphine by stereotaxic hypothalamic lesions in addicted rats. A new theory of addiction, *Mayo Clin. Proc.*, **46**, 653–665 (1971).

98. Killam, E. K., Drug Action on the brain-stem reticular formation, *Pharmacol. Rev.*, **14**, 175–223 (1962).

99. Kosterlitz, H. W. and D. I. Wallis, The action of morphine-like drugs on impulse transmission in mammalian nerve fibers, *Br. J. Pharmacol.*, **22**, 499–510 (1964).

100. Kruglov, N. A. Effect of the morphine group analgesics on the central inhibitory mechanisms, *Neuropharmacology*, **3**, 197–203 (1964).

101. Lotti, V. J., P. Lomax, and R. George, Temperature response in the rat following intracerebral microinjection of morphine, *J. Pharmacol. Exp. Ther.*, **150**, 135–139 (1965).

102. Lotti, V. J., P. Lomax, and R. George, N-Allylnomorphine antagonism of the hypothermic effect of morphine in the rat following intracerebral and systemic administration, *J. Pharmacol. Exp. Ther.*, **150**, 420–425 (1965).

103. Lotti, V. J., P. Lomax, and R. George, Acute tolerance to morphine following systemic and intracerebral injection in the rat, *Int. J. Neuropharmacol.*, **5**, 35–42 (1966).

104. McClane, T. K. and W. R. Martin, Effects of morphine, nalorphine, cyclazocine, and naloxone on the flexor reflex, *Neuropharmacology*, **6**, 89–98 (1967).

105. McKenzie, J. S., The influence of morphine and pethidine on somatic evoked responses in the hippocampal formation of the cat, *Electroencephalogr. Clin. Neurophysiol.*, **17**, 428–431 (1964).

106. McKenzie, J. and N. Beechey, The effects of morphine and pethidine on somatic evoked responses in the midbrain of the cat, and their relevance to analgesia, *Electroencephalogr. Clin. Neurophysiol.,* **14,** 501–519 (1962).

107. Mabry, P. D. and B. A. Campbell, Serotonergic inhibition of catecholamine-induced behavioral arousal, *Brain Res.,* **49,** 381–391 (1973).

108. Magoun, H. W., Caudal and cephalic influences of the brain stem reticular formation, *Physiol. Rev.,* **30,** 359–474 (1950).

109. Martin, W. R. and C. G. Eades, A comparison between acute and chronic physical dependence in the chronic spinal dog, *J. Pharmacol. Exp. Therap.,* **146,** 385–394 (1964).

110. Matthews, W. R., G. Labrecque, and E. Domino, Effects of morphine, nalorphine, and naloxone on neocortical release of acetylcholine in the rat, *Psychopharmacology,* **29,** 113–120 (1973).

111. Martin, W. R., C. G. Eades, H. F. Fraser, and A. Wikler, Use of hindlimb reflexes on the chronic spinal dog for comparing analgesics, *J. Pharmacol. Exp. Ther.,* **144,** 8–11 (1964).

112. Mayer, D. J., T. L. Wolfle, H. Akil, B. Carder, and J. C. Liebeskind, Analgesia resulting from electrical stimulation on the brain stem of the rat, *Science,* **174,** 1351–1354 (1971).

113. Mizoguchi, K. and C. L. Mitchell, An evaluation of the effects of morphine on electrocortical recruitment in the cat and dog, *J. Pharmacol. Exp. Ther.,* **166,** 134–145 (1969).

114. Nash, P., B. Colasanti, and N. Khazan, Long term effects of morphine on the electroencephalogram and behavior of the rat, *Psychopharmacology* (Berlin), **29,** 271–276 (1973).

115. Nakamura, J. and C. L. Mitchell, The effects of morphine, pentobarbitol and chlorpromazine on bioelectric potentials evoked in the brain stem of the cat by electrical stimulation of the gingiva and tooth pulp, *J. Pharmacol. Exp. Ther.,* **178,** 232–240 (1971).

116. Navarro, G. and H. W. Elliott, The effects of morphine, morphinone, and thebaine on the EEG behavior of rabbits and cats, *Neuropharmacology,* **10,** 367–377 (1971).

117. Olds, J. and P. Milner, Positive reinforcement produced by electrical stimulation of septal area and other regions of rat brain, *J. Comp. Physiol. Psych.,* **47,** 419–427 (1954).

118. Olds, J. and R. P. Travis, Effects of chlorpromazine, meprobramate, pentobarbital and morphine on self-stimulation, *J. Pharmacol. Exp. Ther.,* **128,** 397–404 (1960).

119. Paton, W. D. M., The action of morphine and related substances on contraction and on acetylcholine output of coaxially stimulated guinea pig ileum, *Br. J. Pharmacol.,* **12,** 119–127 (1957).

120. Pelikan, E. W., The mechanisms of ganglionic blockade produced by nicotine, *Ann. N.Y. Acad. Sci.,* **90,** 52–69 (1960).

121. Pert, C. B. and S. H. Snyder, Opiate receptor: demonstration in nervous tissue, *Science,* **179,** 1011–1014 (1973).

122. Pinsky, C. and R. C. A. Frederickson, Morphine and nalorphine impair neuromuscular transmission, *Nature; New Biol.,* **231,** 94–96 (1971).

123. Pinto-Corrado, A. and V. G. Longo, An electrophysiological analysis of the convulsant action of morphine, codeine and thebaine, *Arch. Int. Pharmacodyn. Ther.,* **132,** 255–269 (1961).

124. Puri, S. K. and H. Lal, Effect of morphine, haloperidol, apomorphine and benztropine on dopamine turnover in rat corpus striatum: Evidence showing morphine-induced reduction in CNS dopaminergic activity, *Fed. Proc.*, **32**, 758 (1973).

125. Puri, S. K., C. Reddy, and H. Lal, Blockade of central dopaminergic receptors by morphine: effect of haloperidol, apomorphine or benztropine, *Res. Comm. Chem. Path. Pharm.*, **5**, 389–401 (1973).

126. Reis, D. J., P. Hess, and E. Azmitia, Changes in enzymes subserving catecholamine metabolism in metabolism in morphine tolerance and withdrawal in rat, *Brain Res.*, **20**, 309–312 1970.

127. Ritchie, J. M. and C. J. Armett, On the role of acetylcholine in conduction in mammalian nonmyelinated nerve fibers, *J. Pharmacol. Exp. Ther.*, **139**, 201–207 (1963).

128. Samanin, R., W. Gumulka, and L. Valzelli, Reduced effect of morphine in midbrain raphe lesioned rats, *Eur. J. Pharmacol.*, **10**, 339–343 (1970).

129. Samanin, R. and L. Valzelli, Increase of morphine-induced analgesia by stimulation of the nucleus raphe dorsalis, *Eur. J. Pharmacol.*, **16**, 298–302 (1971).

130. Satoh, M., K. Yamatsu, and H. Takagi, Sites of action of Ram-302 and nalorphine as morphine antagonists, *Neuropharmacology*, **9**, 533–538 (1970).

131. Schaumann, W., Inhibition by morphine of the release of acetylcholine from the intestine of the guinea pig, *Br. J. Pharmacol.*, **12**, 115–118 (1957).

132. Simon, E. J. and P. Rosenberg, Effects of narcotics on the giant axon of the squid, *J. Neurochem.*, **17**, 881–887 (1970).

133. Sinclair, J. G., Morphine and meperidine on bulbospinal inhibition of the monosynaptic reflex, *Eur. J. Pharm.*, **21**, 111–114 (1973).

134. Sinitsin, L. N., Effect of morphine and other analgesics on brain evoked potentials, *Int. J. Neuropharmacol.*, **3**, 321–326 (1964).

135. Soteropoulos, G. C. and F. G. Standaert, Neuromuscular effects of morphine and naloxone, *J. Pharmacol. Exp. Ther.*, **184**, 136–142 (1973).

136. Soulairac, A., C. L. Gottesmann, and J. Charpentier, Effects of pain and of several central analgesics on cortex, hippocampus and reticular formation of brain stem, *Int. J. Neuropharmacol.*, **6**, 71–81 (1967).

137. Takagi, H., M. Matsumura, A. Yanai, and K. Ogiu, The effect of analgesics on the spinal cord reflex activity of the cat, *Jap. J. Pharmacol.*, **4**, 176–187 (1955).

138. Teschemacher, H. J., P. Schubert, and A. Hertz, Autoradiographic studies concerning the supraspinal site of the antinociceptive action of morphine when inhibiting the hindleg flexor reflex in rabbits, *Neuropharmacology*, **12**, 123–131 (1973).

139. Trafton, C. L. and P. R. Marques, Effects of septal area and cingulate cortex lesions on opiate addiction behavior in the rat. *J. Comp. Physiol. Psych.*, **75**, 277–285 (1971).

140. Tsou, K. and C. S. Jang, Studies on the site of analgesic action of morphine by intracerebral microinjections, *Scientia Sinica*, **8**, 1099–1109 (1964).

141. Trendelenburg, U., The action of morphine on the superior cervical ganglion and on the nictitating membrane of the cat, *Br. J. Pharmacol.*, **12**, 79–85 (1957).

142. Valdman, A. V., The effect of analgesics on the descending reticular inhibitory system of the brainstem, in *New Data on the Pharmacology of the Reticular Formation of the Cerebrum*, Leningrad Med. Institute, Leningrad, USSR, 1958.

143. Vigouret, J., H. J. Teschemacher, K. Albus, and A. Herz, Differentiation between

spinal and supraspinal sites of action of morphine when inhibiting the hindleg flexor reflex in rabbits, *Neuropharmacology,* **12,** 111–121 (1973).

144. Walker, J. B. and J. P. Walker, Neurohumoral regulation of adenylate cyclase activity in rat striatum, *Brain Res.,* **54,** 386–390 (1973).

145. Wang, S. C., and H. L. Borison, Vomiting center: critical experimental analysis, *Arch. Neurol. Psychiat.,* **63,** 928–941 (1950).

146. Wang, S. C. and V. V. Glaviano, Locus of emetic action of morphine and hydergine in dogs, *J. Pharmacol. Exp. Ther.,* **111,** 329–334 (1954).

147. Wei, E., H. H. Loh, and E. L. Way, Neuroanatomical correlates of morphine dependence, *Science,* **177,** 616–617 (1972).

148. Whittier, J. R. and A. Orr, Hyperkinesia and other physiologic effects of caudate deficit in the adult albino rat, *Neurology* (Minn), **12,** 529–539 (1962).

149. Wikler, A., Sites and mechanisms of action of morphine and related drugs in the central nervous system, *Pharmacol. Rev.,* **2,** 435–507 (1950).

150. Wikler, A., Pharmacologic dissociation of behavior and EEG "sleep patterns" in dogs: morphine, N-allylnomorphine, and atropine, *Proc. Soc. Exp. Biol. Med.,* **79,** 261–265 (1952).

151. Wikler, A., Clinical and Electroencephalographic studies on the effects of mescaline, N-allylnomorphine and morphine in man, *J. Nerv. Ment. Dis.,* **120,** 157–175 (1954).

152. Wikler, A. and R. L. Carter, Effects of single doses of N-allylnomorphine on hindlimb reflexes of chronic spinal dogs during cycles of morphine addiction, *J. Pharmacol. Exp. Ther.,* **109,** 92–101 (1953).

153. Wikler, A. and K. Frank, Hindlimb reflexes of chronic spinal dogs during cycles of addiction to morphine and methadone, *J. Pharmacol. Exp. Ther.,* **94,** 382–400 (1948).

154. Wikler, A., H. Norell, and D. Miller, Limbic system and opioid addiction in the rat, *Exp. Neurol.,* **34,** 543–557 (1972).

Chapter Five

AN EVALUATION
OF TENSION MODELS
OF ALCOHOL CONSUMPTION

HOWARD CAPPELL, *Addiction Research Foundation, Toronto, Canada*

1. INTRODUCTION

Each day, millions of people drink in amounts ranging from the trivial to the pathological. Vast sums of effort and money are spent in an attempt to persuade individuals to drink more or to drink less. Hardly a day passes without mention of alcohol and its effects in the popular media. Although there is evidently no lack of interest in this issue, we still have no clear idea about why people do in fact drink. Few would quibble with the notion that much drinking occurs because it is in some way a *useful,* adaptive behavior; the argument arises only when someone proposes what the "uses" of alcohol might be. Since so many branches of science have been involved, it is hardly surprising that the range of views is wide to the point of utter confusion. But disciplinary differences notwithstanding, perhaps no hypothesis about the function of drinking has been pursued with as much diligence as the one that maintains that many people drink mainly to reduce anxiety and tension. Like many hypotheses about commonplace behavior, this "tension reduction theory" (TRT) owes its origin and longevity more to plausibility than proof. Acceptance of the classical pharmacological proposition that alcohol "may act as an analgesic, a soporific, an anesthetic, a narcotic, or a hypnotic" (85a, p. 26) has probably done much to reinforce the plausibility of the theory. This chapter reviews much of the scientific literature whereby the merits of the TRT may be judged. The review is quite thorough, but if the occasional paper has escaped my attention, I take solace in the fact that no single paper is likely to undermine the position to which a dispassionate review must inexorably lead. I attempt to highlight logical and methodological issues as well as substantive ones. Except in cases in which exceptional circumstances dictate, details of particular experiments are not presented exhaustively; for most of the first section of this chapter this has been done elsewhere (18). Finally, I consider approaches to the understanding and management of drinking which consciously eschew intervening constructs such as tension.

The TRT is essentially based upon two hypotheses. The first of these, which has been dubbed the TRH (18), is that alcohol reduces tension. The second is that organisms drink alcohol in order to benefit from its tension-reducing effect. Evidence bearing on each of these hypotheses will be considered separately.

2. SOME INFORMATIVE QUOTES

For the most part, this chapter deals only with papers in which the mettle of the TRH was tested against data. But an understanding of the natural history of the hypothesis would be incomplete without considering the role which psychodynamic theories have played in its perpetuation. The purpose here is to illustrate what appears to be a relatively uncritical and widely shared view, based largely on clinical practice with alcoholic patients, that drinking and anxiety reduction are closely wed. The Classified Abstract Archive (CAAAL) maintained by the *Quarterly Journal of Studies on Alcohol* served as the guide in the search for these quotes, which, beginning with a source published in 1941, are listed in Table 1. It is remarkable how little the categorical acceptance of this view was altered in subsequent years.

3. EMPIRICAL EVIDENCE

Attempts to gather empirical support for the TRT follow essentially two strategies. In the first, the attempt is to show that the administration of alcohol does indeed reduce tension. The criterion here is a predictable alteration of a behavior believed to be a function of some hypothetical tension state. In the second approach, the actual self-administration of alcohol is the crucial dependent variable, whether this be in an anthropological study of man or a laboratory investigation of mice. Each approach has idiosyncratic logical requirements and characteristic problems of interpretation, and an important goal of this presentation is to identify these.

Does Alcohol Reduce Tension?

If organisms drink alcohol because it reduces tension, it should be possible, and indeed it is essential, to show that alcohol modifies, in a predictable way, behaviors which reflect tension states. The term "tension" is used here as a generic construct which summarizes such diverse concepts as fear,

TABLE 1   SOME QUOTATIONS WHICH INDICATE THE PERVASIVE-
NESS OF THE TRT IN PSYCHODYNAMIC INTERPRETATIONS OF
DRINKING[a]

Quotation	Original Source	Year of Publication
Man's highly developed brain sees too far ahead, causing him anxiety when confronted with problems he feels unable to cope with. Alcohol, by depressing front brain function, helps man to escape this anxiety.	Dent (37)	1941
Tension of a bio-psychosocial nature is at the root of the alcoholic problem. Resolve this tension and you solve the problem of alcoholism.	Stewart (129)	1950
The symptoms that seemingly provoked alcoholism . . . were those of the anxiety syndrome. . . .	Williams (142)	1952
. . . alcohol addicts will have more anxiety than the nonaddicts . . . it is the function of alcohol to reduce this anxiety. . . .	Gibbins (51)	1952
Alcoholism is neither a symptom nor a disease. It is a tension-reducing activity, the source of tension being ordinary human problems.	Ullman (135)	1952
It appears that drinking and intoxication can be put in the service of defense mechanisms against various sources of anxiety.	Higgins (63)	1953
Alcohol is an effective sedative. It is the ability to intoxicate which has caused the use of alcohol to be treasured; the value lies in the anxiety-reducing function of intoxication.	Reed (117)	1953
The patient uses alcohol as a means of avoiding anxiety on an unconscious level and discomfort on a conscious level.	Bruner-Orne and Orne (16)	1954
Alcohol relieves anxiety temporarily and dulls the sense of failure constantly experienced by many who drink pathologically.	Smith (128)	1954
. . . through its pharmacological action, [alcohol] can relieve anxiety of whatever denomination.	Forizs (43)	1958

TABLE 1 (Continued)

Quotation	Original Source	Year of Publication
. . . it seems that alcohol reduces . . . anxiety and so provides the reinforcement which a drive-reducing theory of learning postulates.	Franks (45)	1958
Alcoholism in a phobic is, in effect, also a defensive mechanism against a continual, severe anxiety.	Podolsky (112)	1959
". . . since the alcohol is an instrument of social acceptance and anxiety reduction, the drink is rewarding. . . ."	Heilizer (60)	1964
The individual in stress situations makes a number of different responses, one of which may be the consumption of alcohol, which affords him temporary relief. Repetition of this behavior pattern eventually leads to a conditioned response between *stress* and the *consumption of alcohol*.	Lazarus (80)	1966
Narcotization via drinking is one of the four principal ways of avoiding anxiety in neurotics with pronounced symptoms of anxiety.	Faber (40)	1969
. . . most persons in this sample who drink excessively experience anxiety-affective results. . . . It may be this reason . . . that causes persons to drink progressively more. . . .	Wanberg (140)	1969
Alcohol provokes changes which will allow the "easing" of unpleasant, anxiety-provoking situations . . .	Bacon (6)	1973

[a] In all but three cases (37, 40, 117) the quotations are from original source material. The original sources were inaccessible despite thorough searches in the three cases indicated. Therefore material from the CAAAL cards is cited instead. Those familiar with the reliability of the information on the cards will recognize that this recourse does not fail to adequately represent the original sources. It would not be difficult to produce similar quotations from other authors. The examples chosen here are intended simply to give an idea of the breadth of acceptance of the anxiety-reduction hypothesis among clinical practitioners.

anxiety, frustration, etc., each denoting hypothetical aversive states which motivate behavior. Hypothetically, any manipulation that ameliorates tension will disrupt the behavior that it controls. Specific predictions of course depend upon particular assumptions of the model of tension in question. Usually, although not invariably, the required prediction is clear. A general failure to obtain positive results in this area would make it embarrassing to contend that the self-administration of alcohol is motivated by relief from tension. Since psychologists have been particularly industrious in devising human and animal models and indices of tension states, there is no shortage of relevant source material.

Avoidance and Escape Behavior

Avoidance and escape are two forms of behavior widely believed to be controlled by fear or anxiety. Consequently, the effect of alcohol on these behaviors provide crucial evidence for the TRT. Indeed, there have been a number of animal studies in which alcohol disrupted avoidance or escape at sufficiently high doses (21, 64, 69, 75, 139). Unfortunately, in none of these studies was there an effect of alcohol which could not be accounted for quite readily in terms of nonspecific sensory or motor effects of the drug. In a couple of instances (21, 139) the authors themselves favored such an explanation over one involving an intervening motivational state. A particularly useful kind of experiment in this context is one which attempts to hold constant the topography of a behavior while manipulating its underlying motivation. In two experiments, for example, the effects of alcohol on similar responses controlled by aversive or appetitive motivation were compared (8, 98). Alcohol disrupted performance in both kinds of situation, emphasizing the need to control for alternative explanations which do not require a tension construct.

Occasionally, alcohol has been shown not to impair but rather to enhance avoidance behavior (14, 33, 118). Such results would seem to contradict the TRT, but this is not necessarily the case; if tension and avoidance are nonmonotonically related (1), an agent which reduces tension could enhance avoidance behavior. But in the absence of an explicit test of this position, it becomes necessary to make post hoc assumptions to render the existing data consistent with the TRT. At best, this is an unsatisfying recourse to adopt in order to salvage an hypothesis.

Although negative results do not often find their way into print, there have been four such studies reported on alcohol and avoidance (11, 59, 89, and footnote). In each case alcohol simply failed to affect avoidance in rats;

* Litner, J. S. and R. G. Weisman, The Effects of Alcohol on the Conditioned Excitation and Inhibition of Fear. Paper presented at the meeting of the Canadian Psychological Association, Winnipeg, Manitoba, May 1970.

moreover, each experiment was executed with competence and care equal to that of studies in which positive results were obtained.

The literature on avoidance extinction presents a particularly confusing array of results. In three separate tests (72, 123, 76), alcohol facilitated the extinction of avoidance, which is in general accord with the requirements of the TRT. But more recently, there has been a series of experiments (10–12, 19) in which alcohol had quite the opposite effect. The findings of Cappell et al. (19) are especially damaging to the TRT because in the same experiment, chlordiazepoxide, a drug which is reasonably well established as an agent of anxiety reduction, speeded the extinction of avoidance. Thus, whereas chlordiazepoxide apparently weakened aversive control during extinction, alcohol enhanced it. If the maintenance of avoidance is based on an aversive motivational state, these results are indeed an embarrassment to the TRT.

An experiment by Anisman (5) illustrates a particularly important methodological issue in this area, and in drug research in general. In this generally excellent study, alcohol was found to interfere with both classical and instrumental aspects of avoidance conditioning. Although the results provided apparently unequivocal support for the TRT, a problem of interpretation exists because of the use of only a single dose of alcohol and a single level of fear (operationalized as shock intensity). At the same time, it is often claimed (e.g., 1) that fear level and performance efficiency are nonmonotonically related. Thus impaired avoidance may reflect either high or low levels of fear. Only a design in which several levels of fear are present, that is, a design incorporating more than one drug dose and more than one shock level, can provide evidence on this point. Consequently, using the same number of assumptions in each case, results such as Anisman's may indicate just as readily that alcohol increases fear as that it reduces fear. Counterintuitive as such a position may appear, it is one that has been proposed seriously (12) and for which empirical support (10–19) exists.

Conditioned Suppression

A sensory stimulus repeatedly paired with electric shock will soon come to suppress operant responding for food or water; this phenomenon, first explored by Estes and Skinner (39), is often used as an index of conditioned anxiety or fear. Thus any manipulation which restores responding suppressed in this way may be successful because it reduces fear. In an exhaustive study of conditioned suppression, Lauener (79) reported that alcohol was without effect. Goldman and Docter (53) did find that alcohol reduced conditioned suppression in cats, but at the same time discovered that the same dose of alcohol had a general excitatory effect on responding for food, even in the absence of the conditioned stimulus. Cicala and Hartley (22) were unable to find an effect of alcohol on conditioned suppression, but this was not true for all the drugs that they tested. And finally, Hendry and Van Toller (62) found that alcohol still further depressed responding already attenuated by a conditioned stimulus.

Studies of conditioned suppression, then, have done little to enhance the credibility of the TRT. This cannot be done entirely to faulty methodology, since success has been obtained with other drugs hypothesized to reduce tension, even in the same experiments (22, 79). There is reason, however, to question the adequacy of conditioned suppression as a model for anxiety in psychopharmacological investigations (17). Thus it may be that it is the model, rather than the properties of ethanol, which is called into question by the data.

Extinction and Partial Reinforcement

Like fear or anxiety, experimentally induced frustration appears to qualify as an aversive tension state (4). If alcohol reduces the aversiveness of such states, it should have consequences for behavior frustrated by nonreward. Miller and Miles (95) obtained results which were consistent with the TRT in one behavioral test, but contradictory in another. In an experiment derivative from that of Miller and Miles, Barry, Wagner, and Miller (9) once more tested the effect of alcohol on frustrated behavior. Frustration was apparently inhibited by alcohol, and importantly, an alternative explanation involving dissociation (see below) was excluded by the experimental design. In two other experiments (36, 131), however, alcohol was without effect on behavioral indices of frustration. Thus experiments on frustration do not generally support the TRT, although the most thorough one (9) does.

Audiogenic Seizures

The audiogenic seizure provided one of the earliest models of emotional behavior used to test the TRT in rats. When exposed to intense noise, many rats exhibit a period of frenetic activity followed by a convulsion and a catatonic state. In two independent experiments (34, 57), alcohol did in fact protect against audiogenic seizures. Greenberg and Lester took their results as evidence of alcohol's "mildly sedative" action, and proposed the large inferential leap that this action was the reason for man's moderate use of alcohol. Of course this may be so, but their data on seizure behavior in rats offered slim justification for such a conclusion. Indeed, the question of whether the audiogenic seizure is an appropriate model of emotional behavior is unresolved, so it is difficult to know what to conclude from these experiments.

Conflict and Experimental Neurosis

If not first in order of consideration in this review, experimentally induced conflict may claim primacy as the first laboratory model used in attempts to provide support for the TRT. Typically, the conflict paradigm consists of three experimental phases: training to approach for positive reinforcement (reward), the introduction of punishment for performing the approach response, and finally, testing under the influence of alcohol. Alcohol, if it reduces tension, should suppress the avoidance component of the conflict and remove its inhibitory control over approach. Masserman and his colleagues (83–85) described the aberrant behavioral symptoms produced by this procedure as "experimental neurosis." By showing that alcohol attenuated these symptoms, Masserman provided evidence for the TRT which continues to be cited almost 30 years later. It was Masserman's view that his experimental procedure provided a clinically relevant model for human neurosis, and that the resolution of such neurosis may have disposed man to become a drinker: "Nor is it irrelevant to note that men long ago learned to drink alcoholic beverages either as a 'bracer' to cloud and thereby mitigate the anticipated stresses of impended experiences, or as a hypnotic which blunts and disorganizes neurotic anxieties and symbolic hypersensitivities and thereby permits a regression to less inhibited and temporarily satisfying patterns of behavior" (85). One could not ask for a better statement of the TRT than this.

Work on conflict did not end with these early attempts. In his classic study, Conger (30) showed that a dose of alcohol which weakened avoidance behavior had comparatively little effect on approach; he therefore reasonably concluded that alcohol selectively reduced fear. From data such as these, Conger (31) went on to develop a theory of alcoholism in which tension reduction was the major construct. Other experimenters have also been essentially successful in showing that alcohol may reduce conflict (46–48, 127). However, there has been some question about the mechanism involved. Freed (49) has suggested that dissociation or impairment of discrimination might be involved in this phenomenon, but Grossman and Miller (58) were able to demonstrate conflict resolution with alcohol which could not be accounted for by dissociation. Barry and Miller (7) showed that alcohol ameliorated conflict when approach in a runway was the dependent variable and attributed this to the reduction of fear and anxiety; but when Barry et al. (9) used a lever-press response to measure conflict in a conceptually similar experiment, alcohol depressed appetitively and aversively motivated behavior equally. In comparing the two experiments, Barry et al. (9) attributed the inconsistency to a drug-situation interaction, but they were unable to specify the relevant situational differences.

In two cases, "conflict-induced behavior fixations," which are generated by a variant of the standard conflict procedure, have been studied (41, 99). The authors were able to develop successful therapeutic interventions in both studies, but treatment with alcohol was not one of them.

Although it is unusual to use an experimental conflict procedure with human subjects, one example was provided by Vogel-Sprott (137). Under certain conditions, alcohol restored responding which had been suppressed by a conflict procedure.

The conflict literature appears to be exceptional in providing comfort for adherents of the TRT. With a few exceptions, the empirical outcomes were quite consistent; the question of mechanism has been raised (49), but an explanation involving tension reduction does not seem unreasonable. This success contrasts markedly with other research in which tension was manipulated, and the discrepancy is not easy to explain, since the same underlying mechanism is purported to be involved in all the behavioral models. An elaborated TRT must be able to account for this discrepancy. Although the notion of drug-situation interactions might be invoked here (9) this does not resolve the issue but merely gives it a label.

Human Performance Under Stress

When human subjects are exposed to a slightly delayed auditory feedback of their own verbal production, an "anxiety state," accompanied by a disruption of verbal behavior, may result (66). If anxiety or stress mediates the behavioral disruption, alcohol would be expected to have a meliorative effect according to the TRT, but just the reverse appears to be the case (44, 66–68). There is one experiment in which alcohol appeared to offset an effect of stress on performance (77), but problems of data interpretation (cf. 18) limit the value of this study.

Psychophysiological Indicators

A favorite technique of researchers interested in "objective" measures of affective states is to obtain records of the physical and chemical activities which abound on and under the skin when affect is manipulated. The electrical resistance of the skin has been one of the most popular indices among students of alcohol's effects. Basal skin conductance (BSC) may be used as an index of chronic tension level, while galvanic skin response (GSR) may reflect emotional reactivity to specific environmental stimulation. Greenberg and Carpenter (56) reported confusing data for BSC, but were able to show a substantial reduction in GSR caused by alcohol. They suggested that alcohol reduced "emotional tension." Lienert and Traxel (81) found that alcohol reduced the magnitude of the GSR to verbal stimuli, but since they presented no evidence that the GSR to these stimuli had anything to do with anxiety, their conclusion that alcohol acted as an antianxiety agent remains in doubt. Other experiments using skin conductance have produced results which are mainly equivocal (32, 88) or negative (87).

Experiments on biochemical indicators of stress (42, 50, 52) have not materially advanced the TRT. Indeed, the best experiment in this category (38) indicated that physiologically, alcohol acts as a stressor rather than a stress reducer.

Risk-Taking Behavior

It has been suggested (132) that fear of negative consequences is a major inhibitor of risky behavior. If this is so, alcohol might be expected to increase the willingness to take risks. Such a tendency has been shown in two separate investigations (26, 132), although the authors of the latter work noted a methodological problem in Cohen's experiment. At the same time, they failed to explain why positive results were obtained with bourbon but not with vodka or a solution of synthetic alcohol containing comparable concentrations of alcohol. Two further experiments involving gambling games (70, 126) were unsuccessful in attempting to demonstrate effects of alcohol on risk.

Direct Assessment of Affect in Normal and Alcoholic Subjects

In all the research described to this point, inferences about tension states have been indirect, in that they were based on hypothetical models of affective behavior. Recently, however, there has been a great deal of excellent experimentation in which attempts have been made to obtain direct reports of affect from subjects during periods of alcohol administration. Most of these have involved alcoholic subjects, but there are two important experiments in which normal volunteers were used. Kalin, McClelland, and Kahn (71) provided college students the opportunity to drink at a fraternity party or in an informal group discussion. As assessed by Thematic Apperception Test stimuli, fear-anxiety was reduced by alcohol, but only in the party setting, and only after comparatively heavy drinking. In a similar study, Williams (141) found a decrease in self-ratings of anxiety and depression after a moderate amount of alcohol intake, but a reversal of this trend with heavier consumption. The decrease was taken as support for the TRT, but the subsequent return of anxiety and depression was attributed to alcohol's negative side effects. This appears to be a case of having one's theoretical cake and eating it too, especially in view of the fact that no placebo controls served in Williams' experiment.

Studies of the effects of alcohol on the mood of alcoholics have been most interesting indeed. Mayfield and Allen (86) compared self-reports of mood among groups of alcoholics, depressed patients, and normals, after intravenous administration of alcohol. Mood was improved from its previously disturbed level among depressed patients, but alcoholics failed to benefit affectively from their drug of choice. Menaker (93) was interested in the effect of the anticipation of drinking on alcoholics. Compared to a nonalcoholic control group, alcoholics increased in self-ratings of anxiety in anticipation of a single drink, leading Menaker to speculate that such a mechanism might play a role in the maintenance of drinking. Upon entering a potential drinking situation, the alcoholic would, according to this analysis, experience an increase in anxiety; in turn this would activate his most probable anxiety-reduction response, namely drinking, which would be reinforced by reducing the anxiety engendered by anticipating drinking in the first place. Unfortunately, evidence was provided only about the effects on anxiety of *expecting* to drink. Menaker relied on a selective review in establishing alcohol as a reducer of anxiety in normal humans and animals. For some reason, he took the reports of sober alcoholics (94) as evidence that alcohol may successfully reduce anxiety in this population, but completely overlooked the fact that just the opposite occurred when these alcoholics actually drank heavily in an experimental setting.

More recently, a body of evidence has accumulated to suggest that heavy drinking in alcoholics in fact has an effect strongly opposite to that required by the TRT. The experimental strategy of each of these studies has been relatively uniform. All involved the self-administration of alcohol by subjects diagnosed as alcoholics in the confines of a hospital ward especially designed for experimental research of this type. In each case, the experimenters were careful to obtain base line readings of affective state both before and during drinking. Although the studies were often concerned with other variables as well, the data of interest here were based primarily on self-report of affect by means of standardized mood scales, sometimes supplemented by clinical assessment. One of the earliest investigations of this type was reported by Mendelson et al. (94), who followed affective changes in 10 alcoholics during several experimental phases. During an early alcohol phase which followed a control period, subjects drank from 6 to 30 oz of whiskey per day over a 5-day period; most of the subjects reported that alcohol normally made them feel less tense, but during this initial period, anxiety levels were unaffected by drinking. For 14 subsequent days, the subjects drank 30 oz/day. Anxiety levels, as assessed by clinical and self-report methods, increased. Five days of drinking at a level of 40 oz/day ensued during which anxiety increased yet further, accompanied by depression and increased aggressiveness; notwithstanding the apparently negative affect induced by the experience, the subjects were strongly motivated to drink. Mendelson et al. could not help noting the discrepancy between their observations and the popular assumption that alcohol alleviates anxiety and depression. Their experience was to be confirmed again and again in subsequent research. McNamee, Mello, and Mendelson (90) studied affective changes during drinking in 12 male alcoholics. Interestingly, the subjects expressed the expectation of improved affect and interpersonal relations when questioned during a predrinking phase. But contrary to their predictions, both anxiety and depression increased significantly during the second or third day of drinking, growing even more intense as drinking continued. These consequences, however, did not seem to diminish drinking behavior. The authors reasonably concluded that this increase in distressing affect was paradoxical when viewed in the light of the expectations of the subjects prior to drinking. Consequently, they hypothesized that drinking in alcoholics is "not causally related to attempts to reduce anxiety or depression." This may be a conclusion which is stronger than justified by the data, since as the authors themselves noted, alcohol might have affected these individuals differently in a "real life" environment. Nonetheless, the results are an embarrassment to the TRT. Alcoholics fared somewhat better as predictors of their own behavior in an experiment by Tamerin and Mendelson (130). Each of four alcoholics studied expected a salutary effect of alcohol on anxiety, and psychiatric observation tended to confirm this prediction as true of the initial effect of alcohol during a protracted period of drinking. This effect quickly vanished as anxiety, guilt, and hostility mounted. Interestingly, the subjects seemed to forget the experience of negative affect when they regained sobriety. This disruption of memory has led to an intriguing hypothesis (106) by Peter Nathan, who has repeatedly obtained results which confirm that alcohol increases anxiety and depression in alcoholics (3, 107). The hypothesis, which is based upon the well-documented observation (54, 106, 121) that alcohol causes memory disturbances in alcoholics, is best summarized in the words of those who proposed it (106, p. 611):

To begin with, one might consider the function of alcohol as an anxiety-reducing agent, a function with obvious etiological significance.

Our data show, however, that neither skid-row alcoholics nor their nonalcoholic fellows reduced prevailing levels of anxiety or depression with alcohol, despite much folklore to the contrary. Instead, most alcoholic subjects showed heightened depression, anxiety, and hostility and more symptoms of psychopathology during drinking. Nonalcoholics, by comparison, demonstrated essentially no change in affect with alcohol and only a mild increase in psychopathology.

But if alcohol does not reduce the chronic alcoholic's anxiety and depression or increase his ease with people, why does he continue to drink, especially in view of the serious social, physical, and psychological sequelae of his drinking? Our view is that the phenomena of 'blackout', which accompany most chronic alcoholics' drinking episodes, may explain in part the maintenance of chronic alcoholism in the face of its 'punishing' capabilities. The blackout, one element of which may include a 'state-dependent' event, seems to begin several hours after the beginning of a drinking episode and continue in one form or another as long as the drinking episode itself does. During blackout the alcoholic is entirely conscious and capable of a full range of volitional behavior; after it he may not remember crucial aspects of his behavior during drinking. As a consequence, the alcoholic may remember when he is sober again how good alcohol made him feel when he first began to drink and forget how depressed and anxious he later became, how abusive he was to his wife and children, and how sick he felt during withdrawal.

If true, this hypothesis goes a long way toward resolving the apparent paradox presented by the many studies of self-administration in alcoholics. But there are some general points which should be made in the overall evaluation of this type of research, excellent and stimulating as it is:

1. Perhaps we should not make too much of alcoholics' predictions about what effects drinking will have on them. For instance, one group of investigators (90) noted that these predictions might be conditioned by the alcoholic subjects' responding to expectations placed on them by the experimenters. This need not of course involve explicit communication of expectation, since the subtle operation of communication processes between subject and experimenter is well known (120).

2. Even if alcoholics' expectations about the affective consequences of drinking are accurate, they may not be applicable to a laboratory situation. Perhaps some variables operate in the laboratory to produce affect not normally experienced in the "real life" situation. In fact, some alcoholics reported that they responded differently to alcohol in the study by Mendelson et al. (94) than they would have in their normal drinking environment.

3. For a variety of perfectly good and understandable reasons, the subjects in these studies are characteristically highly selected on a number of criteria. There is no way of telling whether this selection process may produce some bias toward the kind of results which have normally been obtained. It may be, for instance, that alcohol does have a tension-reducing function early in the development of a pattern of excessive drinking which acts as a reinforcer for continued consumption. This consequence of drinking could undergo a reversal as alcoholism progressed, but tension re-

duction would still demand recognition as an important etiological variable.

4. The major salvation of the tension reduction view is Nathan's hypothesis that alcoholics may forget the depression and anxiety associated with drinking, and remember only such positive affect as was experienced. Yet there are two problems with this ingenious suggestion. The first is that it requires selective blackout for the punishing aspects of drinking, and protection of the "positive" memory against blackout. There is no evidence for selectivity in the effects of alcohol on memory (54). A second problem is that this hypothesis must somehow account for why drinking should be free of control from its immediate consequences. It is a widely accepted principle of reinforcement that behavior is controlled by its most immediate consequences; the memory hypothesis requires that this principle not operate while drinking is actually taking place. It is not enough to suggest that drinking episodes recur because of failure to remember past unpleasantness—one must also explain why the immediately punishing effects of drinking do not suppress excessive consumption. One possibility is that other positive reinforcers maintain the behavior in spite of the punishment which it causes, but if this position is taken, there seems to be little point in adding the memory hypothesis to explain why the behavior persists. The problem then becomes to ascertain what these other reinforcers might be. In essence, the "paradox" dissolves to the extent that apparently punishing consequences are not seen as the only events controlling drinking. Perhaps also we should not project our personal views about what would seem to most people to be consequences one would wish to avoid; if all behavior were governed by rational considerations, there would probably be no alcoholics.

Overview of Theoretical and Methodological Issues

Before continuing with an examination of the literature in which the self-administration of alcohol has been the major dependent variable, it is worthwhile to stop and review the theoretical and methodological issues which are pertinent to the scientific evaluation of the material discussed up to this point. With the exception of the conflict literature (and even this was not totally exempt), equivocal, negative, and even contradictory evidence tended to predominate. Of course there is no single explanation which could totally account for this state of affairs, but several points deserve consideration:

1. As an increasing function of dose, alcohol may have effects which are empirically demonstrable but theoretically uninteresting from the point of view of the TRT. Experimenters have invoked both motor impairment

and motor stimulation as explanations for results in avoidance studies. If such mechanisms are satisfactory, the tension construct is not required.

2. Drug-situation interactions can occur such that a general hypothesis which appears confirmed in one experiment will fail in another. Unfortunately, the possibility of such interactions only becomes salient post hoc in an attempt to resolve otherwise troublesome inconsistencies. Although such interactions probably occur, their persuasiveness in accounting for discrepancies is devalued when the reasons for the interaction cannot be specified.

3. A great number of investigators have taken the experimental risk of failing to do full dose-response studies. Thus negative or contradictory results may reflect an arbitrary dose selection. Moreover, the possibility of dose-response interactions limits the generalizability of even the positive results of single dose studies.

4. Experimenters must deal not only with a drug which has a multiplicity of behavioral actions, but the psychological processes and models which are complex and poorly understood. Thus it is not always clear how a particular outcome should be interpreted with respect to the TRT.

5. There have been instances in which the results of experiments would have been much more compelling if alcohol had exerted a selective effect only on aversively controlled behavior, rather than disrupting appetitive responses as well. Many experiments could have been improved by incorporating a test of alcohol's effect on similar responses controlled by the two different sources of motivation.

6. The experimental design of many experiments in this area is "unbalanced" (58). If a response is acquired in the nondrug state and critical tests are made with animals treated with either alcohol or placebo, the conditions of testing resemble those of training more for placebo than for drugged animals. Drug effects on performance may thus reflect mechanisms which have little to do with constructs such as fear or anxiety, but rather are consequences of state-dependent learning (109). Controls for this type of alternative explanation exist (58), but have seldom been used.

7. A very general point has to do with the logic of inferring the cause for a behavior from one of its effects, no matter how reliable. Alcohol has many effects, one of which may well be that it reduces tension. But even if this is so, it is a large inferential leap to conclude that alcohol is consumed because of this property. In sufficient quantities, alcohol causes severe locomotor disturbance and gastric distress. These are *effects* of alcohol, yet few people would seriously propose that anyone drinks to obtain them. It should be evident that the cause for a behavior cannot logically be established by isolating one of its many consequences. Those who favor the TRT appear to have focused exclusively on a single property of alcohol,

one which is not well established at that, without adequate realization of this logical error.

Does Tension Increase Alcohol Consumption?

Although it is crucial to show that alcohol reduces tension, this is clearly not all that is required by the TRT. It remains to be shown that variations in tension are associated positively with variations in the self-administration of alcohol. Only when the manipulation of tension can produce a significant degree of alcohol intake can the role of tension in the etiology of drinking be substantiated. Approaches to this issue may be grouped into three categories.

Analysis of Societal Drinking Patterns

One way to assess the contribution of tension to drinking is to correlate indices of each within and across entire societies or cultural subgroups. It is not the purpose here to completely review the literature in this area, but rather to illustrate both the possibilities and limitations of examples of this research. By far the most famous of such studies is the influential and frequently cited work of Horton (65) which was reported in 1943. Horton began with the basic assumption that the ". . . primary function of alcoholic beverages in all societies is the reduction of anxiety." The major data of Horton's study were indices of sexual and aggressive behavior, which he assumed to be normally inhibited by anxiety. Observing that the probability of sexual and aggressive behavior increases when drinking occurs, Horton concluded that the *motive* for drinking is anxiety reduction. The flaw in this logic has already been discussed. Moreover, no convincing evidence was given to support the assumption that sexual and aggressive behavior are in fact controlled by anxiety. A second source of evidence was based on contingency tables relating indices of cultural features assumed to reflect anxiety with the extent of intoxication typically achieved when drinking occurred in particular cultures. In some analyses a positive association was found, but disconfirmations were no less frequent than confirmations of the relationship. Horton was inclined to discount the latter. There was no evidence that periods of anxiety and drinking coincided in time; if these occurred independently, the positive associations observed would require reinterpretation. Perhaps the most serious difficulty with this study, however, was the index of drinking itself. It did not involve quantification of the frequency or quantity of drinking, but instead estimated the degree of intoxication likely to occur during drinking episodes. The validity of this as an index of consumption can be questioned. In summary, although Horton's study is almost reflexively cited as evidence for the TRT even in experimental investigations, his data were not really very persuasive. Moreover, the validity of Horton's empirical findings has been challenged by Field (41a), who was unable to confirm Horton's position in a thorough anthropological investigation. Jellinek (70a) also challenged Horton's position on strictly theoretical grounds.

Lynn and Hampson (82) attempted to relate anxiety and alcoholism using information gleaned from 11 different countries. The former was measured by a questionnaire administered to university students, and the latter was estimated from deaths attributed to "alcoholism" and liver cirrhosis. Although a positive relationship of marginal significance was obtained, there were several serious problems which compromise the interpretation, the most serious of which was that the anxiety measurements and the mortality statistics were derived from totally different population subgroups. The degree of acceptance of the TRT is evident in a recent study (125) in which alcoholism statistics were actually used as the *exclusive* measure of anxiety within a population. There can be no better evidence of the uncritical acceptance of the TRT than this.

The data from such sociological and anthropological studies do not provide impressive support for the TRT. Indeed, there is a limit to the force of the evidence which can be obtained from research which is essentially limited to correlational methods. Moreover, there are difficult problems in attempting to construct indices of tension, and even of alcohol consumption, adequate to testing derivations from the TRT. Although good studies of this type might advance the TRT, it is difficult to provide compelling evidence when control over potentially relevant variables is virtually impossible.

Correlational Studies of Alcohol Self-Administration

One of the early attempts to show a relationship between tension and drinking in animals was made by Dember and Kristofferson (35), who correlated consumption of ethanol with audiogenic seizure latency. A positive correlation was found, but there was no evidence that the same correlation did not obtain for water consumption. The authors noted an increase in alcohol consumption after seizures when the twelfth and sixteenth days of the experiment were compared, but neglected to point out that in both cases mean consumption was lower than preseizure levels. In any event, alcohol intake was not great at any point in the experiment. Tobach (134) correlated alcohol preference with a number of indices of "emotionality" in rats. Although the investigation had many flaws and significant correlations were obtained in only 4 of 66 tests, such relationship as existed was negative. Korn (78) was able to demonstrate a positive correlation between alcohol preference and a measure of emotional responsivity in rats, but only when the animals were exposed to a series of alcohol concentrations presented in a random rather than gradually increasing schedule. It was speculated that the random method was inherently more stressful and hence brought out the true relationship, since only in stressful conditions should the rats have sought relief in alcohol. But there was no independent confirmation that the schedules differed in stressfulness, nor was there evidence that a similar result might not have been obtained using any non-preferred solution other than alcohol.

Adamson and Black (1) found a significant nonmonotonic relationship between alcohol preference and avoidance learning. If avoidance learning is a measure of tension and if avoidance learning and tension are nonmonotonically related, these results suggest a positive association between tension and alcohol consumption. More recently, however, a careful attempt to replicate these findings failed (55); these experimenters found no relationship at all between alcohol preference and avoidance behavior in rats. A factor analytic study by Poley, Yeudall, and Royce (115) revealed a positive association between "emotionality" and alcohol preference in mice, a finding consistent with the TRT. Yet in a later investigation (114), the same experimenters determined that the relationship between alcohol consumption and emotionality was negative during the latter stages of preference testing; a few positive correlations were obtained, but only when a preference index based on relatively early exposure to alcohol was used. The general conclusion was that there is a relationship between stress *resistance* and alcohol consumption, and not the reverse as is demanded by the TRT. In fact, the results were not completely consistent with any single position. Further, there is no way of knowing whether the results reflected no more than taste preference and had little to do with the pharmacological effects of alcohol. This deficiency, however, is not unique to the Poley and Royce (114) study. Results more consistent with the TRT were obtained by Satinder (122), who showed that the alcohol preference of "emotionally reactive" rats exceeded that of their comparatively nonreactive counterparts. Citing earlier studies (35, 78, 115) as further confirmation, Satinder concluded that the enhanced alcohol preference represented a learned response to stress. As in many studies of this type, no attempt was made to determine whether the amounts consumed actually had the effect of relieving stress; that is, there is no way of telling whether the consumption levels were pharmocologically significant or behaviorally effective.

An overview of these correlational studies suggests that they provide some support for the TRT, but that contrary evidence is also available.

Several methodological problems of a general nature are relevant to this literature, but consideration of these will be deferred until after the next section.

Manipulated Tension and Alcohol Consumption

The previous studies were limited in their impact for all the reasons that compromise the interpretation of any correlational procedure. A much more persuasive methodology involves the actual manipulation of tension levels in an attempt to affect alcohol consumption. A large number of experimenters have adopted this technique. In most instances, the strategy has been to repeatedly apply stimulation which is believed to be stressful to an animal and measure the consequences for alcohol consumption. Repeated exposure to sonic stimulation was shown to increase rats' preference for alcohol (97), but the significance of this result is impossible to assess because no nonstimulated controls were included. In any event, a further increase in the frequency of stimulation was associated with a reversal in preference. The authors attributed this to an adaptation to stress with a consequently lowered need for anxiety reduction, but this is clearly not the only explanation for these data. A particularly unusual stressor was used by Brown (15), who for 2 weeks exposed mice to a 5 min daily spin on a 78 rpm turntable. Weekly records of alcohol consumption revealed a significant increase over base line during the period of the spinning treatment. However, the same result was true of water intake. In a second experiment, Brown found that group housing mitigated the effect of spinning on alcohol consumption, but the effect of spinning among isolated controls once more revealed a nonselective effect on fluid intake, as both alcohol and water consumption increased. Myers (100) reasoned that an extinction procedure might be sufficiently aversive to cause an increased preference for alcohol. During acquisition, rats could press any of three levers which yielded food, water, or alcohol. Each of these substances was then withheld during extinction. Although the animals were comparatively indifferent to the alcohol lever during acquisition, rats that had had prior forced exposure to a 20% solution increased responding on the alcohol lever during the early phase of extinction. Myers concluded that the stress-reducing properties of ethanol had been learned during the period of forced exposure, and that the animals turned to the alcohol lever for relief during the stress extinction. Controls with a history of exposure to alcohol, or with a history of exposure to a 5% solution, did not manifest similar behavior. Myers (101) reported somewhat comparable results elsewhere, and although proponents of the TRT can take comfort in the outcome, the interpretation of these results is subject to some limitations. First, there is a problem in demonstrating that the animals indeed learned to self-medicate to alleviate their stress during the period of forced exposure, since there was no evidence that they experienced any stress during this period. Secondly, the actual *self-administration* of ethanol was not demonstrated. Finally, there was no independent evidence that the extinction procedure was in fact stressful, although it may not be unreasonable to assume that it was.

There have been several attempts to manipulate tension levels by varying the stressfulness of the general living environment of animals. High population density was shown by Rodgers and Thiessen (119) to be a physiological stressor in mice, but it did not affect alcohol preference. The same authors (133) later found that this type of stress, if anything, reduced preference for ethanol. Heminway and Furumoto (61) found that the alcohol intake of rats in low and high density populations was less than that of animals housed in an intermediate density, but they were unable to interpret this nonmonotonic relationship.

A particularly ambitious attempt to test an environmental theory of alcoholism was reported by Clay (25). Using rats as subjects, Clay attempted to simulate a number of features which she believed to characterize human alcoholics: constitutionally low frustration tolerance, a restrictive early environment, a history of youthful exposure to insoluble conflict, the opportunity to learn to drink, and finally, exposure to stress during adulthood with alcohol available. Even granting the validity of the rat analogue, the data failed to confirm the theory. Fixation proneness had a significant effect on alcohol preference but in a direction opposite to prediction. Stress in adulthood was associated with increased preference, but the manipulation was confounded with food deprevation, which could equally well produce an increase in the selection of alcohol. The major contributor to variance in preference was sex, a variable which had no clear role in Clay's alcoholism model. Moreover, the data are difficult for an observer to evaluate, since alcohol/water ratios were presented in the absence of actual intake volumes. Persensky, Senter, and Jones (110) attempted to replicate a portion of Clay's study with controls for food intake, and found that rats exposed to insoluble problems actually preferred ethanol significantly less than controls. They concluded by doubting the adequacy of the TRT. A similar conclusion was reached by Kazmaier, Senter, and Butcher (73) who found that an environmental manipulation of "emotionality" did not affect rats' preference for alcohol. In their words: "The commonly accepted association of EtOH consumption with 'emotionality' fails, again, to be supported."

By far the most common variant of a stress procedure involves the application of a schedule of electric shock. Casey (20) gave rats 16 days of exposure to shock on a variable interval schedule. Preference for alcohol increased over a preshock base line, but only some days after shocks were terminated. Aside from the fact that a questionable data analysis procedure was used to tease out statistical significance, the experiment was compromised by lack of a nonshocked control group. Unavoidable shock appeared to produce an increase in preference in an experiment reported by Powell, Kamano, and Martin (115), but their stress manipulation was confounded and needed controls were lacking. Moreover, a nonstressed control group which was included had the highest mean consumption of alcohol, a finding which is hardly consistent with the TRT. Finally, when Myers and Holman (105) failed to find an effect of intermittent shock on alcohol consumption, they concluded that the application of unavoidable shock may simply have been an inappropriate stressor for their purpose.

The one procedure which has been effective in producing significant increases in alcohol consumption involves avoidance conditioning. Clark and Polish (24) were able to induce drinking to the point of intoxication in rhesus monkeys by exposing them to a demanding schedule of shock avoidance. However, Mello and Mendelson (91) were unable to produce comparable results; they found that a shock avoidance schedule did not add to an effect which was produced by mere exposure to alcohol. The most thorough analysis of the effects of avoidance learning on alcohol consumption has been provided by Myers and his associates (23, 102–104, 108, 136). Although there are still many features of this phenomenon which are unclear, the general finding has been that substantial intake of alcohol may be induced in rats by superimposing a regime of cued, unavoidable shock over a standard avoidance procedure. This is one of the few lines of research in which the investigators have been obviously concerned with *quantities* of alcohol consumed, and it appears that the procedure does indeed cause substantial increases in the absolute quantity of alcohol which rats will self-administer. But even though it has been possible to develop a stress procedure which increases alcohol consumption with reasonable reliability, the experiments in which this technique has been employed typically have failed to include evidence that the induced drinking did in fact mitigate the stressfulness of the procedure. Thus though Myers and Cicero (103) described their data as seeming "to support the notion that alcohol can serve to ameliorate experimentally-induced stress in animals," they actually had no support for the assertion that the enhanced drinking that they produced actually had such an effect. As we have already seen, this is not the first example of faulty logic in connection with the TRT.

Since Masserman and Yum's (85) demonstration that a conflict procedure increased the acceptability of alcohol to cats, two other experiments have reported comparable results (2, 138). In both cases, however, the conflict procedure was confounded with food deprivation, a consequence which is inevitable using a method which punishes approaches to food. Moreover, in neither case was there evidence of clear pharmacological consequences of the increased intake which was observed.

Overview of Studies of Self-Administration

A survey of research in which the self-administration of alcohol has been a dependent variable reveals that there is no straightforward conclusion which can be drawn vis-à-vis the TRT. Some positive results were obtained, but negative, equivocal, and contradictory results were also not uncommon. Following are some general points which must be considered in assessing this literature:

1.   Investigators very often have been content to report preference data without regard for the actual *quantities* of alcohol consumed. Thus even if a *statistically* significant change in preference were obtained, there is often no way of determining the *pharmacological* significance of a preference change. In some cases, no data on fluid intake volumes was presented, so it was impossible to ascertain the true mechanism whereby a preference change occurred.

2.   Alcohol has many effects and properties other than CNS action, but these have been widely ignored in self-administration studies involving stress procedures. For example, few investigators have been concerned with the possibility that stress procedures might alter the responsivity to the taste of alcohol, and there were a few cases in which the caloric value of alcohol provided an alternative explanation for positive results.

3.   The most reliable stress procedure for producing significant alcohol intake (e.g., 23) is highly circumscribed in that a very specific arrangement of contingencies is required. Thus there is some question about the generality of the implications of this success for the TRT, which would seem to require that a much wider variety of stressful situations produce comparable results.

4.   Even in those studies in which stress and alcohol consumption have gone together, there has been no conclusive proof that the results could best be explained by animals purposefully selecting alcohol for its meliorative effects on stress. It has already been mentioned that taste is usually ignored as a variable. In the strictly correlational studies, variables other than "emotionality" might have mediated such positive correlations as were obtained; such is the nature of correlational data. Even in studies in which manipulated stress resulted in increased alcohol consumption, *no evidence was ever presented that this behavior was actually effective in mitigating the effects of the applied stress.* This would appear to be a requisite of solid support for the TRT. A couple of interesting control groups come to mind

in this context, especially when considering results such as those of Cicero et al. (23). It would be useful, for example, to examine the effect of the procedure on a drug matched with alcohol for initial taste preference, but which has quite a different pharmacological effect. For instance, if the procedure increased the intake of CNS stimulants, one might question the role of stress reduction as an explanatory mechanism. Another useful control group would be one in which rats were preloaded with alcohol prior to exposure to a stress procedure. If the pharmacological consequences of alcohol are the mediators of increased drinking, such a treatment should offset the effectiveness of any stress manipulation which normally elevates alcohol intake.

To summarize then, even though it has been possible to show stress-induced increases in alcohol intake in highly restricted circumstances, there is no way to be certain whether reinforcement by stress *reduction* was the reason for the increase. Indeed, the mounting of an experiment which could convincingly show this seems to be quite a formidable task.

4. ALTERNATIVE APPROACHES

Partly due to disenchantment with the TRT, an increasing number of researchers and practitioners have turned toward analyses of drinking behavior which either actively eschew or simply ignore tension constructs. It is worth sampling the developments in this area to determine the scientific and practical merits of such orientations.

Animal Models

In recent years, the application of current thought in reinforcement theory has generated a considerable degree of research on the self-administration of alcohol. Some of this research has been directed explicitly toward discrediting the TRT. For example, Senter, Smith, and Lewin (124) made the avoidance of shock or the acquisition of food contingent upon licking an alcohol solution. When the contingencies were in effect, alcohol intake was high. When the contingencies were removed, the animals that had been rewarded with food persisted at drinking the alcohol solution longer than those that experienced the shock contingency, but in neither case was the persistence great. The authors concluded that the results represented an embarrassment for theories which accord stress reduction a central role in the maintenance of alcohol consumption. But there is clearly a major logical problem in drawing such strong conclusions from data such as these. The major issue, of course, is whether or not the shock avoidance model represents an adequate test of the TRT. This seems not to be the case, since the drinking response was merely an *arbitrarily selected operant*, the performance of which prevented shock presentation. A similar result could readily have been obtained using many fluids instead of alcohol, or indeed, with any number of motor responses. The TRT nowhere maintains that drinking obviates the *occurrence* of aversive stimulation, as in the Senter et al. paradigm, but simply that alcohol will mitigate the aversiveness of various kinds of stimuli. This is not to say that the TRT is adequate but only that the Senter et al. results do not comment directly on its validity. There have been numerous other demonstrations that high levels of alcohol ingestion may be maintained by positive (74, 11) and negative (92, 116) reinforcement contingencies. Such results clearly show that the immediate contingencies of reinforcement can affect alcohol consumption powerfulll. They further suggest that reinforcers other than tension reduction may play a role in the maintenance of excessive drinking. But they do not logically exclude the possibility that alcohol consumption may be reinforced by the reduction of tension.

One possibility which is usually overlooked is that the pharmacological effects of alcohol may be positively reinforcing per se. That this is so for monkeys has been demonstrated amply by Woods, Ikomi, and Winger (143). Without exposing their monkeys to stress or other unusual conditions, they were able to demonstrate the self-administration of large quantities of ethanol. Thus ethanol can clearly act as a powerful reinforcer in the absence of obvious tension or stress. The situation may be unique in that the route of administration was intravenous; moreover, there may be unidentified sources of stress in such a situation. At the same time, it is evident that ethanol may possess some actions which are intrinsically rewarding. If this is so in man as well, perhaps a great deal of drinking may be accounted for by this mechanism. Indeed it is somewhat surprising that this possibility has been virtually ignored in the single-minded search for evidence of the meliorative effects of alcohol.

Clinical Implications of the TRT

One of the best reasons for having a sound theory of behavior is to be able to derive suggestions for behavior change. The TRT has an unequivocal implication: if tension can be relieved by nonalcoholic means, the motivation for drinking will be diminished. Interestingly, it was impossible to locate a straightforward experimental test of this theoretical derivation. Nor were there any clinical demonstrations to support the treatment implications of the TRT. Thus it may be that even if the TRT is adequate, its contribution to date has been primarily academic.

Clinicians with a preference for the techniques of operant conditioning appear to have been moving into the treatment vacuum associated with strict adherence to the TRT. The intention here is not to review the relevant literature exhaustively, but simple to present a treatment philosophy and some illustrations of its application. A good example of this approach is provided in a laboratory experiment recently described by Cohen, Liebson, Faillace, and Allen (28). The description of their experiment was preceded by ana anslysis of the drive-reduction model of alcoholism as a manifestation of a learned drinking response reinforced by anxiety reduction. In their view, this theoretical analysis was discredited by the research described earlier in this paper (e.g., 90), in which alcohol exacerbated tension and anxiety in alcoholics. Rejecting intervening constructs such as anxiety as clinically superfluous, they attempted to demonstrate the efficacy of a contingency management procedure in which only strictly operational relationships were relevant. Briefly, they were able to show that severe alcoholics, when given virtually unrestricted access to alcohol, would consume it in moderation if access to an "enriched environment" were contingent on such drinking. With the contingency removed drinking rose dramatically. Their conclusion was that their results indicated ". . . that, despite its physiological determinants, excessive drinking can be governed by reinforcement contingencies which can be more readily manipulated than craving and anxiety." Clearly, this approach shows an intellectual communality with some of the animal research described in the preceding section. What should be noted is that the authors did not conclude from their results that the TRT was *wrong,* but only that it had little to commend it clinically.

The success of this kind of contingency management has been demonstrated repeatedly (13, 27, 29). Though certainly promising, the procedure shares the limitation associated with any contingency management program: how does one manipulate the contingencies outside of the laboratory?

Another example of this operational approach was provided by Mills, Sobell, and Schaeffer (96), who were able to induce alcoholics to drink moderately in a laboratory setting using an aversive conditioning procedure. They too were left with the question of the durability of such treatment beyond the controlled environment of the hospital. But although operant procedures share an important limitation, their success in controlling drinking in the laboratory suggests that a tension construct is not *necessary* clinically, even if it is relevant academically.

Although hampered by obvious limitations, operant procedures for the management of drinking have been shown to be effective in controlled environments. This approach is partially atheoretical in the sense that intervening psychodynamic constructs are simply irrelevant to the operational tactics. It cannot be asserted from the clinical efficacy of contingency management that the TRT is faulty, but only that it is not entirely necessary.

5. CONCLUSIONS

I have suggested that the TRT be evaluated as an academically sound theory and as a source of clinically relevant suggestions. In the first case, the evidence seems to suggest that the theory is badly flawed. There are but two bodies of research which offer reasonable support for the theory; these are the literature on the effects of alcohol on conflict, and the series of experiments demonstrating enhanced self-administration of alcohol in a very circumscribed stress situation. A large proportion of research bearing on the TRT fails to offer comfort for its supporters; perhaps most damaging are the frequent demonstrations that alcohol induces considerable negative affect in alcoholics. In addition to these substantive issues, errors of logic often have been made in adducing support for the TRT. Thus when judged solely on its merits as a theory, the TRT is substantially undermined. In a sense, this failure is perplexing since the rationale underlying the TRT seems so plausible and so consistent with commonplace experience. But in the final analysis, the evidence can lead to no other conclusion. As for its clinical relevance, the TRT certainly *has* implications, but if these have been applied successfully, the outcome has not been made public. Rather, the most successful behavioral control over drinking has emerged from a tradition which, as a matter of principle, ignores concepts such as tension. This new approach has enjoyed some modest success, but this has been limited to the laboratory. As I have attempted to emphasize, this success does not per se comment upon the merits of the TRT as a theory. It does suggest, however, that we begin to look elsewhere for operationally effective methods of modifying drinking behavior.

REFERENCES

1. Adamson, R. and R. Black, Volitional drinking and avoidance learning in the white rat, *J. Comp. Physiol. Psychol.*, **52**, 734 (1959).
2. Ahlfors, U. G., *Alcohol and Conflict; a Qualitative and Quantitative Study on the Relationship Between Alcohol Consumption and an Experimentally Induced Conflict Situation in Albino Rats,* Finnish Foundation for Alcohol Studies, Helsinki, Finland, 1969.

3. Allman, L. R., H. A. Taylor, and P. E. Nathan, Group drinking during stress: effects on drinking behavior, affect, and psychopathology, *Am. J. Psychiat.*, **129**, 45 (1972).

4. Amsel, A., The role of frustrative nonreward in noncontinuous reward situations, *Psychol. Bull.*, **55**, 102 (1958).

5. Anisman, H., Fear reduction and active avoidance learning following administration of alcohol during prior CS-shock exposure, *Q. J. Stud. Alcohol*, **33**, 783 (1972).

6. Bacon, S. D., The process of addiction of alcohol, *Q. J. Stud. Alcohol*, **34**, 1 (1973).

7. Barry, H. and N. E. Miller, Effects of drugs on approach-avoidance conflict tested repeatedly by means of a "telescope alley," *J. Comp. Physiol. Psychol.*, **55**, 201 (1962).

8. Barry, H. and N. E. Miller, Comparison of drug effects on approach, avoidance and escape motivation, *J. Comp. Physiol. Psychol.*, **59**, 18 (1965).

9. Barry, H., A. R. Wagner, and N. E. Miller, Effects of alcohol and amobarbital on performance inhibited by experimental extinction, *J. Comp. Physiol. Psychol.*, **55**, 464 (1962).

10. Baum, M., Paradoxical effect of alcohol on the resistance to extinction of an avoidance response in rats, *J. Comp. Physiol. Psychol.*, **69**, 238 (1969).

11. Baum, M., Effect of alcohol on the acquisition and resistance-to-extinction of avoidance responses in rats, *Psychol. Rep.*, **26**, 759 (1970).

12. Baum, M., Effect of alcohol on the resistance-to-extinction of an avoidance response; replication in mice, *Physiol. Behav.*, **6**, 307 (1971).

13. Bigelow, G., M. Cohen, I. Liebson, and L. A. Faillace, Abstinence or moderation: choice by alcoholics, *Behav. Res. Ther.*, **10**, 209 (1972).

14. Broadhurst, P. L. and H. Wallgren, Ethanol and the acquisition of a conditioned avoidance response in selected strains of rats, *Q. J. Stud. Alcohol*, **25**, 476 (1964).

15. Brown, R. V., Effects of stress on voluntary alcohol consumption in mice, *Q. J. Stud. Alcohol*, **29**, 49 (1968).

16. Bruner-Orne, M. and M. T. Orne, Directive group-therapy in the treatment of alcoholics: technique and rationale, *Int. J. Group Psychother.*, **4**, 293 (1954).

17. Cappell, H., R. Ginsberg, and C. D. Webster, Amphetamine and conditioned "anxiety," *Br. J. Pharmacol.*, **45**, 525 (1972).

18. Cappell, H. and C. P. Herman, Alcohol and tension reduction: a review, *Q. J. Stud. Alcohol*, **33**, 33 (1972).

19. Cappell, H., A. E. LeBlanc, and L. Endrenyi, Effects of chlordiazepoxide and ethanol on the extinction of a conditioned taste aversion, *Physiol. Behav.*, **9**, 167 (1972).

20. Casey, A., The effect of stress on the consumption of alcohol and reserpine, *Q. J. Stud. Alcohol*, **21**, 208 (1960).

21. Chittal, S. M. and U. K. Sheth, Effect of drugs on conditioned avoidance response in rats, *Arch. Int. Pharmacodyn.*, **144**, 471 (1963).

22. Cicala, G. A. and D. L. Hartley, Drugs and the learning and performance of fear, *J. Comp. Physiol. Psychol.*, **64**, 175 (1967).

23. Cicero, T. J., R. D. Myers, and W. C. Black, Increase in volitional ethanol consumption following interference with a learned avoidance response, *Physiol. Behav.*, **3**, 657 (1968).

24. Clark, R. and E. Polish, Avoidance conditioning and alcohol consumption in rhesus monkeys, *Science*, **132**, 223 (1960).

25. Clay, M. L., Conditions affecting voluntary alcohol consumption in rats, *Q. J. Stud. Alcohol,* **25,** 36 (1964).

26. Cohen, J., *Chance, Skill and Luck: The Psychology of Guessing and Gambling,* Penguin, Baltimore, 1960.

27. Cohen, M., I. A. Liebson, and L. A. Faillace, The role of reinforcement contingencies in chronic alcoholism: an experimental analysis of one case, *Behav. Res. Ther.,* **9,** 375 (1971).

28. Cohen, M., I. A. Liebson, L. A. Faillace, and R. P. Allen, Moderate drinking by chronic alcoholics, *J. Nerv. Ment. Dis.,* **153,** 434 (1971).

29. Cohen, M., I. A. Liebson, L. A. Faillace, and W. Speers, Alcoholism: controlled drinking and incentives for abstinence, *Psychol. Rep.,* **28,** 575 (1971).

30. Conger, J. J., The effects of alcohol on conflict behavior in the albino rat, *Q. J. Stud. Alcohol,* **12.** 1 (1951).

31. Conger, J. J., Alcoholism: theory, problem and challenge. II. Reinforcement theory and the dynamics of alcoholism, *Q. J. Stud. Alcohol,* **17,** 296 (1956).

32. Coopersmith, S., The effects of alcohol on reactions to affective stimuli, *Q. J. Stud. Alcohol,* **25,** 459 (1964).

33. Crow, L. T., Effects of alcohol on conditioned avoidance responding, *Physiol. Behav.,* **1,** 89 (1966).

34. Dember, W. N., P. Ellen, and A. B. Kristofferson, The effects of alcohol on seizure behavior in rats, *Q. J. Stud. Alcohol,* **14,** 390 (1953).

35. Dember, W. N. and A. B. Kristofferson, The relation between free-choice alcohol consumption and susceptibility to audiogenic seizures, *Q. J. Stud. Alcohol,* **16,** 86 (1955).

36. Denenberg, V. H., A. A. Pawlowski, and M. X. Zarrow, Prolonged alcohol consumption in the rat. I. Acquisition and extinction of a bar-pressing response, *Q. J. Stud. Alcohol,* **22,** 14 (1961).

37. Dent, J. Y., *Anxiety and its Treatment: With Special Reference to Alcoholism,* Murray, London, 1941.

38. Ellis, F. W., Effect of ethanol on plasma corticosterone levels, *J. Pharmacol. Exp. Ther.,* **153,** 121 (1966).

39. Estes, W. and B. F. Skinner, Some quantitative properties of anxiety, *J. Exp. Psychol.,* **29,** 390 (1941).

40. Faber, B., Anksiozne manifestacije kod kronicnoz alkoholicara (Manifestations of Anxiety in Chronic Alcoholics), *An. Bolnice Stojanoic,* **8,** 229 (1969).

41. Feldman, R. S., The prevention of fixations with chlordiazepoxide, *J. Neuropsychiat.,* **3,** 254 (1962).

41a. Field, P. B., A New Cross-Cultural Study of Drunkenness, in *Society, Culture, and Drinking Patterns,* D. J. Pittman and C. R. Snyder (Eds.), Chapter 4, John Wiley, New York, 1962.

42. Fleetwood, M. F., Biochemical experimental investigations of emotions and chronic alcoholism, in *Etiology of Chronic Alcoholism,* O. Diethelm (Ed.), Charles C Thomas, Springfield, Ill., 1955, pp. 43–109.

43. Forizs, L., Motivation of the alcoholic for recovery, *Q. J. Stud. Alcohol,* **19,** 133 (1958).

44. Forney, R. B. and F. W. Hughes, Effect of caffeine and alcohol on performance under stress of audiofeedback, *Q. J. Stud. Alcohol,* **26,** 206 (1965).

45. Franks, C. M., Alcohol, alcoholism and conditioning: a review of the literature and some theoretical considerations, *J. Ment. Sci.,* **104,** 14 (1958).

46. Freed, E. X., The effect of alcohol upon approach-avoidance conflict in the white rat, *Q. J. Stud. Alcohol,* **28,** 236 (1967).

47. Freed, E. X., Effect of alcohol on conflict behaviors, *Psychol. Rep.,* **23,** 151 (1968).

48. Freed, E. X., Effect of self-intoxication upon approach-avoidance conflict in the rat, *Q. J. Stud. Alcohol,* **29,** 323 (1968).

49. Freed, E. X., Alcohol and conflict: the role of self-intoxication in a punishment discrimination by rats, *Q. J. Stud. Alcohol* **33,** 756 (1972).

50. Geber, W. F., T. A. Anderson, and B. Van Dyne, Influence of ethanol on the response of the albino rat to audiovisual and swim stress, *Exp. Med. Surg.,* **24,** 25 (1966).

51. Gibbins, R. J., Undersocialization in the incarcerated alcohol addict, unpublished Master's thesis, Queen's University, 1952.

52. Goddard, P. J., Effect of alcohol on excretion of catecholamines in conditions giving rise to anxiety, *J. Appl. Physiol.,* **13,** 118 (1958).

53. Goldman, P. S. and R. F. Docter, Facilitation of bar pressing and "suppression" of conditioned suppression in cats as a function of Alcohol, *Psychopharmacologia* (Berl.), **9,** 64 (1966).

54. Goodwin, D. W., Blackouts and alcohol induced memory dysfunction, in *Recent Advances in Studies of Alcoholism,* N. K. Mello and J. H. Mendelson (Eds.), U.S. Government Printing Office Publication No. (HSM) 71-9045, 1971.

55. Gowdey, C. W. and J. Klaase, Voluntary alcohol consumption and avoidance learning by rats: lack of correlation, *Q. J. Stud. Alcohol,* **30,** 336 (1969).

56. Greenberg, L. A. and J. A. Carpenter, The effect of alcoholic beverages on skin conductance and emotional tension, I. Wine, whiskey, and alcohol, *Q. J. Stud. Alcohol,* **18,** 190 (1957).

57. Greenberg, L. A. and D. Lester, The effect of alcohol on audiogenic seizures in rats, *Q. J. Stud. Alcohol,* **14,** 385 (1953).

58. Grossman, S. P. and N. E. Miller, Control for stimulus-change in the evaluation of alcohol and chlorpromazine as fear-reducing drugs, *Psychopharmacologia* (Berl.), **2,** 342 (1961).

59. Harris, H. E., E. B. Piccolino, H. B. Roback, and D. K. Sommer, The effects of alcohol on counterconditioning of an avoidance response, *Q. J. Stud. Alcohol,* **25,** 490 (1964).

60. Heilizer, F., Conflict models, alcohol, and drinking patterns, *J. Psychol.,* **57,** 457 (1964).

61. Heminway, D. A. and L. Furumoto, Population density and alcohol consumption in the rat, *Q. J. Stud. Alcohol,* **33,** 794 (1972).

62. Hendry, D. P. and C. van Toller, Fixed-ratio punishment with continuous reinforcement, *J. Exp. Anal. Behav.,* **7,** 293 (1964).

63. Higgins, J. W., Psychodynamics in the excessive drinking of alcohol, *Arch. Neurol. Psychiat.,* **69,** 713 (1953).

64. Hogans, A. F., O. M. Moreno, and D. A. Brodie, Effects of ethyl alcohol on EEG and avoidance behavior of chronic electrode monkeys, *Am. J. Physiol.,* **201,** 434 (1961).

65. Horton, D., The functions of alcohol in primitive societies: a cross-cultural study, *Q. J. Stud. Alcohol*, **4**, 199 (1943).

66. Hughes, F. W. and R. B. Forney, Delayed audio feedback (DAF) for induction of anxiety, *J. Am. Med. Assoc.*, **185**, 556 (1963).

67. Hughes, F. W., R. B. Forney, and P. W. Gates, Performance in human subjects under delayed auditory feedback after alcohol, a tranquilizer (benzquinamide) or benzquinamide-alcohol combination, *J. Psychol.*, **55**, 25 (1963).

68. Hughes, F. W., R. B. Forney, and A. B. Richards, Comparative effect in human subjects of chlordiazepoxide, diazepam, and placebo on mental and physical performance, *Clin. Pharmacol. Therap.*, **6**, 139 (1965).

69. Hughes, F. W. and C. B. Rountree, Influence of alcohol-tranquilizer combinations on choice-discrimination in rats, *Arch. Int. Pharmacodyn.*, **133**, 418 (1961).

70. Hurst, P. M., R. Radlow, N. C. Chubb, and S. K. Bagley, Effects of alcohol and d-amphetamine upon mood and volition, *Psychol. Rep.*, **24**, 975 (1969).

70a. Jellinek, E. M., The symbolism of drinking, *Addiction Research Foundation Substudy* 3-2 and Y-65 (1965).

71. Kalin, R., D. C. McClelland, and M. Kahn, The effects of male social drinking on fantasy, *J. Pers. Soc. Psychol.*, **1**, 441 (1965).

72. Kaplan, H. S., The effects of alcohol on fear extinction, unpublished Ph.D. dissertation, Columbia University, 1955.

73. Kazmaier, K., R. J. Senter, and R. Butcher, Induced "emotionality" and ethanol consumption in rats, *Psychon. Sci.*, **29**, 331 (1972).

74. Keehn, J. D., "Voluntary" consumption of alcohol by rats, *Q. J. Stud. Alcohol*, **30**, 320 (1969).

75. Kopmann, E. and F. W. Hughes, Potentiating effect of alcohol on tranquilizers and other central depressants, *Arch. Gen. Psychiat.*, **1**, 7 (1959).

76. Korman, M., Alcohol and anxiety levels in the albino rat, I. Observationally defined anxiety, *Tex. Rep. Biol. Med.*, **18**, 34 (1960).

77. Korman, M., I. J. Knopf, and R. B. Austin, Effects of alcohol on serial learning under stress conditions, *Psychol. Rep.*, **7**, 217 (1960).

78. Korn, S. J., The relationship between individual differences in the responsivity of rats to stress and intake of alcohol, *Q. J. Stud. Alcohol*, **21**, 605 (1960).

79. Lauener, H., Conditioned suppression in rats and the effect of pharmacological agents thereon, *Psychopharmacologia* (Berl.) **4**, 311 (1963).

80. Lazarus, A. A., Towards the understanding and effective treatment of alcoholism, *S. Afr. Med. J.*, **39**, 736 (1965).

81. Lienert, G. A. and W. Traxel, The effects of meprobamate and alcohol on galvanic skin response, *J. Psychol.*, **48**, 329 (1959).

82. Lynn, R. and S. Hampson, National anxiety levels and prevalence of alcoholism, *Br. J. Addict.*, **64**, 305 (1970).

83. Masserman, J. H., Drugs, brain, and behavior: an experimental approach to experimental psychoses, *J. Neuropsychiat.*, **3**, S104 (1962).

84. Masserman, J. H., M. G. Jacques, and M. R. Nicholson, Alcohol as a preventive of experimental neuroses, *Q. J. Stud. Alcohol*, **6**, 281 (1945).

85. Masserman, J. H. and K. S. Yum, The influence of alcohol on experimental neuroses in cats, *Psychosom. Med.*, **8**, 36 (1946).

85a. McCarthy, R. G. (Ed.), *Drinking and Intoxication,* College and University Press, New Haven, Conn., in association with Rutgers Center of Alcohol Studies, New Brunswick, N.J. 1959.

86. Mayfield, D. and D. Allen, Alcohol and affect: a psychopharmacological study, *Am. J. Psychiat.,* **123,** 1346 (1967).

87. McDonnell, G. J. and J. A. Carpenter, Anxiety, skin conductance, and alcohol: a study of the relation between anxiety and skin conductance and the effect of alcohol on the conductance of subjects in a group, *Q. J. Stud. Alcohol,* **20,** 38 (1959).

88. McGonnell, P. C. and H. D. Beach, The effects of ethanol on the acquisition of a conditioned GSR, *Q. J. Stud. Alcohol,* **29,** 845 (1968).

89. McMurray, G. A. and L. B. Jacques, The effects of drugs on a conditioned avoidance response, *Can. J. Psychol.,* **13,** 186 (1959).

90. McNamee, H. B., N. K. Mello, and J. H. Mendelson, Experimental analysis of drinking patterns in alcoholics: concurrent psychiatric observations, *Am. J. Psychiat.,* **124,** 1063 (1968).

91. Mello, N. K. and J. H. Mendelson, Factors affecting alcohol consumption in primates, *Psychosom. Med.,* **28,** 529 (1966).

92. Mello, N. K. and J. H. Mendelson, The effects of drinking to avoid shock on alcohol intake in primates, in *Biological Aspects of Alcohol,* M. K. Roach, W. M. McIsaac, and P. J. Creaven (Eds.), Chap. 14, University of Texas Press, Austin, 1971.

93. Menaker, T., Anxiety about drinking in alcoholics, *J. Abnorm. Psychol.,* **72,** 43 (1967).

94. Mendelson, J. H., L. LaDou, and P. Solomon, Experimentally induced chronic intoxication and withdrawal in alcoholics, Part 3, Psychiatric Findings, *Q. J. Stud. Alcohol,* Suppl. 2, 40 (1964).

95. Miller, N. E. and W. R. Miles, Alcohol and removal of reward: an analytical study of rodent maze behavior, *J. Comp. Psychol.,* **21,** 179 (1936).

96. Mills, K. C., M. B. Sobell, and H. H. Schaeffer, Training social drinking as an alternative to abstinence for alcoholics, *Behav. Ther.,* **2,** 18 (1971).

97. Moore, W. T., B. M. Moore, J. B. Nash, and G. A. Emerson, Effects of maze running and sonic stimulation on voluntary alcohol intake of albino rats, *Tex. Rep. Biol. Med.,* **10,** 59 (1952).

98. Moskowitz, H., and H. Asato, Effect of alcohol upon the latency of responses learned with positive and negative reinforcers, *Q. J. Stud. Alcohol,* **27,** 604 (1966).

99. Murphree, O. D., and J. E. Peters, The effect of electroconvulsions, insulin comas and certain chemical agents on fixations in the rat, *J. Nerv. Ment. Dis.,* **124,** 78 (1956).

100. Myers, R. D., Changes in learning, extinction, and fluid preference as a function of chronic alcohol consumption in rats, *J. Comp. Physiol. Psychol.,* **54,** 510 (1961).

101. Myers, R. D., Effects of meprobamate on alcohol preference and the stress of response extinction in rats, *Psychol. Rep.,* **8,** 385 (1961).

102. Myers, R. D., Influence of stress on alcohol preference in rats, in *Alcohol and Alcoholism,* R. E. Popham (Ed.), Chapter 13, Addiction Research Foundation, Toronto, 1970.

103. Myers, R. D., and T. J. Cicero, Effects of tybamate on ethanol intake in rats during psychological stress in an avoidance task, *Arch. Int. Pharmacodyn.,* **175,** 440 (1968).

104. Myers, R. D. and T. J. Cicero, Effects of serotonin depletion on the volitional intake of rats during a condition of psychological stress, *Psychopharmacologia* (Berl.), **15,** 373 (1969).

105. Myers, R. D. and R. B. Holman, Failure of stress of electric shock to increase ethanol intake in rats, *Q. J. Stud. Alcohol,* **28**, 132, (1967).

106. Nathan, P. E., M. S. Goldman, S. A. Lisman, and H. A. Taylor, Alcohol and alcoholics: a behavioral approach, *Trans. N.Y. Acad. Sci.,* **34**, 602 (1972).

107. Nathan, P. E., N. A. Titler, L. M. Lowenstein, P. Solomon, and A. M. Rossi, Behavioral analysis of chronic alcoholism: interaction of alcohol and human contact, *Arch. Gen. Psychiat.,* **22**, 419 (1970).

108. Opsahl, C. A. and G. I. Hatton, Volitional ethanol increase during acquisition and extinction of avoidance responding, *Physiol. Behav.,* **8**, 87 (1972).

109. Overton, D. A., State-dependent or "dissociated" learning produced with pentobarbital, *J. Comp. Physiol. Psychol.,* **57**, 3 (1964).

110. Persensky, J. J., R. J. Senter, and R. B. Jones, Alcohol consumption in rats after experimentally induced neurosis, *Psychon. Sci.,* **15**, 159 (1969).

111. Persensky, J. J., R. J. Senter, and R. B. Jones, Induced alcohol consumption through positive reinforcement, *Psychon. Sci.,* **11**, 109 (1968).

112. Podolsky, E., The phobic chronic alcoholic, *Med. Times N.Y.,* **87**, 1651 (1959).

113. Poley, W. and J. R. Royce, Alcohol consumption, water consumption, and emotionality in mice, *J. Abnorm. Psychol.,* **79**, 195 (1972).

114. Poley, W., L. T. Yeudall, and J. R. Royce, Factors of emotionality related to alcohol consumption in laboratory mice, *Mult. Behav. Res.,* **5**, 203 (1970).

115. Powell, B. J., D. K. Kamano, and L. K. Martin, Multiple factors affecting volitional consumption of alcohol in the Abrams Wistar rat, *Q. J. Stud. Alcohol,* **27**, 7 (1966).

116. Ramsay, R. W. and H. vanDis, The role of punishment in the aetiology and continuance of alcohol drinking in rats, *Behav. Res. Ther.,* **5**, 229 (1967).

117. Reed, R. E., The problem of addictive drinking. I. Beverage alcohol in simple and complex societies, *N.C. Med. J.,* **14**, 101 (1953).

118. Reynolds, G. S. and P. van Sommers, Effects of ethyl alcohol on avoidance behavior, *Science,* **132**, 42 (1960).

119. Rodgers, D. A. and D. D. Thiessen, Effects of population density on adrenal size, behavioral arousal, and alcohol preference in inbred mice, *Q. J. Stud. Alcohol,* **25**, 240 (1964).

120. Rosenthal, R. and R. L. Rosnow (Eds.), *Artifact in Behavioral Research,* Academic Press, New York, 1969.

121. Ryback, R. S., Alcohol amnesia: observations in seven drinking inpatient alcoholics, *Q. J. Stud. Alcohol,* **31**, 616 (1970).

122. Satinder, K. P., Behavior-genetic-dependent self-selection of alcohol in rats, *J. Comp. Physiol. Psychol.,* **80**, 422 (1972).

123. Scarborough, B. B., Lasting effects of alcohol on the reduction of anxiety in rats, *J. Genet. Psychol.,* **91**, 173 (1957).

124. Senter, R. J., F. W. Smith, and S. Lewin, Ethanol ingestion as an operant response, *Psychon. Sci.,* **8**, 291 (1967).

125. Serebro, B., Total alcohol consumption as an index of anxiety among urbanised Africans, *Br. J. Addict.,* **67**, 251 (1972).

126. Sjöberg, L., Alcohol and gambling, *Psychopharmacologia* (Berl.), **14**, 284 (1969).

127. Smart, R. G., Effects of alcohol on conflict and avoidance behavior, *Q. J. Stud. Alcohol,* **26**, 187 (1965).

128. Smith, J. A., *Alcoholism,* Lippincott, Philadelphia, 1954.

129. Stewart, D. A., Alcoholism as a psychological problem, *Can. J. Psychol.,* **4,** 75 (1950).

130. Tamerin, J. S. and J. H. Mendelson, The psychodynamics of chronic inebriation: observations of alcoholics during the process of drinking in an experimental group setting, *Am. J. Psychiat.,* **125,** 886 (1969).

131. Taylor, A., R. Lehr, D. F. Berger, and C. A. Terry, Effects of alcohol on the partial reinforcement effect, *Psychon. Sci.,* **11,** 371 (1968).

132. Teger, A. I., E. S. Katkin, and D. G. Pruitt, Effects of alcoholic beverages and their congener content on level and style of risk taking, *J. Pers. Soc. Psychol.,* **11,** 170 (1969).

133. Thiessen, D. D. and D. A. Rodgers, Alcohol injection, grouping, and voluntary alcohol consumption of inbred strains of mice, *Q. J. Stud. Alcohol,* **26,** 378 (1965).

134. Tobach, E., Individual differences in behavior and alcohol consumption, *Q. J. Stud. Alcohol,* **18,** 19 (1957).

135. Ullman, A. D., The psychological mechanism of alcohol addiction, *Q. J. Stud. Alcohol,* **13,** 602 (1952).

136. Veale, W. L. and R. D. Myers, Decrease in ethanol intake following administration of p-chlorophenylalanine, *Neuropharmacol.,* **9,** 317 (1970).

137. Vogel-Sprott, M., Alcohol effects on human behaviour under reward and punishment, *Psychopharmacologia* (Berl.), **11,** 337 (1967).

138. Von Wright, J. M., L. Pekanmaki, and S. Malin, Effect of conflict and stress on alcohol consumption in rats, *Q. J. Stud. Alcohol.,* **32,** 420 (1971).

139. Wallgren, H. and S. Savolainen, The Effect of ethyl alcohol on a conditioned avoidance response in rats, *Acta Pharm. Toxicol.,* **19,** 59 (1962).

140. Wanberg, K. W., Prevalence of symptoms found among excessive drinkers, *Int. J. Addict.,* **4,** 169 (1969).

141. Williams, A. F., Social drinking, anxiety, and depression, *J. Pers. Soc. Psychol.,* **3,** 689 (1966).

142. Williams, E. Y., The anxiety syndrome in alcoholism, *Psychiat. Q.,* **24,** 782 (1950).

143. Woods, J. H., F. Ikomi, and G. Winger, The reinforcing property of ethanol, in *Biological Aspects of Alcohol,* M. K. Roach, W. M. McIsaac, and P. J. Creaven (Eds.), Chapter 16, University of Texas Press, Austin, 1971.

Chapter Six

COST OF ALCOHOLIC BEVERAGES AS A DETERMINANT OF ALCOHOL CONSUMPTION

HUNG-HAY LAU, *Informetrica Limited, Consultants in Economic Research, Ottawa, Ontario, Canada*

1. INTRODUCTION

Alcohol consumption has been studied in many ways, varying from a survey of sales by a number of families in some communities (5) to the extensive statistical work of Aarni Nyberg (14). In this paper, I can only survey the wide range of alcohol consumption studies by considering the effects on consumption due to price and income changes. The first part of this chapter consists of a survey of previous works in this area, pointing out the sources of differences among various estimates of price and income elasticities which measure the sensitivity of demand for alcoholic beverages to changes in price and income, respectively. The second part of the paper describes my estimation of the various elasticities based on Canadian data.

2. SURVEY OF ANALYSES OF DEMAND FOR ALCOHOLIC BEVERAGES

Empirical studies on the consumption of alcoholic beverages in different countries have produced different results and conclusions. This phenomenon can be attributed not only to a host of cultural and economic differences, and to the difference in the time period of analysis, but also to differences in the method of analysis.

Family Budget Data and Market Statistics

Empirical demand analysis derives its results from two main sources of statistical data: household survey statistics and time series data. In family budget data, the price is considered to be the same for all consumers and to be constant over the entire period under survey. Hence demand is not a function of price but is mainly a function of income. Consequently, the importance of price over consumption cannot be determined. The elasticities calculated from budget data are more analogous to long-term rather than short-term elasticities calculated from time series data. It assumes that if a low-income household attains the income level of a high-income household, it will adopt the expenditure pattern of the latter. This assumes away the period of time that is required for adjusting spending habit to the new income level. Therefore, the elasticity estimates obtained from budget data must be viewed as long-term elasticities.

From family budget data, one can obtain estimates of the income elasticities for alcoholic beverages for different social groups. For example, Nyberg (14) obtains estimates of income elasticity of demand for alcoholic beverages of 0.81, 1.29, and 0.82, respectively, for Finnish workers, salaried employees, and professionals for 1955. Harris' (9) estimates, presented in Table 1, show that income elasticities of demand for alcoholic drinks are different for regions of different degrees of urbanization.

However, it should be pointed out that elasticity estimates of demand for alcoholic beverages obtained from most family expenditure surveys are unlikely to be reliable because of serious understatement of spending on such beverages. The discrepancy between the true figure and the reported figure is so large as to throw considerable doubt on the estimates from this source. With regard to the demand for alcoholic beverages, it is better to rely on estimates of elasticities obtained from time series analyses.

Quantity and Expenditure Elasticities

From budget or time series data, two different types of elasticity estimates can be obtained. Elasticities of demand for alcoholic beverages can then be

TABLE 1 INCOME ELASTICITY OF DEMAND FOR ALCOHOLIC DRINKS, JAMAICA, 1958

Functional Form	Metropolitan	Main Towns	Rural
Double-log	1.837	2.464	2.238
Semi-log	1.026	2.592	1.752

Source: D. J. Harris, Econometric analysis of household consumption in Jamaica, *Soc. Econ. Stud.*, **1964,** 265–273.

divided into two types, namely, expenditure and quantity elasticities, according to whether the regressand is measured in terms of expenditure or in terms of volume. Although they both measure the dependence of demand upon income changes, they are meant to answer somewhat different questions. Expenditure elasticity shows the responsiveness of consumer spending with respect to changes in the purchasing power of the buyer and in price, quantity elasticity refers to the physical volume consumed. For the purpose of macroeconomic analysis concerned with consumers' propensity to consume, expenditure elasticity is more relevant. For the control of alcoholism and related problems, it is the quantity elasticity that is of greater relevance.

One may note that expenditure data cover both on-sale and off-sale (direct retail sale to consumers) beverage alcohol. Expenditure data therefore include the value of marketing services bought along with the purchase of alcoholic beverages consumed on premise. Expenditure elasticity may be interpreted as to contain two additive components, namely, quantity elasticity of demand and quality elasticity of demand. This can be illustrated below. Expenditure V is equal to quantity Q multiplied by price P which embodies the changes in the quality of the good. Let Y be income; then by definition, the expenditure elasticity can be expressed as

$$\frac{Y}{V} \times \frac{dV}{dY} = \frac{Y}{P \times Q} \times \frac{d(P \times Q)}{dY} = \frac{Y}{P \times Q} \left(P \frac{dQ}{dY} + Q \frac{dP}{dY} \right)$$

$$= \frac{Y}{Q} \frac{dQ}{dY} + \frac{Y}{P} \frac{dP}{dY} = E_y' + E_y''$$

where E_y' is the quantity elasticity and E_y'' is the quality elasticity which measures the proportionate change in prices at which consumers purchase the commodity in response to a change in income. In general, quantity elasticity is smaller than the corresponding expenditure elasticity. This is primarily because a rise in income or a fall in price not only leads to a higher volume of consumption but also shifts consumption toward more expensive qualities resulting in a more than proportionate increase in expenditure.

Table 2 presents various estimates of price and income elasticities derived from time series expenditure data. It may be observed that studies based on the Houthakker-Taylor hypothesis (11) produce estimates of both short-term and long-term elasticities. The short-term elasticities measure the reaction in the year of change in income (or price), whereas long-term elasticities measure the long-term effect of all previous changes after the reactions to the initial change have been felt. Such estimates are the result of the Houthakker-Taylor hypothesis which considers that there are dy-

TABLE 2   DEMAND ELASTICITIES DERIVED FROM EXPENDITURE DATA

Author and Country	Beverage	Expenditure Elasticity	Own-Price Elasticity
Malmquist, Sweden			
1923–1939[a]	Liquor	0.300	0.631
1923–1940[a]	Liquor	0.286	0.557
Bentzel, Sweden, 1931–1954	Beer and soft drink	0.679	—
	Wine and spirits	1.052	
Stone and Rowe, U.K.,	Beer	0.52 (LR) 0.68 (SR)	−0.40 (LR) −0.31 (SR)
1950–1956	Wine and spirits	2.18 (LR) 3.23 (SR)	1.05 (LR) −0.47 (SR)
Rowe, U.K., 1900–1960	Tobacco and drink	1900: 1.54	1900: −0.69
		1938: 1.23	1938: −0.26
		1960: 0.74	1960: −0.18
Houthakker–Taylor, U.S.,	Alcoholic beverages	0.68	—
1929–1960			
Taylor, Sweden, 1931–1958	Beer and soft drink	0.8879 (LR) 0.6361 (SR)	−1.1287 (LR) −0.5853 (SR)
Tran Van Hoa, Australia,	Wine and spirits	1.4988 (LR) 1.0825 (SR)	−0.6271 (LR) −0.8501 (SR)
1949–1965	Tobacco and drink		

214

National	0.13			−0.66
New South Wales	0.002			−0.001
Victoria	0.182			−0.062
Queensland	0.249			−0.123
South Australia	0.387			−0.258
Western Australia	0.641			−0.253
Tasmania	0.846			−0.270
Schweitzer, Canada, 1934–66 Alcoholic beverages	0.94 (LR)	0.88 (SR)	−0.21 (LR)	−0.19 (SR)

[a] During the period of analysis, the sale of liquor in Sweden was regulated by state rationing.

Sources: Malmquist, S., *A Statistical Analysis of the Demand for Liquor in Sweden*, University of Uppsala, Uppsala, Sweden, 1948.

Bentzel, R., *Den privata konsumtionen i Sverige 1931–65*, Almqvist and Wiksells, Stockholm, 1957.

Stone, R. and D. A. Rowe, Dynamic demand functions: some econometric results, *Econ. J.*, **1958**, 256–270.

Rowe, D. A., Private Consumption, in *The British Economy in 1975*, W. Beckerman (Ed.), 1965, pp. 177–200.

Houthakker, H. S. and L. D. Taylor, *Consumer Demand in the United States, 1929–1970*, Harvard University Press, Cambridge, 1966.

Taylor, L. D., Personal consumption expenditure in Sweden, 1931–1958, *Rev. Int. Stat. Inst.* **1968**, 19–36.

Tran Van Hoa, Interregional elasticities and aggregation bias: a study of consumer demand in Australia, *Aust. Econ. Paper*, **1968**, 206–226.

Schweitzer, T. T., *Personal consumer expenditure in Canada, 1926–1975*, Staff study number 26, Part I, Economic Council of Canada, Ottawa, 1969.

namic features in the expenditure pattern of consumers. The hypothesis considers that current consumption is affected not only by current expenditure and prices, but also by past consumption. In principle, the elasticity estimates derived from dynamic models are different from those obtained from static models. Conceptually, the elasticities estimated from a static equation should lie between the short-term and long-term elasticities because they represent some kind of an average of the long-term and short-term elasticities of the dynamic model.

Since the deleterious effect of alcohol consumption depends upon the quantity of pure alcohol consumed, students interested in the control of alcohol problems should focus attention on the relationship between the volume of alcoholic beverages consumed and factors that determine variations in its consumption.

Before we present the quantity elasticities obtained from time series regression analysis, it may be worthwhile to mention some attempts to establish the dependency of the consumption of alcohol on income and the price of alcohol by finding the degrees of correlation between consumption and income and consumption and price. Based on 1966 data for Poland, Tolkan (25) finds that per capita quantity consumption of alcohol is correlated highly with per capita purchasing power. Seeley (19) also obtains a high degree of correlation between per adult Canadian consumption of absolute alcohol and a constructed price variable over the period 1929–1956. This price variable is the ratio of the real price of absolute alcohol per gallon to real personal disposable income per adult. If one were to use this price-income ratio to explain consumption, it would be impossible to isolate the effect of price changes over consumption from that of income change. Expressed as the ratio of price to income, the use of this variable implies that the elasticity with respect to real price obtained with constant real income must necessarily be equal in magnitude and opposite in sign to the elasticity with respect to real income obtained with constant price. One implication of the negative relationship between consumption and the price-income ratio is that per adult consumption of absolute alcohol would increase even when the real price of alcohol is increased as long as there is a more than proportionate increase in real income. In order to measure the different effects which changes in price and income have over consumption, price and income should be treated as two separate determinants.

In Table 3, we have the estimates of the income and price elasticities of demand for various types of alcoholic beverages. It should be pointed out that the quantity series used by Richard Stone (22) and by Walsh and Walsh (27) are not the quantities sold to consumers but are the apparent consumption of alcoholic beverages. These series represent merely domestic production plus imports less exports. Such an estimate of consumption may involve errors depending on the variability of inventories held by retailers. In certain years, retailers increase their inventories to replenish the stock or to create reserves, resulting in an upward bias of consumption for those years. This will introduce some bias into the elasticity estimates.

Among the several alternative dynamic models tested, Nyberg prefers the formulations (those listed in Table 3) which constrain the coefficient on the last period purchase to the value of 0.7 implying a stock adjustment coefficient of 0.3. This coefficient of 0.7 is different from those obtained from statistical methods of estimation. The reason for using *a priori* coefficients is simply because Nyberg has more confidence in the value of 0.7 than in those derived from time series regressions. The validity of the estimates of income and price elasticity stands and falls with the validity of the assumption about the coefficient.

Most of the studies contained in Table 3 do not distinguish between per capita consumption changes from consumption changes attributed to changes in population since the dependent variable is the total quantity consumed by consumers as a whole. Walsh and Walsh, however, have used mid-year population as a deflator of total consumption to purge the influence of changes in population on the total volume of consumption. The authors recognize that ideally one should use adult population as the deflator.

In the economic literature, an attempt has been made to measure the price elasticity of demand for liquor in the United States without recourse to regression analysis. This is embodied in the work of Simon (20), which in essence applies the formula of price elasticity to measure the effect of independent observations of changes in state liquor tax on the consumption of liquor. In general, the price elasticity is obtained by dividing the percentage change in consumption by the percentage change in price. To purge the effect of other influences on changes in consumption, Simon introduces an adjustment into the calculation of the percentage change in consumption. The price elasticity is obtained in two steps. First, compute the percentage change in state liquor consumption for a 12-month period after a change in tax and deduct it from the corresponding change in comparison states where no changes in tax had taken place over the period under observation. Second, divide the resulting change in liquor consumption by the size of the tax change which is expressed as percentage of the retail price. Using 24 independent observations of tax changes of 23 U.S. states during the period 1955–1961, Simon obtains price elasticities ranging from 0.97 (for Rhode Island) to −4.35 (for Alaska), with a median value of

TABLE 3 DEMAND ELASTICITIES DERIVED FROM QUANTITY DATA

Author and Country	Beverage	Income Elasticity	Own-Price Elasticity
Malmquist, Sweden, 1923–1939[a]	Liquor	0.300	−0.369
	Wine	1.323	−0.716
Stone, U.K., 1920–1938	Beer	0.136	−0.727
	Spirits	0.54	−0.72
Niskanen, U.S.	Spirits	—	−1.74
Nyberg, Finland, 1949–1962	Vodka	0.417	−0.126
	Other spirits	1.296	−0.95
	Wines	0.97	−0.826
Static model	Malt beverages	0.219	−0.49
	Total off-sales	1.052	−1.173
	Total on-sale	0.938	−0.987
	Total sales (absolute alcohol)	1.009	−1.108

Dynamic model				
Vodka	0.84 (LR)	0.253 (SR)	−2.003 (LR)	−0.601 (SR)
Other spirits	1.62 (LR)	0.486 (SR)	−3.65 (LR)	−1.096 (SR)
Wines	1.29 (LR)	0.386 (SR)	−3.28 (LR)	−0.985 (SR)
Malt beverages	0.64 (LR)	0.191 (SR)	+0.01 (LR)	+0.003 (SR)
Total off-sales	1.14 (LR)	0.341 (SR)	−3.28 (LR)	−0.985 (SR)
Total on-sale	0.87 (LR)	0.261 (SR)	−1.26 (LR)	−0.379 (SR)
Total sales	1.03 (LR)	0.309 (SR)	−2.503 (LR)	−0.751 (SR)
Walsh-Walsh, Ireland, 1953–1967				
Beer	0.78		−0.17	
Spirits	1.94		−0.57	

[a] During the period of analysis, the sale of liquor in Sweden was regulated by state rationing.

Sources: Malmquist, S., A Statistical Analysis of the Demand for Liquor in Sweden, University of Uppsala, Uppsala, Sweden, 1948.
Stone, R., The analysis of market demand, J. R. Stat. Soc., 108 (Part III–IV), 286–382 (1945).
Niskanen, W. A., Taxation and the Demand for Alcoholic Beverages P-182, The Rand Corp., Santa Monica, Calif., 1960.
Nyberg, A., Alkoholijuomien kulutus ja H'mat, The Finnish Foundation for Alcohol Studies, Helsinki, 1967.
Walsh, B. M. and D. Walsh, Economic aspects of alcohol consumption in the republic of Ireland, Econ. Soc. Rev., 1970, 115–138.

−0.79 (for Missouri). Simon considers the median value of the price elasticity of demand of −0.79 to be the best estimate for the United States as a whole.*

It may be observed that the reliability of the estimate obtained from this procedure is contingent upon the availability of suitable comparison states. One may doubt whether factors (such as income and taste changes) other than price changes have the same impact on liquor consumption on various states.

3. PER ADULT CONSUMPTION OF ALCOHOLIC BEVERAGES, CANADA, 1949–1969

This part of the chapter describes an econometric study which estimates the elasticities of demand for three different types of alcoholic beverages based on Canadian data for the period 1949–1969. It differs from all previous studies in two respects. First, the dependent variable is *per adult* quantity consumption which is the volume consumption of alcoholic beverages deflated by the population of age 15 and over. Secondly, an attempt is made to cope with the statistical problem of multicollinearity in order to isolate the influences of price and income on per adult consumption of beer.

The aggregate demand for alcoholic beverages is the outcome of innumerable individual decisions which are affected by a large number of transient and long-term influences. Although transient influences cancel out for consumers as an aggregate, many important influences on the consumption of alcoholic beverages can be identified. In the present state of the art, price, income, and the price of substitutes have been identified as important determinants of the consumption of alcoholic beverages. The basic time series data required for analysis therefore include the quantity of alcoholic beverages consumed, the individual prices of these beverages, and the price of substitutes as well as personal disposable income.

Time Series Data

A brief description of the time series data used in the regression analysis is in order. Data on the quantity of alcoholic beverages consumed in Canada are based on sales figures published by Statistics Canada in various issues

* In a subsequent paper (21), Simon attempts to explain the variations in per capita liquor consumption among U.S. states. The multiple regression analysis based on 1961 cross-section data for 47 U.S. states concludes that liquor prices (expressed both by the composite-index price and the price of the best selling liquor) do not contribute toward explaining variations in per capita state consumption of liquor.

of the *Annual Reports on the Control and Sale of Alcoholic Beverages in Canada* (Queen's Printer and Controller of Stationery, Ottawa). The pre-1962 figures are obtained from tables published by the Brewers' Association of Canada rather than from Statistics Canada data since the data based on the former source are "adjusted to include estimates for provinces where figures are not published" (3, p. 119) by Statistics Canada.

As these sales data are published for each fiscal year ending on March 31, they have to be converted to calendar year estimates. The method of conversion is quite simple and straightforward. It takes the sum of $\frac{1}{4}$ of the current fiscal year estimate with $\frac{3}{4}$ of the estimate for the next fiscal year. The formula used is

$$CY1969 = \tfrac{1}{4} FY1969 + \tfrac{3}{4} FY1970$$

where

CY1969 = volume of beverage consumed in calendar year 1969
FY1969 = volume of retail sale of alcoholic beverage in fiscal year ending on March 31, 1969
FY1970 = volume of the retail sale of alcoholic beverage in fiscal year ending on March 31, 1970

Since practically all the alcoholic beverages sold are consumed by the adult population, the calendar year consumption is converted to per *adult* consumption by employing mid-year estimates of population of age 15 and over as the deflator. Per adult consumption of alcoholic beverages is then used as the dependent variable in the regressions. The availability of sales data has restricted the terminal year of the analysis to 1969 since sales data have been published only up to the fiscal year ending on March 31, 1970.

The price series for beer and spirits for Canada are obtained from Statistics Canada, Catalogue Number 62-002, *Price and Price Indexes,* for the periods 1949–1952 and 1958–1971, whereas the figures for 1953–1957 are supplied by Statistics Canada. Because no individual price indexes for alcoholic beverages were compiled prior to 1949, the beginning year of the regression analysis is constrained to 1949. In the compilation of the price indexes, alcoholic beverages are disaggregated into beer and liquor only. Since the sales value of wine represents a very small proportion of the total value of liquor sales, the liquor price index is used as the price index for spirits with insignificant departure from reality. The indexes for beer and spirits are deflated by the consumer price index to reflect the changes in the prices of beer and spirits relative to the movements in the price of consumer goods as a whole. Since no individual price index is compiled for wine, the price movement of wine can be obtained by deriving the average price of wine per gallon. This is obtained by dividing the total estimated calendar year sales of wine in dollar terms by the total estimated calendar year volume sales, measured in gallons. The resulting average price is deflated by the consumer price index with 1961 as unity and set to an index with 1961 as 100. This price index can be constructed only for calendar years 1953–1969, so the sample period for the wine analysis includes only 17 observations. In the analyses of spirits and beer, the sample period is 1949–1969 with 21 observations.

As the price of one alcoholic beverage relative to that of another may be expected to affect the quantities of individual alcoholic beverages consumed, the relative beer-spirits price is included as an additional explanatory variable in the analysis of per adult consumption of beer and spirits. Although the price index in the regression analysis for per adult consumption of wine is based on the average price of wine per gallon and is therefore different from the price indexes constructed for beer and spirits, the wine-beer and the wine-spirits relative price variables are incorporated and tested. These relative price variables are set to 100 in 1961. The inclusion of the relative price of different kind of alcoholic beverages is also useful as a means of testing whether these beverages are substitutes or complements.

Economic analysis suggests that it is the real personal disposable income that is the income determinant of consumption of alcoholic beverages. This includes personal income (which includes transfer payments) less personal direct taxes deflated by the consumer price index. It appears that it is the personal disposable income per capita rather than per adult that is the more appropriate determinant of per adult consumption of alcoholic beverages. Therefore the national income estimates are converted to the per capita basis at 1961 prices by deflating the income series by the total population and by the consumer price index with 1961 as unity.

The transformed data series utilized to run the regressions are shown in Tables 4 and 5. Per adult calendar year consumption of pure alcohol is obtained by summing up per adult consumption of spirits, beer, and wine, each multiplied by their alcohol contents, which are 0.40, 0.05, and 0.16, respectively.

Estimation and Evaluation of Statistical Results

In the regressions, a time trend variable assuming a value of unity in the beginning year of the sample period is added to the list of explanatory variables. The incorporation of the time trend variable is to take explicit account of taste trend as a device to reduce the variability in the universe and to isolate the effect of price changes.

TABLE 4 PER ADULT ANNUAL CONSUMPTION OF ALCOHOLIC BEVERAGES, CANADA 1949–1969 (GALLONS)

Year	Beer	Spirits	Wine	Absolute Alcohol
1949	18.0910	0.952386	0.506235	1.36650
1950	17.8443	0.987085	0.517351	1.36982
1951	18.2279	1.01160	0.523783	1.39984
1952	19.3673	1.05261	0.523668	1.47319
1953	19.8296	1.07654	0.526125	1.50627
1954	19.0271	1.07206	0.541305	1.46679
1955	19.3979	1.11360	0.556040	1.50430
1956	19.7854	1.17682	0.576087	1.55217
1057	19.8897	1.19957	0.601678	1.57058
1058	19.1007	1.25842	0.659578	1.56393
1959	19.7640	1.24240	0.668543	1.59212
1960	19.8996	1.24303	0.692230	1.60280
1061	19.9502	1.26439	0.719573	1.61840
1962	20.3272	1.29970	0.743381	1.65518
1963	20.8522	1.36130	0.789456	1.71344
1964	21.2357	1.34956	0.781154	1.72659
1965	21.2909	1.49174	0.878154	1.80174
1966	21.6642	1.56576	0.931782	1.85860
1967	21.9082	1.63053	0.973926	1.90345
1968	21.7415	1.61724	1.008410	1.89532
1969	22.1904	1.62661	1.131800	1.94125

Sources: Statistics Canada, Catalogue Number 63-202, *Annual Reports on the Control and Sale of Alcoholic Beverages in Canada*, Queen's Printer and Controller of Stationery, Ottawa.

Brewers' Association of Canada, *Brewing in Canada*, Ronalds-Federated Limited, Montreal, 1965.

Statistics Canada, Catalogue Number 91-201, *Estimated Population of Canada by Provinces*, September 1970.

Statistics Canada, Catalogue Number 91–203, *Population Estimates by Marital Status, Age and Sex for Canada and Provinces*.

Statistics Canada, Catalogue Number 91-511, *Population 1921–1966, Revised Estimates of Population by Sex and Age, Canada and the Provinces*.

TABLE 5 PRICE INDEXES AND PER CAPITA PERSONAL DISPOSABLE INCOME IN 1961 PRICES, CANADA 1949–1969

Year	Beer	Wine	Spirits	Wine/Spirits	Beer/Spirits	Wine/Beer	Income ($)
1949	107.313		106.163		101.083		1189.49
1950	107.789		104.987		102.668		1217.34
1951	106.182		100.568		105.582		1251.95
1952	103.769		98.658		105.180		1297.41
1953	104.698	97.173	99.630	97.533	105.086	92.8127	1334.60
1954	104.394	98.593	99.265	99.322	105.166	94.4438	1299.90
1955	104.351	100.403	99.134	101.280	105.262	96.2169	1366.56
1956	103.052	100.382	98.347	102.068	104.784	97.4089	1449.74
1957	101.548	100.413	99.597	100.820	101.959	98.8826	1450.15
1958	101.074	98.493	97.613	100.901	103.545	97.4464	1470.53
1959	100.531	99.460	99.622	99.838	100.912	98.9356	1486.60

1960	100.404	99.035	100.161	98.875	100.242	98.636	1500.18
1961	100.000	100.000	100.000	100.000	100.000	100.000	1475.00
1962	100.049	103.294	101.660	101.607	98.415	103.243	1560.39
1963	98.717	102.715	100.534	102.169	98.192	104.050	1600.09
1964	98.587	104.983	102.557	102.366	96.129	106.487	1634.80
1965	96.592	105.726	101.676	103.983	95.000	109.456	1718.36
1966	93.536	104.967	100.180	104.778	93.369	112.220	1788.34
1967	91.334	105.921	98.960	107.034	92.294	115.971	1830.88
1968	93.422	106.358	103.164	103.096	90.556	113.847	1879.66
1969	92.510	103.477	101.434	102.014	91.201	111.855	1926.05

Sources: Statistics Canada, Catalogue Number 62-002, *Price and Price Indexes*, Queen's Printer and Controller of Stationery, Ottawa.

Statistics Canada, Catalogue Number 63-202, *Annual Report on the Control and Sale of Alcoholic Beverages in Canada.*

Communication from National Income and Expenditure Division of Statistics Canada on June 29, 1972.

The estimation technique employed is the traditional ordinary least squares (OLS) with income, price, relative prices, and a time trend as the explanatory variables for the consumption of alcoholic beverages. Both the simple linear and the logarithmic linear functional forms are tested in the specifications presented in Tables 6, 7, and 11 to get the mathematical form that best describes the relationship. Whenever biases caused by the possible existence of the problem of serial correlations of the residuals are detected, the Hildreth-Lu method of correcting the biases is applied (10). The equation number of such regressions are marked with an apostrophe in Tables 6, 7, and 11 and the estimation technique is abbreviated as OLS H-L. The t ratios of the coefficients are set out underneath each coefficient in parenthesis. The addition of *** to the t ratio implies that the coefficient is significant at over 99% probability level, whereas those of ** and * indicate 95% and 90% probability levels, respectively. Values underneath the t ratios are estimates of elasticities calculated at the means. The coefficient of determination of the estimated equation, the coefficient of determination adjusted for degrees of freedom, the standard error of estimate, and the Durbin-Watson statistics are abbreviated as R^2, $\bar{R}^2$, SEE, and DW, respectively.

The statistical results are found to be very satisfactory. The coefficients of determination adjusted for degrees of freedom ($\bar{R}^2$) are extremely high in all cases for the three types of alcoholic beverages, particularly for spirits and wine. The standard errors of estimate of the regressions are very small, representing minute percentages of the respective means. The regression results indicate that the choice between linear arithmetic or linear logarithmic functions is of little importance since both specifications yield highly consistent conclusions. In most cases, the estimates of the mean elasticity obtained from the linear equations are of the same order of magnitude as those given by the log-linear specifications. It should be pointed out, however, that in general the mean elasticities obtained from a simple linear function will differ from the constant elasticities obtained from a logarithmic-linear function as indicated by the regression coefficient. The mean elasticity and the constant elasticity will be of similar magnitude only when the ratios between the observed variables do not change violently over the sample period.

The income variable is found to be the most important determinant of per adult consumption of alcoholic beverages of any kind. As shown in equations S5 and S6 in Table 6, the income variable alone explains about 99% of the total variations in the per adult consumption of spirits. In the case of beer, the proportion of variations explained by the income variable alone is about 99%, as indicated by equations B9 and B10 in Table 7. In Table 9, equations W9 and W10 show that the income variable alone accounts for 96% of the total variations in per adult consumption of wine.

Spirits

The regression results of per adult consumption of spirits are shown in Table 6. The most promising specification of the model is described in equation S3 where per adult consumption of spirits is a linear function of real personal disposable income per capita, the real price of spirits, and the relative beer-spirits price. The model works extremely well as these three explanatory variables together explain more than 99% of the total variations in per adult consumption of spirits. All these three explanatory variables are highly significant at the > 99.9% level. The income coefficient has the expected positive sign and the price coefficient has the expected negative sign. The consistently negative sign on the relative beer-spirits variable signifies that beer and spirits are complements rather than substitutes similar to the finding of the Walsh-Walsh study (27).

With the simple linear functional form, the time trend variable has not been found to be statistically significant as shown in equation S1. Actually, the inclusion of the time trend as an additional explanatory variable reduces the coefficient of determination adjusted for degrees of freedom, indicating that this variable does not contribute to the explanation of per adult consumption of spirits.

The income and price elasticities calculated at the means are 0.68 and −1.45, respectively. This income elasticity means that, *ceteris paribus,* a 1% increase in real personal disposable income per capita will result in a 0.68% increase in per adult consumption of spirits. The price elasticity of −1.45% implies that a 1% increase in the price of spirits will lead to a more than proportionate decrease (i.e., 1.45%) in the consumption of spirits, other variables remaining constant. An increase in the price of spirits will bring about an absolute reduction in expenditure on the consumption of spirits.

The statistical evidence reveals conclusively that the consumption of spirits is very sensitive to price changes. Not only is the estimated coefficient on the price variable highly significant at the > 99.9% level, but also the price variable is found, by applying the Farrar-Glauber test of interdependence (8), to be negligibly affected by the problem of multicollinearity that is almost inherent in practically all econometric time series regression analyses.

The coefficient on the time trend variable in equation S1 means that per adult consumption of spirits increases by 0.0012 gal annually. Using the mean of per adult spirits consumption for computation, this coefficient indicates that per adult spirits consumption is increasing at the annual rate of 0.94%. In equation S1, the time trend coefficient of 0.0058 signifies that per adult consumption of spirits has been increasing at the annual rate of 0.58% cumulatively.

TABLE 6 REGRESSION ANALYSIS OF THE CONSUMPTION OF SPIRITS, CANADA, 1949–1969

Equation Number	Estimation Technique	Functional Form	Constant Term	Real Income per Capita	Price of S / CPI	Price of B / Price of S	Time Trend	R^2	$\bar{R}^2$	DW Statistics	SEE as % of Mean
S1	OLS	Simple linear	4.141	0.0005416	−0.01796	−0.01901	0.001193	0.9941	0.9927	2.40	1.4676%
			(3.964)***	(4.179)***	(4.011)***	(3.977)***	(0.3528)				
				0.6462	−1.4277						
S2	OLS	Log-linear	5.941	0.5860	−1.173	−1.011	0.005817	0.9946	0.9932	2.11	6.25%
			(1.572)	(3.432)***	(3.548)***	(3.239)***	(1.876)*				
S3	OLS	Simple linear	4.163	0.0005695	−0.01823	−0.01925		0.9941	0.9930	2.41	1.429%
			(4.1)***	(5.697)***	(4.244)***	(4.176)***					
				0.6795	−1.4491						
S4	OLS	Log-linear	3.909	0.8380	−1.129	−1.001		0.9934	0.9922	1.89	6.697%
			(1.007)	(7.411)***	(3.195)***	(2.991)***					
S5	OLS	Simple linear	−0.2154	0.0009807				0.9876	0.9894	1.84	1.959%
			(5.593)***	(38.85)***							
				1.1701							
S6	OLS	Log-linear	−8.339	1.171				0.9894	0.9888	1.97	8.028%
			(41.030)***	(42.13)***							

Coefficients of Independent Variables (Values in parentheses are t ratios. Values beneath the t-ratios are mean elasticities.)

Dependent variable is gallons of spirits per adult. Beer, spirits, and the consumer price index are abbreviated as B, S, and CPI, respectively.

***Coefficient significant at over 99% probability level.
**Coefficient significant at over 95% probability level.
*Coefficient significant at over 90% probability level.

The Durbin-Watson statistics (7) computed for these equations show no existence of the problem of serial correlations of the residuals at the 1% level.

Although it is equation S3 that is the best specification of the model given the high coefficient of determination adjusted for degrees of freedom and the small standard error of estimate, some remarks about the rest of the specifications may be relevant. In all cases, the income variable, the price variable, and the beer-spirits relative price variable are highly significant at 99.9% probability level regardless of the choice of functional form. The income variable alone accounts for more than 98% of the entire variations in per adult consumption of spirits. The addition of the price and the relative beer-spirits price variables reduces about 50% of the residual variations.

In all these equations, the income and price variables consistently have the expected signs. The income and price elasticities obtained from the simple linear functional form are very similar to those obtained from the log-linear functional form. The variations in the price elasticities are very small ranging from the low of -1.13 in equation S4 to the high value of -1.45 in equation S3. From equations S1 to S4, the estimated income elasticities similarly vary very little from the low value of 0.586 in equation S2 to the high of 0.84 in equation S4.

Beer

Table 7 lists the regression results of the consumption of beer per adult. These results show that there is some moderate degree of serial correlation of the residuals in all the 10 regressions. To correct the bias introduced by the problem of first-order serial correlation of the residuals, the Hildreth-Lu (10) procedure is applied to all these cases. Assuming, for instance, that equation B1 is of a first-order Markov process so that the residuals ϵ_t is independently distributed,

$$\mu_t = \rho\mu_{t-1} + \epsilon_t. \tag{1}$$

Thus all the variables in equation B1 can be transformed as

$$V_t = V^*_t - \rho V_{t-1} \tag{2}$$

so that they will have an independently distributed error. The transformed equation becomes

$$(B_t - \rho B_{t-1}) = \alpha + \beta(Y_t - \rho Y_{t-1}) - \gamma(PB_t - \rho PB_{t-1})$$
$$+ \delta(PBPS_t - \rho PBPS_{t-1}) - \lambda(T_t - \rho T_{t-1}) \tag{3}$$

where B, Y, PB, $PBPS$, T, t and t-1 stand for per adult consumption of beer, per capita real income, real price of beer, beer-spirits relative price,

TABLE 7   REGRESSION ANALYSIS OF THE CONSUMPTION OF BEER PER ADULT, CANADA, 1949–1969

Equation Number	Estimation Technique Value of ρ	Functional Form	Constant Term	Real Income per Capita	Price of B CPI	Price of B Price of S	Time Trend	R^2 $\bar{R}^2$	DW Statistics SEE as % of Mean
B1	OLS	Simple linear	14.80 (1.111)	0.004193 (1.549) 0.31572	−0.05203 (0.5514) −0.26054	0.03757 (0.8831)	0.03694 (0.5374)	0.9292 0.9115	1.42 1.8837%
B1′	OLS H-L $\rho = 0.64298$	Simple linear	12.86 (2.533)**	0.004406 (1.587) 0.34188	−0.09544 (1.187) −0.4592	−0.1108 (1.278)	−0.1582 (1.145)	0.6901 0.6074	1.71 4.9016%
B2	OLS	Log-linear	0.3403 (0.1022)	0.3917 (1.657)*	−0.2026 (0.4427)	0.1571 (0.7546)	−0.0003789 (0.08831)	0.9265 0.9081	1.38 0.6419%
B2′	OLS H-L $\rho = 0.65095$	Log-linear	1.639 (1.347)	0.4014 (1.829)*	−0.4340 (1.104)	−0.5482 (1.241)	−0.009080 (1.288)	0.6711 0.5834	1.66 1.7367%
B3	OLS	Simple linear	14.67 (1.125)	0.005051 (2.359)** 0.38032	−0.06059 (0.6656) −0.30337	0.03856 (0.9266)		0.9279 0.9152	1.37 1.8438%
B3′	OLS H-L $\rho = 0.44539$	Simple linear	14.25 (1.902)*	0.003139 (1.347) 0.2403	−0.07317 (0.8935) −0.35824	−0.02993 (0.4121)		0.8096 0.7739	1.77 3.1455%
B4	OLS	Log-linear	0.2212 (0.07488)	0.4081 (2.879)***	−0.1997 (0.4509)	0.1550 (0.7723)		0.9265 0.9135	1.38 0.6229%

Coefficients of Independent Variables (Values in parentheses are t ratios. Values beneath the t ratios are mean elasticities.)

	Estimator	Form	(1)	(2)	(3)	(4)	(5)	R^2	$\bar{R}^2$	DW	
B4'	OLS H-L, $\rho = 0.39077$	Log-linear	1.282 (0.6044)	0.3162 (1.788)*	−0.2773 (0.6747)		−0.03023 (0.08574)	0.8246	0.7917	1.74	0.9892%
B5	OLS	Simple linear	19.16 (1.559)	0.003442 (1.348) 0.25917	−0.04710 (0.5033) −0.23583	−0.03955 (0.5797)		0.9257	0.9126	1.27	1.8714%
B5'	OLS H-L, $\rho = 0.39874$	Simple linear	13.32 (2.026)*	0.003945 (1.499) 0.31466	−0.07902 (0.9244) −0.38782	−0.008154 (0.08889)		0.8298	0.7978	1.78	2.9154%
B6	OLS	Log-linear	0.4740 (0.1444)	0.3974 (1.704)*	−0.08298 (0.1958)	−0.0000038 (0.00092)		0.9239	0.9105	1.29	0.6337%
B6'	OLS H-L, $\rho = 0.40367$	Log-linear	0.9926 (0.5656)	0.3889 (1.736)*	−0.3232 (0.7900)	−0.001876 (0.3759)		0.8202	0.7865	1.74	1.0065%
B7	OLS	Simple linear	19.15 (1.587)	0.00434 (2.180)** 0.3268	−0.05615 (0.6201) −0.28114			0.9243	0.9159	1.21	1.8366%
B7'	OLS H-L, $\rho = 0.39077$	Simple linear	13.45 (2.077)*	0.003784 (2.123)** 0.2891	−0.0767 (0.9579) −0.3766			0.8330	0.8134	1.77	2.7926%
B8	OLS	Log-linear	0.4753 (0.1637)	0.3973 (2.849)***	−0.08299 (0.2016)			0.9239	0.9154	1.29	0.6159%
B8'	OLS H-L, $\rho = 0.37788$	Log-linear	1.184 (0.6845)	0.3266 (2.356)**	−0.2804 (0.7166)			0.8300	0.8100	1.74	0.940%
B9	OLS	Simple linear	11.68 (20.75)***	0.005553 (15.06)*** 0.4181				0.9227	0.9186	1.26	1.8066%
B9'	OLS H-L, $\rho = 0.35702$	Simple linear	7.661 (13.63)***	0.005405 (9.659) 0.41243				0.8383	0.8293	1.78	2.6408%

TABLE 7 (Continued)

Equation Number	Estimation Technique Value of ρ	Functional Form	Constant Term	Real Income per Capita	Price of B / CPI	Price of B / Price of S	Time Trend	R^2 $\bar{R}^2$	DW Statistics SEE as % of Mean
B10	OLS	Log-linear	−0.1082 (0.5286)	0.4248 (15.17)***				0.9237 0.9197	1.31 0.60%
B10′	OLS H-L ρ = 0.34413	Log-linear	−0.04944 (0.2367)	0.4203 (9.684)***				0.8390 0.8300	1.75 0.8790%

Coefficients of Independent Variables (Values in parentheses are *t* ratios. Values beneath the *t* ratios are mean elasticities.)

Dependent variable is gallons of beer per adult. Beer, spirits, and the consumer price index are abbreviated as B, S, and CPI, respectively.

***Coefficient significant at over 99% probability level.

**Coefficient significant at over 95% probability level.

*Coefficient significant at over 90% probability level.

the time trend, year t, and year t-1, respectively. The optimum value of ρ for equation B1 is found to be 0.643 as shown in Table 7. The optimum values of ρ for the other equations are also listed in Table 7.

The persistent indication of the existence of the problem of serial correlation of the residuals reveals that some important determinants of per adult beer consumption may have been omitted from the regressions. It may appear that the consumption of beer is also influenced to a large extent by various kinds of beer advertisement. Unfortunately, this cannot be tested since there is no historical series on expenditure on beer advertisement. The only available information pertaining to advertising expenditure by manufacturers of alcoholic beverages is shown in Table 8. It can be observed that whereas the ratios of advertising expenditure to shipments change very little for the distilleries and the wineries over the period 1954–1965, the ratio exhibits a rapid increase for the breweries rising in 1965 to 300% its value for 1954. This trememdous increase in the ratio of advertising expenditure to shipment may reflect the importance of advertising expenditure on the sale of beer.

The statistical fit is considered to be rather satisfactory since more than 90% of the total variations in the consumption of beer is explained by equations B1, and B2. As shown in equations B9 and B10, the income variable alone accounts for 91% of the total variations in per adult beer consumption. It appears that the income variable is the most important determinant of beer consumption. The inclusion of the price variables and the time

TABLE 8 ADVERTISING EXPENDI-TURE AS PERCENT OF SHIPMENT, CANADA

Industry	1954[a]	1965[b]
Breweries	2.19%	6.56%
Distilleries	3.50%	2.74%
Wineries	2.89%	3.99%

[a] Source: Communication from Statistician, Service Trade Section, Merchandising and Service Division, Economic Statistics Branch, Statistics Canada.
[b] Source: Statistics Canada, Catalogue No. 63-216, *Advertising Expenditure in Canada, 1965*, Queen's Printer and Controller of Stationery, Ottawa.

trend does not add significantly towards explaining beer consumption. The price of beer, the relative beer-spirits price, and the time trend are therefore unlikely to be important determinants of beer consumption. In these regressions, the coefficients on the real income and on the real price variables consistently assume the expected signs.

In equation B1 the high coefficient of determination and the low level of significance of the variables symptomatizes the existence of substantial multicollinearity among the explanatory variables. To pinpoint the existence and the location of singularity within the independent set, the Farrar-Glauber method (8) of measuring the interdependence within the matrix is applied. The results are presented in Table 9.

The chi-square transformation for the matrix of correlation coefficients over the entire set is as high as 157 providing evidence that the problem of multicollinearity is particularly severe. The F statistics within the matrix used to measure the dependence of each independent variable on the others

TABLE 9   PER ADULT BEER CONSUMPTION, CANADA 1949–1969

Measure of Dependence

$R^2 = 0.9292$ $\bar{R}^2 = 0.9115$ $F (4, 16) = 52.494$ $SEE = 0.378$
$= 1.88\%$ of mean
$B = 14.80 + 0.004193\ Y - 0.05203\ PB - 0.03757\ PBPS + 0.03694\ T$
$\quad (1.11)\quad (1.549)\qquad (0.5514)\qquad\quad (0.8831)\qquad\qquad (0.5374)$

Measures of Interdependence

Determinant of correlation matrix = 0.000219
Chi Square (6) = 157

$$F_Y\quad (3, 17) = 275$$
$$F_{PB}\quad (3, 17) = 159$$
$$F_{PBPS}\ (3, 17) = \ \ 30$$
$$F_T\quad (3, 17) = 138$$

Pattern of Independence

	Y	PB	PBPS	T
Y	0.9798	−3.2123	−1.3659	3.0074
PB	−0.6146	0.9656	0.2442	−0.7067
PBPS	−0.3145	0.0591	0.8428	0.1777
T	0.5893	−0.1689	0.0431	0.9607

The abbreviations B, Y, PB, $PBPS$, and T stand for per adult consumption of beer in gallons, real personal disposal income per capita, real price of beer, beer-spirits relative price, and the time trend, respectively.

amply illustrate that income, real price of beer, the relative beer-spirits price, and the time trend are highly multicollinear though the relative beer-spirits price variable is less severely affected by multicollinearity compared with the other explanatory variables. The effect of multicollinearity is to diminish the identifiability of the separate influence of each explanatory variable over the dependent variable. Therefore, the estimates of the coefficients of the regressions are unreliable.

To minimize the problem of multicollinearity of the four explanatory variables, a subset of their principal components are used as explanatory variables following the method employed by Professor Dhrymes (6). The principal components are simply linear combinations of the four explanatory variables which capture most of the variability in the explanatory variables included in the regression. This study employs only the first two of the four principal components as explanatory variables since these two principal components account for 98.9% of the total movements of the four explanatory variables. The dimensionality of the problem is therefore reduced from four to only two with very little loss of explanatory power.

Since principal components are generally very sensitive to different units of measurement, the original variables are transformed to the same unit of measurement in terms of standardized deviates. The principal components of the standardized deviates of these four explanatory variables are then computed. The characteristic roots and vectors defining the principal components of income, real price, relative beer-spirits price, and the time trend are shown in Table 10. The first principal component alone accounts for 95.6% of the variance of the four series, and the first two principal components (PC_1 and PC_2) together account for 98.9% of such variance. Therefore, nearly all the information contained in the four series is embodied in the first two principal components, so that only these two are used as explanatory variables in the actual regression. This procedure helps approximate closely the identification of the coefficients of all the individual explanatory variables by reducing the incidence of collinearity through the reduction in the dimensionality of the data from four to two.

The parameter estimates using the first two principal components of the simple linear functional form of equation B1 and with the dependent variable expressed in standardized deviates are as the following:

$$\frac{B - \bar{B}}{s_B} = 0.4733 + 2.229 \, PC_1 + 1.836 \, PC_2 \qquad (4)$$

$$(2.187)^* \quad (14.84)^{***} \quad (2.243)^{**}$$

$$R^2 = 0.9260 \qquad \bar{R}^2 = 0.9178 \qquad SEE = 0.2939 \qquad DW = 1.38.$$

The parameter estimates of both of these principal components are highly

TABLE 10 CHARACTERISTIC ROOTS AND VECTORS ASSOCIATED WITH THE PRINCIPAL COMPONENTS OF Y, PB, PBPS, AND T

	PC_1	PC_2	PC_3	PC_4
Characteristic roots	3.8255	0.1289	0.0314	0.0142
Percent of variance accounted for	95.6	98.9	99.6	100.0
Characteristic vectors	0.5072	−0.5042	−0.4857	0.5027
	0.2127	−0.2752	0.8699	0.3498
	0.0612	−0.6975	0.0508	−0.7122
	0.8329	−0.4285	0.0699	−0.3431

The abbreviations B, Y, PB, $PBPS$, T, PC_1, PC_2, PC_3, and PC_4 stand for per adult consumption of beer in gallons, real personal disposal income per capita, real price of beer, beer-spirits relative price, the time trend, the first, second, third, and fourth principal component, respectively.

significant. The third and the fourth principal components have not been found to be statistically significant when used individually or in conjunction with the other components as explanatory variables. This together with the fact that the coefficient of determination thus obtained is almost identical with that obtained in equation B1 show that negligible explanatory power is sacrificed by discarding the third and the fourth principal components.

The coefficients obtained in equation 4 are then converted to the implied coefficients for the four original explanatory variables. By definition, the principal components are linear combinations of the standardized deviates of the four variables, that is,

$$PC_i = \psi_{1_i} \frac{Y - \bar{Y}}{s_Y} + \psi_{2_i} \frac{PB - \overline{PB}}{s_{PB}} + \psi_{3_i} \frac{PBPS - \overline{PBPS}}{s_{PBPS}}$$

$$+ \psi_{4_i} \frac{T - \bar{T}}{s_T} \tag{5}$$

where

$i = 1, 2$, for the first and second principal components
$\bar{Y}$ = the sample mean of Y
s_Y = the sample standard deviation of Y; and likewise for the other variables. Applying the results obtained from equation 4, we have

$$2.229 \, PC_1 + 1.836 \, PC_2 = \quad (2.229 \, \psi_{11} + 1.836 \, \psi_{12}) \, \frac{Y - \bar{Y}}{s_Y}$$

$$+ (2.229 \; \psi_{21} + 1.836 \; \psi_{22}) \frac{PB - \overline{PB}}{s_{PB}}$$

$$+ (2.229 \; \psi_{31} + 1.836 \; \psi_{32}) \frac{PBPS - \overline{PBPS}}{s_{PBPS}}$$

$$+ (2.229 \; \psi_{41} + 1.836 \; \psi_{42}) \frac{T - \bar{T}}{s_T}. \tag{6}$$

Substituting the values of the characteristic vectors shown in Table 10 into equation 6, we get

$$2.229 \; PC_1 + 1.836 \; PC_2 = 0.2048376 \frac{Y - \bar{Y}}{s_Y} - 0.0311589 \frac{PB - \overline{PB}}{s_{PB}}$$

$$- 1.266969 \frac{PBPS - \overline{PBPS}}{s_{PBPS}}$$

$$+ 2.64326 \frac{T - \bar{T}}{s_T}. \tag{7}$$

By substituting equation 7 into equation 4, we have

$$\frac{B - \bar{B}}{s_B} = 0.4733 + 0.2048 \frac{Y - \bar{Y}}{s_Y} - 0.0312 \frac{PB - \overline{PB}}{s_{PB}}$$

$$- 1.267 \frac{PBPS - \overline{PBPS}}{s_{PBPS}} + 2.643 \frac{T - \bar{T}}{s_T} \tag{8}$$

$$R^2 = 0.9260 \qquad SEE = 0.2939 \qquad DW = 1.38.$$

Although the coefficients on the first two principal components are highly significant as shown in equation 4, there is no way of inferring the significance of the coefficients of these four variables from equation 8.

The coefficients in equation 8 imply a mean income elasticity of 0.205, a mean price elasticity of -0.031, and a mean elasticity with respect to changes in the relative beer-spirits price of -1.27. The income and price elasticities assume the expected positive and negative signs, respectively. The low income elasticity of 0.205 implies that a 1% increase in income will lead to a 0.205% increase in per adult consumption of beer. This mean income elasticity is not very different from those obtained from the equations listed in Table 7. The extremely low mean price elasticity of -0.031 means that a 1% increase in the price of beer will only lead to a 0.031% decrease in per adult consumption of beer. This demonstrates that per adult consumption of beer is extremely insensitive to changes in the real price of beer. Price changes will have almost no influence on per adult beer consumption. The negative sign on the coefficient of the beer-spirits price variable indicates that beer and spirits are substitutes. But the statistical significance of this variable is unknown. This does not provide a strong basis for arguing that beer and spirits are substitutes. The positive coefficient on the time trend variable reveals that there is a trend toward increasing per adult consumption of beer holding the other variables constant. Since the variables in equation 8 are expressed in standardized deviates with mean zero, the annual increase in beer consumption cannot be computed at the mean. However, the coefficient on the time trend variable in equation B1 in Table 7 implies an annual rate of increase in per adult consumption of beer of 0.2%.

Wine

The regression results obtained in the analysis of per adult consumption of wine are presented in Table 11. Equation W6 gives the highest statistical fit with a coefficient of determination adjusted for degrees of freedom of 99.22%, whereas equation W7 gives the highest coefficient of determination adjusted for degrees of freedom of 98.21% for the simple linear functional form. Equation W6 states that real per capita income, the real price of wine, the relative wine-beer price, and the time trend together account for over 99% of the total variations in per adult consumption of wine. When the simple linear form is employed, the relative wine-beer price does not appear to contribute to the explanation of wine consumption since its inclusion in equation W5 reduces the resulting coefficient of determination adjusted for degrees of freedom. In equation 7, over 98% of the entire variations in per adult consumption of wine is explained by income, the real price of wine and the time trend. Real per capita income is found to be a very important determinant of per adult wine consumption. In equations W9 and W10, the income variable alone explains over 96% of the variations in wine consumption. The addition of the real price of wine and the time trend has reduced about 50% of the residual variation. Real per capita income, real price, and the time trend are found to assume the expected signs and to be highly significant in all the specifications in Table 11. Equation W7 is preferred in view of the small standard error of estimate and the high coefficient of determination adjusted for degrees of freedom. There are no autocorrelations of the residuals.

The mean income elasticity is found to be 1.43 and the mean price elasticity to be −1.65 as shown in equation 7. Per adult consumption of wine is found to be both income and price elastic. *Ceteris paribus,* a 1%

increase in income would result in a 1.43% increase in per adult wine consumption whereas a 1% increase in the real average wine price would bring about a 1.65% reduction in per adult wine consumption. Calculated at the mean, the coefficient on the time trend variable implies that *ceteris paribus,* per adult consumption of wine is increasing at an annual rate of 2.1%.

The relative wine-spirits price variable and the relative wine-beer price variable have not been found to be statistically significant at the generally accepted level of 90%. The relative wine-beer price variable is marginally significant at 81% level only in equation W6. The negative sign on the coefficient on the wine-spirits variable suggests that wine and spirits are substitutes, and the positive sign on the coefficient on the wine-beer price variable suggests that wine and beer are complements. Since the level of significance is very low, no firm conclusions on the complementarity and substitutability of the beverages can be deduced, particularly in view of the fact that the price index of wine is not strictly comparable with the spirits and beer price indexes.

There is very little variation in the estimated price and income elasticities in equations W1–W8 when the same functional form is employed. Though the estimated price elasticities obtained from both the linear and the log-linear functional forms are quite similar, the income elasticities given by the linear functional form are twice as large as those given by the log-linear function form. As pointed out above, the estimated elasticities given by the linear and the log-linear functional forms will be similar only when the ratios between all the observed variables do not change violently during the sample period. The choice of the kind of elasticities depends, of course, on the choice of the functional form that best describes the relationship between the dependent and independent variables. In the present case, the simple linear form is preferred.

Summary of the Regressions

The main findings of the above regressions for the three different types of alcoholic beverages can be grouped in Table 12. The statistical fit is rather satisfactory for per adult consumption of the three kinds of beverages particularly for spirits and wine. The income elasticity is the highest for wine, and the lowest for beer. This suggests that beer is more of a necessity since the consumption of necessities if known to be less responsive to income changes. The income elasticities also imply that spirits are more of a necessity than is wine.

The contrast in the price elasticities is very striking. Whereas both spirits and wine are highly price elastic, beer is found to be extremely inelastic to

TABLE 11   REGRESSION ANALYSIS OF THE CONSUMPTION OF WINE PER ADULT, CANADA, 1949–1969

Equation Number	Estimation Technique Value of ρ	Functional Form	Constant Term	Real Income per Capita	Price of W / CPI	Price of W / Price of S	Price of W / Price of B	Time Trend	R^2	$\bar{R}^2$	DW Statistics / SEE as % of mean
W1	OLS	Simple linear	1.058 (2.037)**	0.0005712 (2.890)*** 1.1966	−0.01382 (1.982)* −1.87246	−0.006285 (0.8335)	0.007015 (0.9216)	0.01310 (2.127)**	0.9866	0.9805	1.64 3.3396%
W2	OLS	Log-linear	1.453 (0.5889)	0.4868 (1.730)*	−1.886 (3.036)***	−0.1940 (0.2904)	0.8578 (1.226)	0.03323 (5.420)***	0.9942	0.9915	1.87 −6.9002%
W3	OLS	Simple linear	0.8128 (1.833)*	0.0006955 (4.845)*** 1.4570	−0.01079 (1.766)* −1.4619	−0.001907 (0.3277)		0.01519 (2.667)**	0.9856	0.9808	1.55 3.3186%
W4	OLS	Log-linear	−0.1173 (0.05452)	0.6885 (2.955)***	−1.517 (2.735)	0.3083 (0.5728)		0.03647 (6.458)***	0.9934	0.9912	1.55 −7.0431%
W5	OLS	Simple linear	0.8504 (1.889)*	0.0006138 (3.256)*** 1.2859	−0.01489 (2.199)** −2.0174		0.003018 (0.5171)	0.01554 (2.901)***	0.9858	0.9810	1.32 3.2969%

Coefficients of Independent Variables (Values in brackets are t ratios. Value beneath the t-ratios are mean elasticities.)

	Estimation	Model						R^2 / $\bar{R}^2$	D-W / %
W5′	OLS H-L ρ = 0.86143	Simple linear	0.1761 (2.790)***	0.0002018 (1.114)	−0.01582 (2.877)**	0.002621 (0.5615)	0.04623 (3.407)***	0.8454 0.7891	2.24 15.99%
W6	OLS	Log- linear	1.204 (0.5415)	0.36677 0.4975 (1.855)*	−1.6526 −1.920	0.7331 (1.380)	0.03419 (6.888)***	0.9941 0.9922	1.75 −6.6317%
W7	OLS	Simple linear	0.7787 (1.872)*	0.0006813 (5.159)***	−0.01220 (2.899)***		0.01581 (3.055)***	0.9854 0.9821	1.42 3.2026%
W8	OLS	Log- linear	−0.06469 (0.03090)	1.4273 0.7359 (3.469)***	−1.65297 −1.293 (3.374)***		0.03522 (6.941)***	0.9932 0.9916	1.75 −6.8557%
W9	OLS	Simple linear	−0.6949 (10.47)***	0.0009186 (21.96)***				0.9698 0.9678	1.56 4.2914%
W10	OLS	Log- linear	−14.31 (21.04)***	1.9244 1.903 (20.59)***				0.9658 0.9635	1.43 −14.297%

Dependent variable is gallons of wine per adult. Wine, beer, spirits, and the consumer price index are abbreviated as W, B, S, and CPI respectively.

***Coefficient significant at over 99% probability level.
**Coefficient significant at over 95% probability level.
*Coefficient significant at over 90% probability level.

TABLE 12   PER ADULT CONSUMPTION OF ALCOHOLIC BEVERAGES, CANADA, 1949–1969

Beverages	Spirits	Beer	Wine
$\bar{R}^2$	0.9930	0.9178	0.9821
Income elasticity	0.6795***	0.2048	1.4273***
Price elasticity	−1.4491***	−0.0312	−1.6530***
Annual rate of change	+0.94%	+0.2%	+2.1%***
Complements/ substitutes	Complements*** (spirits-beer)	Substitutes (beer-spirits)	Substitutes (wine-spirits) Complements (wine-beer)

*** Coefficient significant at over 99% probability level.

price changes. Per adult consumption of beer is entirely insensitive to changes in the price of beer. On the contrary, a 1% increase in the price of spirits or in the price of wine will lead to a more than proportionate reduction in per adult consumption of spirits and wine since the price elasticities exceed unity. *Ceteris paribus,* a rise in the real price of beer will lead to an almost proportionate increase in consumer expenditure on beer, whereas a price increase in wine or in spirits will lead to some reduction in total expenditure on these beverages.

These results show that of all kinds of alcoholic beverages, the consumption of wine is most sensitive to changes in price. This conclusion appears to support Schmidt's (17) finding of the importance of wine consumption as a determinant of liver cirrhosis mortality. As pointed out by Schmidt *et al.,* a large proportion of wine sold through legal outlets is consumed by drinkers who choose wine as the least expensive source of beverage alcohol for economic reasons (5). This phenomenon accounts for the high price elasticity of demand for wine.

The time trend variable is found to have a positive sign in all kinds of alcoholic beverages, suggesting that per adult consumption of these beverages would have increased in the absence of changes in other variables. The annual rate of increase in per adult wine consumption is 2.1%. This value is highly significant but the coefficients on the time trend terms for beer and for spirits are not significant. Over the sample period, per adult consumption of wine increased 124%. For beer and spirits, the increases are 23 and 71%, respectively.

The overall results show that beer and spirits are complementary to each other. The equations for per adult wine consumption suggest that wine and spirits are substitutes whereas wine and beer are complements.

4. DISCUSSION

A knowledge of the extent to which changes in the price of alcoholic beverages affect the consumption of beverage alcohol may be important in two respects. First, since taxes on alcoholic beverages enter into the final price paid by consumers, this knowledge can help determine the rate of tax that will yield the maximum tax revenue. The determination of the maximum revenue point in alcohol taxation has been the concern of legislators dealing with public finance (28, 29). As long as the demand for alcoholic beverages is price inelastic as is the demand for beer in Canada, it is possible to increase government revenue by higher taxes. Secondly, since Schmidt and de Lint found that the distribution of alcohol consumption is unimodal, indicating that a reduction in the level of consumption would necessarily bring about a reduction in the number of excessive drinkers (4), our knowledge of the price elasticity of demand for alcoholic beverages can serve as a measure of the effectiveness of price policies on the control of alcoholism and other alcohol problems. Given the high price elasticity of demand for wine and spirits, there is little doubt that, *ceteris paribus,* an increase in the price of wine and spirits can bring about a significant reduction in the per adult consumption of these beverages and by implication some mitigation of the deleterious influence of alcohol consumption on the welfare of the people. One should note, however, that there are other factors such as rising real income per capita which are important determinants of per adult alcohol consumption. In view of the high income elasticity of demand for wine, there would be a rapid increase in per adult consumption of wine associated with rising per capita real income, unless there is a more than proportionate increase in the real price of the beverage.

REFERENCES

1. Adamu, S. O., Expenditure elasticities of demand for household consumer goods, *Niger. J. Econ.,* **1966,** 50–60.

2. Bentzel, R., *Den privata konsumtionen i Sverige 1931–65,* Almqvist and Wiksells, Stockholm, 1957.

3. Brewers' Association of Canada, *Brewing in Canada,* Ronalds-Federated Limited, Montreal, 1965.

4. de Lint, J. and W. Schmidt, The distribution of alcohol consumption in Ontario. *Q. J. Stud. Alcohol,* **29,** 968–973 (1968).

5. de Lint, J., W. Schmidt, and F. Jorge, *Statistics of Alcohol Buying in Toronto,* Addiction Research Foundation, Toronto, 1967.

6. Dhrymes, P. J., Price and quality changes in consumer capital goods: an empirical study, in *Price Indexes and Quality Changes,* Z. Grilliches (Ed.), Harvard University Press, Cambridge, Mass., 1971, pp. 88–149.

7. Durbin, J. and G. S. Watson, Testing for serial correlation in least squares regression, II, *Biometrika,* **38,** 159–178 (1951).

8. Farrar, D. E. and R. R. Glauber, Multicollinearity in regression analysis: the problem revisited, *Rev. Econ. Stat.,* 92–107 (1967).

9. Harris, D. J., Econometric analysis of household consumption in Jamaica, *Soc. Econ. Stud.,* **1964,** 265–273.

10. Hildreth, C. and J. Y. Lu, *Demand Relations with Autocorrelated Disturbances,* Department of Agricultural Economics, East Lansing, Mich., 1960.

11. Houthakker, H. S. and L. D. Taylor, *Consumer Demand in the United States, 1929–1970,* Harvard University Press, Cambridge, Mass., 1966.

12. Malmquist, S., *A Statistical Analysis of the Demand for Liquor in Sweden,* University of Uppsala, Uppsala, Sweden, 1948.

13. Niskanen, W. A., *Taxation and the Demand for Alcoholic Beverages P-182,* The Rand Corp., Santa Monica, Calif., 1960.

14. Nyberg, A., *Alkoholijuomien kulutus ja Hinnat,* The Finnish Foundation for Alcohol Studies, Helsinki, 1967.

15. Popham, R. E., W. Schmidt, and J. Lint, The prevention of alcoholism: epidemiological studies of the effects of government control measures, Substudy 2-2 & 4 10-71, Addiction Research Foundation, Toronto, 1971.

16. Rowe, D. A., Private consumption, in *The British Economy in 1975,* W. Beckerman (Ed.), 1965, pp. 177–200.

17. Schmidt, W. and J. Bronetto, Death from liver cirrhosis and specific alcoholic beverage consumption: an ecological study, *Am. J. Public Health,* **52,** 1473–1482 (1962).

18. Schweitzer, T. T., *Personal Consumer Expenditure in Canada, 1926–1975,* Staff study number 26, Part I, Economic Council of Canada, Ottawa, 1969.

19. Seeley, J. R., Death by liver cirrhosis and the price of beverage alcohol, *Can. Med. Assoc. J.,* **83,** 1361–1366 (1960).

20. Simon, J. L., The price elasticity of liquor in the U.S. and a simple method of determination, *Econometrica,* 193–205 (Jan. 1966).

21. Simon, J. L., The economic effects of state monopoly of packaged-liquor retailing, *J. Polit. econ.,* 188–194 (April 1966).

22. Stone, R., The analysis of market demand, *J. R. Stat. Soc.,* **108**(Part III–IV), 286–382 (1945).

23. Stone, R. and D. A. Rowe, Dynamic demand functions: some econometric results, *Econ. J.,* **1958,** 256–270.

24. Taylor, L. D., Personal consumption expenditure in sweden, 1931–1958, *Rev. Int. Stat. Inst.,* **1968,** 19–36.

25. Tolkan, M., "Polityka cen a wzrost spozycia alkoholu," *Probl. Alkohol. nr,* **1969,** 7–10.

26. Tran Van Hoa, Interregional elasticities and aggregation bias: a study of consumer demand in Australia, *Aust. Econ. Paper,* **1968,** 206–226.

27. Walsh, B. M. and D. Walsh, Economic aspects of alcohol consumption in the republic of Ireland, *Econ. Soc. Rev.,* 115–138 (Oct. 1970).

28. Webb, A. D., The consumption of alcoholic liquors in the United Kingdom, *J. R. Stat. Soc.,* **1913,** 207–220.

29. Williamson, K. M., The effects of varying the rate of the tax on spirits, *J. Am. Stat. Assoc.,* **1920,** 451–464.

ACKNOWLEDGMENT

This paper is partly based on an unpublished substudy of the author, "Time Series Regression Analysis of Per Adult Canadian Consumption of Alcoholic Beverages 1949–1969," which was financed by the Alcoholism and Drug Addiction Research Foundation of Ontario, Canada. The author wishes to gratefully acknowledge his indebtedness to Dr. Schmidt for invaluable advice and comments on the basic study and for enkindling his interest in research works on alcohol problems.

Chapter Seven

METHODS FOR THE TREATMENT OF CHRONIC ALCOHOLISM: A CRITICAL APPRAISAL

FREDERICK BAEKELAND, LAWRENCE LUNDWALL, AND BENJAMIN KISSIN, *Division of Alcoholism and Drug Dependence, Department of Psychiatry, Downstate Medical Center, State University of New York, Brooklyn, New York*

The past 20 years and the last 10 in particular have witnessed an impressive increase in interest both in treating and understanding chronic alcoholism. The early part of this period saw the introduction of disulfiram and citrated calcium carbimide. A little later, tranquilizers and antidepressants came to the fore. At the same time there was a rapid increase in the vogue for group as opposed to individual psychotherapy. (The latter, along with Alcoholics Anonymous, had been an established therapeutic mainstay since World War II.) The un-critical acclaim that at first greeted each new approach was later tempered by increasingly reserved judgments as controlled studies began to accumulate. During this time, sizable federal, state, and municipal funds have been spent in this country on both inpatient and outpatient treatment programs. It is time for those of us who work with alcoholics to ask ourselves how well these different treatments work and under what circumstances, but before we try to answer these questions, we must consider some methodological issues that are relevant to all the treatment studies we propose to examine.*

* In this overview of the treatment of chronic alcoholism, given the size of the pertinent literature, the fact that we cannot claim expertise in any more than a very small corner of it, and that we have neither the time nor the inclination to write an "exhaustive" review, which would be exhausting to the readers of this book and would in itself be book length, we have eschewed the temptation to discuss all possible aspects of the treatment of alcoholism. Rather, we try to focus on conceptual and methodological issues so that researchers may be helped to design better and more definitive studies in the future. In general, we report only on those that

1. METHODOLOGICAL ISSUES

Sources of Sampling Bias

Definitions and Diagnosis

Although varying definitions of alcoholism are a real obstacle to comparing the results of prevalence studies (58), which may deal with rather different populations, they probably do not pose much of a problem in facilities that specialize in the treatment of alcoholism. There, alcoholism is usually taken to mean a condition where the use of alcohol deviates from norms of the patient's key social groups, role performance (home, work, social) is impaired, the individual suffers emotional and/or physical damage, and he is unable to stop drinking excessively for extended periods of time (364). On the other hand, referring units such as hospital emergency rooms, where physicians tend to see alcoholism as a disorder of derelicts, are apt to preferentially diagnose it in lower class persons (52, 396). Patients in whom the diagnosis is missed are more likely to be married, employed, and not socially isolated (30). It is likely that similar diagnostic stereotyping biases referrals from other institutional sources as well. The use of brief standardized questionnaires can obviate many such failures to diagnose correctly and refer alcoholics (259, 330).

Volunteers

Many treatment studies have used volunteers as experimental subjects and nonvolunteers as control subjects. The kind of bias this sort of nonrandom patient assignment to treatments can introduce is illustrated by a study of

---

used tests of statistical significance and control groups. However, we of course include descriptive reports on programs, and in a few treatment studies where interesting but little studied treatment methods were at issue, we decided to rise above our principles. In some cases, data were not analyzed by the authors of papers but presented in such a way that we could do analyses of them. It hardly seems necessary to justify the restrictions we imposed on our review of the literature. However, the reader who feels that they are too severe should consider that Viamontes (371), who reviewed 89 studies of drugs in the treatment of alcoholism, found that 94.5% of uncontrolled studies reported positive results, in contrast to only 5.8% of those that used control groups. Along similar lines, Foulds (102), who examined clinical psychiatric research studies done between 1951 and 1956, found that fully 83% of the uncontrolled pieces of research reported successful outcomes as opposed to only 25% of those that used controls.

We are indebted to Drs. Gennaro Ottomanelli and Milton M. Gross for their critical and constructive comments on this paper.

This research was supported by United States Public Health Service Grant MH-16477. Dr. Baekeland is the recipient of a Level 2 Research Scientist Development Award 5-KO 2 MH23901.

Myerson and Mayer (266). They reported an astonishingly high long-term success rate of 45.4% in skid row alcoholics offered a halfway house after hospitalization as compared to the usual dismal outcome of those who did not volunteer and only were dried out in a hospital. Is this strong evidence for the efficacy of halfway houses? Probably not, since the volunteers came from smaller families, had a better occupational status, and were more likely to be married, all factors which, we shall see, favor better outcomes in every kind of treatment. On the other hand, in a study of the effects of LSD on alcoholism, volunteers had used drugs more often and had had more illegal activity than nonvolunteers (80), activities leading to a poor prognosis for patients treated by any method.

Exclusion Criteria

Many studies and treatment programs exclude certain kinds of patients. Those excluded usually include patients with chronic brain syndrome, internal medical complications, psychosis, psychopathy, or skid row alcoholism, that is, types of patients who tend to do poorly in any treatment situation. Studies conducted in private facilities, on the other hand, are apt to exclude lower socioeconomic status (SES) patients, thus guaranteeing better outcomes. Social Class 3, 4, and 5 patients, especially the last two categories, tend to be overrepresented in public facilities. Hence, since most studies have been conducted in public institutions, our scientific knowledge of alcoholism treatment may be applicable to only half of all alcoholics treated. Another source of sampling bias is the exclusion of women from most studies. Of 35 studies focusing only on inpatient treatment, we found that only eight included female patients. Yet women comprise about one-sixth of the total alcoholic population (165, 166). A number of studies indicate consistent group differences between male and female alcoholics. Thus the female alcoholic is likely to have started drinking later than her male counterpart but to have sought treatment earlier. She reports more depressive symptoms, and available data suggest that alcoholism in women may often occur in the presence of a primary affective disorder (329).

Patient Treatment Rejection

Proportions of acceptable patients ranging from 14.8 to 20.4% reject proffered inpatient treatment (192, 291). Patients accepted for inpatient treatment and who ostensibly have accepted it may then change their minds and fail to report for treatment. Those who fail to report have higher incomes and greater marital stability than those who do (247). Treatment rejectors score higher on self-acceptance (229). Furthermore, patients who volunteer beyond a required period of time may be sicker and less psychologically minded than those who do not (66). Thus, treatment rejection and failing to report for treatment may involve denial of illness, but they may also entail elimination of patients who would do better in treatment, something that can introduce a negative bias into inpatient treatment studies.

From 25 to 67.7% of inpatient program completers have been reported to refuse proffered outpatient aftercare (237, 292, 368). Similarly, from 19.5 to 29% of outpatients referred from other sources were found to refuse treatment (36, 57, 283). It is not certain what kind of bias is introduced when inpatients who do and do not refuse outpatient aftercare are lumped together in inpatient outcome studies. However, in one study extent of subsequent outpatient treatment was positively related to long-term improvement (292), and another group of researchers reported that outpatient treatment rejectors did worse than acceptors at follow-up (57). They may have been sicker than those who accepted treatment, in which case their refusal would tend to eliminate poor prognosis patients from outpatient clinics. Some nonhospitalized patients who reject outpatient treatment, like some of their inpatient counterparts, may on the other hand be healthier persons. Both possibilities need investigation in studies trying further to spell out the characteristics of treatment acceptors and rejectors as well as the external (hospital, clinic) factors that promote or discourage treatment rejection.

Dropouts

The patient who refuses treatment is probably quite different from one who does not show up for a first appointment. The latter can be considered the most extreme and earliest form of dropout. Indeed, he is likely to drop out of treatment if he subsequently makes and keeps an appointment (15).

In 14 voluntary inpatient programs, reported dropout rates ranged from 13.7 to 39.2% with a mean of 28% (32, 136, 159, 161, 192, 261, 290, 292, 298, 302, 313, 335, 359, 386). In five outpatient studies they were higher and have varied from 52 to 75% of patients by the fourth session (15, 29, 118, 351, 385). In both inpatient and outpatient settings, dropouts, who have a worse outcome than program completers (32, 351, 360), have often been excluded from calculations of success rates, something that spuriously inflates positive outcome. That patients who drop out of treatment may later return with eventual success or may go to other treatment facilities where they may be successfully treated is rarely taken into account and should be investigated as an important problem in its own right. Kendall and Staton's (182) finding that 40% of those denied treatment at a hospital eventually got it elsewhere within 7 years is suggestive in this regard.

Study Patients Who Die

Alcoholics have a much higher death rate than the population at large (328), with higher than expected rates for cancer of the upper digestive and respiratory tracts, arteriosclerotic heart disease, pneumonia, cirrhosis of the liver, gastric or duodenal ulcer, accidents, and suicide. Accordingly, in one study of alcoholics discharged from hospitals, at least 5.1% and possibly as many as 7.3% died over a 3-year follow-up period. Eighty percent of them were among patients lost to follow-up (209). In another study of outpatients treated over a 5-year period with a follow-up interval of from 1 to 5 years, 12% of them died (123). Nørvig and Nielson (269), who followed up their patients after 2.75 to 5.25 years, found that 19% had died and that suicide was the most frequent cause of death (36% of deaths). They felt that 50% of the deaths were alcohol related. Dead patients often have been excluded from calculations of success rates in outcome studies of alcoholism treatment programs. It appears that at least half the patients who die at follow-up should be considered treatment failures. However, we need more accurate information on this score.

Patients Lost to Follow-Up

Two things make alcoholics hard to follow up: their high geographical mobility and their reluctance to reveal that they have resumed drinking. Thus in 41 inpatient studies patients lost to follow-up ranged from 0 to 65.8% with a mean of 17.0% (s.d. = 17.1%) (32, 68, 72, 75, 82, 83, 85, 121, 123, 125, 151, 167, 177, 184, 192, 195, 205, 237, 250, 261, 269, 277, 281, 288, 290, 292, 295, 298, 302, 309, 313, 315, 319, 321, 331, 359, 366, 368, 380, 388, 398), and from 0 to 77.5% with a mean of 36.9% (s.d. = 23.7%) in 10 outpatient programs (1, 12, 35, 49, 57, 126, 215, 297, 312, 351), a difference that is significant at $p < .005$ (two-tailed t test). It is apparent that follow-up failures are a serious problem in treatment studies, especially those conducted on outpatients. Clearly, patients lost to follow-up are an important source of biased sampling that tends to inflate outcome figures if it is not taken into account. Should the patient lost to follow-up be considered a treatment failure? The answer seems to be yes. Miller et al. (247) found that untraceable and uncooperative patients had poorer marital status and work histories and had more trouble with the law, all factors conferring a poorer prognosis, and Pittman and Tate (288) reported that 12 out of 13 patients they were unable to interview were functioning poorly in the community. Similarly, Dunne (83), in a study of an alcoholism program for police department employees, found that none of the patients retired for drinking responded to his questionnaires. In fact, 25% of them were in jail and another 25% were either dead or hospitalized. Along the same lines, Pfeffer and Berger (283), who solicited follow-up interviews of treated company employees by telephone and letter, found that no patient ultimately fired for drinking participated in the follow-up study, whereas Wolff and Holland (398) found that abstinence was reported twice as often by expatients who responded to a simple questionnaire as by those who did not. Furthermore, patients on whom other reliable information was available were 2.4 times as likely to be abstinent. On balance, these studies suggest that most, if not all, patients lost to follow-up should be considered treatment failures. This makes especially good sense since the dropout, who has a poor prognosis, is most likely to be impossible to follow up (118).

The operation of biasing factors is seen most clearly if programs with low (0–10%) follow-up failure rates are compared with those that have high ($\geq 30\%$) ones. Of 17 studies with low patient losses, 9 had populations heavily enriched with Class 1, 2, and 3 patients (72, 82, 237, 281, 295, 298, 368, 380, 388), while of 8 with high patient losses, 7 had largely lower class populations, 3 of them skid row (161, 177, 302), and 7 were reports on programs in public institutions (161, 167, 177, 195, 269, 314, 398). In one study with high attrition rates (167), the reported rate of 51.2% may have been due to these patients not getting the then sensational LSD while others were. On the other hand, almost one-half of Nørvig and Nielsen's (269) large sample attrition was accounted for by an unusually long follow-up period with a consequently high death rate. Factors other than high socioeconomic status favoring low patient losses in these studies were intensive individual treatment in the setting of a prospective study conducted in a university hospital (261), volunteer subjects (151, 266), having patients wait 6–9 months for admission (32), high occupational stability in Air Force personnel with 8–10 years service (277), and exclusion of dropouts from the follow-up (184). In outpatient studies low follow-up failure rates have been due to factors such as the use of company employees with high occupational stability (12) and very persistent follow-up techniques in a prospective study (57). High follow-up failure rates have been caused by exclusive reliance on questionnaires (283) and failure to interview dropouts (126).

That sample biasing factors can seriously distort outcome figures if they are not properly taken into account can best be appreciated by some descriptive statistics on methodological sinning. When the percentage success rates claimed by the authors of 14 inpatient studies (68, 83, 177, 184, 250, 269, 290, 295, 298, 319, 331, 335, 359, 366) were corrected for dropouts, deaths, and patients otherwise lost to follow-up, they dropped from 47.8 to 31.6% ($p \leq 0.005$, two-tailed t test), a relative decrease in reported effectiveness of more than one-third.

Sources of Unreliability

Evaluation procedures have varied widely with the result that published studies range from poor to excellent in reliability and validity and hence can be hard to compare with each other. Five such factors account for most of the between study noncomparability.

Outcome Measures

A much vexed question in the field of alcoholism is how best to measure the outcome of treatment. Does it suffice to determine abstinence or some other measure of alcohol intake, or should a more comprehensive and broad based assessment be made that includes the patient's role functioning at work and at home as well as his physical status and general psychiatric symptomatology? Published studies have varied widely with respect to the outcome measures they used. There are several arguments against the use of abstinence as the sole criterion of outcome: (1) because of patient denial it is less reliable than other measures such as occupational status, stability, and performance; failure in these areas is not so fraught with shame, and it can be determined from employers, who may keep objective and accurate records on such matters. (2) A patient may improve on one measure but not on others. (3) Abstinence is no guarantee of a good life adjustment. Thus Gerard et al. (119) reported that of a group of alcoholic outpatients abstinent for at least a year, 54% were "overtly disturbed" (had excessive community or social activities), 24% were "conspicuously inadequate" (led meager lives), 12% were "AA successes" (had little or no social life apart from AA), and only 10% were "independent successes." This widely quoted paper should not be taken at face value since the authors present no solid evidence that these patients had had better life adjustments *before* they became alcoholics. The same criticism can be made of Gerard and Saenger's (118) report that 12–32% of patients in eight clinics improved with respect to drinking but functioned poorly in one or more of five other areas. Similar criticisms can be leveled at Moore and Ramseur's (261) report that 6 out of 15 abstinent patients were only slightly improved and Pfeffer and Berger's (283) assertion that 30% of their abstinent patients were only slightly improved. However, Gerard and Saenger's (118) finding that 4–24% of abstinent patients deteriorated in other areas cannot be ignored. (4) Some alcoholics can become normal drinkers. This was reported by Davies (71) in 7 out of 93 of his hospital patients, by Selzer and Holloway (331) in 9.1% of theirs, by Gerard and Saenger (118) in 5% of patients in eight outpatient clinics they studied, by Pfeffer and Berger (283) in 7 out of 60 patients, by Moore and Ramseur (261) in 51 of theirs, by Reinert and

Bowen (301) in 3 out of 155, by Bailey and Stewart (18) in 7% of nonpatients previously identified as probable alcoholics, by Kendall and Staton (181, 182) in 8% of patients rejected for hospital treatment, by Goodwin et al. (130) in 18.2% of felons thought to be alcoholics, by Lemere (201) in 3% of deceased alcoholics, and by Cahalan (42) in 50% of those surveyed with past or present drinking problems. Reluctance to accept these results has been based on adherence to the loss of control theory of alcoholism. Recently this has apparently been challenged by findings that the blind administration of disguised vodka does not increase alcoholics' desire to drink (91, 245), that on an experimental alcoholization ward craving did not occur with the first drink but only after large quantities of whiskey were consumed over a period of many days (242), and that in a similar setting one-third of the patients never took a drink and one-third began drinking but stopped (131). However, all these experiments were conducted in highly artificial settings with little resemblance to everyday life with its privation, stresses, and insecurity. They were, rather, protected supportive environments where the patient could seek out company and support if he wished. We should also be aware that the drinking behavior of patients in the above-mentioned "normal drinking" studies was sampled only once during their moderate drinking. In long-term longitudinal studies it has been found that drinking status in a given individual can be quite variable over time even when group means do not change (100, 385), so that the drinking status of these "normal drinkers" could change quickly in response to renewed life stress, be it occupational, marital, or other. [One has only to think of the findings of Rosenberg et al. (317), who reported that half the abstinent alcoholics in a halfway house returned to drinking within 2 weeks after it was burned down.] Indeed, in those studies which provide case histories (18, 71, 181), of 19 subjects, 7 changed to less vulnerable occupations, 4 embarked on less stressful sexual lives with new partners, and 3 lost their tolerance for alcohol. Five others were exposed to "treatment" influences (religious conversion, AA, fear of medical consequences). It also should be noted that none of Davies' patients had drunk until impelled to stop by internal or external factors and that only one of them had a history of clear-cut withdrawal symptoms. [Apropos, Reinert and Bowen's (301) 3 patients who reverted to normal drinking all had short histories of heavy drinking.] Alternatively, they may have been controlled or steady drinkers, who have been found to differ from intermittent or periodic drinkers with respect to a number of clinical and psychological variables (226, 348, 375, 379). Another argument in favor of the abstinence criterion is that abstinence and other measures of alcohol intake have been found to be strongly related to work adjustment (21, 32, 56, 123, 298, 315) and to health status, interpersonal relationships, and social stability (56,

118, 123, 126). On the other hand, Rossi et al. (319) in a follow-up study of hospitalized alcoholics, presented data that implied that those who achieved abstinence improved significantly in only 4 of 20 areas when compared with other patients (147). Finally, Pattison et al. (279) studied outcome in three institutions, one a private aversion conditioning hospital treating upper class "high bottom" alcoholics, the second an outpatient clinic, and the third a halfway house handling lower class, socially deteriorated patients. They found that the private patients improved most with respect to physical health, and the halfway house patients most in drinking status, vocational status, and interpersonal relationships.

Until further research has settled this issue, it seems safest to use multifactorial outcome measures unless very large numbers or treatment effects are contemplated. Many such scales have been used. Whatever their details, they should be simple and noninferential and stick to easily ascertainable facts. They can be quite reliable (389). An alternative approach is to factor analyze clinical questionnaires as Foster et al. (101) did. They identified seven factors which they called drinking behavior, observed (i.e., observer rated) improvement, job and productivity, self-claimed improvement and control of drinking problem, decrease in sociopathy, intrapersonal adjustment (psychological symptoms), and social involvement. This approach seems quite promising but further work needs to be done along these lines.

Follow-up Interval

The treated alcoholic who becomes abstinent is notoriously prone to relapse. The following figures will give some idea of how rapidly he may lose the ground he seems to have gained in the hospital once he is again exposed to the slings and arrows of the outside world. Of those who relapse after discharge from hospital 50% do so by 1 month (290), 66% do by 3 months (315) [in the case of committed multiple drunkenness offenders, 60% within a week (250)], 67 and 88% by six months (72, 331), and 95% by 1 year (331). The figures of Selzer and Holloway (331) and Rohan (315) are probably underestimates since they are based on questionnaire data. Davies et al. (72) found that a patient's drinking status at 6 months correctly predicted his 2-year outcome in better than 80% of cases. In outpatients, Charnoff et al. (53) found a 100% failure rate in patients who attended clinic for 3 months with improvement but dropped out as opposed to a 23% failure rate in patients who had attended for 6 months with improvement. Ritson (309) found 52% abstinent and 22% improved at 6 months as opposed to 46 and 16% at 1 year, and Walton et al. (380) reported figures of 54% and 18% at 6 months and 51% and 17% at 1.5 years. Similarly,

Willems et al. (388) found that 1 year abstinence predicted 2 year abstinence with 76% accuracy, a result very similar to that of an AA study (41), and 1 year abstinence and improvement (i.e., any improvement) gave a 90% accurate 2 year prediction. Similar results have been reported by McCance and McCance (237). Gerard and Saenger (117), who analyzed their own data as well as that of Davies et al. (72) and Gibbons and Armstrong (121), also found that patient status at 2 years was close to that at 1 year. However, even 90% predictive accuracy may not be good enough in a study comparing the efficacy of two treatment regimens if they are not very different in effectiveness or if the outcome measures used are not very reliable. Furthermore, it should be kept in mind that most of these reports of consistency of abstinence after 1 year have been based on point samples of patients' drinking behavior.* Hence, it is not surprising that Burton et al. (37), who studied the effect of marriage counseling with alcoholics and their spouses, found that even to the point of 5-year follow-ups, broken marriages were more likely the longer the follow-up interval. Fitzgerald et al. (100), in a 4-year follow-up of alcoholics treated in hospital, found that only 30.4% of patients kept the same sobriety status from year to year. Though 76.9% were abstinent at 1 year, only 22.5% were abstinent in each of the next 3 years. It would appear that the issue of the optimal maximal follow-up interval should be reinvestigated using sustained or interval abstinence or improvement (and other outcome measures as well) rather than that obtained at discrete points in time. [That the patient's drinking pattern should be taken into account is suggested by McCance and McCance's (237) finding that periodic drinking is not predictive of outcome at 6 months but is at 1 year.] Provisionally, though, a 1 year follow-up seems reasonably safe. The finding that a minimum of 6 months is predictive of significant improvement has interesting theoretical implications as it suggests that this cutoff point may be determined by ease of readdiction. It has been shown that alcoholics are readdicted to alcohol much more rapidly than volunteers can be made physically dependent on it (162, 243). Clearly, this is an area in which more research is badly needed.

Nonuniform Sources of Information

The cheapest but least valid way to secure follow-up information on patients is by mailed questionnaires. With questionnaires, reported rates of nonresponding have ranged from 26.1% at 6 years (68) to 39% at 1 year (313, 360). After 3 months, rates of nonresponding rapidly increase. Mailings to relatives, who are apt to be more residentially stable and cooperative than patients, who rate low in these respects (315), result in

---

* The two exceptions are those of Bill C. (41) and Willems et al. (388).

higher return rates than those to discharged patients (68). However, relatives are likely to be less well informed than the patient (138). Most studies have used a variety of sources of information on patients. These have included phone calls to or personal interviews with them, phoning, interviewing, or writing relatives or members of community agencies, hospital records in the case of readmitted patients, and finally, death registries. Interviews are better than phone calls, letters, or questionnaires but are also most expensive. One prospective study tried to deal with the problem of interviewing patients by using only subjects who lived within 100 miles of the hospital (290), a procedure that probably tended to bias their sample in favor of patients who were not willing to make the commitment to treatment involved in a long trip. Among treatment studies, those that have used blind ratings shine out like beacons in the night. Yet blind ratings are a sine qua non for eliminating rater bias and a surefire way to help cut down spurious differences between new and enthusiastically endorsed treatments and older ones. A related source of error is the interviewer's private definition of alcoholism: his own alcohol intake has been found to be related to subjects' reported frequency of drinking (67). Because of the varied sources of follow-up information used in most studies, a considerable aura of uncertainty hovers around their results. Ideally, only subjects and their relatives should be interviewed, but this supposes stable patients. Hence in the usual population this prescription would entail a high follow-up failure rate.

The Reliability of Drinking Histories

It is often assumed that the alcoholic's drinking history is unreliable either because he wants to minimize the extent of his problem (at the beginning of treatment) or to minimize the extent to which he has lost ground (at follow-up). Since change scores should be used in any treatment study, this means a double source of unreliability. The evidence on this issue is contradictory. Guze et al. (138), who were able to interview both subjects and their relatives in the case of 90 out of 221 felons, detected among them 39 alcoholics, 26% of whose responses disagreed with those of their relatives with respect to a 17-item history. However, in only 6% of questions did the subject give a negative response and the relative a positive one, but since the sample was biased in favor of more socially stable felons (those with contactable relatives), the most severe alcoholics, those who would be totally rejected by their families and might be most unreliable in their answers, likely were missed. On the other hand, Guze and Goodwin (137), who reinterviewed these felons 8–9 years later, found that the more extensive the original drinking problem, the more likely the subject was to be consistent in his answers at follow-up. They concluded that the original felon-relative inconsistency was largely a manifestation of mild or borderline alcoholism. However, Bailey et al. (17), who identified alcoholics in a population survey, reported 37% disagreement at a first interview as opposed to 25% at a second one 3 years later. Finally, Summers (353), who interviewed 15 skid row alcoholics on admission and again 2 weeks later with a 14-item questionnaire, found that only 1/15 patients gave the same answers as on admission while 14/15 changed 50% of their responses. More important, though only 4/15 changed their estimate of the number of years of heavy drinking, in the second interview half gave a more severe history, and half a better one than they had in the first place, a finding that suggests denial may not have been the only source of unreliability in this population. Confusion and memory impairment in the wake of acute alcohol withdrawal may have played a hand. Certainly, a number of studies suggest variable impairment of brain function in hospitalized alcoholics. Thus Weingartner et al. (382) found a reversible memory impairment involving hold information (storage) which disappeared with 3 weeks' abstinence. Reversible impairment of intellectual and cognitive functioning have also been reported by others (168, 183, 359). It may be dangerous to generalize from Summers' (353) small sample study for a second reason: she studied a special and atypical patient (the skid row alcoholic) who could be expected to be especially unreliable. The issue of patient-collateral differences in alcohol history items ostensibly settled by Guze et al. (138) is more seriously raised by Schaefer et al.'s (327) observation that in a group of patients rated on a multifactorial outcome measure, 50% were improved at 1 year in the opinion of the investigators as opposed to only 19.2% in the eyes of the patients' relatives. The issue of the reliability of historical information given by alcoholics and their relatives seems to be an open one. It deserves careful reexamination with testing at a number of points in time, and study of interviewer factors in a large sample of inpatients and outpatients that includes sufficient numbers in all SES categories and age groups.

Inexact Specification of Treatment Methods

A recurrent problem in studies comparing different treatments is their frequent failure to give more than the most cursory information about the method whose efficacy is being tested. Thus, over and over one reads about the use of "group therapy" without being told which of its numerous variants is meant. The same problem repeatedly crops up with the terms "counseling" and "individual psychotherapy," which can connote a variety of different approaches. Such conceptual vagueness may be the result of researchers' overriding emphasis on the results of treatment rather than on what goes on in the course of it, that is, on so-called process variables, but in any case this is an aspect of treatment about which no paper's method section can be too detailed or too exhaustive.

Confounded Treatment and Nontreatment Factors

A troublesome problem inherent in treatment studies reporting long-term outcome is the operation of unknown nonmedical factors that promote improvement during the follow-up interval. These may include AA attendance and various changes in life situation. As already noted, change of occupation may be an important element as persons in certain occupations suffer unusually high risks of alcoholism (148). In survey studies there is ample evidence that alcoholism may abate spontaneously without formal treatment. For example, at reinterview after 3 years, 26.7% of Bailey et al.'s subjects now denied alcoholism (18) and Cahalan (42) discovered that drinking problems taper off sharply in men after age 50, especially in higher SES subjects. He found that changes in drinking behavior were highly susceptible to social influences. Similarly, Smart (336) reported that from 1951 to 1961, 2%/year of alcoholics in Frontenac County, Ontario, apparently recovered without formal treatment, and Goodwin et al. (130) found that on 8 year follow-up 18.4% of their alcoholic felons had been abstinent for at least 2 years and 45% were drinking moderately (at least once a month but no more than twice a week and without intoxication). Of the seven abstinent subjects, two had gotten formal treatment, thus reducing the figure to 13.2% Improved subjects were more likely to be white (an indication of higher SES) and older, and to have superior social adjustment and less general psychopathology, all predictors of better outcome in persons treated for alcoholism. Similarly, other studies of untreated alcoholics have reported spontaneous sustained abstinence figures of 11% over an unspecified interval (201) and 15% at 7 years (182). However, in Kendall and Staton's (182) study, which examined the fate of patients referred for hospitalization but refused it, only one out of nine abstinent patients improved without medical or lay treatment. In all, 23% of their subjects showed marked improvement. They were probably sicker than those of Goodwin et al. (130) since they had been forced to seek hospital treatment. Finally, Kissin et al. (189) found a 4% 1 year improvement rate in untreated lower class outpatients. It thus appears that about 2%/year of follow-up abstinence figures should be lopped off the results of treatment studies and perhaps as much as 5%/year from overall improvement figures. Although it would certainly be worthwhile to do so, only one study has tried to weigh the role of extraneous influences in treatment successes. Bruun (35) estimated that over a 3 year interval, 31.4% of improved patients who saw a psychiatrist up to 10 times in one clinic and 9.2% of those who made up to 32 visits, mostly to a nurse but also to internists, social workers, and group sessions, in another clinic, improved due to extraneous factors. However, he arbitrarily decided that less than five clinic visits could not exert a therapuetic influence. More carefully designed studies along the same lines should be done; they could be of special value since they might give clinicians valuable information about factors, some of which are under their control, but are not ordinarily taken into account by them, and which help their patients get better.

General Design Considerations

Treatment studies have been either retrospective or prospective, increasingly the latter in recent years as research has become more extensive and more sophisticated. In the retrospective study, information about patients is examined after their discharge. Its quality therefore suffers because desired data are frequently lacking in charts, where they were collected according to nonuniform criteria and for clinical rather than research purposes. In such situations, only those questions validly can be asked that are permitted by consistently recorded and unequivocal chart variables. These are all too often only demographic. Retrospective studies can never be truly controlled since admission to different treatments was nonrandom. Trying to settle the problem by matching patients on a number of variables never ensures they are the relevant ones, and in essence is not much more than trying to make a silk purse out of a sow's ear. Hence the only strictly legitimate place for a retrospective treatment study is in a program survey, whose intent is merely descriptive. (This is not to say that valuable correlational studies cannot be done with retrospectively obtained information.) More specific treatment issues must be settled by prospective studies where decisions about patient selection, assignment and follow-up, personnel, test instruments, rating methods, design and statistical procedures, and the like are made beforehand. Despite their advantages and the good intentions of the researchers who conduct them, in practice the excellent designs of prospective studies often are not followed in detail because of the increasing resistance of clinical personnel to interference with their familiar routines and with their right freely to decide what treatment they think the patient should have. The clinician's concern on this score is not unfounded, as Bergin (24) has shown. He reviewed controlled studies of psychotherapy (mostly in neurotics and schizophrenics) and found that it made some worse, others better.

Another design issue is the question of over what period of pretreatment time historical information should be gathered with which to compare subsequent outcome. Should the interval sampled simply be at admission, when only a point sample of behavior can be observed, or should it cover a period before admission? The longer the interval chosen, the greater the likelihood that memory for details will err, so that the information desired must become cruder and cruder as the interval extends if it is to be at all valid. The same considerations apply to information gotten from collaterals. On the other hand, alcohol most affects recent memory (322). Probably the best procedure is to use at least two or three different preadmission time spans, to use only information which can be independently verified by a nonpatient source, and to apply systematic tests and measurements on admission, 3 weeks later, on discharge, and at the end of the follow-up interval; at 3 weeks because of reversible changes in brain function, and at discharge because of the possibility of being unable to contact the patient at the end of the follow-up period.

Finally, therapists vary a great deal in their effectiveness depending on their attitudes, personality traits, and level of experience. Luborsky et al. (212) have summarized the extensive evidence for this in the psychotherapy of nonalcoholics. Therapist factors may also determine the outcome of drug treatment (158, 305, 334) and even whether or not a patient drops out of psychotherapy (22, 176, 265). Although therapist characteristics have scarcely been investigated in the treatment of alcoholics (65), there is no reason to suppose that they would not be equally important there. Hence patients should be assigned randomly to therapists and, ideally, therapists to treatments. Failing this, therapist × treatment, therapist × patient, and therapist × patient × treatment interactions must be estimated by an analysis of variance and taken into account in the calculation of treatment effects. As a last resort, the patients of only one therapist can be studied (12). However, although this procedure has the advantage of simplicity and holds therapist attitudes and style constant, it may yield conclusions from which it is dangerous to generalize.

2. INPATIENT TREATMENT

Inpatient facilities include state, Veterans Administration, and private hospitals, and halfway houses. State hospitals have the lowest staff to patient ratios, but their staffing pattern is similar to that of VA and private hospitals, which employ doctors, psychologists, social workers, and nurses. Halfway houses often are run by recovered alcoholics and depend almost exclusively on AA and other group methods. Group therapy currently is stressed in all hospitals, but more so in public institutions, which must operate on less money per patient. At present, the trend is toward specialized units or facilities with suggested patient stays ranging from 60 to 90 days. The fundamental questions in hospital treatment are the following. (1) How effective is it? (2) How much of its reported effectiveness can be attributed to treatment and how much to the kind of patient treated? (3) Is any particular kind of pretreatment regimen better than any other? (4) Is hospital treatment better than outpatient treatment? (5) How necessary is posthospital outpatient follow-up treatment?

Effectiveness of Inpatient Treatment

When the reported improvement rates of 30 studies (68, 72, 82–85, 125, 151, 167, 177, 184, 237, 250, 261, 266, 269, 288, 290, 295, 298, 302, 310, 319, 331, 335, 359, 366, 368, 380, 388) with an average follow-up period of 2.2 years were corrected for sample attrition, they dropped from 48.8 to 41.5%, a relative decrease of 14.9%. With a further correction for spontaneous improvement (possibly an overcorrection in the case of skid row and state hospital populations), they dropped still further to 29.9%, a final relative decrease of 54.3% in reported outcome. Thus about 30% of patients appear to improve with hospitalization, or, dispensing with the debatable correction for spontaneous improvement, 41.5%. Either figure seems a very reasonable one.

Patient and Treatment: Which is the Tail and Which is the Dog?

Good as these figures appear, it seems natural to wonder whether we should applaud the treatment programs or the patients they treat. There are two possible approaches to this issue. First, we can see what have commonly been found to be good prognostic indicators. Then we can examine high and low outcome studies to see whether they differ more in respect to treatment methods used or to the populations dealt with. With regard to prognostic factors, it has been found repeatedly that social (residential/occupational/marital) stability is positively related to outcome (32, 72, 82, 93, 123, 125, 184, 195, 237, 261, 281, 290–292, 298, 318, 331). Similarly, in those studies where there was enough spread profitably to examine it, SES (itself related to social stability) has a strong positive relationship to outcome (123, 125, 237, 250, 292, 366). Conversely, a poor prognosis is associated with factors such as legal trouble (66, 82, 237, 290, 321, 366, 288) and psychopathic features (125, 264, 290, 298), themselves interrelated.* With this in mind, let us look at the four studies with the best out-

---

* Other prognostic indicators of good long term outcome in inpatient treatment are the following: higher IQ (146), better education (146); older patient (21, 103, 125, 298, 366); later onset of heavy drinking (103, 295, 331, 366); noninstitutional referral (129); no court convic-

comes and the four with the worst. Papas (277), Rae (295), Willems et al. (388), and Davies et al. (72) found (corrected) improvement rates of 32.4, 46.4, 55.8, and 68%, respectively. Papas's (277) patients were Air Force personnel with 10–18 years of service, and the other three study populations were heavily larded with Class 1, 2, and 3 patients. All four investigations in addition had rather extensive exclusion criteria and stressed group therapy. The four studies with the worst outcome were those of Mindlin (250), Katz (177), Rubington (321), and Rhodes and Hudson (302), which had (corrected) improvement rates of 18, 7.9, 2.2 (abstinence), and 0%. They had virtually no exclusion criteria. Mindlin's (250) population was heavily seasoned with skid row type patients, Katz's (177) were all skid row alcoholics treated in a Salvation Army service center, and Rubington's (321) were tuberculous alcoholics treated in a sanatorium. Group therapy also was used in all these settings. The differences in success rates of about 50% between the good and poor outcome programs, much larger than that ever reported between different treatment regimens even in uncontrolled studies, strikingly affirms the dominant role played by prognostic factors (or sampling bias, if you will) in outcome. However, possible treatment effects are suggested by the fact that patients in the first four investigations probably received more intensive treatment than those in the last four and that among the latter, Mindlin's (250) patients got the most intensive treatment, Katz's (177) and Rubington's (321) an intermediate amount, and Rhodes and Hudson's (302) the least. However, because of the confounding of treatment effects and patient by treatment effects, these differences are at best suggestive. Another way to examine this variant of the nature-nurture problem is to consider studies of comparable populations, neither skid row nor upper class, executed up through 1963, when treatment tended to be either custodial or less intense than later on, with those carried out from 1964 to the present. The former (68, 261, 269, 319, 331, 366, 368) have an average success rate of 26.2% (s.d. = 6.7%), the latter (184, 290, 313, 359) one of 33.9% (s.d. = 8.6%), a nonsignificant difference which (disregarding the small N's that temper the nonsignificance) is unimpressive in view of the fact that 3/7 studies in the first group (68, 269, 331) were either purely custodial or entirely lacking in specific psychological treatment.

---

tions (56); social stability (84); at least 6 months' prior abstinence (319); abstinence for at least 1 week before admission (21); fewer previous hospitalizations (88, 195, 237); lower current symptom levels (129, 366); does not drink while in hospital (131); admits alcoholism on admission (319); less self-esteem (290); high on extroversion and low neuroticism (84); lower Sc and Ma scale scores on the MMPI (146); moderately self-critical rather than grossly self-punitive (380); lower hostility scores (310); capacity to maintain interpersonal relationships (129); and mother dead or, if living, seen less than once a month (21).

Treatment Length and Outcome

A related issue is that of the relationship between treatment length or intensity and outcome. Is there a point of diminishing returns, and if so, when is it? Several investigators (88, 261, 298) reported that longer hospitalization gave a better prognosis, Pemberton (281) that more intensive treatment favored a good outcome. Several other studies indicated that patients who stay longer than 4 months do markedly better (98, 177). Other investigations gave equivocal answers to these questions. Thus Tomsovic (360) found length of stay predictive of outcome, but only in nonresponders to his questionnaires (they tended to be dropouts), whereas Ritson (309), who excluded dropouts from his outcome analyses, found that length of inpatient stay was not predictive of outcome. Similarly, Willems et al. (388), who compared short stay (20 days) and long stay (80 days) patients, both of whom were discharged to outpatient treatment for the balance of the year, found no difference in outcome between the two groups. Although patients were randomly assigned to treatments, all the patients lost to follow-up were in the long stay group (most of these were deaths), which suggests that the long stay patients were sicker and hence had a poorer prognosis. Therefore, if they had been equivalent to the short stay patients, it is conveivable that they would have had a better outcome. The last three studies were conducted in higher SES populations than the first two, so that it is tempting to conclude that higher SES patients require relatively short hospitalizations (perhaps because they are subject to more favorable extra hospital environmental influences), whereas low SES patients need longer stays in order to better their abilities to deal with more difficult life situations. However, the confounding of hospital stay with other factors such as motivation, the presence or absence of sociopathy, and so forth, necessarily make such conclusions rather tenuous. This is an important practical issue that warrants careful reexamination in a prospective study built around it.

The Relative Effectiveness of Different Treatment Regimens

Three studies are relevant to the issue of the specific effectiveness of individual psychotherapy in hospitalized alcoholics (205, 261, 327). Moore and Ramseur (261) examined a program that treated only veterans with intensive psychoanalytically oriented individual psychotherapy in a high staff/patient ratio setting and excluded deteriorated, psychotic, or low IQ patients. At 3½ years, 30% of their patients were improved, not a very impressive result in comparison with Cowen's (68) and Selzer and Holloway's (331) results of 25.2 and 25.9% with custodial state hospital treatment of patients admitted without any exclusion criteria and most of whom never received aftercare [unlike about half of Moore and Ramseur's (261) patients]. However, because of population differences [the psychotherapy patients were 10–15 years younger and young patients tend to do worse (93, 247, 298, 302, 366)], we must hedge our bets on this comparison and must therefore look to controlled studies for better evidence on the matter. Schaefer et al. (327) studied the effects of self-confrontation experiences by videotape. At one year, they judged that 13/26 experimental patients were doing well as opposed to 5/26 controls. Although not significant, in view of the small N's this difference would be interesting enough to suggest replication with a larger sample were it not for the fact that according to collaterals, 5/26 patients and 5/26 controls were improved. Levinson and Sereny (205) reported on an experimental 6 week program in which experimental patients got insight oriented individual therapy, group therapy, didactic lectures, RT, and OT, whereas controls got only RT and OT. One year after discharge there were no between group differences. Although the effects of group therapy were confounded with those of individual therapy and other therapeutic influences, it is striking that psychotherapy did not seem to help. It is possible, of course, that treatment was too short or that the patients were unsuitable.

The effectiveness of group therapy in the treatment of alcoholics is rarely questioned, to the point that it has become almost an article of dogma. Yet the evidence in favor of it is extremely marginal. Thus, whereas four studies showed changes in psychological test measures applied during or at the end of hospitalization (10, 89, 90, 252), two follow-up studies give no support to the idea that group therapy helps much. In one (397), patients received either intensive group therapy for 1 month and then once a month or else no group therapy. Comparative 6 month abstinence rates were 14.6 and 6.6%, a nonsignificant difference (our calculations, χ^2 test of significance). Despite this, and notwithstanding the fact that patient assignment was nonrandom, the author advanced these results to further the cause of group therapy! Recently, Dichter et al. (75) studied the effect of 40–50 hr continuous encounter group sessions and reported 10 month (corrected) improvement rates of 47%. They did not use controls. (However, in all fairness, theirs was a preliminary report.) Such success rates in an uncontrolled study are not particularly surprising. Certainly, well designed controlled studies addressed to the problem of the efficacy of various kinds of psychotherapy in inpatients deserve to be done.

Hospital versus Outpatient Treatment

Because hospitalization is so much more expensive and disruptive of the life of the patient and his family than outpatient treatment, it is important to know how important the former is beyond the absolutely necessary initial drying out period. Only two studies bear directly on this question (84, 85, 308, 310). Ritson (308, 310) looked at 6 month and 1 year outcomes in two groups of patients, one of which received outpatient care and the other inpatient treatment (group therapy and AA). They found no significant between group difference. However, treatments were not the same (group therapy for inpatients but individual therapy for outpatients), and patients were probably not assigned to them on a random basis since inpatients had to agree to a year of outpatient treatment (which they did not get) and be capable of forming good relationships. Edwards and Guthrie (85), however, did randomly assign well matched patients either to 2 months of inpatient or outpatient treatment (patients got group therapy and AA in both cases) and found nonsignificant between group differences at 6 and 10 months. Thus the evidence so far does not support the idea that prolonged inpatient treatment offers any special advantage for most patients. Clearly, though, more work should be done in this area, especially with the aim of establishing which patients really need long-term treatment as opposed to those who can get along just as well without it.

How Necessary is Aftercare?

An allied question is that of the necessity of active aftercare. Pokorny et al. (292) approached this issue by comparing a 60 day inpatient program supplemented by outpatient group therapy with 90 day hospitalization without aftercare (290). Similar outcome figures were obtained in both programs, which used similar patients, the same facility, and the same personnel and treatment methods. Hansen and Teilmann (143) examined the effect of hospital plus outpatient aftercare versus hospital treatment alone in criminal alcoholics. Using recidivism as their outcome measure, they found that follow-up treatment helped the group that got it, one with a worse general prognosis. Several reports indicate that patients who got group therapy after discharge did better (123, 261, 309). However, this might simply be because they were better motivated patients who tend to persist in treatment. Fox and Smith (105) reported on a group of patients treated either with inpatient treatment, outpatient treatment, or a combination of the two. A χ^2 analysis of their data shows that patients receiving combined treatment did better. However, since patient assignment was not on a random basis, this simply might indicate that they were highly motivated patients who opted to stay in treatment after discharge from hospital. On the other hand, Pittman and Tate (288) did execute a carefully designed study in which patients were randomly assigned either to 7-10 days of hospitalization or to 3-6 weeks of inpatient care with subsequent outpatient treatment. (The main emphasis was on group therapy in both settings.)

This meant in essence that the hospital-only patients were getting not a great deal more than detoxification. At 1 year there was no between group difference in outcome. Their results should be tempered by their finding that of the 19 patients who remained abstinent for the whole follow-up period, 18 had extensive follow-up contact with the outpatient clinical staff or with some community group. On the other hand, Dubourg (82), in a follow-up study of 79 hospital treated alcoholics, found that among the 25 with a good outcome, only three had received regular outpatient treatment (as had three failures), and six got support from agencies and 13 from relatives only. Such apparently conflicting findings may be explicable by the fact that Dubourg's (82) patients were of much higher SES than those of Pittman and Tate (288). To confuse the issue even more, when three studies where patients got no formal aftercare (82, 85, 310) are compared with four where they definitely received aftercare (72, 237, 368, 388) (all six dealt with populations of equivalent SES) there is no apparent difference in improvement (54.2% ± 19.5 versus 48.7% ± 12.8 n.s., Mann-Whitney U test). The issue of the optimal combination of hospital and outpatient treatment is one that deserves careful reexamination taking into account individual differences and patient subgroups.

3. OUTPATIENT TREATMENT

The number of outpatient alcohol clinics in the United States has doubtless grown since 1963, when Bahn et al. (16) put their number at 39 out of 1429 outpatient psychiatric clinics. Their figures give a very cogent rationale for specialized alcohol clinics: 51% of alcoholics treated at alcohol clinics improved as opposed to only 29% of those seen in general psychiatric clinics, where they amounted to only 3% of patients seen. The negative bias of medical and paramedical personnel against alcoholics is well known (43, 191, 263, 287).

Dropping Out of Treatment

Two of the biggest problems in the outpatient treatment of alcoholics are engaging the patient in treatment in the first place and, once in treatment, keeping him there. Under ordinary circumstances, only a very low percentage of alcoholics referred by hospitals ever show up at the clinics they are referred to, in one study, only 5% of alcoholics seen in a big city hospital emergency room that served a lower class population (50, 51). In this same study the simple expedient of having the patient seen by a psychiatrist and social worker increased the rate of successful referrals to 65%

Similarly, one preliminary visit of a social worker to female alcoholics in a correctional institution increased the yield from 1 to 59% (73). Of the ER patients, 27.3% ended up in continued treatment, of those in the correctional institution, 18%. Several variables have been found to contribute to dropping out at the referral stage. They include anger in the voice of the referring physician [a reflection of his attitude toward the patient (225)] and dilatory scheduling of initial appointments (231, 233). (The latter is certainly much easier to control than the former, which points up the need for intensive educational efforts to rid the medical profession of its false stereotype of the alcoholic as a skid row individual.) On the other hand, writing or telephoning the patient to remind him about his first appointment increased successful referral (193, 194).

As already noted, outpatients tend to drop out of treatment very rapidly. Certain factors have been found to be associated with dropping out of outpatient treatment. Many of these are the same ones found in hospital programs. They include nonabstinence on admission (15), compulsory treatment [i.e., non-self or family referral (126, 401)], lower SES or factors related to it (15, 29, 118, 126, 189, 284), social isolation and lower marital stability (15, 126, 401), negative treatment attitudes [poor motivation, denial, ambivalence about treatment counterdependence, resistance to proffered help (15, 28, 312)], previously having dropped out of treatment (400), severity of illness (15, 126), arrest history (126), and the cognitive style of field dependence (172).* Thus the composite picture of the outpatient who is most likely to drop out of treatment is that of a field dependent, counterdependent, highly symptomatic, socially isolated lower class person of poor social stability who is highly ambivalent about treatment and has some psychopathic features. The skid row alcoholic is the most extreme example of this kind of patient.

Does the dropout derive less benefit from treatment than his counterpart who persists in attending an alcohol clinic? The answer seems to be yes, since a number of studies have reported significant and positive correlations between attendance and improvement rates (57, 110, 118, 164, 189, 357). On the other hand, Storm and Cutler (351) found that 12% of dropouts were improved at 6 month follow-up, a finding that could reflect both their initial motivation in coming and the effects of even brief treatment. Good attendance and good outcome may not be causally related, however, since they may both simply be but one of a number of attributes of good prognosis patients who would improve in any case. That dropping out can be a sign of health rather than of illness is highlighted by Tarnower and Toole's (355) finding that of patients who continued attending their clinic 10 or more years (6.1% of their patients), 70% were passive-dependent per-

* F. Baekeland and L. Lundwall, unpublished results.

sonalities, 23% inadequate personalities, and 7% schizoid personalities, all of whom pursued a marginal adjustment. Clearly, attendance should be manipulated as an independent variable if the issue of treatment length is ever to be settled.

A number of simple measures have been found helpful in keeping the outpatient in treatment. These include group as opposed to individual intake sessions (112), additional services to the patient [being seen early by the social worker, seeing relatives (381)], and writing letters to patients who miss appointments (276).

Basic Issues of Outpatient Treatment

Some of the same basic questions apply to outpatient as to inpatient treatment. (1) How well does it work? (2) Which determines treatment outcome more, type and amount of treatment or patient characteristics? (3) Is one kind of treatment better than another?

Effectiveness of Outpatient Treatment

Here, as in the case of inpatient programs, sample attrition should be, but was not, taken into account in many reports. Follow-up failure rates in 11 outpatient studies that reported them (1, 12, 35, 49, 57, 126, 215, 283, 297, 312, 351) were significantly higher than in the inpatient studies surveyed (36.9% vs. 17.0%, $p < .005$, two-tailed t test), doubtless a reflection both of higher dropout rates and of having less time to get information from, and to establish a working relationship with, the patient. No common factor seemed to tie together either studies with very high attrition rates [$\geq 60\%$ in 6–46 months (126, 283, 312)] or those with very low ones [$\leq 15\%$ in 1–2 years (12, 35, 57)]. However, Robson et al.'s (312) follow-up period was very long (10–47 months), Pfeffer and Berger (283) treated company referrals where the company did not pressure employees to cooperate in the follow-up, and Goldfried (126) apparently simply did not try to contact dropouts. On the other hand, Asma et al. (12) studied a treatment program for company employees where the company furnished full information on them; Clancy et al. (57) conducted a prospective study in a university clinic as did Bruun (35). Taking sample attrition into account in those studies where the authors did not do so, the mean reported outcome for 18 clinics (12, 35, 49, 57, 118, 215, 249, 283, 297, 351) was one of 41.6% (s.d. = 15.3%) improvement, a figure that dropped to 36% if an assumed 5%/year spontaneous improvement rate is taken into account. It is interesting that these success rates are not significantly different from those calculated from eight inpatient studies with about the same proportion of good and poor prognosis populations and which definitely did not offer aftercare (82,

85, 167, 237, 269, 288, 290, 310): 41.6% vs. 33.8% (n.s., two-tailed t test, figures corrected for sample attrition).

Treatment Length and Outcome

Treatment length repeatedly has been found to be positively related to outcome in outpatient treatment studies (105, 118, 189, 309, 357). Yet since it and other prognostic factors were confounded, it is hard to know what to make of these findings. Partial rather than simple correlational analyses looking at a full battery of known prognostic factors would have helped settle this issue but remain to be done. In this respect, it is interesting that Gibbins and Armstrong (121), who excluded patients who attended less than three sessions, found no relationship between abstinence gain and extent of outpatient contact. If other authors had likewise eliminated rapid dropouts from their analyses, perhaps their results would have vanished. Gibbins and Armstrong's (121) findings also imply that short-term intensive hospitalization (which their patients had) is enough for better motivated, better prognosis patients but that it is just those who do not get outpatient aftercare who might benefit most from it. In theory, such issues can be decided only by institution and evaluation of outpatient aftercare programs in which patients are randonly assigned to compulsory and voluntary treatment. A very rough look at this question can be gotten by examining the relationship between treatment length and outcome in studies rather than individuals. Twenty-four inpatient studies (21, 74, 82, 85, 95, 105, 123, 167, 192, 203, 205, 237, 248, 250, 269, 277, 288, 294, 296, 313, 321, 368, 380, 388) and 7 outpatient studies (35, 37, 105, 118, 283, 297, 350) gave information either on abstinence or improvement or both at long-term follow-up. Among 14 inpatient studies with good prognosis populations (21, 74, 82, 85, 95, 123, 167, 203, 237, 277, 295, 368, 380, 388) and nine with medium prognosis populations (105, 167, 192, 205, 237, 248, 269, 288, 315), correlations between treatment length and abstinence and between treatment length and improvement were, respectively, 0.46 and 0.06 (n = 11 and 10) and 0.40 and 0.27 (n = 7 and 7). Similarly, in the outpatient studies, which were too few for separate analyses for prognostic groups, the correlations were 0.46 and 0.27. These results, which are most tentative, suggest that treatment length is related more to abstinence than to lesser degrees of improvement which, perhaps, may depend more on environmental factors.

Patient versus Treatment as Outcome Predictor

An array of factors has been reported to favor good outcome in outpatient treatment of alcoholism. By now some of them will sound familiar. They include SES and social stability (15, 118, 126, 189, 232, 249), abstinence on admission or length of abstinence in the year befroe treatment (15, 126, 289), motivation* (15, 118, 126, 232, 249), spouse in treatment (357), 40–45 years old (189), and periodic drinking (189).† On the other hand, sociopathic features confer a poor outcome (15, 189, 249, 310), as does having a punitive wife (310).

Of the 19 clinics surveyed (12, 35, 49, 57, 118, 215, 249, 283, 297, 351), the two with the highest improvement figures, 52.0 (12) and 72.0%,‡ were, respectively, one where patients had first completed inpatient treatment at $100/week and would accept disulfiram, hence highly motivated higher SES patients, and another where patients were telephone company employees, 56% of whom had been employed by their firm for 10–29 years, thus a group of more than middle income with exceptional occupational stability. On the other hand, the two clinics with the poorest outcomes, 17.7 (297) and 22.2%§ were ones which catered largely to skid row type patients. Treatment methods, on the other hand, were different within each set of two clinics (disulfiram vs. psychotherapy and medication vs. psychotherapy). Again, it would seem that the nature of the patient is much more important than that of the treatment used on him.

The Relative Value of Different Treatments

Currently, outpatient treatment of alcoholism runs the gamut from classical individual psychotherapy through group and couple therapy to behavior therapy and drug treatment. Very often, especially if the patient is

---

* Motivation is a term commonly used by clinicians and its circular use has been rightly criticized by Pittman and Sterne (287). It is not always clear what clinicians mean by the word motivation. Often they are not as explicit as Mindlin (249), who stipulated that it include at least one of the following: (1) wanting to change beyond stopping drinking, (2) realizing that one must take an active part in treatment, and (3) being willing to make sacrifices for the sake of treatment. The reader will recognize these as the usual canons of psychoanalytically oriented psychotherapy. On the other hand, the term motivation is often used in connection with positive accepting attitudes toward treatment and those who render it. In addition, a distinction certainly should be made between extrinsic motivation (pressure from wife, boss, etc.), which is what initially drives most alcoholics to treatment, and intrinsic motivation, a desire to get better for one's own sake, into which extrinsic motivation is often converted in the course of treatment. Finally, motivation in the above sense and motivation as a personality trait in the sense of a general tendency to persevere in endeavors once they are undertaken may be only distantly related. The relative prognostic value of motivation in these various meanings of the word should be investigated.

† The last is probably an artifact of data analysis depending on the 1 year follow-up interval used. Thus Willems et al. (389) found that periodic drinking was not a predictor of good outcome at 6 months but was at 1 year in their patients.

‡ Gerard and Saenger (118), Clinic G.

§ Gerard and Saenger (118), Clinic C.

not lower class, he receives both some kind of psychotherapy and medication and, usually, social work counseling. The social worker, rather than the psychiatrist or clinical psychologist, has more and more come to be the mainstay of psychotherapy.

There have been relatively few controlled studies which evaluated different treatment regimens in outpatient settings. Bruun (35) tried to assess the relative effectiveness of two programs in which patients were assigned randomly either to 10 sessions of individual therapy by a psychiatrist in one clinic or to another clinic with multidisciplinary approach (three visits to an internist, seven to a social worker, two to group therapy, and 20 to a nurse). When improvement due to extraneous therapeutic influences was taken into account, multidisciplinary treatment turned out to be more effective than individual psychotherapy. Unfortunately, as already noted, Bruun (35) made certain questionable assumptions in his calculation of improvement due to extraneous factors. A more trenchant indication of the relative ineffectiveness of individual psychotherapy with the alcoholic is given in a report by Hayman (144). In a survey of members of the Southern California Psychiatric Association, he found that among those who treated alcoholics (mostly by psychoanalytically oriented individual psychotherapy), over one-half had no success with any of their alcoholic patients, and of those who did report successes, these occurred in no more than 10% of cases. These results with higher SES patients, if at all representative, are a telling indictment of psychoanalytically oriented individual psychotherapy of alcoholics when it is not supplemented by other kinds of treatment.

An interesting and promising psychotherapeutic approach is that which tries to treat the wife as well as the husband. Edwards et al. (86), in a thorough and critical review of the literature, showed that the classical description of the alcoholic's wife advanced between 1937 and 1959 as an aggressive, domineering woman who married her husband to mother or control him is without foundation. Nevertheless, there seems to be a good rationale for couple treatment. Rae and Drewery (296) have shown that if wives of alcoholics are divided into those above and below the median of the MMPI psychopathic deviate (Pd) scale and are compared with wives of normals, the former see themselves as more masculine, as do their husbands, who see themselves as feminine. However, high Pd wives deny that their husbands are feminine, an attitude that may work counter to therapists' efforts to get patients to recognize problems in this area. Pd scale scores also seem connected with alcoholic patients' wives' perception of their husbands' independence or dependence. Control husbands scored much more independent than dependent, control wives much more dependent than independent, as one might expect of those who conform to conventional sex role stereotypes. However, alcoholic husbands saw themselves as equally independent and dependent. High Pd wives recognized this conflict, but low Pd wives denied it, something that may have negated these patients' efforts to achieve independence if they had high Pd wives or have enhanced them if they had low Pd wives. Hence it is not surprising that in another study (295) successfully treated inpatients had wives with lower Pd scores. However, having a low Pd wife was a prognostic indicator only in marriages marked by employment instability and sexual disturbance. In line with Rae's (295) findings, it is interesting that Smith (339), who asked the wives of married inpatients to attend a wives' group (65.2% of them did so), found that at 4–9 months follow-up, the husbands of wives who cooperated were doing significantly better. However, since wives were not assigned randomly to treatments, it is not clear whether the results are due to wife group therapy or to the fact that cooperative wives would have proved, for example, to have had lower Pd scores on the MMPI than uncooperative ones. Conversely, Pemberton (281) found that assistance and support of alcoholic women by their husbands promoted better results. Gallant et al. (114) reported on treatment of 118 couples, of whom at least one in each was alcoholic, with group psychotherapy at the rate of 2 hr every 2 weeks. Their high reported success rate of 44.9% at 2–20 months might in part be attributed to the fact that these were highly selected patients discharged from their inpatient service, where patients are not discharged until the spouse visits the unit for a family session. Similarly, Burton and Kaplan (37), who studied group counseling at the rate of 1½ hr/week with alcoholics and their spouses, focusing on husband-wife interactions, at follow-up found fewer marital problems in 61.7%, drinking improvement in 46.8%, and reduced social pathology in 38.2% It should be kept in mind that this was a highly selected group of patients. One controlled study (64) bears out these reports of the effectiveness of alcoholic couple group psychotherapy, though in a hospital setting. Controls received the usual 4 weeks of daily group therapy, didactic lectures, RT, and OT. Experimental subjects got the same program for 3 weeks, then an intensive 4 day workshop with wives and their husbands which consisted of two couple therapy sessions, session videotape analyses, group lectures and discussions about alcoholism, discussions of game-playing in alcoholism joint recreational counseling, AA and Al-anon meetings, and meetings with representatives from follow-up treatment agencies. At 7 month follow-up, experimental subjects were significantly more abstinent (55%), and a higher proportion of them were attending follow-up treatment and had been employed 1 month. Obviously, in this experiment, couple treatment was effective, but it is difficult to know which aspect of it was most responsible for the observed treatment effects or to what extent subject selection had a hand.

In summary, then, it does seem that multidisciplinary treatment is more effective than individual psychotherapy and that involvement of spouses in treatment is worthwhile.

The Issue of Compulsory Treatment

One of the most difficult problems facing the clinician is the treatment of the skid row patient. His expense to society and his suffering are great. As already indicated, he does poorly with any kind of treatment. The problem is such a desperate one that clinicians and municipal authorities have experimented with compulsory treatment of this otherwise poorly motivated kind of patient who accounts for the bulk of arrests for drunkenness and vagrancy. One of the earliest such attempts was that reported by Maier and Fox (223). Patients with more than two but less than 50 arrests in the past 5 years were put on probation for 3 months and made to attend 34 group meetings and five individual therapy sessions at an alcohol clinic. Missing three appointments was considered a violation of probation. Although 44.8% of patients broke probation, 3 months after probation 37.9% of them were improved. In a similar program in another city (163) a significant reduction in arrest rates during the 6 months after release was reported in selected patients who received counseling, the intensiveness of which proved to be related to outcome. It is striking that education, job level, job stability, and marital status did not preduct outcome. However, this may simply be a reflection of the fact that patients who rated even moderately high on these items were probably only a tiny fraction of the sample studied. More recently, Esterly (92) reported that parolees or probationers graduating from an alcoholic rehabilitation unit had about one-third as many arrests after treatment as before, whereas in a control group the number of arrests went up slightly. However, assignment to treatment was apparently not random and because of the way the results were presented, it is impossible to say how well the outcome figures would have held up had a 31.8% dropout rate been taken into account. Other recent experiments of this kind have been less promising. Thus, although Gallant et al. (109) reported that a small sample of 19 state penitentiary alcoholics paroled to compulsory individual therapy at an alcohol clinic as opposed to a group compelled only to keep the first appointment there, did better under compulsory treatment with respect to recidivism, drinking, and unemployment 6 months after treatment, a later and larger-scale experiment with 210 house of detention skid row alcoholics was very disappointing (111). In this well designed study with multifactorial outcome measures, at 1 year only 8% of patients could be followed up and only 6.1% were successful. Unfortunately, the number of patients found at follow-up in the three groups used (compulsory outpatient treatment, compulsory hospital treatment, voluntary outpatient treatment) was too small to permit valid between group comparisons. At first glance, these discrepancies are puzzling until we realize that Jackson et al.'s (163) patients were screened so as to have a good prognosis; on the other hand, Maier and Fox's (223) 29 Georgia patients had to be white and only six of them were unskilled, and Gallant et al.'s (109) prison inmates had been imprisoned for at least 4 years and hence had been abstinent for at least that long and knew that the penalty for parole violation was a long sentence. On the other hand, their skid row patients were unselected and suffered only a short sentence if they relapsed. The conclusion seems to be that skid row alcoholics, if carefully selected, can benefit from compulsory treatment.

4. ALCOHOLICS ANONYMOUS (AA)

General Considerations

Of all the treatment methods we have chosen to consider, AA, a self-help organization founded in 1935, is one of the oldest and best established. Its importance can best be appreciated if we consider a few statistics. It is estimated that there are 9 million alcoholics in the United States (268). In 1970, the last year about which complete information is available, 278,000 patients with a primary diagnosis of alcoholism were being treated in psychiatric facilities (299). (The number with a secondary diagnosis of alcoholism is not known.) Jones and Helrich (171) estimated that about 70, 000 alcoholics were being seen by private practitioners. Thus about 350,000 alcoholics receive medical and/or psychiatric treatment for alcoholism per se. On the other hand, AA's current membership is about 650,000 (2) so that in terms of primary treatment it reaches almost twice as many alcoholics as does the medical profession (7.2% of the alcoholic population vs. 3.9%).

Jones (170) from a sociological point of view has pointed out that AA has much in common with religious sects. Indeed, AA has a strongly religious orientation and its precepts (the so-called twelve steps) involve the alcoholic's admission that he cannot control his drinking by himself, his admitting his wrongs and making amends, his submission to and reliance on God, and his carrying the message to other alcoholics (the sponsor system). Parenthetically, it is interesting that Gozali and Sloan (132) found that alcoholics are more internally as opposed to externally oriented on Rotter's Internal-External Control Scale than normals. They make the point that the alcoholic's excessive belief in his control over the outcome of events may be partially responsible for his behavior, so that feedback from its consequences do not modify it. It is just this aspect of the alcoholics' behavior that AA tries to change. Although loose or inexplicit definitions of the concept of motivation have been rightly criticized (349), some such construct does seem involved in both AA attendance and therapeutic change. Motivation may be external [Lemere et al. (202), for example, found a positive correlation between threatened loss of job or spouse and good prognosis], or it may be more a function of enduring personality traits. Clinicians repeatedly comment on the alcoholic's extraordinary propensity to overuse the psychological defense mechanisms of denial, but only a few research studies have addressed themselves to this issue (140). Via MMPI analysis, Button (40) concluded that alcoholics with better insight were more candid and less defensive than those with poor understanding of their problems. More important, several authors (195, 261) found that among hospitalized alcoholics extent of denial on admission did not predict long-term outcome, but rather decrease in denial during hospitalization did so. More recently, Willems et al. (388) reached the identical conclusion.* They stressed that change in denial was the single most powerful prognostic indicator they could find in their patients.† Hence it is just AA's insistence that the patient reduce his denial that may give it much of its therapeutic leverage. Along with an emphasis on the patient's dropping the barriers of denial, personal responsibility is stressed. Although the role denial reduction plays in AA's effectiveness is fairly clear, that of the sponsor system is not as well understood.

The use of AA either on a voluntary or compulsory basis (the former is much more common) is an explicit and integral part of most inpatient and many outpatient programs. AA has been called "probably the single most effective method of treatment that we have" (104) by a well-known expert in the field of alcoholism who was merely voicing an opinion widely shared by other workers in the field. Yet, surprisingly little is known about AA in a systematic way, as it has consistently avoided scientific study. At a descriptive level, Hayman (145) has pointed out that via AA the alcoholic

---

* However, Rossi et al. (319) did find that patients who admitted their alcoholism on admission had a better prognosis.

† The skeptic might object that reduction in denial is not a predictor but merely a concomitant of therapeutic change or of therapist-patient agreement about causes and goals. The important questions for the researcher should be: what kind of patient diminishes his denial under treatment, under what treatments, and with what kinds of therapists? Here AA's cooperation could be of enormous value.

becomes a member of an important subculture; he belongs to an in-group which can function for him as an auxiliary, external superego. Important, he feels, is the destruction of fantasies of omnipotence, atonement of guilt, and the construction of powerful reaction formations in a setting that promises love, care, and help. A number of characteristic defense mechanisms seem to be turned into their opposites: denial into open acknowledgment and projection into self-blame. Heavy emphasis is put on the use of reaction formation: hostility and destructiveness are replaced by profession of love. The role of these and other psychological phenomena in AA deserves the systematic scientific study that has up to now been denied them. The findings of Tokar et al. (358) may be relevant. They analyzed an emotion-states-by-behavior data matrix in alcoholics and normals. Their results suggested that when an alcoholic feels friendly, he withdraws, and that when something is wrong, he hides. The pertinence of this finding to AA, where both social interaction and calling a friend if one feels like a drink are encouraged, is obvious.

AA Population Characteristics

Who seeks out AA, and who sticks with it? Most studies of psychological factors in AA members have been carried out on hospital or clinic populations (4, 44, 139, 163, 251, 365). AA members for whom AA is less helpful, those who are sicker, or those who are less strongly affiliated with it may be overrepresented in such studies. A few have looked at nonpatients, that is, AA volunteers, in themselves probably a biased sample which preferentially includes more successful AA members (175, 220, 221, 230). With these reservations in mind, we note that past or present AA members are less likely to be married (139) and, if successful (at least 2 years sobriety), more likely to have been solitary drinkers (163), a finding that suggests the role of AA in resocializing the alcoholic. Not surprisingly, the patient who has sought out AA is less well informed about alcoholism than the one who has had previous psychotherapy but is less so than the patient who has never been treated. Compared to non-AA members, AA attenders were found to have weaker aggressive needs, to be less dysphoric and more verbally productive, and to have stronger hypomanic trends (230), all features that would favor successful membership in socially oriented AA groups. People who join AA seem to be more field dependent than those who do not (175). Canter (44) found that the hospital patient who participated in AA rather than in disulfiram therapy, group therapy, or conditioned reflex treatment had a higher IQ and was more authoritarian. Trice (362, 363) devoted several studies to the process of affiliation with AA. He made the important distinction between those who stick with AA (affiliates, attended at least twice a month over the past year) and nonaffiliates (attended less than once every 6 months in the past 3 years). He sees AA affiliation as consisting of three phases: (1) the pre-AA phase, (2) the phase of initial contact, and (3) the phase in which meetings have been attended for several weeks. The affiliate was found to be one who could share emotional reactions with others, had lost his drinking friends (and thus was increasingly socially isolated and had lost an important support for his drinking), and was exposed to favorable descriptions of AA. He had no close friend or relative who had quit drinking on his own and hence had no competing will power model of treatment. He had a better history of childhood churchgoing and was more likely to have a wife or girl friend who accompanied him to meetings and supported his affiliation with AA. (We recall the wife's important role in the outcome of hospitalized patients and will find this an important factor in disulfiram treatment.) The affiliate was not found to be class conscious (362). [However, it should be kept in mind that AA membership is restricted mainly to classes 2–4 and that 30% of its members have executive, professional, or technical jobs. Class 5 skid row persons do not often seek out AA (170, 285)]. Yet affiliates had higher status jobs. The fact that AA appeals to socially isolated persons is highlighted by the finding that whereas affiliates scored higher on affiliation motives than did nonaffiliates, both groups scored relatively low on affiliation compared to controls (363). In another and more methodologically sophisticated study of AA affiliates and nonaffiliates which used a stepwise multiple regression analysis of 26 social-demographic and 55 psychological variables, Trice and Roman (365) found that psychological rather than social-demographic factors accounted for more of the experimental variance.* Implicated were guilt proneness, intensive labeling, and physical stability. Quite opposed to the accepted stereotypes about AA were the findings that 0/3 variables indicated social stability and only 1/5 middle-class background as predictors of affiliation. However, the authors were studying a state hospital population (thus one weighted away from middle-class status and possibly one consisting of persons who failed in AA because of high levels of somatic and/or psychological symptoms which drove them into a hospital). It may be that the socially, medically, and psychiatrically stable middle-class AA affiliate only infrequently ends up in state hospitals, a possibility that deserves investigation. It is well-known to clinicians but not well publicized by them that AA tends to discourage members' attendance at alcohol clinics, which offer alternative forms of treatment. (AA's fear that addiction-prone members may become inde-

---

* Similarly, Overall et al. (273) have shown that although both historical and psychological items help to account for the variance in outpatient psychopathology, it is more efficiently accounted for by the former.

pendent on tranquilizers is probably well founded in some cases. What is needed, though, is hard data on this issue. Who is most and least likely to become dependent on tranquilizers? How common is such dependence, and what are its medical and psychiatric implications?) AA's attitudes toward alcohol clinics may be one factor that tends to select different kinds of patients for AA and clinic treatments. Trice and Roman's (365) finding that affiliators were high on guilt proneness, intensive labeling, and physical stability goes along with this idea. Psychiatrists, psychologists, and social workers tend to adopt a much less directive posture with alcoholics than does AA and they attack the alcoholic's denial much more gently with an approach calculated not to make him feel guilty. (He is led to believe that he has "emotional problems" rather than that he is defective in "will power.") Hence patients low on denial may be overrepresented among AA members and underrepresented in alcohol clinic populations, a bias that in itself would give the AA member a better prognosis. Since AA does not offer medical treatment, it is possible that the patient with high levels of psychiatric and somatic symptoms may drop out of it for the sake of more specific treatment of else supplement his attendance with visits to medical clinics. The contrast between clinic and AA populations is further suggested by a study on outpatient alcoholics conducted by Allen and Dootjes (4). They found that clinic attendance correlated negatively with autonomy and positively with deference (on the Gough Adjective Check List). Subjects who agreed with AA were higher on autonomy and lower on deference. The implication is that there was an inverse relationship between AA affiliation and clinic attendance. Hence it is possible that AA members (past or present) who attend alcohol clinics are either AA nonaffiliates in Trice's sense of the word or else former affiliates who derived no benefit from it, a point that should be kept in mind in trying to sort out findings that relate AA membership to other variables in outpatient treatment studies. Much work needs to be done on the problem of the similarities and differences between AA members and alcoholics who go to medical clinics.

Predictors of Success in AA

Only two studies have looked directly at the issue of who is and who is not likely to benefit from AA. Machover et al. (221), who used an extensive battery of psychological tests on remitted AA members, unremitted alcoholics, normal controls, and homosexuals (Mattachine Society members), concluded that remitted AA members were less defensive. In other words, they either had been low on denial in the first place or had reduced it as the result of attending AA. They also reported that remitted AA members were not socially inhibited (the best discriminant) and were more likely to be identified with their mothers, to be obsessive-compulsive, and to use overcontrol, rationalization, and reaction formation. These are valuable studies which deserve repetition with larger and less biased samples.

In summary, it seems that the new AA affiliate is most likely to be a single, Class 2–4 individual who has lost his drinking friends and has a supportive wife or girl friend. He is not highly symptomatic, and is a socially dependent guilt-prone person with obsessive-compulsive and authoritarian personality features, prone to use rationalization and reaction formation.

The Effectiveness of AA

Now that we have some idea about who goes to AA and who does best in it, how well does it work? We recall Fox's (104) statement to the effect that AA is the most valuable treatment method available in the field of alcoholism. One often finds similar statements in medical and psychiatric papers. For example, Gellman (116) estimated that as many as 75% of AA attenders are cured and AA itself claims that 60% of those attending AA achieve sobriety within 1 year (3). What are the facts? Because AA has consistently declined to let itself be scientifically studied, the facts are, alas, pitifully few. The only available and useful source of hard data on the effectiveness of AA as a primary treatment method known to us is a report by an AA member, Bill C. (41). We are indebted to him for providing the data he did but equally frustrated because he chose to report only on members who attended AA at least 10 times, so that we can have no idea of the overall dropout rate in the AA group he reported on. Of the 393 members who attended at least 10 meetings, 122 stayed sober for at least 1 year and were still sober, while another 14 had stayed sober for a least 1 year but had slipped and were currently attending. Thus this gives an improvement rate of 34.6%, a cumulative 7.4 year attrition rate of 65.4%, and a yearly attrition rate of 8.8% among members who came at least 10 times. On the face of it, then, allowing for probable sampling variation among AA groups, AA seems to do about as well as alcohol clinics. However, we should recall that Class 5 patients, who have a poor prognosis, tend to avoid AA. So do those who reject religious values and are especially apprehensive about social and group interaction and hence are probably unaffiliated, that is, those who do not belong to any organization. Thus at least three kinds of poorer prognosis persons tend to avoid AA or quickly drop out of it, something that makes AA populations much better prognosis ones than those in typical alcohol clinics. We recall also that AA members may be lower on denial than clinic patients, yet another favorable prognostic feature. Seen in this light, a 34.6% improvement rate becomes a little less impressive, especially if one keeps in mind the fact that the base from which the 41.6% outpatient figure was computed included 18 programs, ⅚ of which had typical poorer prognosis clinic populations. The apparently better results of alcohol clinics is not so surprising if one considers that they offer a much wider range of services (medical, psychiatric, social work) and a variety of treatment methods (conventional individual and group psychotherapy, couple and family therapy, behavior therapy, and drug treatment). Clearly, the issue of the effectiveness of AA as a primary treatment method cannot be further clarified easily unless it opens its doors to researchers. Until that time, the researcher, whose professional stance must be the infuriating and unpopular one of the man from Missouri, will take with a grain of salt claims of very high success rates so often expressed by AA members.

The issue of the value of AA as a secondary treatment method is a separate one. As an adjunct to other kinds of treatments it is likely that it is useful in a much wider range of patients. However, unconfounded results are lacking in this area. What is needed is a multivariate analysis of clinic or hospital patients which examines the relationship between parameters of AA attendance and outcome while correcting for the influence of other correlated population characteristics related both to AA attendance and outcome.

In summary, then, as a primary treatment method, compared to alcohol clinic treatment, AA seems to be applicable to a narrower range of patients in whom it may not be as effective, although this issue remains to be clarified. However, as a supplementary treatment method it may be applicable to a much wider range of alcoholics. These are questions which are crying out for more research to be done on them.

AA Attendance as a Predictor of Success in Other Settings

Many clinicians take past or present contact with AA to be one of several indicators of good motivation. In many studies patients were involuntary and usually they were asked whether they had ever attended AA rather than how frequently they had done so, a procedure that would not identify AA affiliates but rather patients' willingness voluntarily to label themselves as alcoholics. On the other hand, Bateman and Petersen (21) and Rossi et al. (319), who asked voluntary patients whether or not they had regularly attended AA, found that regular attenders had a better long-term outcome. The former's findings are weakened by their exclusion of program dropouts and patients lost to follow-up from their data analysis, a procedure that eliminated poor prognosis patients, who may have included regular AA attenders. Haertzen et al. (142), who examined this question in a large-scale and very well designed study of hospital patients, found that AA membership was not significantly related to responses on their Addiction Research Center Inventory, which measures subjective experiences associated with drugs and alcohol withdrawal. Thus the issue of prior AA attendance as a predictor of the outcome of inpatient treatment remains to be settled. On the other hand, posthospital AA attendance has been found to be associated with better outcome in 3/4 clinical studies that looked at it (32, 184, 360). It is interesting that they were conducted in VA hospitals, while the negative report (331) came from a state hospital, which tends to take sicker, lower class, and more deteriorated alcoholics than VA programs, in other words, just the kind of patient who would tend not to attend AA anyway. In outpatients, the picture seems much the same. There we find that previous AA contact was not predictive of success in two studies with predominantly lower class populations (189, 232), but was in three others that dealt with somewhat higher SES patients (15, 118, 312). Since frequency of prior AA attendance was not determined, these results suggest that, provided he has more environmental supports, or alternatively, that he belongs to the SES category that would go to AA, a patient's willingness to label himself as an alcoholic in the past gives him a better prognosis in outpatient treatment. Here again, the role of prior AA affiliation and nonaffiliation remains to be determined. In any case, no sure answer is forthcoming until a study is conducted in which AA attendance and SES are not confounded.

5. BEHAVIORISTICALLY ORIENTED PSYCHOTHERAPY

General Considerations

In our discussion of inpatient and outpatient treatment, without going into details, we have mentioned repeatedly the use of individual and group psychotherapy on the assumption that the reader is familiar with the practice, if not the theory, of their major variants. Logically, in the same sections, we should have included studies that used psychotherapeutic approaches based on principles of learning theory and hence on experimental psychology rather than on clinical medicine. That we did not do so and instead have reserved for them a special section at this point is not because, in our opinion, there is compelling evidence that they are more effective than other treatment methods, but simply because the reader may be less familiar with their details.

Behavioral approaches to alcoholism are hardly new. The use of aversion therapy dates back more than 40 years, of drugs even farther. The principal forms of behavioral therapy are (1) Aversion therapy. This includes the following variants: classical aversive conditioning, instrumental avoidance conditioning, instrumental escape conditioning, aversive imagery techniques, and relaxation aversion. (2) Systematic desensitization. (3) Operant conditioning techniques. Because these terms may be unfamiliar, we briefly define them.

In *simple classical aversive conditioning,* not drinking alcohol in the presence of alcohol along with disgust at the sight, smell, taste, or thought of alcohol is the conditioned stimulus (CS) and an aversive stimulus (nausea and vomiting, paralysis, painful electric shock) is the unconditioned stimulus (UCS) (160, 204, 248, 323, 372). This and other aversive techniques depend on the establishment of classical (Pavlovian) conditioned responses. The CS precedes the UCS. In *instrumental avoidance conditioning* the patient can avoid shock if he turns off the stimulus (stimuli range from photographs of spirits to the sight of a bottle) within 8 sec of its presentation (219). In *instrumental escape conditioning* (25), the patient learns to spit out his favorite drink in order to terminate shocks. In *aversive imagery techniques* (5–8, 46, 47) the patient is first given relaxation training by deep breathing and inhaling, after which he is required to imagine various situations involving drinking and finally is asked to visualize these situations and then various unpleasant consequences involving nausea, vomiting, and social shame and degradation. In *relaxation aversion* (25) the procedure is the same as in instrumental escape conditioning except that the aversion training is preceded by training in progressive relaxation. In *systematic desensitization* (399), anxiety evoking stimuli are graded according to the intensity of the anxiety they induce in the patient. He is then asked to imagine the least disturbing stimulus (event, feeling, fantasy, interpersonal situation) while at the same time undergoing a relaxation response in which he has been trained previously and which is thought to be incompatible with anxiety. The procedure is repeated until the patient reports that the stimulus no longer makes him feel anxious. In the next session it is repeated but with the next most anxiety provoking stimulus on the hierarchical list of graded stimuli. Relaxation procedures include progressive relaxation, hypnosis, or carbon dioxide inhalation. In *operant conditioning* techniques an alternative behavior to drinking is established by selectively rewarding it. Approaches based on classical conditioning have depended on the assumption that punishment leads to avoidance of the punished response and thus have stressed passive avoidance training; those based on operant conditioning have emphasized instead active avoidance learning, in which learning rather than inhibiting a response is the aim. Theoretically, there is no reason both approaches cannot be combined, although this does not seem to have been done in large series of patients.

Aversive Conditioning

The oldest method of aversive conditioning is through the use of drugs (apomorphine, emetine, and the like) to induce nausea and vomiting just after the subject smells, tastes, swills, and swallows an alcoholic beverage. The procedure is an arduous one for both therapist and patient and carries with it potential medical hazards. Needless to say, in published studies patients have never been assigned randomly to such treatments. Voegtlin and Broz (373) surveyed the results of more than 3,000 upper SES patients treated with such techniques and reported an overall abstinence rate of 44.8%, which fell to 25–30% by the end of 10 years. Lemere and Voegtlin (203) reported 51% overall abstinence rates in more than 4,000 patients dropping to 23% at 10 years. Thimann (356), who used similar methods in 282 higher SES patients, also reported 1–7 year abstinence rates of 45.4%, and Stojiljkovic (350) reported 51.5% abstinence for at least 18 months in patients of lower SES than those treated by either Lemere or Thimann. Reported relapse rates have ranged from 3.2% (356) to 21.4% (203) and 33.3% (350), so that the corrected figures for Lemere and Voegtlin's (203) and Thimann's (356) series, which included retreated relapsed patients, must be revised to 30.6% and 42.2%, respectively. Stojiljkovic's (350) results are more impressive since he dealt only with outpatients who had been treated unsuccessfully by other methods. His program included 2 sessions a week for 6 weeks, testing for conditioned aversion with placebo, and supplementary reconditioning if necessary, followed by stabilization sessions at 15, 30, 60, and 90 days, thus a 6-month course of treatment. It is impossible securely to assess Lemere's and Thimann's results since their patients were highly motivated higher SES persons who might have done well under any kind of treatment. The level of their motivation is suggested by the fact that only 10.9% of Thimann's patients failed to finish the total conditioning series. Similarly, Stojiljkovic (350), who used emetics, reported only a 15.1% dropout rate in his outpatients. Furthermore, the effects of aversive conditioning, as Lemere and Voegtlin (203) point out themselves, were confounded with those of a number of other factors, including sympathetic staff attitudes, interpatient effects, and staff efforts to rehabilitate the patient on his job, with his family, and in his recreations, comments that also apply to Thimann's (356) patients. Similarly, Stojiljkovic's (350) patients joined a kind of AA organization and were seen by a social worker. These considerations aside, the results seem no better than those reported with other hospital treatment methods in similar patients. However, Stojiljkovic's (350) patients were clearly quite unlike those reported in other outpatient studies with respect to motivation.

Since apomorphine and emetine, particularly the former, are CNS depressants which produce nausea of gradual onset, they are theoretically not well suited for aversive conditioning: central depressants inhibit the formation of conditioned responses and precise timing of the CS-UCS interval (it should be about 0.5 sec), which is important for optimal conditioning. Franks (108) has outlined other requirements for effective conditioning. They include distributed rather than massed trials (to avoid the accumulation of reactive inhibition), prominence of the CS with respect to background stimuli, a realistic overall training situation and the use of a number of different forms and attributes of alcohol as of the CS. Finally, partial or intermittent reinforcement is most effective. The cogency of these recommendations is illustrated by the results of Quinn and Kerr (294), who treated 22 poor prognosis alcoholics, of whom 60% were readmissions, with apomorphine at the rate of 6 days a week for 3 months. Of the 15 patients (68.2%) who completed 50 reinforcements, all but 1 resumed drinking within a short time, this despite the fact that they also received group and individual therapy. A later report (293) on patients who had received apomorphine aversion therapy and got a long-lasting aversion to whiskey, showed that these patients had switched to other alcoholic beverages, clear evidence of a failure of generalization of aversion from one type of alcoholic beverage to another, something that may help to explain their poor results.

An even more drastic aversive conditioning procedure, but one in which the CS-UCS interval can be timed precisely and the UCS has a sudden onset, involves the use of the intravenously administered muscle relaxant succinyl choline as the UCS just after the presentation of the CS. Terrifying total paralysis with full consciousness immediately ensues for 60–90 seconds. Needless to say, the procedure is not without risk, requires the services of an anesthesiologist, and is acceptable only to most atypical patients. Two series without random assignment of patients reported improvement rates of 17.3% at 4 months (154) and 16.7% abstinence at 1 year (95). Holzinger's (154) results were actually worse than those of other patients treated by more conventional methods. Farrar et al.'s (95) better results may be due to the fact that their patients had a secondary rather than a primary diagnosis of alcoholism (reactive rather than primary alcoholics). Controlled studies have been even less encouraging. Thus Laverty (197) treated patients either with three alcohol presentations followed by scoline apnea with concurrent presentation of alcohol, three alcohol presentations and scoline apnea, or four alcohol presentations only. At one year, all three groups showed a significant increase in abstinence without substantial between group differences. However, the aversion groups had a significant decrease in the amount of alcohol ingested on drinking days, while the controls did not. Thus there seems to have been some effect of conditioning, but the results would be more convincing if gains had been registered in other areas than alcohol consumption (these were not quantified). Madill et al. (222) experimented with another design in which three groups of patients received either CS and UCS, UCS alone, or CS alone. At 3 months, there was no significant change in beverage or drinking pattern. Clancy et al. (56) tried to control for the volunteer effects by treating four groups: (1) CS and UCS (2 day hospital stay); (2) volunteers, CS (2 day hospital stay); (3) regular hospital treatment; and (4) regular hospital treatment in patients who refused aversion treatment. In this extremely well designed experiment without any sample attrition, a model for this kind of research, at 1 year follow-up group 1 did better than groups 3 and 4 but no better than group 2, which controlled for the conditioning procedure, which was thus shown to be ineffective in distinction to better motivation.

The results of electric aversion therapy are no more promising. Thus Devenyi and Sereny (74), who controlled for the conditioning procedure but not for volunteering, and used reinforcement sessions, reported only a 16.6% abstinence rate with a dropout rate of 86.6% within the first three reinforcement sessions. An interesting refinement was supplied by Mills et al. (248), who used a control group whose comparability to their experimental subjects was not shown. Building on their previous findings that when alcoholics and social drinkers are compared, the former are found to drink straight drinks in gulps and large quantities, the latter mixed drinks in small sips and small overall quantities (344, 345), they tried to train alcoholics to drink normally. This they did in a hospital setting in a simulated bar by shocking undesired responses (gulping rather than sipping, too frequent sipping, or gulping). The intended course of treatment was one of 14 2 hour sessions. Four out of 14 subjects dropped out before the sixth session and the nine completers showed conditioning effects. Booster sessions after discharge from hospital were not used. At 6 weeks, 5/13 experimental subjects were improved as opposed to 2/13 controls, a nonsignificant difference. Three of the improved patients did not drink moderately, which they supposedly had been trained to do, but instead were abstinent, something that casts grave doubts on the highly publicized procedure which otherwise might have been faulted for omitting reinforcement sessions. In a refinement of this experiment (345) volunteer patients in a voluntary hospital, chosen either to be appropriate to a goal of abstinence (identification with AA, requested abstinence, poor social support for controlled drinking) or of controlled drinking (previous history of controlled drinking, good social support for controlled drinking) not only were given aversive conditioning on a variable avoidance schedule but also were interviewed when drunk, looked at videotape replays of these episodes, were subjected to an artificial failure experience, and in the remaining sessions (the bulk of treatment) there was emphasis on defining prior setting events for heavy drinking and training subjects in alternative, socially acceptable responses to these situations. Patients were randomly assigned to these treatments or to the control condition, which included group therapy, AA, and so forth, which experimental subjects also received. At 6 months follow-up, 75% of the controlled drinker experimental patients were functioning well versus 31.6% of controls, and 80% of the abstinence experimental subjects were functioning well as opposed to only 20% of the controls, both significant differences. Equally striking results were reported by Lovibond and Caddy (210), who trained alcoholics to discriminate their blood alcohol concentrations from 0 to 0.98%. They were then shocked on a variable intermittent schedule if they drank to levels above 0.065%. These largely self-referred patients were told that treatment alone could not ensure control of their drinking behavior but that its purpose was to provide them with a stop mechanism to help their own efforts at self-control. They were given 6–12 sessions and 30–70 shocks. Family members were actively involved in treatment. At 4–15 months, 21/31 (67.7%) of patients were rarely exceeding 0.07% blood alcohol levels and only 3/31 subjects had failed to complete the full course of treatment. On the other hand, control subjects, who received shocks on a random basis for the first three sessions but contingent on blood alcohol levels thereafter, dropped out very rapidly (8/13 before the third session) and quickly returned to their normal drinking pattern after initially reducing it. These seem like very impressive results. However, Sobell and Sobell's (345) abstinence experimental subjects were better educated than their controls and one would like to know whether experimental and control subjects had equivalent periods of hospitalization and also whether the same therapists administered experimental and control treatments (details not mentioned in their long report). Furthermore, does the subject who had hoped for a novel kind of treatment but instead receives an old one feel that he is being given short shrift and hence become discouraged? Surely Lovibond and Caddy's (210) control subjects must have realized quickly that they were merely receiving painful shocks which were in no way therapeutic, so that one wonders in what sense their sessions filled the bill as control *treatments*. The question of the strict comparability of experimental and control groups keeps cropping up in all kinds of treatment research except for double blind drug studies, where both patient and therapist expectancies are controlled. Until the latter, in particular, is controlled and volunteers are not used, it will be hard to know what to make of the findings of experiments like the present ones, which, on the face of it, describe very promising approaches to the treatment of alcoholism. The emphasis in both experiments, not just on the conditioning procedure, but also on other aspects of the patient and his treatment, is probably indicative of a trend in behavior therapy away from simplistic procedures to ones more geared to the specifics of individual patients' clinical histories and personalities.

Blake (25) pioneered in the introduction of instrumental escape conditioning with shock. He reported that at 1 year 27% of his patients were improved, not a striking result (26). He also studied shock with relaxation-electrical aversion and reinforcement sessions (25). At one year, results were no different from those with electric aversion, with a pooled improvement rate of 56%, one that might be expected with the highly motivated Class 1 and 2 subjects he used. His results are similar to those reported by McCance and McCance (237), who randomly assigned patients either to electric aversion or to group therapy and found both treatments quite effective in good prognosis patients. A strong proponent of behavior therapy might object that Blake's subjects were not treated under realistic conditions. They should consult the experiment published by Vogler et al. (378), who used a control group, gave instrumental escape conditioning with shock in a simulated public bar, and used a random reinforcement schedule with 20 sessions of 20 sips per session over a 2-week period. At 8 months, experimental subjects did no better than controls in terms of the number of relapses they had suffered, although they did have a significantly greater number of days to relapse. Poor results could be related to the fact that few patients returned for booster sessions, perhaps only another way of saying that subject characteristics (motivation) were much more important than specific treatment effects.

An apparent drawback of all the aversive techniques discussed is the unpleasantness of the procedures, which tend to have low patient acceptability and to induce high dropout rates. On the face of it, then, verbal conditioning techniques would seem to hold more promise. Aversive imagery techniques include both so-called aversive imagery per se and the use of hypnosis. Anant (6) initially reported that 25/26 alcoholics who completed his program abstained for 8–15 months, whereas in a later study (8) only 20% were found to be abstinent at 6–23 month follow-up. The poorer outcome in the second study may be due to the fact that he failed to use booster sessions. Ashem and Donner (11) used aversive imagery techniques in a controlled study of patients who previously had been treated unsuccessfully with other methods (AA, clinic treatment, or private psychotherapy). Besides group therapy, they received nine formal sessions (as well as practicing by themselves). At 6 month follow-up, 6/15 (40%) were abstinent as opposed to none of the controls. Considering that patients were assigned randomly to treatments and that these were presumably poor prognosis patients, the procedure seems promising and warrants further and more extensive study, which it will no doubt receive in the future.

Hypnosis has been tried sporadically in the treatment of alcoholism for a long time. However, reasonably well designed experiments are rare. Smith-Moorehouse (342) reported on his results with hypnosis in alcoholic out-patients. In his procedure he tells the patient that whenever he sees or smells alcohol he will remember that he is an alcoholic and that if he wants to keep fit, well, and happy, he should not take the first drink. He points out that suggesting to the patient under hypnosis not to drink again may produce severe conflicts in him, which in turn can lead to increased tension and anxiety and renewed drinking. He reported a 6 month to 2 year improvement rate in experimental subjects of 53.4% as compared with 37.5% in controls, a significant difference. The hypnotic subjects were self-selected, but on the other hand, if they had been more highly motivated than the controls, one would expect that their dropout rate would have been lower than that of the latter. Dropout rates were in fact the same (37%). In a better designed study which used random assignment of patients to treatments, Edwards (85), on the other hand, found no lasting benefit of hypnosis at 1 year, this despite the fact that 6 days of hypnotic suggestion with apparently adequate suggestions followed by weekly and then montly reinforcement had been used. However, an overriding emphasis on absolute abstinence may have worked counter to the author's intentions.

In summary, it seems that chemical aversion does no better than other methods but that it has not yet been tested fairly because of the absence of controlled experiments, whereas succinyl choline aversion and instrumental escape conditioning with shock offer no special treatment advantages that outweigh their unpleasantness. However, aversive imagery techniques seem both more palatable and promising. In experiments that failed, one is struck by the small number of treatments. The role of booster sessions and patient-therapist interaction in aversion treatment should be studied carefully. That chemical and electric aversion therapies have not shown any special worth despite their apparently good theoretical foundation is cause for reflection. Their failure to live up to their initial promise may be due to the following. (1) They can generate high general levels of anxiety as opposed to the specific anxiety conditioned to the alcoholic beverage. (2) Eysenck and Rachman (94) have reviewed evidence showing that if behavior (drinking, for example) is motivated by anxiety, aversive conditioning can augment rather than reduce such behavior. (3) If a subject is habituated to receiving punishment together with a reward, punishment during extinction can actually increase resistance to extinction (346). Many alcoholics learn to associate both reward and punishment with drinking. (4) Punishing a response originally established by punishment, such as drinking because of a painful experience, may strengthen rather than weaken the response. (5) Adaptation to punishment may take place. (6) In practice, aversive therapy has focused on only one aspect of excessive drinking, the actual act of drinking. The drinking response, as Franks (108) points out, is but one item in a complex series of closely interrelated responses, which are established earlier and are essential to the act of drinking, (a behaviorist's way of saying, "Treat the whole man.") In other words, these techniques have tended to ignore the history of the symptom and the full social context in which it occurs, something that ordinary psychotherapy, which is on less firm theoretical grounds, has not neglected to do. A more sophisticated approach to behavioral treatment has been suggested by Keehn et al. (180), who applied Cautela and Kastenbaum's (48) Reinforcement Survey Schedule to a group of alcoholics. This schedule consists of three lists of objects, activities, or situations rated on a 5 point scale according to the amount of pleasurable feelings each provides, and of four lists of things he thinks about 5, 10, 15, or 20 times a day. Keehn (179) found the following order of preference of themes: occupational status, loving intimacy, pleasure from nature, favorable social attention, faith and good works, and competitive performance, a hierarchy that corresponds to the general experience of any psychotherapist who has extensive experience with alcoholics. (They are, after all, people who tend to be downwardly mobile with respect to work, they need love but don't know how to get or give it, they want to escape from their cares, like children they have a strong need for favorable attention, they would like to make up for their failures in life, and, like other people, they want to compete, only much less so, because of strong dependency needs that increase the risk of competition and also because of a history of repeated failure.) While 22.5% of his subjects didn't like any alcoholic beverage very much, 45% said drinking gave them as much or more pleasure as other alternatives. Keehn (179) points out that for the first group of patients it would be inappropriate to make alcohol aversive but that they should rather be helped to attain their aspirations by some other route, occupational success, for example.

Systematic Desensitization

There seem to have been few reports on large-scale studies using systematic desensitization alone in alcoholics. An exception is that of Storm and Cutler (351), who reported no effect of systematic desensitization using Wolpe's (399) methods. They attributed their lack of success to the relatively low anxiety-tension levels of the desensitization group, something that made identification of special foci of anxiety difficult. On theoretical grounds, one would expect desensitization techniques to apply only to highly self-aware patients who are excellent self-observers, who are not physically dependent on alcohol, and who, to boot, do not drink to alleviate depression or to allow the release of inhibited sexual or aggressive drive expression under conditions of diminished self-criticism. Hence their negative results are not surprising. The technique deserves reexamination in a suitable population as it is by now a well established kind of psychotherapy.

Operant Conditioning

A major criticism of all the aversive techniques is that they rather shortsightedly focus on the extinction of a response (drinking) without giving the patient an alternative way of reducing anxiety or teaching him any behavior incompatible with drinking. This criticism is met by operant conditioning, which shapes desired alternative responses by rewarding them. Extensive studies of the effectiveness of this approach with alcoholics remain to be reported. However, a very promising pilot study was reported by Cohen et al. (59–61) who tried to answer the question, can moderate drinking be maintained for 5 days, in five Class 5 inpatient alcoholics. As a reinforcer, they used participation in an enriched environment. All five subjects drank moderately during the experimental treatment. Another experiment showed that it was the absence of reinforcement contingencies for moderation, rather than living in an impoverished environment, that gave rise to excessive drinking.

Individual Differences

A neglected area in systematic treatment research in general is the study of individual differences in response to treatment. This is particularly germane to aversion techniques, where individual differences in conditionability have not been taken into account sufficiently. Considering the amount of time, money, and effort that have been lavished on behavioral techniques and promise to be in the future, it is truly astonishing that so little is known about individual differences in conditionability among alcoholics. However, Vogel (374–377) reported that introverts (according to the Maudsley Personality Inventory) conditioned more easily than extroverts and that it took longer for their responses to extinguish. Interestingly, she found that introverts tended to be daily rather than periodic drinkers. In distinction to extroverts, they tended to be solitary drinkers with a later onset of frequent blackouts.

An obvious extension of behavioral techniques would be the combination of aversive, systematic desensitization, and operant conditioning techniques in patients. This obviously calls for very careful study of the patient and the details of his history and doubtless will be done in the future.

6. DRUG TREATMENT

The use of drugs to modify alcoholism has a long history. Drug treatment of alcoholism has been one of the most carelessly and mechanically treated areas of research, careless because of the enormous proliferation of uncontrolled studies, and mechanical because of the blind application of double blind techniques with utter disregard of many other equally important methodological requirements. Because three comprehensive reviews concluding that there is no evidence that drug treatment helps in the treatment of alcoholism (77, 262, 371) have already appeared, we were at first tempted merely to refer to them and let it go at that. Two considerations led us to try to pile Pelion on Ossa. First of all, contrary to these reviews, there are some demonstrated positive effects of drugs on outcome in alcoholics. Few, it is true, but they still exist. Secondly, the methodological issues need clarification.

Implicit Assumptions

The basic assumption of most drug treatments involving tranquilizers and antidepressants is the drive reduction theory of alcoholism, which runs something like this: (1) alcoholics suffer from dysphoric symptoms such as anxiety, depression, and, if physically dependent, symptoms of partial withdrawal. Alcohol reduces such symptoms. Therefore drugs that reduce these symptoms will diminish the patient's drive to consume alcohol. Alcoholics do seem to be more anxious and depressed than normal controls (186, 383) and a factor analytic study of two depression scales applied to inpatient alcoholics found 3/4 factors previously reported in eight factor analytic studies of patients with a primary diagnosis of depression (122). Another factor analytic study of alcoholic outpatients' Q sort self-depictions of the effects of alcohol on their sober, drunk, and ideal selves revealed four factors, one of which involved, inter alia, reduction of depression, anxiety, and tension (218). On the other hand, a recent review (45) indicates that the evidence in human studies for the tension-reduction hypothesis of alcoholism is conflicting. Hore (155) found that though there was no significant correlation between the number of stressful life events experienced (personal interactions, health events, residential change events, work events) and frequency of relapse in 22 patients, in 7 of them there did seem to be one. In much the same way, the group evidence that underlying emotional states contributed to relapses was equivocal (156). However, Mayfield (234, 235) has reported that intravenous alcohol administration decreased depressive affect in both depressed moderate and excessive drinkers but only at lower doses. In 21 patients with excessive drinking and depressive disorder, he found that in only seven patients were depressive episodes and excessive drinking associated (236). All this suggests that antidepressants might be applicable only to a certain subgroup of depressed alcoholics, those who drink more or less continuously at moderate levels. Uninvestigated individual differences in tension reduction via alcohol may also explain some of the conflicting reports reviewed by Cappell and Herman (45). Indeed, Vannicelli (370) studied the effects of alcohol in hospitalized alcoholics in divided doses over 2 days and found that half his subjects were anxious when intoxicated, whereas the reverse was true in the other half. Change in anxiety after the first drink was a good predictor of overall change in anxiety after several drinks. Subjects who changed the least in anxiety scored the highest on the California Psychological Inventory Cm Scale, indicating a greater tendency for them to be dependable, moderate, steady, etc., a result consistent with Cutter et al.'s (70) finding that inhibition rather than power needs was a determinant of whether subjects did or did not take a second drink. Thus it is possible that tranquilizers might be effective only in less inhibited and, perhaps, socially stable patients. At first glance, the validity of the suggestions we have just made might seem questionable, especially in view of reports that in alcoholics negative affects increase as they continue drinking (238, 243, 369). Since they may preferentially remember the short-term rather than the long-term effects of alcohol on them (382) (one of the major problems in doing psychotherapy with them) or, put differently, since only the immediate effects of alcohol significantly reinforce alcohol consumption, such observations are probably irrelevant. Much more to the point are reports to the effect that alcohol causes an immediate, albeit transitory, reduction in dysphoric affects (23, 186, 234, 235). Our suggestions about the effectiveness of tranquilizers and antidepressants could be checked easily in the course of large-scale drug studies on alcoholic populations.

Other Methodological Issues

Two things more than anything else have vitiated most studies of the drug treatment of alcoholics: high dropout rates and so-called nonspecific effects. Dropout rates in hospital studies have ranged from 9.7% in 1 month to 62.5% in 2 weeks (33, 213, 325, 332, 333). Since these studies were executed on similar populations, such widely different dropout rates seem to reflect more than anything else patient and investigator enthusiasm or the lack of it. The lowest rates, 9.7 and 18.1% (33, 213), were in investigations of the much touted LSD. The highest, 62.5% in 2 weeks, accrued to the much less vaunted and more familiar drug triiodothyronine (325). Dropout rates in outpatient studies (by far the most common kind) have been much higher. If unusually low values are excluded, they present the following rather dismal picture: by the first visit, 36.5% (31); by 1 week, 46.8% (76, 200, 258); by 2 weeks, 57.6% (53, 62, 78, 257); by 1 month, 50.1% (31, 141, 311, 367); by 3 months, 61.3% (53, 76, 311); and 89.2% at 6 months (53, 76, 79, 311). These figures, derived from studies conducted among skid row or predominantly lower class populations, should be contrasted with Bartholomew and Guile's (20) report of a 17.5% dropout rate in a better prognosis population at a time when enthusiasm about chlordiazepoxide was waxing high, or with Hoff's (150) 0% dropout rate in a nonblind study conducted in a population where those not given the new drug dropped out at the rate of 48%. The important roles played by SES, patient selection, and adjunctive treatment are illustrated by two studies with reserpine, a drug with annoying side effects. Ritter (311) found that 97% of his lower SES Home Term Court patients who received only reserpine or placebo on a double blind basis had dropped out by 6 months, whereas Greenhouse and Pilot (134), whose patients were voluntary, more carefully selected, of higher SES, and seen either by a psychiatrist or social worker, indicated that only 42.2% had dropped out at the end of a year. Here again, enthusiasm and subject SES factors seem to play a major role. It is interesting that combined hospital and outpatient studies have reported much lower 6 month dropout rates than inpatient studies, 26.3% (87, 113, 282, 354). Two of these four studies (282, 354) were carried out in higher than average SES populations so that more favorable subject factors as well as the long-term commitment of the investigators to patients treated with a promising new drug probably were responsible. Although differential drug and placebo rates have not been found in some studies (256, 311, 325, 354), such high dropout rates have had the effect of curtailing the time span of many of them to the point where they were in effect 1-, 2-, or 3-week affairs or else of reducing sample size to a point where drug effects, even if they existed, would be difficult to pick up, that is, below the 50 patient group size usually considered necessary in drug research with heterogeneous populations (274). In this regard, it is noteworthy that Swinson (354), who had a low dropout rate, found a definite effect of metronidazole on drinking patterns at 12 months but not at 6 months. One wonders whether other drugs now felt (by researchers, not clinicians) to be ineffective in the treatment of alcoholism would have proved of benefit had they only been put to the test in longer-term studies in non-skid row and lower class populations, in other words, with patients who would stay in treatment and thus allow a fair test of the drugs.

General disregard of so-called nonspecific effects may have been even more crippling to the validity of studies of drug treatment of alcoholics by virtue of their vitiating real drug-placebo differences in a number of ways.

First of all—and this is generally overlooked—many patients do not take medication as it is prescribed, either omitting it altogether, taking too little, or taking it at irregular intervals (178, 304, 306, 387), and patients who deviate from prescribed dosages are most likely to drop out of treatment (304, 391). Published drug studies for the most part do not seem to take this into account. Many do not even try to correct for missed visits. Secondly, alcoholic patients on active medication may drop out of treatment more rapidly and more often than those on placebo, depending on their SES characteristics (53, 185). If not taken into account, such differential dropout rates can obscure true drug-placebo differences. Early dropping out of treatment can be especially misleading in studies evaluating the effectiveness of drugs with a slow onset of therapeutic action, such as antidepressants, a point especially relevant in a population which tends to suffer from depression. Thirdly, physicians are usually resentful about having to give their patients a placebo and communicate this resentment of drug studies to their patients, another factor contributing to high dropout rates and the paradoxical relative ineffectiveness of active medications in such studies. Fourth, the effect of physician attitudes on the effectiveness of active medications has been shown clearly in the case of antidepressants (334). It is particularly important to take into account therapist differences since therapeutic style [detached vs. active, type A therapist vs. type B (384)] determines both attrition rate (158, 241) and placebo response (305), and differential assignment of patients to therapists, depending on patient and therapist characteristics, often takes place in supposedly well designed studies (305). Fifth, placebo reactors may report so much improvement on placebo that drug-placebo differences are obscured (240, 241). Sixth, patients with an established pattern of dropping out of treatment and who are most likely to drop out (303) are included in drug studies. Finally, inadequate dosage regimens below levels affording adequate symptomatic relief for many patients have often been used, something that may contribute to high dropout rates within the first month of treatment (15). On the other hand, if these factors were taken into account, along with others already mentioned, it seems reasonable to expect that drug treatment might prove effective in the outpatient treatment of carefully selected alcoholics in studies involving less than the N of 50–100 usually recommended.

Outcome in Drug Studies

In view of the foregoing, it is not surprising that few double blind studies have shown drugs to be effective in the treatment of chronic alcoholism. Rather, it is amazing that any of them have panned out.

Disulfiram and Citrated Calcium Carbimide

Disulfiram (DS) and citrated calcium carbimide (CCC) are different from other drugs studied in the treatment of alcoholism in two respects: (1) their effect on drinking is an indirect or potential one; and (2) neither has been subjected to a double blind study. If a patient takes either, he experiences a highly unpleasant physiological reaction, the knowledge or fear of which, it is hoped, will keep him from drinking. However, once having discontinued the medication (for 48 hr in the case of disulfiram, for 24 hr in that of CCC), he is free to drink again with impunity. Hence, unless he takes either drug on a compulsory basis, he is not compelled not to drink and knows it. Thus it can be argued that any effects of either drug in nondouble blind studies simply reflect the patient's motivation not to drink or, at least, to control his drinking when he feels most driven to it, the strength of his bond with the therapist who administers it, the strength of the latter's belief in efficacy of DS, and the former's suggestibility. Clearly, a priori it is hard to imagine any rationale for using either DS or CCC except in patients who have moderately good but not perfect control of their drinking and who are neither forgetful about taking medication nor fooling themselves that they want to stop drinking. Absolute medical contraindications to their use have been outlined elsewhere. In practice this usually only includes arteriosclerotic heart disease (214). Studies with controls suggest that the patient who does better on disulfiram is older, better motivated, better able to form dependent relationships, and more likely to have had blackouts and to have compulsive personality traits (14, 393). Depression confers a worse outcome in DS therapy (14, 393). Uncontrolled studies suggest that more socially stable and better motivated patients do better, and those with sociopathic features do worse (214). None of these prognostic indicators is remarkable in itself; in fact, most of them are quite familiar. Specific only, perhaps, are the contraindication of depression and the proviso of blackouts. Goodwin et al. (129) found that blackouts tend to be a relatively late manifestation of alcoholism. They also indicate rapid heavy intake (129). Therefore, it is possible that the patient with blackouts is more apt to be one who cannot stop after the first drink or two. Whether this is simply a common late manifestation of alcoholism or a personality trait remains to be investigated.

Only seven studies of disulfiram have used any kind of control group (14, 118, 120, 121, 149, 152, 393). In all but one the control conditions were nondrug treatments (120). Patients received either DS plus regular treatment or regular treatment only (114, 118, 120, 121, 149, 152), or DS in contrast to some other kind of treatment (393). All these studies concluded that DS was effective, but in such designs any differences found between experimental and control groups cannot be attributed *only* to the drug per se. The important role of motivation is suggested by Hoff and McKeown's (152) finding that within their control group, patients who wanted DS but were denied it for various reasons did better than those who refused it. On the other hand, two other studies reached the surprising conclusion that willingness to take DS does not indicate above average motivation for treatment in general. In one of them (1), one group wanted DS and got it, another wanted it but did not get it, and a third neither wanted nor got it. At 6–18 months after the beginning of treatment the authors could discern no relationship between a variety of outcome measures and what were felt to be motivational variables (state of sobriety on admission, groups 1 and 2 vs. 3, type of referral, regularity, number of clinic contacts, and pattern and length of disulfiram taking). The results, however, are weakened by a high dropout rate (39.4%), which may not have been distributed equally between groups, and by the fact that immediate dropouts and patients already doing well were excluded from the study. A more convincing study by Gerrein et al. (120) ostensibly overcame the formidable design problems involved in evaluating the efficacy of DS. They considered 6 groups: (1) patients who received a supply of DS once a week and took it without supervision; (2) those who got DS twice a week, when they took it under supervision; (3) DS acceptors who got regular treatment once a week, or (4) twice a week; (5) those who refused DS and were seen once a week, or (6) twice a week. If percentage attendance is used as an outcome measure, patients who took DS under supervision did better than those who took it without supervision, who in turn did no better or worse than the remaining four groups. Patients willing to take DS but not given it did no better than those who didn't want to take it. Those refused DS were told that the clinic was interested in the percentage of patients willing to take DS and that it might be available to them at a later date depending on how they were doing. To an alcoholic such a prescription means rejection. Hence this group did not really control for motivation. The issue of motivation in DS treatment needs further study as an aspect of the broader problem of what are the components of what we call motivation, and what determines the differential motivation that patients have for different treatments.

A major problem in DS treatment is that the patient may take himself off it and drink. Indeed, Baekeland et al. (14) found that the proportion of dry appointments their patients kept varied from 0.51 in the group with the poorest outcome, to 0.89 in that that did best. Hence, ideally, something else with strong reward value should be made contingent on the patient's taking his DS. In everyday terms, he should be gently forced to take his DS. Such a strategy was reported by Bourne et al. (31) in a study of jailed skid row alcoholics put on probation and given DS daily for 30 or 60 days (after which they could either continue or stop treatment) either without legal obligation, by a family member, or else by the courthouse probation officer with return to jail as the penalty for missing appointments. Patients were also given vocational counseling, and AA and psychotherapy were urged upon them. Nine months after the start of treatment both groups had an abstinence rate of 50%, unusually high in this kind of patient. One month dropout rates were similar (50%, 40.9%), and 8.1% of the patients drank while on DS and hence had DS-alcohol reactions. The conclusion that voluntary supervised treatment is as effective as compulsory treatment, however, is not warranted since the voluntary patients, who had available family members to give them DS, had not been given long-term sentences. Hence they probably had a better prognosis for two reasons: (1) since they had available relatives, they must have been less socially deteriorated; and (2) since they were not sentenced, they must have had more control over their behavior, which was less psychopathic, when drinking. A promising approach to the currently serious problem of the development of alcoholism among heroin addicts (13, 127) on methadone maintenance treatment was reported by Liebson et al. (207), who found that patients among whom receiving their methadone was made contingent on their taking disulfiram had much better control of their drinking than those simply urged to take it on a noncontingent basis. One can imagine that such approaches could be extended to patients in alcohol clinics who are dependent on minor tranquilizers such as chlordiazepoxide.

A potentially useful approach is that of surgical implantation of DS to ensure long-term effective blood levels. Widely used in Europe, an extensive trial in the English speaking world was reported only recently by Malcolm and Madden (224). In what must have been a highly motivated group of patients (83% of them had taken oral DS) they reported postoperative abstinence periods that were significantly longer than the longest 2 year preoperative abstinence period. 19.6% of patients drank once. Contraindications were those for oral disulfiram (respiratory, cardiac or renal disease, cirrhosis, diabetes, epilepsy, mental subnormality, and psychosis) and the patient's living alone. In practice, the authors state, they only had to consider the last. (On an anecdotal level, many clinicians using oral DS have felt those patients not living alone do better on it. This is an open issue for research.) The fact that infection was a problem in 14.9% of patients and that tablet extrusion occurred in another 14.9% emphasizes that this is a procedure best reserved for those who have failed by every other treatment method, thus truly a court of last resort.

CCC produces an alcohol reaction which is like that of DS but is milder (9, 34, 63, 124, 196, 206, 227, 228, 253, 254, 267, 280, 340, 341), shorter lived (124, 228), and of more rapid onset (63, 97). Its duration of action is only about half that of DS (63, 280). In view of CCC's shorter duration of action it is hard to imagine any rationale for its use except in some persons in whom DS is contraindicated. No properly controlled studies comparing its effectiveness with that of DS are known to us.

Metronidazole

The case of metronidazole is an excellent example of how poor experimental design can lead to the erroneous conclusion that a probably effective drug is useless. First introduced with the claim that it reduced craving for alcohol, a spate of uncontrolled studies found it effective. Then when controlled studies were done, nine (87, 109, 199, 208, 282, 289, 320, 352, 367) found it ineffective as opposed to one study that did not (354). The democratic procedure, if one were to blindly believe in the efficacy of double blind studies, would be to count heads and ignore the one paper that reported positive results. However, let us examine it and the others critically. Swinson (354), first of all, elected to study a population not too likely to drop out or to be impossible to follow up: the first 60 male alcoholics discharged from an inpatient unit willing to be studied and likely to stay in the area for at least 12 months. His patients did not include Class 4 or 5 patients and had an established relationship with the investigator, all factors militating against dropping out of treatment. Patients were told they might expect to feel less like drinking on the medication than previously. Drinking was assessed on a 5-point scale, weekly at first, and then at 3 month intervals by interview with patient and spouse/next of kin and patient. At 1 month there was no significant group difference but a trend in favor of metronidazole, which increased at 6 months and turned out to be significant at 1 year. Dropout rates were only 5% at 1 month and 35% at 3 months. (Class 1 and 2 patients were least likely to drop out.) Now let us consider the studies with negative results. All of them used treatment periods that were too short and ranged from 2 to 6 months, and all but one of them (282) used skid row or largely lower class populations. In one study (367) a 50% dropout rate in the first month reduced the effective sample size to only 23 patients. Two trials (109, 246) which found metronidazole no better than chlordiazepoxide and neither better than routine treatment suggest that the latter drug, too, may have been tested for too short a time in other published studies on it. Although Swinson's (354) work should be replicated, it appears that metronidazole may be effective on a long-range basis. How does it work? Several investigators found that it had a tranquilizing effect (115, 199) and that it interfered with the taste of or for alcohol (199, 289, 352, 367). Further work needs to be done in this area, especially in view of Lehman and Ban's (199) finding that clinical factors such as early onset of alcoholism were predictive of these effects in their patients. (Patients who had been drinking for less than 13 years had a significant decrease in anxiety and alcohol consumption.)

Lysergic Acid Diethylamide (LSD)

The history of LSD treatment of alcoholism starts with sensational anecdotal reports, followed by enthusiastic and almost always successful uncontrolled studies, and finally, by consistently unsuccessful controlled trials. A number of the latter (33, 275) showed transient short-term effects, but they, like the others (54, 153, 169, 213, 270, 338, 361), were not able to demonstrate long-term efficacy. If nothing else, this research, which made a number of schizophrenic patients decompensate, has drawn attention to the hazards of using hallucinogens in borderline or compensated schizophrenics.

Antidepressants and Tranquilizers

Considering the pitfalls of routine double blind drug research in alcoholic populations, it is hardly surprising that the only solid results are from short-term studies which have addressed themselves to symptoms of anxiety and depression in inpatients specially selected to exceed cutting scores on these symptoms. Thus imipramine proved effective in a 6 week trial in depressed female alcoholic outpatients (390) and at 3 weeks in depressed male alcoholic inpatients (38), and doxepin was more effective than chlordiazepoxide in treating symptoms of anxiety and depression at 3 weeks in male alcoholic inpatients (39). Similarly, Overall et al. (272) in a large-scale and methodologically sophisticated study of hospital alcoholics recently reported that chlordiazepoxide in low doses (10 mg t.i.d.) was ineffective in reducing symptoms of anxiety and depression but mesoridazine or amitryptaline did help. The issues of effective dosage and cross tolerance were raised but not settled. An intriguing recent double blind study by Kline et al. (190) of the effects of lithium on alcoholics, who were first hospitalized and then discharged to outpatient treatment and who received the drug for 1 year, concluded that the patients on lithium did much better than those on placebo in terms both of drinking episodes and rehospitalizations. However, our reanalysis of Kline et al.'s (190) data using a Yates correction for continuity in the calculation of the χ^2 tests shows that among patients who completed the program, patients on lithium did better than placebo patients only at $.05 \leq p \leq .10$ rather than $p \leq .05$ as reported. However, in a preliminary study with a 58.9% 1-year dropout rate, this is a minor point compared to the fact that when dropouts are *included* in the analysis, the significance of the difference between the two groups' readmission rates *increases* to $p \leq .025$. Careful examination of the data shows that this happened because a much smaller proportion of the lithium dropouts were rehospitalized than of the placebo dropouts. Since both groups had the same dropout rate (59.0 vs. 58.8%), the conclusion is unavoidable that patients assigned to lithium treatment were a better prognosis group than those assigned to placebo, so that the between group differences obtained could be (but may not be) due entirely to sampling bias rather than to drug effects. (The two groups were matched only on age and number of previous hospitalizations.) The finding that lithium program completers had significantly fewer drinking episodes in the follow-up interval than did patients on placebo must be tempered by this possibility. Furthermore, if dropouts are included, the between group difference in number of drinking episodes vanishes. Finally, there was no between group difference in change in scores on two depression inventories, this notwithstanding the fact that the rationale of the study was the repeated report that the drug is effective in mania and depression. We have indulged in such a lengthy analysis of this paper not to discourage further investigation of the effects of lithium on alcoholics (we in fact plan such a study ourselves), but rather to reemphasize how important it is to keep dropout rates low in drug studies, to control for sampling bias (a recurrent theme in this paper), and to match experimental and control groups on as many potentially relevant variables as possible. By contrast, reported effects in unstable lower class patient populations have been scanty indeed. However, Ditman (76) found that unselected and mostly skid row patients on chlordiazepoxide had a lower short-term dropout rate than those on placebo, imipramine, thioridazine, or diethylpropion. On the other hand, thioridazine was most effective in keeping hostile, irritable, unsociable, and lonely patients in treatment. Similarly, Haden and Fowler (141) found that outpatients with withdrawal symptoms were less likely to drop out before the fifth session if they were given promazine than if they were not. Such findings suggest that in a reliable population of nonplacebo responders with low dropout rates and adequate levels of target symptoms, antidepressants and tranquilizers would have a significant effect on specific symptom levels and, possibly, on long-term outcome. Both assumptions remain to be fairly and properly tested.

7. CRITERION GROUPS AND OUTCOME

We have emphasized again and again the need for optimal studies of any kind of treatment to take into account special subgroups of alcoholics most likely to benefit from it. Also important is the person who treats the alcoholic. Clues in this direction have been provided by Gerard and Saenger (118), who reported that in terms of outcome, patients treated by internists did best, by social workers next best, and by psychiatrists worst of all. This may be nothing more than a reflection of the fact that the total population of the eight clinics they studied was heavily weighted in the direction of lower class patients who are not very "psychologically minded," expect to be treated in the traditional medical model with drugs, and find psychological concepts of illness alien. Thus, among lower class patients who received psychotherapy, type B therapists (active, personality-oriented problem solving approach, more expressive) did better than type A therapists (regulative, mechanical interests) (239). Similarly, in drug treatment, active therapists do better than those who adopt a more passive role vis-à-vis the lower class patient (158). Along the same lines, Mayer and Myerson (232) found that low status patients were less likely to be treated by physicians, but among them only, those treated by physicians or who had a positive relationship with the therapist did best. On the other hand, disulfiram was the most successful treatment in low stability patients. The authors' finding that (short-term) reduction in alcohol intake was unrelated to attendance highlights the crucial, little investigated, and poorly understood question of the relative importance of patient-therapist and patient-treatment matches. For example, would the relationship between authoritarianism and the reluctance of physicians who don't specialize in treating alcoholics to treat them (133) carry over in the form of less obvious but still negative attitudes among more authoritarian alcoholism specialists? That it might is suggested by the finding that effective volunteer women alcohol counselors scored better on dominance, effective male counselors on femininity-nurturance (65). An allied problem is that of the advisability of using recovered alcoholics without professional training as counselors. Although this is currently fashionable in some quarters, there is, to our knowledge, no hard data supporting this practice and a very hard look should be taken at it. Indeed, Ottomanelli* recently showed that among heroin addicts maintained on methadone, those with psychiatric symptoms did worse with ex-addict counselors than with counselors who had professional training.

The problem of treatment acceptability has rarely been taken into account in treatment studies. Yet it is known that women tend to prefer individual psychotherapy to group therapy (69), that AA is unacceptable to most Class 1 and 5 patients (286), and that disulfiram is accepted by only a small fraction of patients (211), although the generalizability of this last-mentioned finding in lower class alcoholics is questionable since Gerrein et

---

* G. Ottomanelli, The Use of the MMPI as a Predictor of Outcome in a Methadone Maintenance Program, unpublished doctoral dissertation, New York University, 1973.

al. (120) found that 40.5% of alcoholic outpatients were willing to take disulfiram. Kissin's group is one of the few to have looked at the issues of treatment acceptability and patient-treatment match (172, 186, 187, 189). By using a design in which patients were randomly assigned to drug treatments or to psychotherapy, but either had or did not have the option of switching to an alternative form of treatment to that originally assigned, it was found that treatment acceptors did better than treatment rejectors and also that the greater the number of treatment choices, the better the outcome (188). Led to this line of investigation by repeated failures to show the expected effectiveness of antidepressants and tranquilizers in heterogeneous, largely lower class populations (185), they found that the successful drug patient tends to be older than 45, to be a professional, clerical, or skilled rather than unskilled worker, to have stable employment, and to have higher arithmetic scores on the WAIS, whereas the successful psychotherapy patient tends to be older than 45, white, vocationally stable, and self-referred, and scores high on fantasy ideation and also object assembly and picture completion in the WAIS (hence more field independent); on the other hand, the successful rehabilitation ward patient is vocationally stable, field independent, and has higher arithmetic scores. In other words, the patient who does best in psychotherapy is the most socially competent and psychologically sophisticated, the patient who does best on drugs is socially competent but less psychologically minded, and the patient who does best in a rehabilitation program is relatively socially incompetent but psychologically minded. (Group therapy is the mainstay of treatment there.) Patients who initially accepted psychotherapy (i.e., either did not become rapid dropouts or insisted on some other kind of treatment) were of higher SES, had higher IQs, and scored higher on fantasy ideation than those who do not accept psychotherapy, whereas rehabilitation acceptors had lower occupational status and were more field independent (less field dependent) than those who rejected it. No differences were found between drug acceptors and rejectors, but a recently completed double blind drug study in the same clinic showed drug treatment acceptors (nondropouts) to be more field independent than rejectors*, and on a clinical level Sarwer-Foner (324) has categorized patients who are threatened by medication. Systematic research needs to be done in this area. Along the same lines, other studies in this clinic have shown that dropouts from outpatient drug therapy are a nonhomogeneous group who drop out of treatment at different times for quite different reasons (15).

Another useful approach might be to look at known subgroups of alcoholics and see whether they do better or worse in various kinds of treat-

---

* Field dependence is positively related to behavioral dependence (394).

ments. The choice of groups might be determined as a first approximation by available nonsystematic information about their prognostic value in general populations of alcoholics or in various kinds of treatment regimens. The potentially relevant variables need not only be demographic, sociological, clinical, and psychological. Indeed, physiological variables have been relatively neglected in outcome studies. An interesting lead in this respect is provided by a recent report of Mendelson and Mello (244), which showed that alcoholics with a primary type 4 hyperlipoproteinemia had a striking elevation of triglycerides in their sera during long periods of alcohol consumption as compared with controls. They suggested that this fairly common and genetically related lipid abnormality may be a significant factor in the pathogenesis of alcohol hyperlipemia and alcohol-induced fatty liver. Gross et al. (135) have cited unpublished results of Mello and Mendelson to the effect that alcoholics with this metabolic defect are not able to drink as much or as long as other alcoholics. Gross et al. (135) suggest that such alcoholics are less likely to develop severe withdrawal or might be periodic rather than daily drinkers. Other groups potentially worth studying might include women as opposed to men (329), female primary alcoholics vs. male primary alcoholics vs. female depressive alcoholics vs. sociopathic alcoholics (307, 392), belligerent vs. nonbelligerent alcoholics (164), high occupation risk alcoholics vs. low occupation risk patients (148, 316), field independent vs. field dependent alcoholics (19, 27, 55, 173, 175, 300, 395), skid row alcoholics vs. Class 4 vs. Class 1 and 2 alcoholics (96), and regular vs. periodic alcoholics (226, 348). All these have been shown to differ both clinically and psychologically from each other. It is an old saw that there is no such thing as the alcoholic personality, but it has nonetheless become increasingly apparent that there may be differentiable subtypes of alcoholics. Thus alcoholics can be distinguished reliably by certain psychological tests (99, 216, 255, 272). On the basis of MMPI scale scores and their response or lack of response to treatment, Frame and Osmond (106) made the interesting and potentially fruitful distinction between psychopathic reaction types, who are unable to adjust only under stress, and psychopathic personalities, whose maladaptive behavior is more or less constant in all life situations. Rohan (314) has reported similar findings, and Kurland (195) found that a decrease in MMPI Pd scale scores during hospitalization gave a better prognosis. Factor analytic studies have revealed a number of factors derived from clinical history and psychological test items (93, 157, 217) and with or without multiple discriminant analysis they have uncovered a number of subtypes of alcoholics (93, 128, 198, 278, 326, 347). Rather than blindly apply treatments wholesale to hospital and outpatient populations (which is more administratively convenient), it is time that the issue of the patient-treatment fit be investigated using some of these variables. Clinicians intuitively recognize the importance of this issue, as witnessed by Smart et al.'s (337) report that Class 1 outpatients are more often treated by psychiatrists, Class 3 patients by internists, and that group therapy is given most often to Class 2 patients and least often to those in Class 3. Perhaps such an arrangement is based on little more than the operation of erroneous treatment stereotypes. On the other hand, it may indicate the clinician's intuitive recognition that different kinds of patients find certain kinds of treatments more acceptable and do better in them than others. Definitive answers to such questions can come only from further rigorously designed treatment research.

8.   SUMMARY AND CONCLUSIONS

The English language literature from 1953 to the present on methods for the treatment of chronic alcoholism is reviewed critically. The methodological problems inherent in treatment studies are discussed, in particular, sources of sampling bias and unreliability. Most studies were badly biased in favor of lower class nonpsychotic male patients, something that should be rectified in the future. Many studies failed to take into account various kinds of sample attrition and hence reported spuriously inflated success rates. It appears that multifactorial outcome measures are superior to abstinence alone as a criterion of success and that a 1 year follow-up interval is the absolute minimum acceptable. Unsettled questions needing more study are (1) the reliability of the drinking history, (2) the problem of the relative contributions of treatment and nontreatment factors during the follow-up period, and (3) the allied issue of spontaneous improvement. We recommend that only prospective studies be done and that information on the patient be sampled on admission, 3 weeks to 1 month later, just before discharge, and at follow-up.

Over and over we were impressed with the dominant role the patient, as opposed to the kind of treatment used on him, played both in his persistence in treatment and in his eventual outcome. Thus in inpatient studies good prognosis patients (higher SES and social stability) had improvement rates varying from 32.4 to 68% but poor prognosis patients (largely skid row alcoholics) had rates ranging from 0 to 18%. The effectiveness of hospital treatment programs, despite the introduction of new methods, seemed no better from 1960 to 1973 than it was from 1953 to 1963, and no differences were found in the effectiveness of different kinds of treatment regimens. There was some evidence that higher SES patients may need shorter hospitalizations and little aftercare, although these questions need more research.

Outpatient clinics had higher improvement rates (41.6%) than did inpatient programs despite their higher dropout rates (36.9 vs. 17.0%). Outpatient programs with the highest improvement rates had good prognosis patients (higher SES, better motivation, higher social stability), whereas those with the poorest outcomes catered largely to skid row patients. There was suggestive evidence in favor of multidisciplinary approaches, involvement of the spouse in treatment, and forced treatment of selected skid row alcoholics.

On the basis of the available evidence, which is limited, it seems possible that the population served by AA is quite different from that which goes to hospitals and clinics, and also that the general applicability of AA as a treatment method is much more limited than has been supposed in the past. Available data do not support AA's claims of much higher success rates than clinic treatment. Indeed, when population differences are taken into account, the reverse seems to be true. Of all the treatment methods reviewed, AA is most in need of further systematic study.

Behavioral approaches, if one takes into account that they are usually tried on highly selected volunteers, seem to give about the same results as other treatment methods. However, succinyl choline aversion is ineffective whereas aversive imagery techniques and those combining aversive and operant conditioning show promise.

Because of high dropout rates and the operation of uncontrolled nonspecific factors, double blind drug studies conducted in heterogeneous, unselected, and predominantly lower class clinic populations have not fairly tested the utility of antidepressants or tranquilizers in the treatment of chronic alcoholism. Future studies should concentrate on carefully selected criterion groups.

In the absence of controlled studies, it is still an open question whether the major determinant of success in the use of disulfiram is not simply the strength of the therapist-patient relationship. In any case, better results seem to be obtained if it is taken under supervision. The successful disulfiram patient, besides having characteristics which confer a good prognosis with any kind of treatment, is likely not to be depressed and to have compulsive personality features. Disulfiram may be particularly effective in heroin addict alcoholics maintained on methadone when receiving methadone is made contingent on taking disulfiram.

Metronidazole may be better than placebo on a long-term basis. The short time spans used in almost all drug studies suggests a reexamination of the utility of antidepressants and tranquilizers in better designed long-term studies with select populations.

Patients who do well on drugs, psychotherapy, or rehabilitation programs seem to have different characteristics, and success rates go up with the number of treatment options given the patient. More work needs to be done in this area. Future research could profitably examine the response to various kinds of treatments of already known criterion groups derived from factor analytic and other types of studies.

If differences in improvement rates indeed depend more on the kind of patient being treated than on the kind of treatment being used—and this did seem to us to be the case—an obvious question arises: since the treatments studied have all been applied somewhat indiscriminately to rather heterogeneous populations but nonetheless seem to help many patients, why are they as effective as they are? In other words, what do they have in common and how do they work? We do not presume to be able to answer these questions beyond noting that when a patient is hospitalized, he is detoxified, withdrawn from various life stresses, given practical help and guidance with respect to some of the problems of his everyday life, and may be given a modicum of hope via someone who is interested in him and his future. The last two factors also apply to outpatient treatment. Frank (107) has stressed the role of patient expectations, hope, suggestion, persuasion, and the like in psychotherapy. On the other hand, Drew (81) on the basis of epidemiologic evidence has suggested that alcoholism tends to be a self-limiting disease without explaining adequately why this might be so. Trying to answer the question of how different treatments work and what they have in common seems to us a major challenge to research that should not be ignored in the future.

Some other research questions that seem to us especially interesting and important to answer are the following. (1) What is the relative effectiveness of group versus individual psychotherapy in inpatient and outpatient treatment? (2) What is the optimal combination of hospital and outpatient treatment? (3) How strongly related are treatment length and outcome? (4) What kinds of patients are most likely to become dependent on tranquilizers and to abuse them? (5) Conversely, can receiving tranquilizers be made contingent on taking disulfiram in such patients? (6) How important are booster sessions and the patient-therapist relationship in behavior therapy? (7) To what kinds of patients is AA most applicable as a primary as opposed to secondary form of treatment? (8) How effective are recovered alcoholics as counselors as compared with professionally trained personnel?

REFERENCES

1. Aharan, C. H., R. D. Ogilvie, and J. T. Partington, Clinical indications of motivation in alcoholic patients, *Q. J. Stud. Alcohol,* **28,** 486–492 (1967).

2. Alcoholics Anonymous, The Fellowship of Alcoholics, New York, 1972.

3. Alcoholics Anonymous, Profile of an AA Meeting, Alcoholics Anonymous World Services, Inc., New York, 1972.

4. Allen, L. R. and I. Dootjes, Some personality considerations of an alcoholic population, *Percept. Mot. Skills*, **27**, 707–712 (1968).

5. Anant, S. S., The treatment of alcoholics by a verbal aversion technique: a case report, *Manas*, **13**, 79–86 (1966).

6. Anant, S. S., A note on the treatment of alcoholics by a verbal aversion technique, *Can. J. Psychol.*, **8**, 19–22 (1967).

7. Anant, S. S., Treatment of alcoholics and drug addicts by verbal aversion technique, Paper read at the 7th International Congress of Psychotherapy, Wiesbaden, 1967.

8. Anant, S. S., Treatment of alcoholics and drug addicts by verbal aversion techniques, *Int. J. Addict.*, **3**, 381–388 (1968).

9. Armstrong, J. D., The protective drugs in the treatment of alcoholism, *Can. Med. Assoc. J.*, **77**, 228–232 (1957).

10. Armstrong, R. G. and D. B. Hoyt, Personality structure of male alcoholics as reflected in the IES test, *Q. J. Stud. Alcohol*, **24**, 239–248 (1960).

11. Ashem, B. and L. Donner, Covert sensitization with alcoholics: a controlled replication, *Behav. Res. Ther.*, **6**, 7–12 (1968).

12. Asma, F. E., R. L. Eggert, and R. R. Hilker, Long term experience with rehabilitation of alcoholic employees, *J. Occup. Med.*, **13**, 581–585 (1971).

13. Baden, M. M., Methadone-related deaths in New York City, in *Methadone Maintenance*, S. Einstein (Ed.), Marcel Dekker, New York, 1971, pp. 143–152.

14. Baekeland, F., L. Lundwall, B. Kissin, and T. Shanahan, Correlates of outcome in disulfiram treatment of alcoholism, *J. Nerv. Ment. Dis.*, **153**, 1–9 (1971).

15. Baekeland, F., L. Lundwall, and T. Shanahan, Correlates of patient attrition in the outpatient treatment of alcoholism, *J. Nerv. Ment. Dis.*, **157**, 99–107 (1973).

16. Bahn, A. K., C. L. Anderson, and V. B. Norman, Outpatient psychiatric clinic services to alcoholics, *Q. J. Stud. Alcohol*, **24**, 213–226 (1963).

17. Bailey, M., P. Haberman, and J. Sheinberg, Identifying alcoholics in population surveys, *Q. J. Stud. Alcohol*, **27**, 300–315 (1966).

18. Bailey, M. B. and J. Stewart, Normal drinking by persons reporting previous problem drinking, *Q. J. Stud. Alcohol*, **28**, 305–315 (1967).

19. Bailey, W., F. Hustmyer, and A. Kristoffersen, Alcoholism, brain damage and perceptual dependence, *Q. J. Stud. Alcohol*, **22**, 387–393 (1961).

20. Bartholomew, A. A. and L. A. Guile, A controlled evaluation of "Librium" in the treatment of alcoholics, *Med. J. Aust.*, **48**, 578–581 (1961).

21. Bateman, N. I. and D. M. Petersen, Variables related to outcome of treatment for hospitalized alcoholics, *Int. J. Addict.*, **6**, 215–224 (1971).

22. Baum, O. E., S. B. Stanton, T. L. D'Zmura, and E. Shumaker, Psychotherapy dropouts and lower socioeconomic patients, *Am. J. Orthopsychiat.*, **36**, 629–635 (1966).

23. Berg, N. L., Effects of alcohol intoxication on self-concept; studies of alcoholics and controls in laboratory conditions, *Q. J. Stud. Alcohol*, **32**, 442–453 (1971).

24. Bergin, A. E., Some implications of psychotherapy research for therapuetic research, *J. Abnorm. Psychol.*, **71**, 235–246 (1966).

25. Blake, B. G., The application of behavior therapy to the treatment of alcoholism, *Behav. Res. Ther.*, **3**, 75–85 (1965).

26. Blake, B. G., A follow-up of alcoholics treated by behavior therapy, *Behav. Res. Ther.*, **5**, 89–94 (1967).

27. Blane, H. T. and M. E. Chafetz, Dependency conflict and sex-role identity in drinking delinquents, *Q. J. Stud. Alcohol*, **32**, 1025–1039 (1971).

28. Blane, H. T. and W. R. Meyers, Behavioral dependence and length of stay in psychotherapy among alcoholics, *Q. J. Stud. Alcohol*, **24**, 503–510 (1963).

29. Blane, H. T. and W. R. Meyers, Social class and the establishment of treatment relations by alcoholics, *J. Clin. Psychol.*, **20**, 287–290 (1964).

30. Blane, H. T., W. F. Overton, and M. E. Chafetz, Social factors in the diagnosis of alcoholism, I. Characteristics of the patient, *Q. J. Stud. Alcohol*, **24**, 640–663 (1963).

31. Bourne, P. G., J. A. Alford, and J. Z. Bowcock, Treatment of skid-row alcoholics with disulfiram, *Q. J. Stud. Alcohol*, **27**, 42–48 (1966).

32. Bowen, W. T. and L. Androes, A follow-up study of 79 alcoholic patients: 1963–1965, *Bull. Menninger Clinic*, **32**, 26–34 (1968).

33. Bowen, W. T., R. A. Soskin, and J. W. Chotlos, Lysergic acid diethylamide as a variable in the hospital treatment of alcoholism; a follow-up study, *J. Nerv. Ment. Dis.*, **150**, 111–118 (1970).

34. Brunner-Orne, M., Evaluation of calcium carbimide in the treatment of alcoholism, *J. Neuropsychiat.*, **3**, 163–167 (1962).

35. Bruun, K., Outcome of different types of treatment of alcoholics, *Q. J. Stud. Alcohol*, **24**, 280–288 (1963).

36. Burton, G., H. M. Kaplan, and E. H. Hudd, Marriage counseling with alcoholics and their spouses—I. A critique of the methodology of a follow-up study, *Br. J. Addict.*, **63**, 151–160 (1968).

37. Burton, G. and H. M. Kaplan, Marriage counseling with alcoholics and their spouses—II. The correlation of excessive drinking behavior with family pathology and social deterioration, *Br. J. Addict.*, **63**, 161–170 (1968).

38. Butterworth, A. T., Depression associated with alcohol withdrawal; imipramine therapy compared with placebo, *Q. J. Stud. Alcohol*, **32**, 343–348 (1971).

39. Butterworth, A. T. and R. D. Watts, Treatment of hospitalized alcoholics with doxepin and diazepam; a controlled study, *Q. J. Stud. Alcohol*, **32**, 78–81 (1971).

40. Button, A. D., A study of alcoholics with the Minnesota Multiphasic Inventory, *Q. J. Stud. Alcohol*, **17**, 263–281 (1956).

41. C., Bill, The growth and effectiveness of Alcoholic Anonymous in a Southwestern city, *Q. J. Stud. Alcohol*, **26**, 279–284 (1965).

42. Cahalan, D., *Problem Drinkers: A National Survey*, Jossey-Bass, San Francisco, 1970.

43. Cahn, S., *The Treatment of Alcoholics: An Evaluation Study*, Oxford University Press, New York, 1970.

44. Canter, F., Personality factors related to participation in treatment of hospitalized male alcoholics, *J. Clin. Psychol.*, **22**, 114–116 (1966).

45. Cappell, H. and P. C. Herman, Alcohol and tension reduction: a review, *Q. J. Stud. Alcohol*, **33**, 33–64 (1972).

46. Cautela, J. R., Treatment of compulsive behavior by covert sensitization, *Psychol. Rec.*, **16**, 33–41 (1966).

47. Cautela, J. R., Covert sensitization, *Psychol. Rep., 20,* 459–468 (1967).

48. Cautela, J. R. and R. A. Kastenbaum, A reinforcement survey schedule for use in therapy, training and research, *Psychol. Rep., 20,* 1115–1130 (1967).

49. Cellar, F. A. and A. H. Grant, The treatment of alcoholism in an outpatient clinic, *J. Mich. Med. Soc., 51,* 722–723, 729 (1952).

50. Chafetz, M. E. and H. T. Blane, Alcohol-crisis treatment approach and establishment of treatment relations with alcoholics, *Psychol. Rep., 12,* 862 (1963).

51. Chafetz, M. E., H. T. Blane, H. S. Abraham, J. Golner, E. Lacy, W. F. McCourt, E. Clark, and W. Meyers, Establishing treatment relations with alcoholics, *J. Nerv. Ment. Dis., 134,* 395–409 (1962).

52. Chafetz, M. E., H. T. Blane, and M. Hill, Social factors in the diagnosis of alcoholism, *Q. J. Stud. Alcohol, 26,* 72–79 (1965).

53. Charnoff, S. M., B. Kissin, and J. I. Reed, An evaluation of various psychotherapeutic agents in the long term treatment of chronic alcoholism. Results of a double blind study, *Am. J. Med. Sci., 246,* 172–179 (1963).

54. Cheek, F. E., H. Osmond, M. Sarett, and R. S. Albahary, Observations regarding the use of LSD-25 in the treatment of alcoholism, *J. Psychopharmacol., 1,* 56–74 (1966).

55. Chess, S. B., C. Neuringer, and G. Goldstein, Arousal and field dependency in alcoholics, *J. Gen. Psychol., 85,* 93–102 (1971).

56. Clancy, J., E. Vanderhoof, and P. Campbell, Evaluation of an aversive technique as a treatment for alcoholism; controlled trial with succinylcholine-induced apnea, *Q. J. Stud. Alcohol, 28,* 476–485 (1967).

57. Clancy, J., R. Vornbrock, and E. Vanderhoof, Treatment of alcoholics; a follow-up study, *Dis. Nerv. Syst., 26,* 551–561 (1965).

58. Clark, W., Operational definitions of drinking problems and associated prevalence rates, *Q. J. Stud. Alcohol, 27,* 648–668 (1966).

59. Cohen, M., I. A. Liebson, L. A. Faillace, and R. P. Allen, Moderate drinking by chronic alcoholics, *J. Nerv. Ment. Dis., 153,* 434–444 (1971).

60. Cohen, M., I. A. Liebson, L. A. Faillace, and W. Speers, Alcoholism: controlled drinking and incentives for abstinence, *Psychol. Rep., 28,* 575–580 (1971).

61. Cohen, M., I. A. Liebson, and L. A. Faillace, A technique for establishing controlled drinking in chronic alcoholics, *Dis. Nerv. Syst., 33,* 46–49 (1972).

62. Cohen, S., K. S. Ditman, H. B. Mooney, and J. R. B. Whittlesey, Prothiperidyle (Timovan) in the treatment of alcoholism: a preliminary report, *J. New Drugs, 1,* 235–237 (1961).

63. Collins, J. M. and L. M. Brown, Calcium carbimide a new protective drug in alcoholism, *Med. J. Aust., 1,* 835–838 (1960).

64. Corder, B. F., R. F. Corder, and N. D. Laidlaw, An intensive treatment program for alcoholic and their wives, *Q. J. Stud. Alcohol, 33,* 1144–1146 (1972).

65. Corner, B. J., Screening volunteer alcoholism counselors, *Q. J. Stud. Alcohol, 30,* 420–425 (1969).

66. Corotto, L. V., An exploratory study of the personality characteristics of patients who volunteer for continued treatment, *Q. J. Stud. Alcohol, 24,* 432–442 (1963).

67. Cosper, R., Interviewer bias in a study of drinking practices, *Q. J. Stud. Alc., 30,* 152–157 (1969).

68. Cowen, J., A six-year follow-up of a series of committed alcoholics, *Q. J. Stud. Alcohol*, **15**, 413–423 (1954).

69. Curlee, J., Sex differences in patient attitudes toward alcoholism treatment, *Q. J. Stud. Alcohol*, **32**, 643–650 (1971).

70. Cutter, H. S. G., J. C. Kay, E. Rothstein, and W. C. Jones, Alcohol, power and inhibition, *Q. J. Stud. Alcohol*, **34**, 381–389 (1973).

71. Davies, D. L., Normal drinking in recovered alcohol addicts, *Q. J. Stud. Alcohol*, **23**, 94–104 (1962).

72. Davies, D. L., M. Shephard, and E. Myers, The two years prognosis of fifty alcohol addicts after treatment in hospital, *Q. J. Stud. Alcohol*, **17**, 485–502 (1956).

73. Demone, H. W., Experiments in referral to alcoholism clinics, *Q. J. Stud. Alcohol*, **24**, 485–502 (1963).

74. Devenyi, P., and G. Sereny, Aversion treatment with electro-conditioning for alcoholism, *Br. J. Addict.*, **65**, 289–292 (1970).

75. Dichter, M., G. Z. Driscoll, D. J. Ottenberg, and A. Rosen, Marathon therapy with alcoholics, *Q. J. Stud. Alcohol*, **32**, 66–77 (1971).

76. Ditman, K. S., Evaluation of drugs in the treatment of alcoholics, *Q. J. Stud. Alcohol*, *Suppl. No. 1*, 107–116 (1961).

77. Ditman, K. S., Review and evaluation of current drug therapies in alcoholism, *Psychosom. Med.*, **28**, 667–677 (1966).

78. Ditman, K. S. and H. B. Mooney, Effects of phenyltoxamine in alcoholics, *Q. J. Stud. Alcohol*, **20**, 276–280 (1959).

79. Ditman, K. S., H. B. Mooney, and S. Cohen, New drugs in the treatment of alcoholism, in *Neuropsychopharmacology*, Vol. 3, Elsevier, New York, 1962, pp. 352–355.

80. Ditman, K. S., T. Moss, E. Forgy, L. Zunin, W. Funk, and R. Lynch, Characteristics of alcoholics volunteering for lysergide treatment, *Q. J. Stud. Alcohol*, **31**, 414–422 (1970).

81. Drew, L. R. H., Alcoholism as a self-limiting disease, *Q. J. Stud. Alcohol*, **29**, 956–967 (1968).

82. Dubourg, G. O., After-care for alcoholics—a follow-up study, *Br. J. Addict.*, **64**, 155–163 (1969).

83. Dunne, J. A., Counseling alcoholic employees in a municipal police department, *Q. J. Stud. Alcohol*, **34**, 423–434 (1973).

84. Edwards, G., Hypnosis in treatment of alcohol addiction; controlled trial, with analysis of factors affecting outcome, *Q. J. Stud. Alcohol*, **27**, 221–241 (1966).

85. Edwards, G. and S. Guthrie, A comparison of inpatient and outpatient treatment of alcohol dependence, *Lancet*, **1**, 467–468 (1966).

86. Edwards, P., C. Harvey, and P. C. Whitehead, Wives of alcoholics: a critical review and analysis, *Q. J. Stud. Alcohol*, **34**, 112–132 (1973).

87. Egan, W. P. and R. Goetz, Effect of metronidazole on drinking by alcoholics, *Q. J. Stud. Alcohol*, **29**, 899–902 (1968).

88. Ellis, A. S. and J. Krupinski, The evaluation of a treatment program for alcoholics: a follow-up study, *Med. J. Aust.*, **1**, 8–13 (1964).

89. Ends, E. J. and C. W. Page, A study of three types of group psychotherapy with hospitalized male inebriates, *Q. J. Stud. Alcohol*, **18**, 263–277 (1957).

90. Ends, E. J. and E. W. Page, Group psychotherapy and concomitant psychological change, *Psychol. Monogr.*, **73**, No. 480 (1959).

91. Engle, K. B. and T. K. Williams, Effect of an ounce of vodka on alcoholics' desire for alcohol, *Q. J. Stud. Alcohol*, **33**, 1099–1105 (1972).

92. Esterly, R. W., The alcoholic rehabilitation program in the Prince George's County Division of Parole and Probation, *Md. State, Med. J.*, **20**, 81–84 (1971).

93. Evenson, R. C., H. Altman, I. W. Sletten, and R. R. Knowles, Factors in the description and grouping of alcoholics, *Am. J. Psychiatry*, **130**, 49–54 (1973).

94. Eysenck, H. J. and S. Rachman, *The Causes and Cures of Neurosis*, Routledge & Kegan Paul, London, 1965.

95. Farrar, C. H., B. J. Powell, and L. K. Martin, Punishment of alcohol consumption by apneic paralysis, *Behav. Res. Ther.*, **6**, 13–16 (1968).

96. Feeney, F. E., D. F. Mindlin, V. H. Minear, and E. E. Short, The challenge of the skid-row alcoholic: A social psychological and psychiatric comparison of chronically jailed alcoholics and cooperative alcohol clinic patients, *Q. J. Stud. Alcohol*, **16**, 645–667 (1955).

97. Ferguson, J. K. W., A new drug for alcoholism treatment. 1. A new drug for the treatment of alcoholism, *Can. Med. Assoc. J.*, **74**, 793–795 (1956).

98. Ferneau, E. W., Jr., and H. F. Desroches, The relationship between abstinence and length of hospitalization, *Q. J. Stud. Alcohol*, **30**, 447–448 (1969).

99. Finney, J. C., D. F. Smith, D. E. Skeeters, and C. D. Auvenshine, MMPI alcoholism scales: factor structure and content analysis, *Q. J. Stud. Alcohol*, **32**, 1055–1060 (1971).

100. Fitzgerald, B. J., R. A. Pasewark, and R. Clark, Four-year follow-up of alcoholics treated at a rural state hospital, *Q. J. Stud. Alcohol*, **32**, 636–642 (1971).

101. Foster, F. M., J. L. Horn, and K. W. Wanberg, Dimensions of treatment outcome: a factor analytic study of alcoholics' responses to a follow-up questionnaire, *Q. J. Stud. Alcohol.*, **33**, 1079–1098 (1972).

102. Foulds, G., Clinical research in psychiatry, *J. Ment. Sci.*, **104**, 259–265 (1958).

103. Foulds, G. A. and C. Hassall, The significance of age of onset of excessive drinking in male alcoholics, *Br. J. Psychiat.*, **115**, 1027–1032 (1969).

104. Fox, R., Treatment of alcoholism in *Alcoholism: Basic aspects and treatment*, H. E. Himwich (Ed.), Publication #47 of the American Association for the Advancement of Science, Washington, D.C, 1957.

105. Fox, V. and M. A. Smith, Evaluation of a chemopsychotherapeutic program for the rehabilitation of alcoholism, *Q. J. Stud. Alcohol*, **20**, 767–780 (1959).

106. Frame, M. C. and W. M. G. Osmond, Alcoholism. Psychopathic personality and psychopathic reaction type, *Med. Proc. Jhbg.*, **2**, 257–261 (1956).

107. Frank, J. D., *Persuasion and Healing: A Comparative Study of Psychotherapy*, John Hopkins Press, Baltimore, 1961.

108. Franks, C. M., Alcoholism, in *Symptoms of Psychopathology: A Handbook*, C. G. Costello (Ed.), John Wiley, New York, 1970, pp. 160–190.

109. Gallant, D. M., M. P. Bishop, E. Camp, and C. A. Tisdale, A six-month controlled evaluation of metronidazole (Flagyl) in chronic alcoholic patients, *Curr. Ther. Res.*, **10**, 82–87 (1968).

110. Gallant, D. M., M. P. Bishop, M. A. Faulkner, L. Simpson, A. Cooper, D. Lathrop, A. M. Brisolara, and J. R. Bossetta, A comparative evaluation of compulsory (group

therapy and/or Antabuse) and voluntary treatment of the chronic alcoholic municipal court offender, *Psychosomatics, 9*, 306–310 (1968).

111. Gallant, D. M., M. P. Bishop, A. Mouledoux, A. A. Faulkner, A. Brisolara, and W. A. Swanson, The revolving-door alcoholic, *Arch. Gen. Psychiat., 28*, 633–635 (1973).

112. Gallant, D. M., M. P. Bishop, B. Stoy, M. A. Faulkner, and L. Paternostro, The value of a "first contact" group intake session in an alcoholism outpatient clinic: Statistical confirmation, *Psychosomatics 7*, 349–352 (1969).

113. Gallant, D. M., M. Faulkner, B. Stoy, M. P. Bishop, and D. Langdon, Enforced clinic treatment of paroled criminal alcoholics, *Q. J. Stud. Alcohol, 29*, 77–83 (1968).

114. Gallant, D. M., A. Rich, E. Bey, and I. Terranova, Group psychotherapy with married couples: a successful technique in New Orleans alcoholism clinic patients, *J. La. State Med. Soc., 122*, 41–44 (1970).

115. Gelder, M. G. and G. Edwards, Metronidazole in the treatment of alcohol addiction; a controlled trial, *Br. J. Psychiat., 114*, 473–475 (1968).

116. Gellman, G. I. P., *The Sober Alcoholic: An Organizational Analysis of Alcoholics Anonymous*, College and University Press, New Haven, Conn., 1964.

117. Gerard, D. L., and G. Saenger, Interval between intake and follow-up as a factor in the evaluation of patients with a drinking problem, *Q. J. Stud. Alcohol, 20*, 620–630 (1959).

118. Gerard, D. L. and G. Saenger, *Outpatient Treatment of Alcoholism*, Univ. of Toronto Press, Toronto, 1966.

119. Gerard, D. L., G. Saenger, and R. Wile, The abstinent alcoholic, *Arch. Gen. Psychiat., 6*, 83–95 (1962).

120. Gerrein, J. R., C. M. Rosenberg, and V. Manohar, Disulfiram maintenance in outpatient treatment of alcoholism, *Arch. Gen. Psychiat., 28*, 298–802 (1973).

121. Gibbins, R. J. and J. D. Armstrong, Effects of clinical treatment on behavior of alcoholic patients, an exploratory methodological investigation, *Q. J. Stud. Alcohol, 18*, 429–450 (1957).

122. Gibson, S. and J. Becker, Alcoholism and depression; the factor structure of alcoholics' responses to depression inventories, *Q. J. Stud. Alcohol, 34*, 400–408 (1973).

123. Gillis, L. S. and M. Keet, Prognostic factors and treatment results in hospitalized alcoholics, *Q. J. Stud. Alcohol, 30*, 426–437 (1969).

124. Glatt, M. M., Disulfiram and citrated calcium carbimide in the treatment of alcoholism, *J. Ment. Sci., 105*, 476–481 (1959).

125. Glatt, M. M., Treatment results in an English mental hospital alcoholic unit, *Acta Psychiat. Scand., 37*, 143–148 (1961).

126. Goldfried, M. R., Prediction of improvement in an alcoholism outpatient clinic, *Q. J. Stud. Alcohol, 30*, 129–139 (1969).

127. Goldstein, A., Blind controlled dosage comparisons with methadone in 200 patients, in *Proceedings of the Third National Conference on Methadone Treatment*, Public Health Service Publication No. 2172, Washington, D.C., U.S. Government Printing Office, 1972, pp. 31–37.

128. Goldstein, S. G. and J. D. Linden, Multivariate classification of alcoholics by means of the MMPI, *J. Abnorm. Psychol., 74*, 661–669 (1969).

129. Goodwin, D. W., B. Crane, and S. B. Guze, Alcoholic "blackouts": A review and clinical study of 100 alcoholics, *Am. J. Psychiat., 126*, 191–198 (1969).

130. Goodwin, D. W., J. B. Crane, and S. B. Guze, Felons who drink: an 8-year follow-up, *Q. J. Stud. Alcohol*, **32**, 136–147 (1971).

131. Gottheil, E., B. F. Murphy, T. E. Skoloda, and L. O. Corbett, Fixed interval drinking decisions. II. Drinking and discomfort in 25 alcoholics, *Q. J. Stud. Alcohol*, **33**, 325–340 (1972).

132. Gozali, J. and J. Sloan, Control orientation as a personality dimension among alcoholics, *Q. J. Stud. Alcohol*, **32**, 159–161 (1971).

133. Gray, R. M., P. M. Moody, M. Sellars, and J. R. Ward, Physician authorization and the treatment of alcoholics, *Q. J. Stud. Alcohol*, **30**, 981–983 (1969).

134. Greenhouse, R. H. and M. L. Pilot, Reserpine as an adjunct in the treatment of alcoholism, *Q. J. Stud. Alcohol*, **18**, 468–474 (1957).

135. Gross, M. M., E. Lewis, J. Hastey, and M. Nagarajan, Acute alcohol withdrawal syndrome, in *The Biology of Alcoholism*, B. Kissin and H. Begleiter (Eds.), Vol. 3, Chapter 3, 1973.

136. Gross, W. F. and V. J. Nerviano, The prediction of dropouts from an inpatient alcoholism program by objective personality inventories, *Q. J. Stud. Alcohol*, **34**, 514–515 (1973).

137. Guze, S. B. and D. W. Goodwin, Consistency of drinking history and diagnosis of alcoholism, *Q. J. Stud. Alcohol*, **33**, 111–116 (1972).

138. Guze, S. B., V. B. Tuason, M. A. Stewart, and B. Picken, The drinking history: a comparison of reports by subjects and their relatives, *Q. J. Stud. Alcohol*, **24**, 249–260 (1963).

139. Gynther, M. D. and P. I. Brilliant, Marital status, readmission to hospital, and intrapersonal and interpersonal perceptions of alcoholics, *Q. J. Stud. Alcohol*, **28**, 52–58 (1967).

140. Gynther, M. D., C. H. Presher, and R. L. McDonald, Personal and interpersonal factors associated with alcoholism, *Q. J. Stud. Alcohol*, **20**, 321–333 (1959).

141. Haden, H. H. and R. D. Fowler, Prozine as an adjunct to psychotherapy with alcoholic outpatients in the withdrawal stage, *Q. J. Stud. Alcohol*, **23**, 442–448 (1962).

142. Haertzen, C. A., N. T. Hooks, J. J. Monroe, G. B. Fuller, and H. Sharp, Nonsignificance of membership in alcoholics anonymous in hospitalized alcoholics, *J. Clin. Psychol.*, **24**, 99–103 (1968).

143. Hansen, H. A. and K. Teilmann, A treatment of criminal alcoholics in Denmark, *Q. J. Stud. Alcohol*, **15**, 245–287 (1954).

144. Hayman, M., Current attitudes to alcoholism of psychiatrists in Southern California, *Am. J. Psychiat.*, **112**, 484–493 (1956).

145. Hayman, M., *Alcoholism: Mechanism and Management*, Charles C Thomas, Springfield, Ill., 1966.

146. Heilbrun, A. B., Prediction of rehabilitation outcome in chronic court-case alcoholics, *Q. J. Stud. Alcohol*, **32**, 328–333 (1971).

147. Hill, M. J. and H. T. Blane, Evaluation of psychotherapy with alcoholics: a critical review, in *Frontiers of Alcoholism*, M. E. Chafetz, H. T. Blane, and M. J. Hill (Eds.), Science House, New York, 1970, pp. 160–199.

148. Hitz, D., Drunken sailors and others; drinking problems in specific occupations, *Q. J. Stud. Alcohol*, **34**, 496–505 (1973).

149. Hoff, E. C., The use of disulfiram (Antabuse) in the comprehensive therapy of a group of 1,020 alcoholics, *Conn. State, Med. J., 19,* 793–798 (1955).

150. Hoff, E. C., The use of pharmacological adjuncts in the psychotherapy of alcoholics, *Q. J. Stud. Alcohol Suppl.* 1, 138–150 (1961).

151. Hoff, E. C. and J. C. Forbes, Some effects of alcohol on metabolic mechanisms with applications to therapy of alcoholics. III. The effect of poly-vitamin supplementation in the diet of alcoholics upon their clinical course, in *Origins of Resistance to Toxic Agents,* M. G. Sevag, R. D. Reid, and O. E. Reynolds (Eds.), Academic Press, New York, 1955, pp. 184–193.

152. Hoff, E. C. and C. E. McKeown, An evaluation of the use of tetraethylthiuram disulfide in the treatment of 560 cases of alcohol addiction, *Am. J. Psychiat., 109,* 670–673 (1953).

153. Hollister, L. E., J. Shelton, and G. Kriger, A controlled comparison of lysergic acid diethylamide (LSD) and dextroamphetamine in alcoholism, *Am. J. Psychiat., 125,* 1352–1357 (1969).

154. Holzinger, R., R. Mortimer, and W. Van Dusen, Aversion conditioning treatment of alcoholism, *Am. J. Psychiat., 124,* 246–247 (1967).

155. Hore, B. D., Life events and alcoholic relapse, *Brit. J. Addict., 66,* 83–88 (1971).

156. Hore, B. D., Factors in alcoholic relapse, *Br. J. Addict., 66,* 89–96 (1971).

157. Horn, J. L. and K. W. Wanberg, Dimensions of perception of background and current situation of alcoholic patients, *Q. J. Stud. Alcohol, 31,* 633–658 (1970).

158. Howard, K., K. Rickels, J. E. Mock, R. S. Lipman, L. Covi, and N. C. Baum, Therapeutic style and attrition rate from psychiatric drug treatment, *J. Nerv. Ment. Dis., 150,* 102–110 (1970).

159. Hoy, R. M., The personality of inpatient alcoholics in relation to group psychotherapy, as measured by the 16-PF., *Q. J. Stud. Alcohol, 30,* 401–407 (1969).

160. Hsu, J. J., Electroconditioning therapy of alcoholics: A preliminary report, *Q. J. Stud. Alcohol, 26,* 449–459 (1965).

161. Hunsicker, A. L., D. E. Hurd, and D. Morse, Group therapy with alcoholic tuberculous patients, *Am. Rev. Respir. Dis., 95,* 313–316 (1967).

162. Isbell, H., H. Fraser, A. Wikler, R. Belleville, and A. Eisenman, An experimental study of the etiology of "run fits" and delirium tremens, *Q. J. Stud. Alcohol, 15,* 1–33 (1955).

163. Jackson, J. K., Type of drinking patterns of male alcoholics, *Q. J. Stud. Alcohol, 19,* 269–302 (1958).

164. Jackson, J. K., R. J. Fagan, and R. C. Burr, The Seattle police department rehabilitation project for chronic alcoholics, *Fed. Probation, 22,* 36–41 (1958).

165. Jellinek, E. M., Recent trends in alcoholism and in alcohol consumption, *Q. J. Stud. Alcohol, 8,* 1–43 (1947).

166. Jellinek, E. M., The estimate of the number of alcoholics in the U.S.A. for 1949 in the light of the Sixth Revision of the International Lists of Causes of Death, *Q. J. Stud. Alcohol, 11,* 215–218 (1952).

167. Jensen, S. E., A treatment program for alcoholics in a mental hospital, *Q. J. Stud. Alcohol, 23,* 315–320 (1962).

168. Jenssen, C. O., B. Cronholm, S. Izikowitz, K. Gordon, and A. Rosen, Intellectual

changes in alcoholics; psychometric studies in mental sequels of prolonged intensive abuse of alcohol, *Q. J. Stud. Alcohol,* **23,** 221–242 (1962).

169. Johnson, F. G., LSD in the treatment of alcoholism, *Am. J. Psychiat.,* **126,** 481–487 (1969).

170. Jones, R. K., Sectarian characteristics of Alcoholics Anonymous, *Sociology,* **4,** 181–195 (1970).

171. Jones, R. W. and A. R. Helrich, Treatment of alcoholism by physicians in private practice, *Q. J. Stud. Alcohol,* **33,** 117–131 (1972).

172. Karp, S. A., B. Kissin, and F. E. Hustmyer, Jr., Field dependence as a predictor of alcoholic therapy dropouts, *J. Nerv. Ment. Dis.,* **150,** 77–83 (1970).

173. Karp, S. A., D. C. Poster, and A. Goodman, Differentiation in alcoholic women, *J. Pers.,* **31,** 386–393 (1963).

174. Karp, S. A., H. A. Witkin, and D. R. Goodenough, Alcoholism and psychological differentiation: effect of alcohol on field dependence, *J. Abnorm. Psychol.,* **70,** 262–265 (1965).

175. Karp, S. A., H. A. Witkin, and D. R. Goodenough, Alcoholism and psychological differentiation: effect of achievement of sobriety on field dependence, *Q. J. Stud. Alcohol,* **26,** 580–585 (1965).

176. Katz, J. and R. Solomon, The patient and his experiences in an outpatient clinic, *A.M.A. Arch. Neurol. Psychiatry,* **80,** 86–92 (1958).

177. Katz, L., The Salvation Army men's social service center: II. Results, *Q. J. Stud. Alcohol,* **27,** 636–647 (1966).

178. Kearney, T. and J. C. Bonime, Problems of drug evaluation in outpatients, *Dis. Nerv. Syst.,* **27,** 604–606 (1966).

179. Keehn, J. D., Reinforcement of alcoholism; schedule control of solitary drinking, *Q. J. Stud. Alcohol,* **31,** 28–39 (1970).

180. Keehn, J. D., F. F. Bloomfield, and M. A. Hug, Use of the reinforcement survey schedule with alcoholics, *Q. J. Stud. Alcohol,* **31,** 602–615 (1970).

181. Kendall, R. E., Normal drinking by former alcohol addicts, *Q. J. Stud. Alcohol,* **26,** 247–257 (1965).

182. Kendall, R. E. and M. C. Staton, The fate of untreated alcoholics, *Q. J. Stud. Alcohol,* **27,** 30–41 (1966).

183. Kish, G. B. and T. M. Cheney, Impaired abilities in alcoholism: measured by the General Aptitude Test Battery, *Q. J. Stud. Alcohol,* **30,** 384–388 (1969).

184. Kish, G. B. and H. T. Hermann, The Fort Meade alcoholism treatment program: a follow-up study, *Q. J. Stud. Alcohol,* **32,** 628–635 (1971).

185. Kissin, B., S. M. Charnoff, and S. M. Rosenblatt, Drug and placebo responses in chronic alcoholics, *Am. Psychiat. Assoc. Psychiat. Res. Rep.,* **24,** 44–60 (March 1968).

186. Kissin, B. and A. Platz, The use of drugs in the long term rehabilitation of chronic alcoholics, in *Psychopharmacology: A Review of Progress 1957–1967,* D. H. Efron (Ed.), Public Health Service Publication 1836, Washington, D.C., 1968, 835–851.

187. Kissin, B., A. Platz, and W. H. Su, Social and psychological factors in the treatment of chronic alcoholism, *J. Psychiat. Res.,* **8,** 13–27 (1970).

188. Kissin, B., A. Platz, and W. H. Su, Selective factors in treatment choice and outcome in alcoholics, in *Recent Advances in Studies of Alcoholism,* N. K. Mello and J. H.

Mendelson (Eds.), U.S. Government Printing Office, Publication #(HSM) 71-9045, Washington, D.C., 1971, 781–802.

189. Kissin, B., S. M. Rosenblatt, and S. Machover, Prognostic factors in alcoholism, *Wash. D.C. Am. Psychiat. Assoc. Psychiat. Res. Rep.*, **24**, 22–43 (1968).

190. Kline, N. S., J. C. Wren, T. B. Cooper, E. Vargas, and O. Canal, Evaluation of lithium therapy in chronic alcoholism. *Clinical Medicine*, **81**, 33–36 (1974).

191. Knox, W. J., Attitudes of psychiatrists and psychologists toward alcoholism, *Am. J. Psychiat.*, **127**, 1675–1679 (1971).

192. Knox, W. J., Four-year follow-up of veterans treated on a small alcoholism ward, *Q. J. Stud. Alcohol*, **33**, 105–110 (1972).

193. Koumans, A. J. R. and J. J. Muller, Use of letters to increase motivation for treatment in alcoholics, *Psychol. Rep.*, **16**, 1152 (1965).

194. Koumans, A. J., J. J. Muller, and C. F. Miller, Use of telephone calls to increase motivation for treatment in alcoholics, *Psychol. Rep.*, **21**, 327–328 (1967).

195. Kurland, A. A., Maryland alcoholics: follow-up study I. *Psychiat. Res. Rep.*, **24**, 71–82 (1968).

196. Lader, M. H., Alcohol reactions after single and multiple doses of calcium cyanamide, *Q. J. Stud. Alcohol*, **28**, 468–475 (1967).

197. Laverty, S. G., Aversion therapies in the treatment of alcoholism, *Psychosom. Med.*, **28**, 651–666 (1966).

198. Lawlis, G. F. and S. E. Rubin, 16-PF study of personality patterns in alcoholics, *Q. J. Stud. Alcohol*, **32**, 318–327 (1971).

199. Lehmann, H. E. and T. A. Ban, Chemical reduction of the compulsion to drink with metronidazole; a new treatment modality in the therapeutic program of the alcoholic, *Curr. Ther. Res.*, **9**, 419–428 (1967).

200. Leivonen, P., P. Stenij, and C. J. Thesleff, Experience with three drugs in ambulatory treatment of alcoholism, *Acta Psychiat. Scand.*, **42**(*Suppl. 192*), 177–181 (1966).

201. Lemere, F., What happens to alcoholics, *Am. J. Psychiat.*, **109**, 674–676 (1953).

202. Lemere, F., P. O'Holloran, and M. A. Maxwell, Motivation in the treatment of alcoholism, *Q. J. Stud. Alcohol*, **19**, 428–431 (1958).

203. Lemere, F. and W. L. Voegtlin, An evaluation of the aversion treatment of alcoholism, *Q. J. Stud. Alcohol*, **11**, 199–204 (1950).

204. Lemere, F., W. L. Voegtlin, W. R. Broz, P. O'Holloran, and W. E. Tupper, The conditioned reflex treatment of chronic alcoholism: VII. Technic, *Dis. Nerv. Syst.*, **3**, 243–247 (1942).

205. Levinson, T. and G. Sereny, An experimental evaluation of "insight therapy" for the chronic alcoholic, *Can. Psychiat. Assoc. J.*, **14**, 143–145 (1969).

206. Levy, M. S., B. L. Livingstone, and D. M. Collins, A clinical comparison of disulfiram and calcium carbimide, *Am. J. Psychiat.*, **123**, 1018–1022 (1967).

207. Liebson, I., G. Bigelow, and R. Flamer, Alcoholism among methadone patients: a specific treatment method, *Am. J. Psychiat.*, **130**, 483–485 (1973).

208. Linton, P. H. and J. D. Hain, Metronidazole in the treatment of alcoholism, *Q. J. Stud. Alcohol*, **28**, 544–546 (1967).

209. Lipscomb, W. R., Mortality among treated alcoholics: A three-year follow-up study, *Q. J. Stud. Alcohol*, **20**, 596–603 (1959).

210. Lovibond, S. H. and G. Caddy, Discriminated aversive control in the moderation of alcoholics' drinking behavior, *Behav. Ther.*, **1**, 437–444 (1970).

211. Lubetkin, B. S., P. C. Rivers, and C. M. Rosenberg, Difficulties of disulfiram therapy with alcoholics, *Q. J. Stud. Alcohol*, **32**, 168–171 (1971).

212. Luborsky, L., M. Chandler, A. Auervach, and J. Cohen, Factors influencing the outcome of psychotherapy: a review of quantitative research, *Psychol. Bull.*, **75**, 145–185 (1971).

213. Ludwig, A., J. Levine, L. Stark, R. Lazar, A clinical study of LSD treatment in alcoholism, *Am. J. Psychiat.*, **126**, 59–69 (1969).

214. Lundwall, L. and F. Baekeland, Disulfiram treatment of alcoholism; a review, *J. Nerv. Ment. Dis.*, **153**, 381–394 (1971).

215. Lynn, L. and P. M. Smith-Moorehouse, A survey of treatment of alcoholism at an outpatient clinic, *Br. J. Addict.*, **61**, 197–200 (1966).

216. MacAndrew, C., The differentiation of male alcoholic outpatients from nonalcoholic psychiatric outpatients by means of the MMPI, *Q. J. Stud. Alcohol*, **26**, 238–246 (1965).

217. MacAndrew, C., Self-reports of male alcoholics: a dimensional analysis of certain differences from nonalcoholic male psychiatric outpatients, *Q. J. Stud. Alcohol*, **28**, 43–51 (1967).

218. MacAndrew, C. and H. Garfinkel, A consideration of changes attributed to intoxication as common-sense reasons for getting drunk, *Q. J. Stud. Alcohol*, **23**, 252–266 (1962).

219. MacCulloch, M. J., M. P. Feldman, J. F. Orford, and M. L. MacCulloch, Anticipatory avoidance learning in the treatment of alcoholism: a record of therapeutic failure, *Behav. Res. Ther.*, **4**, 187–196 (1966).

220. Machover, S., F. S. Puzzo, and F. Plumeau, Clinical and objective studies of personality variables in alcoholism. I. Clinical investigation of the "alcoholic personality," *Q. J. Stud. Alcohol*, **20**, 505–519 (1959).

221. Machover, S., F. S. Puzzo, and F. Plumeau, Clinical and objective studies of personality variables in alcoholism. II. Clinical study of personality correlates of remission from active alcoholism, *Q. J. Stud. Alcohol*, **20**, 520–527 (1959).

222. Madill, M. F., D. Campbell, S. G. Laverty, R. E. Sanderson, and S. L. Vanderwater, Aversion treatment of alcoholics by succinylcholine-induced apneic paralysis; an analysis of early changes in drinking behavior, *Q. J. Stud. Alcohol*, **27**, 483–509 (1966).

223. Maier, R. A. and V. Fox, Forced therapy of probated alcoholics, *Med. Times/N.Y.*, **86**, 1051–1054 (1958).

224. Malcolm, M. T. and J. S. Madden, The use of disulfiram implantation in alcoholism, *Br. J. Psychiat.*, **123**, 41–55 (1973).

225. Malmoe, S., R. Rosenthal, H. T. Blane, M. E. Chafetz, and I. Wolf, The doctor's voice: postdictor of successful referral of alcoholic patients, *J. Abnorm. Psychol.*, **72**, 78–84 (1967).

226. Marconi, J., K. Fink, and L. Moya, Experimental study on alcoholics with an inability to stop, *Br. J. Psychiatry*, **113**, 543–545 (1967).

227. Marconi, J., G. Solari, and S. Gaete, Comparative clinical carbimide. II. Reaction to alcohol, *Q. J. Stud. Alcohol*, **22**, 46–51 (1961).

228. Marconi, J., G. Solari, S. Gaete, and L. Piazza, Comparative clinical study of the ef-

fects of disulfiram and calcium carbimide. I. Side effects, *Q. J. Stud. Alcohol,* **21,** 642–654 (1960).

229. Matefy, R. E., R. A. Kalish, and J. M. Cantor, Self-acceptance in alcoholics who accept and reject help, *Q. J. Stud. Alcohol,* **32,** 1088–1091 (1971).

230. Mathias, R. E. S., An experimental investigation of the personality structure of chronic alcoholics, Alcoholics Anonymous, neurotic and normal groups, Doctoral dissertation, Univ. of Buffalo (1955).

231. Mayer, J., Initial alcoholism clinic attendance of patients with legal referrals, *Q. J. Stud. Alcohol,* **33,** 814–816 (1972).

232. Mayer, J. and D. J. Myerson, Outpatient treatment of alcoholics; effects of status, stability and nature of treatment, *Q. J. Stud. Alcohol,* **32,** 620–627 (1971).

233. Mayer, J., M. A. Needham, and D. J. Myerson, Contact and initial attendance at an alcoholism clinic, *Q. J. Stud. Alcohol,* **26,** 480–485 (1965).

234. Mayfield, D. G., Psychopharmacology of alcohol. I. Affective change with intoxication, drinking behavior and affective state, *J. Nerv. Ment. Dis.,* **146,** 314–321 (1968).

235. Mayfield, D. G., Psychopharmacology of alcohol. II. Affective tolerance in alcohol intoxication, *J. Nerv. Ment. Dis.,* **146,** 322–327 (1968).

236. Mayfield, D. G. and L. L. Coleman, Alcohol use and affective disorder, *Dis. Nerv. Syst.,* **29,** 467–474 (1968).

237. McCance, C. and P. F. McCance, Alcoholism in North-East Scotland; its treatment and outcome, *Br. J. Psychiat.* **115,** 189–198 (1969).

238. McGuire, M. T., S. Stein, and J. H. Mendelson, Comparative psychosocial studies of alcoholic and nonalcoholic subjects undergoing experimentally induced ethanol intoxication, *Psychosom. Med.,* **28,** 13–26 (1966).

239. McNair, D. M., D. M. Callahan, and M. Lorr, Therapist "type" and patient response to psychotherapy, *J. Consult. Psychol.,* **26,** 425–429 (1962).

240. McNair, D. M., S. Fisher, R. J. Kahn, and L. F. Droppleman, Drug-personality interaction in intensive outpatient treatment, *Arch. Gen. Psychiat.,* **22,** 128–135 (1970).

241. McNair, D. M., R. J. Kahn, L. F. Droppleman, and S. Fisher, Compatibility, acquiescence and drug effects, in *Neuropsychopharmacology,* H. Brill, J. O. Cole, P. Deniker, H. Hippins, and P. B. Bradley (Eds.), New York, Excerpta Medical Foundation, 536–542, 1967.

242. Mendelson, J. H., Experimentally induced chronic intoxication and withdrawal in alcoholics, *Q. J. Stud. Alcohol, Suppl. No. 2,* 1–126 (1964).

243. Mendelson, J. H., J. LaDou, and P. Solomon, Experimentally induced chronic intoxication and withdrawal in alcoholics. Part 3. Psychiatric findings, *Q. J. Stud. Alcohol, Suppl. No. 2,* 40–52 (1964).

244. Mendelson, J. H. and N. K. Mello, Alcohol-induced hyperlipemia and beta lipoproteins, *Science,* **180,** 1372–1374 (1973).

245. Merry, J., The "loss of control" myth, *Lancet,* 1257–1258 (June 4, 1966).

246. Merry, J. and A. Whitehead, Metronidazole and alcoholism, *Br. J. Psychiat.,* **114,** 859–861 (1968).

247. Miller, B. A., A. D. Pokorny, J. Valles, and S. E. Cleveland, Biased sampling in alcoholism treatment research, *Q. J. Stud. Alcohol,* **31,** 97–107 (1970).

248. Mills, K. C., M. B. Sobell, and H. H. Schaeffer, Training social drinking as an alternative to abstinence for alcoholics, *Behav. Ther.,* **2,** 18–27 (1971).

249. Mindlin, D. F., The characteristics of alcoholics related to prediction of therapeutic outcome, *Q. J. Stud. Alcohol,* **20,** 604–619 (1959).

250. Mindlin, D. F., Evaluation of therapy for alcoholics in a workhouse setting, *Q. J. Stud. Alcohol,* **21,** 90–112 (1960).

251. Mindlin, D. F., Attitudes toward alcoholism and toward self: differences between three alcoholic groups, *Q. J. Stud. Alcohol,* **25,** 136–141 (1964).

252. Mindlin, D. F. and E. Belden, Attitude changes with alcoholics in group therapy, *Calif. Ment. Health Res. Dig.,* **3,** 102–103 (1965).

253. Minto, A. and F. J. Roberts, "Temposil," a new drug in the treatment of alcoholism, *J. Ment. Sci.,* **106,** 288–295 (1960).

254. Mitchell, E. H., Use of citrated calcium carbimide in alcoholism, *J. Am. Med. Ass.,* **168,** 2008–2009 (1958).

255. Monroe, J. J., G. E. English, and C. A. Haertzen, The language of addiction scales; validity generalization of effects of labeling as drug addict or alcoholic, *Q. J. Stud. Alcohol,* **32,** 1048–1054 (1971).

256. Mooney, H. B., S. Cohen, K. S. Ditman, and J. R. B. Whittlesey, Methocarbamol (Robaxin) in the treatment of alcoholics, *J. New Drugs,* **1,** 276–278 (1961).

257. Mooney, H. B. and K. S. Ditman, Tybamate, a meprobamate analog, in the treatment of alcoholics, *J. New Drugs,* **5,** 233–235 (1965).

258. Mooney, H. B., K. S. Ditman, and S. Cohen, Cyphroheptadine in the treatment of alcoholics, *J. New Drugs,* **4,** 46–51 (1964).

259. Moore, R. A., The diagnosis of alcoholism in a psychiatric hospital: a trial of the Michigan Alcoholism Screening Test (MAST), *Am. J. Psychiat.,* **128,** 1565–1569 (1972).

260. Moore, R. A. and T. C. Murphy, Denial of alcoholism as an obstacle to recovery, *Q. J. Stud. Alcohol,* **22,** 597–609 (1961).

261. Moore, R. A. and F. Ramseur, Effects of psychotherapy in an open-ward hospital in patients with alcoholism, *Q. J. Stud. Alcohol,* **21,** 233–252 (1960).

262. Mottin, J. L., Drug-induced attenuation of alcohol consumption, *Q. J. Stud. Alcohol,* **34,** 444–472 (1973).

263. Mulford, H. A., *Identifying Problem Drinkers,* USPHS Publ. #1000, Washington, D.C., 1966.

264. Muzekeri, L. H., The MMPI in predicting treatment outcome in alcoholism, *J. Consult. Psychol.,* **29,** 281 (1965).

265. Myers, J. K. and F. Auld, Some variables related to outcome of psychotherapy, *J. Clin. Psychol.,* **11,** 51–54 (1955).

266. Myerson, D. J. and J. Mayer, Origins, treatment, and destiny of skid-row alcoholic men, *N. Engl. J. Med.,* **275,** 419–425 (1966).

267. Nason, Z. M., Temposil; new chemotherapy for treatment of alcoholism, *J. Kans. Med. Soc.,* **59,** 391–392 (1958).

268. National Council on Alcoholism Fact Sheet, *Facts on Alcoholism,* August 1972.

269. Nørvig, J. and B. Nielsen, A follow-up study of 221 alcohol addicts in Denmark, *Q. J. Stud. Alcohol,* **17,** 633–642 (1956).

270. O'Reilly, P. O. and A. Funk, LSD in chronic alcoholism, *Can. Psychiat. Assoc. J.,* **9,** 258–261 (1964).

271. Overall, J. E., MMPI personality patterns of alcoholics and narcotic addicts, *Q. J. Stud. Alcohol*, **34**, 104–111 (1973).

272. Overall, J. E., D. Brown, J. D. Williams, and L. T. Neill, Drug treatment of anxiety and depression in detoxified alcoholic patients, *Arch. Gen. Psychiat.*, **29**, 218–221 (1973).

273. Overall, J. E., B. W. Henry, and H. Ford, Background variables and outpatient psychopathology, *Psychol. Rep.*, **28**, 303–309 (1971).

274. Overall, J. E. and L. E. Hollister, Psychiatric drug research: sample size requirements for one vs. two raters, *Arch. Gen. Psychiat.*, **16**, 152–161 (1967).

275. Pahnke, W. N., A. A. Kurland, S. Unger, C. Savage, and S. Grof, The experimental use of psychedelic (LSD) psychotherapy, *J. Am. Med. Assoc.*, **212**, 1856–1863 (1970).

276. Panepinto, W. C. and M. J. Higgins, Keeping alcoholics in treatment: Effective follow-through procedures, *Q. J. Stud. Alcohol*, **30**, 414–419 (1969).

277. Papas, A. N., An Air Force alcoholic rehabilitation program, *Mil. Med.*, **136**, 277–281 (1971).

278. Partington, J. T. and F. G. Johnson, Personality types among alcoholics, *Q. J. Stud. Alcohol*, **30**, 21–34 (1969).

279. Pattison, E. M., R. Coe, and R. A. Rhodes, Evaluation of alcoholism treatment: Comparison of three facilities, *Arch. Gen. Psychiat.*, **20**, 478–488 (1969).

280. Peck, R. E., Use of CCC in treatment of alcoholic patients of Meadowbrook Hospital, *N.Y. State J. Med.*, **62**, 1626–1629 (1962).

281. Pemberton, D. A., A comparison of the outcome of treatment in female and male alcoholics, *Br. J. Psychiat.*, **113**, 367–373 (1967).

282. Penick, S. B., R. N. Carrier, and J. B. Sheldon, Metronidazole in the treatment of alcoholism, *Am. J. Psychiat.*, **125**, 1063–1066 (1969).

283. Pfeffer, A. Z. and S. Berger, A follow-up study of treated alcoholics, *Q. J. Stud. Alcohol*, **18**, 624–648 (1957).

284. Pisani, V. D. and G. U. Motansky, Prediction of premature termination of outpatient follow-up group psychotherapy among male alcoholics, *Int. J. Addict.*, **5**, 731–737 (1970).

285. Pittman, D. J. and C. W. Gordon, *Revolving Door: A Study of the Chronic Police Case Inebriate*, Monographs of the Yale Center of Alcohol Studies #2, New Haven, Free Press, Glencoe, Ill., 1958.

286. Pittman, D. J. and M. Sterne, *Alcoholism: Community Agency Attitudes and Their Impact on Treatment Services*, U.S.P.H.S. Publ. #1263, Washington, D.C., 1963.

287. Pittman, D. J. and M. Sterne, Concept of motivation: Sources of institutional and professional blockage in the treatment of alcoholics, *Q. J. Stud. Alcohol*, **26**, 41–57 (1965).

288. Pittman, D. J. and R. L. Tate, A comparison of two treatment programs for alcoholics, *Q. J. Stud. Alcohol*, **30**, 888–899 (1969).

289. Platz, A., W. C. Panepinto, B. Kissin, and S. M. Charnoff, Metronidazole and alcoholism: an evaluation of specific and non-specific factors in drug treatment, *Dis. Nerv. Syst.*, **31**, 631–636 (1970).

290. Pokorny, A. D., B. A. Miller, and S. E. Cleveland, Response to treatment of alcoholism: a follow-up study, *Q. J. Stud. Alcohol*, **29**, 364–381 (1968).

291. Pokorny, A. D., B. A. Miller, T. E. Kanas, and J. Valles, Dimensions of Alcoholism, *Q. J. Stud. Alcohol*, **32**, 699–705 (1971).

292. Pokorny, A. D., B. A. Miller, T. Kanas, and J. Valles, Effectiveness of extended aftercare in the treatment of alcoholism, *Q. J. Stud. Alcohol*, **34**, 435–443 (1973).

293. Quinn, J. T. and R. Henbest, Partial failure of generalization in alcoholics following aversion therapy, *Q. J. Stud. Alcohol*, **28**, 70–75 (1967).

294. Quinn, J. T. and W. S. Kerr, The treatment of poor prognosis in alcoholics by prolonged apomorphine aversion therapy, *J. Irish Med. Assoc.*, **53**, 50–54 (1963).

295. Rae, J. B., The influence of the wives on the treatment outcome of alcoholics: a follow-up study at two years, *Br. J. Psychiat.*, **120**, 601–613 (1972).

296. Rae, J. B. and J. Drewery, Interpersonal patterns in alcoholic marriages, *Br. J. Psychiat.*, **120**, 615–621 (1972).

297. Rankin, J. G., N. N. Santamoria, D. M. O'Day, and M. C. Doyle, Studies in alcoholism. I. A general hospital medical clinic for the treatment of alcoholism, *Med. J. Aust.*, **1**, 157–162 (1967).

298. Rathod, N. H., E. Gregory, D. Blows, and G. H. Thomas, A two-year follow-up study of alcoholic patients, *Br. J. Psychiat.*, **112**, 683–692 (1966).

299. Redick, R. W., Utilization of psychiatric facilities by persons diagnosed with alcohol disorders, *National Institute of Mental Health Mental Health Statistics, Series B., No. 4*, U.S. Dept. of Health, Education and Welfare, Rockville, Md., 1973.

300. Reilly, D. H. and A. A. Sugerman, Conceptual complexity and psychological differentiation in alcoholics, *J. Nerv. Ment. Dis.*, **144**, 14–17 (1967).

301. Reinert, R. E. and W. T. Bowen, Social drinking following treatment for alcoholism, *Bull. Menn. Clinic*, **32**, 280–290 (1968).

302. Rhodes, R. J. and R. M. Hudson, A follow-up study of tuberculous Skid-Row alcoholics. I. Social adjustment and drinking behavior, *Q. J. Stud. Alcohol*, **30**, 119–128 (1969).

303. Rickels, K., Drugs in the treatment of neurotic anxiety and tension: controlled studies, in *Psychiatric Drugs*, P. Solomon (Ed.), Grune & Stratton, New York, 1966, pp. 225–235.

304. Rickels, K., Non-specific factors in drug therapy of neurotic patients, in *Non-Specific Factors in Drug Therapy*, K. Rickels (Ed.), Charles C Thomas, Springfield, Ill., 1968, pp. 3–26.

305. Rickels, K. and R. B. Cattell, Drug and placebo response as a function of doctor and patient type, in *Psychotropic Drug Response*, P. R. A. May and J. R. Wittenborn (Eds.), Charles C Thomas, Springfield, Ill., 1969, pp. 126–140.

306. Rickels, K., E. Raab, P. E. Gordon, K. G. Laquer, R. V. DeSilverio, and P. Hesbacher, Differential effects of chlordiazepoxide and fluphenazine in two anxious patient populations, *Psychopharmacologia* (Berl.), **12**, 181–192 (1968).

307. Rimmer, J., T. Reich, and G. Winokur, Alcoholism vs diagnosis and clinical variation among alcoholics, *Q. J. Stud. Alcohol*, **33**, 658–666 (1972).

308. Ritson, B., The prognosis of alcohol addicts treated by a specialized unit, *Br. J. Psychiat.*, **114**, 1019–1029 (1968).

309. Ritson, B., Involvement in treatment and its relation to outcome amongst alcoholics, *Br. J. Addict.*, **64**, 23–29 (1969).

310. Ritson, B., Personality and prognosis in alcoholism, *Br. J. Psychiat.*, **118**, 79–82 (1971).

311. Ritter, N. S., Experience with reserpine in the treatment of alcoholism, *Q. J. Stud. Alcohol,* **17,** 195–197 (1956).

312. Robson, R. A. H., I. Paulus, and G. G. Clarke, An evaluation of the effect of a clinic treatment program on the rehabilitation of alcoholic patients, *Q. J. Stud. Alcohol,* **26,** 264–278 (1965).

313. Rohan, W. P., A follow-up study of hospitalized problem drinkers, *Dis. Nerv. Syst.,* **31,** 259–267 (1970).

314. Rohan, W. P., MMPI changes in hospitalized alcoholics: a second study, *Q. J. Stud. Alcohol,* **33,** 65–76 (1972).

315. Rohan, W. P., Follow-up study of problem drinkers, *Dis. Nerv. Syst.,* **33,** 196–199 (1972).

316. Roman, P. M. and H. M. Trice, The development of deviant drinking behavior: occupational risk factors, *Arch. Environ. Health,* **20,** 424–435 (1970).

317. Rosenberg, C. M., V. Manohar, J. O'Brien, F. Cobb, and S. Weinberger, The Hello House fire: response of alcoholics to crisis, *Q. J. Stud. Alcohol,* **34,** 199–202 (1973).

318. Rosenblatt, S. M., M. M. Gross, B. Malenowski, M. Broman, and E. Lewis, Marital status and multiple psychiatric admissions for alcoholism, *Q. J. Stud. Alcohol,* **32,** 1092–1096 (1971).

319. Rossi, J. J., A. Stach, and N. J. Bradley, Effects of treatment of male alcoholics in a mental hospital: a follow-up study, *Q. J. Stud. Alcohol,* **24,** 19–108 (1963).

320. Rothstein, E. and D. D. Clancy, Combined use of disulfiram and metronidazole in treatment of alcoholism, *Q. J. Stud. Alcohol,* **31,** 446–447 (1970).

321. Rubington, E., Referral, post treatment contacts and length of stay in a halfway house, *Q. J. Stud. Alcohol,* **31,** 659–668 (1970).

322. Ryback, R. S., The continuum and specificity of the effects of alcohol on memory, *Q. J. Stud. Alcohol,* **32,** 995–1016 (1971).

323. Sanderson, R. E., D. Campbell, and S. G. Laverty, An investigation of a new aversive conditioning treatment for alcoholism, *Q. J. Stud. Alcohol,* **24,** 261–275 (1963).

324. Sarwer-Foner, G. J., Psychodynamics of psychotropic medication: an overview, in *Clinical Handbook of Psychopharmacology,* A. Dimascio and R. I. Shader (Eds.), Science House, New York, 1970, pp. 161–182.

325. Satterfield, J. H. and S. B. Guze, Treatment of alcoholic patients with tridothyronine, *Dis. Nerv. Syst.,* **22,** 227 (1961).

326. Schaefer, E. S., Personality structure of alcoholics in outpatient psychotherapy, *Q. J. Stud. Alcohol,* **15,** 304–319 (1959).

327. Schaefer, H. H., M. B. Sobell, and L. C. Sobell, Twelve month follow-up of hospitalized alcoholics given self-confrontation experiences by videotape, *Behav. Ther.,* **3,** 283–285 (1972).

328. Schmidt, W. and J. deLint, Causes of death in alcoholics, *Q. J. Stud. Alcohol,* **33,** 171–185 (1972).

329. Schuckit, M., The alcoholic woman: a literature review, *Psychiat. Med.,* **3,** 37–43 (1972).

330. Selzer, M. L., The Michigan Alcoholism Screening Test: the quest for a new diagnostic instrument, *Am. J. Psychiat.,* **127,** 1653–1658 (1972).

331. Selzer, M. L. and W. H. Holloway, A follow-up of alcoholics committed to a state hospital, *Q. J. Stud. Alcohol,* **18,** 98–120 (1957).

332. Shaffer, J. W., W. R. Freinek, S. Wolf, N. H. Foxwell, and A. A. Kurland, A controlled evaluation of chlordiazepoxide (Librium) in treatment of convalescing alcoholics, *J. Nerv. Ment. Dis.*, **137**, 494–507 (1963).

333. Shaffer, J. W., T. E. Hanlon, S. Wolf, N. H. Foxwell, and A. A. Kurland, Nialamide in the treatment of alcoholism, *J. Nerv. Ment. Dis.*, **135**, 222–232 (1962).

334. Sheard, M. A., The influence of doctor's attitude on the patient's response to antidepressant medication, *J. Nerv. Ment. Dis.*, **136**, 555–560 (1963).

335. Simpson, W. S. and P. W. Webber, A field program in the treatment of alcoholism, *Hosp. Commun. Psychiat.*, **22**, 170–173 (1971).

336. Smart, R. G., The evaluation of alcoholism treatment programs, *Addictions* (Toronto), **17**, 41–51 (1970).

337. Smart, R. G., W. Schmidt, and M. K. Moss, Social class as a determinant of the type and duration of therapy received by alcoholics, *Int. J. Addict.*, **4**, 543–556 (1969).

338. Smart, R. G., T. Storm, E. F. W. Baker, and L. Solursh, A controlled study of lysergide in the treatment of alcoholism. I. The effects on drinking behavior, *Q. J. Stud. Alcohol*, **27**, 469–482 (1966).

339. Smith, C. G., Marital influences on treatment outcome in alcoholism, *J. Irish Med. Assoc.*, **60**, 433–434 (1967).

340. Smith, J. A., E. Mansfield, and H. D. Herrick, Treatment of chronic alcoholics with citrated calcium carbimide (Temposil), *Am. J. Psychiat.*, **115**, 822–824 (1959).

341. Smith, J. A., J. A. Wolford, M. Weber, and D. McLean, Use of citrated calcium carbimide (Temposil) in the treatment of chronic alcoholism, *J. Am. Med. Assoc.*, **165**, 2181–2183 (1957).

342. Smith-Moorhouse, P. M., Hypnosis in the treatment of alcoholism, *Br. J. Addict.*, **64**, 47–55 (1969).

343. Sobell, M. B., H. H. Schaefer, and K. C. Mills, Differences in baseline drinking behaviors between alcoholics and normal drinkers, *Behav. Res. Ther.*, **10**, 257–267 (1972).

344. Sobell, L. C., M. B. Sobell, and H. H. Schaefer, Alcoholics name fewer mixed drinks than social drinkers, *Psychol. Rep.*, **28**, 439–494 (1971).

345. Sobell, M. B. and L. C. Sobell, *Individualized Behavior Therapy for Alcoholics: Rationale, Procedures, Preliminary Results and Appendix*, State of California Dept. of Mental Hygiene, Sacramento, 1972.

346. Solomon, R. L., Punishment, *Psychologist*, **19**, 239–253 (1964).

347. Stein, K. B., V. Royzynko, and L. A. Pugh, The heterogeneity of personality among alcoholics, *Br. J. Soc. Clin. Psychol.*, **10**, 253–259 (1971).

348. Stein, L. I., D. Niles, and A. M. Ludwig, The loss of control phenomenon in alcoholics, *Q. J. Stud. Alcohol*, **29**, 598–602 (1968).

349. Sterne, M. W. and D. J. Pittman, The concept of motivation: a source of institutional and professional blockage in the treatment of alcoholics, *Q. J. Stud. Alcohol*, **26**, 41–57 (1965).

350. Stojiljkovic, S., Conditioned aversion treatment of alcoholics, *Q. J. Stud. Alcohol*, **30**, 900–904 (1969).

351. Storm, T. and R. E. Cutler, *Systematic Desensitization in the Treatment of Alcoholics: an Experimental Trial*. Alcoholism Foundation of British Columbia, Vancouver, 1968.

352. Strassman, H. D., B. Adams, and A. W. Pearson, Metronidazole effect on social drinkers, *Q. J. Stud. Alcohol*, **31**, 394–398 (1970).

353. Summers, T., Validity of alcoholics' self-reported drinking history, *Q. J. Stud. Alcohol,* **31,** 972–974 (1970).

354. Swinson, R. P., Long term trial of metronidazole in male alcoholics, *Br. J. Psychiat.,* **119,** 85–89 (1971).

355. Tarnower, S. M. and H. M. Toole, Evaluation of patients in alcoholism clinic for more than ten years, *Dis. Nerv. Syst.,* **29,** 28–31 (1968).

356. Thimann, J., Conditioned reflex treatment of alcoholism. I. Its rationale and technic, *N. Engl. J. Med.,* **241,** 368–370 (1949).

357. Thomas, R. E., L. H. Gliedman, S. D. Imber, A. R. Stone, and J. Freund, Evaluation of the Maryland Alcoholic Rehabilitation Clinics, *Q. J. Stud. Alcohol,* **20,** 65–76 (1959).

358. Tokar, J. T., A. J. Brunse, V. J. Stefflre, D. A. Napior, and J. A. Sodergren, Emotional states and behavioral patterns in alcoholics and nonalcoholics, *Q. J. Stud. Alcohol,* **34,** 133–143 (1973).

359. Tomsovic, M., Hospitalized alcoholic patients. I. A two-year study of medical, social and psychological characteristics, *Hosp. Comm. Psychiat.,* **19,** 197–203 (1968).

360. Tomsovic, M., A follow-up study of discharged alcoholics, *Hosp. Comm. Psychiat.,* **21,** 94–97 (1970).

361. Tomsovic, M. and R. V. Edwards, Lysergide treatment of schizophrenic and nonschizophrenic alcoholics: a controlled evaluation, *Q. J. Stud. Alcohol,* **31,** 932–949 (1970).

362. Trice, H. M., A study of the process of affiliation with Alcoholics Anonymous, *Q. J. Stud. Alcohol,* **18,** 39–54 (1957).

363. Trice, H. M., The affiliation motive and readiness to join Alcoholics Anonymous, *Q. J. Stud. Alcohol,* **20,** 313–320 (1959).

364. Trice, H. M., *Alcoholism in America,* McGraw-Hill, New York, 1966.

365. Trice, H. M. and P. M. Roman, Sociopsychological predictors of affiliation with Alcoholics Anonymous: A longitudinal study of "treatment success," *Soc. Psychiat.,* **5,** 51–59 (1970).

366. Trice, H. M., P. M. Roman, and J. A. Belasco, Selection for treatment: A predictive evaluation of an alcoholism treatment regimen, *Int. J. Addict.,* **4,** 303–317 (1969).

367. Tyndel, M., J. G. Fraser, and C. J. Hartleib, Metronidazole as an adjuvant in the treatment of alcoholism, *Br. J. Addict.,* **64,** 57–61 (1969).

368. Vallance, M., Alcoholism: a two-year follow-up study of patients admitted to the psychiatric department of a general hospital, *Br. J. Psychiat.,* **111,** 348–356 (1965).

369. Vanderpool, J. A., Alcoholism and the self-concept, *Q. J. Stud. Alcohol,* **30,** 59–77 (1969).

370. Vannicelli, M. L., Mood and self-perception of alcoholics when sober and intoxicated. I. Mood change. II. Accuracy of self-perception, *Q. J. Stud. Alcohol,* **33,** 341–357 (1972).

371. Viamontes, J. A., Review of drug effectiveness in the treatment of alcoholism, *Am. J. Psychiat.,* **128,** 1570–1571 (1972).

372. Voegtlin, W. L., The treatment of alcoholism by establishing a conditioned reflex, *Am. J. Med. Sci.,* **199,** 802–809 (1940).

373. Voegtlin, W. L. and W. R. Broz, The conditioned reflex treatment of chronic alcoholism. X. An analysis of 3125 admissions over a period of ten and a half years, *Ann. Intern. Med.,* **30,** 580–597 (1949).

374. Vogel, M. D., The relation of personality factors to GSR conditioning of alcoholics: an exploratory study, *Can. J. Psychol.*, **14**, 275–280 (1960).

375. Vogel, M. D., GSR conditioning and personality factors in alcoholics and normals, *J. Abnorm. Soc. Psychol.*, **63**, 417–421 (1961).

376. Vogel, M. D., The relationship of GSR conditioning to drinking patterns of alcoholics, *Q. J. Stud. Alcohol*, **22**, 401–410 (1961).

377. Vogel, M. D., The relationship of personality factors to drinking patterns of alcoholics: an exploratory study, *Q. J. Stud. Alcohol*, **22**, 394–399 (1961).

378. Vogler, R. E., S. E. Lunde, G. R. Johnson, and P. L. Martin, Electrical aversion conditioning with chronic alcoholics, *J. Consult. Clin. Psychol.*, **34**, 302–307 (1970).

379. Walton, H. J., Personality as the determinant of the form of alcoholism, *Br. J. Psychiat.*, **114**, 761–766 (1968).

380. Walton, H. J., E. B. Ritson, and R. I. Kennedy, Response of alcoholics to clinic treatment, *Br. Med. J.*, **2**, 1171–1174 (1966).

381. Wedel, H. L., Involving alcoholics in treatment, *Q. J. Stud. Alcohol*, **26**, 468–479 (1965).

382. Weingartner, W., L. A. Faillace, and H. G. Markley, Verbal information retention in alcoholics, *Q. J. Stud. Alcohol*, **32**, 293–303 (1971).

383. Weingold, H. P., J. M. Lechin, H. A. Bell, and R. C. Coxe, Depression as a symptom of alcoholism: search for a phenomenon, *J. Abnorm. Psychol.*, **73**, 195–197 (1968).

384. Whitehorn, J. C. and B. J. Betz, Further studies of the doctor as a crucial variable in the outcome of treatment with shizophrenic patients, *Am. J. Psychiat.*, **117**, 215–223 (1960).

385. Wilby, W. E. and R. W. Jones, Assessing patient response following treatment, *Q. J. Stud. Alcohol*, **23**, 325–334 (1962).

386. Wilkinson, A. E., W. M. Prado, W. O. Williams, and F. W. Schnadt, Psychological test characteristics and length of stay in alcoholism treatment, *Q. J. Stud. Alcohol*, **32**, 60–65 (1971).

387. Willcox, D. R. C., R. Gillan, and E. H. Hore, Do psychiatric outpatients take their drugs?, *Br. Med. J.*, **2**, 790–792 (1966).

388. Willems, P. J. A., F. J. J. Letemendia, and F. Arroyave, A two-year follow-up study comparing short with long stay in-patient treatment of alcoholics, *Br. J. Psychiat.*, **122**, 637–648 (1973).

389. Willems, P. J. A., F. J. J. Letemendia, and F. Arroyave, A categorization for the assessment of prognosis and outcome in the treatment of alcoholism, *Br. J. Psychiat.*, **122**, 649–654 (1973).

390. Wilson, I. C., B. A. Lacoe, and L. Riley, Tofranil in the treatment of postalcoholic depressions, *Psychosomatics*, **11**, 488–494 (1970).

391. Winkelman, N. W., A clinical and socio-cultural study of 200 psychiatric patients started on chlorpromazine 10½ years ago, *Am. J. Psychiat.*, **120**, 861–869 (1964).

392. Winokur, G., J. Rimmer, and T. Reich, Alcoholism IV: Is there more than one type of alcoholism?, *Br. J. Psychiat.*, **118**, 525–531 (1971).

393. Winship, G. M., Antabuse treatment, in *Hospital Treatment of Alcoholism; A Comparative, Experimental Study*, R. S. Wallerstein (Ed.), Menninger Clinic Monogr. Ser., No. 11, Basic Books, New York, 1957, pp. 23–51.

394. Witkin, H. A., R. B. Dyk, H. F. Faterson, D. R. Goodenough, and S. A. Karp, *Psychological Differentiation*, John Wiley, New York, 1962.

395. Witkin, H., S. Karp, and D. Goodenough, Dependence in alcoholics, *Q. J. Stud. Alcohol,* **20,** 493–504 (1959).

396. Wolf, I., M. E. Chafetz, H. T. Blane, and M. J. Hill, Social factors in the diagnosis of alcoholism in social and non-social situations, *Q. J. Stud. Alcohol,* **24,** 61–79 (1965).

397. Wolff, K., Hospitalized alcoholic patients. III. Motivating alcoholics through group psychotherapy, *Hosp. Comm. Psychiat.,* **19,** 206–209 (1968).

398. Wolff, S., and Holland, L., A questionnaire follow-up of alcoholic patients, *Q. J. Stud. Alcohol,* **25,** 108–118 (1964).

399. Wolpe, J., *Psychotherapy by Reciprocal Inhibition,* Stanford University Press, Stanford, Calif., 1958.

400. Zax, M., The incidence and fate of the reopened case in an alcoholism treatment center, *Q. J. Stud. Alcohol,* **23,** 634–639 (1962).

401. Zax, M., R. Marsey, and C. F. Biggs, Demographic characteristics of alcoholic outpatients and the tendency to remain in treatment, *Q. J. Stud. Alcohol,* **22,** 98–105 (1961).

INDEX

morphine, 155
see also Limbic system
Homocide, Indian, 22
in Navaho drinking, 19, 40, 44
Homosexuals, 279
Hospital, clinical research, alcoholics and
    tension reduction, 187, 188, 189,
    201, 202
    treatment of chronic alcoholism, 249,
        250, 252, 253-256, 258, 259, 261-
        267, 270, 273, 275-278, 281, 284,
        286, 287, 293, 294, 300, 304-307
Hospital, drinking driver, 135, 137, 142
Hostility, 188, 277
Houthakker-Taylor hypothesis, 213
Human performance under stress, 185
Husband and wife, alcoholism treatment,
    272, 273, 274
    see also Couple therapy
Hyperalgesia, 159
Hyperglycemia, morphine-induced, 159,
    161
Hyperlipemia, alcohol, 304
Hyperlipoproteinemia in alcoholics, 304
Hyperkinesia, 157
Hypnosis, 283, 288, 289
Hypothalamus, alcohol effects on, 149
    duiresis, 149
    hypothalamic-hypophyseal function,
        149
    hypothalamic neurones, 149
    nephron, 149
    sodium channels, 149
    sodium-sensitive neurones, 149
    opiate effects on, 158, 159, 160, 167
    adipsia, 159
    adrenal hormone, 158
    aphagia, 159
    catecholamine depletion, 158
    eating and drinking, 158
    electrical activity, hypothalamic neu-
        rones, 159
    gonadal function, 158
    gonadotropin release, 158
    hyperalgesia, 159
    hyperglycemia, 159
    hypothermia, 158
    ovulation, 158
    serotonin depletion, 158
    thermoregulation, 158, 167

thyroid hormone, 158
Hypothermia, opiates, 157, 158
    serotonin and catecholamine depletion,
    158

Iceland, drinking driver, 131
Information Transmission Approach, 111,
    113, 116, 117
Injury, risk of, in auto accidents, 124
Imipramine, treatment, 300, 301
Impaired driving, *see* Blood alcohol concen-
    tration; Conviction; Drinking driver;
    Legislation; Road traffic accidents
Impairment, driving, 126, 127, 130, 131,
    133
    alcohol and drugs, 127
Impairment of brain function in alcoholics,
    188-190, 258, 261
Impairment of discrimination, 184
Implied consent law, drivers, 132, 134
Imprisonment, drinking drivers, 131, 135,
    143
Improvement of alcoholics, 255, 256, 259,
    262, 263, 268, 269, 270, 271, 273,
    288, 305, 306, 307
    see also Outcome
Income and prices, *see* Cost of alcoholic
    beverages
Index of consumption, drinking, 192
India, drinking in, 7, 13, 26, 27, 46, 48
Indians, American, drinking in, 2, 7, 12, 14-
    19, 22, 24, 25-29, 31, 32, 37-41, 43-
    46, 53, 54, 58, 59
    Aleuts, 49
    Apaches, 2, 42, 43, 52
    Aymara Indians, 26
    Aztec, 29
    Camba, 14, 15, 27, 28, 38, 49, 58
    Canadian Indians, 25, 28
    Chamula, 2, 15, 22, 28, 38
    Cherokee, 39
    Chichicastenango, 15, 22, 38
    Chippewa, 51
    Choco, 39
    Colombian Indians, 26
    Cree, 25
    Delawares, 39
    Giriama, 49
    Guarani, 39
    Iroquois, 17, 18, 29, 31, 32, 38, 39, 46